Political Spiritualities

Political Spiritualities

The Pentecostal Revolution in Nigeria

RUTH MARSHALL

The University of Chicago Press   Chicago and London

RUTH MARSHALL is assistant professor of religion and political science at the University of Toronto and coeditor of *Between Babel and Pentecost: Transnational Pentecostalism in Africa and Latin America.*

The University of Chicago Press, Chicago 60637
The University of Chicago Press, Ltd., London
© 2009 by The University of Chicago
All rights reserved. Published 2009
Printed in the United States of America

18 17 16 15 14 13 12 11 10 09   1 2 3 4 5

ISBN-13: 978-0-226-50712-5 (cloth)
ISBN-13: 978-0-226-50713-2 (paper)
ISBN-10: 0-226-50712-2 (cloth)
ISBN-10: 0-226-50713-0 (paper)

Library of Congress Cataloging-in-Publication Data

Marshall, Ruth, 1964–
  Political spiritualities : the Pentecostal revolution in Nigeria / Ruth
Marshall.
    p. cm.
  Includes bibliographical references and index.
  ISBN-13: 978-0-226-50712-5 (cloth : alk. paper)
  ISBN-13: 978-0-226-50713-2 (pbk. : alk. paper)
  ISBN-10: 0-226-50712-2 (cloth: alk. paper)
  ISBN-10: 0-226-50713-0 (pbk. : alk. paper)
  1. Pentecostalism—Nigeria. 2. Pentecostalism—Political aspects—
Nigeria. 3. Christianity and politics—Nigeria. 4. Nigeria—Religious
life and customs. 5. Nigeria—Church history. I. Title.
  BR1644.5.N6M37 2009
  276.69'082—dc22

                                                        2008043576

♾ The paper used in this publication meets the minimum requirements of the American National Standard for Information Sciences—
Permanence of Paper for Printed Library Materials, ANSI Z39.48-1992.

FOR CHLOË, ELISE, AND ANNA

Contents

Acknowledgments

Over the fifteen years of research that has gone into this study, I have accumulated so many debts that it is impossible to recognize them all here. I must thank first my adoptive extended family in Nigeria, whose friendship and support made this work possible: the Onuzos, to whom I owe my original interest in the subject; Kehinde and Taiwo Johnson, who taught me everything I needed to know about Lagos but was afraid to ask; Tokunbo, Yomi, 'Lara, Segun, Clement, and a host of other friends. I owe a great deal to Professor Claude Ake, whose spirit is present in these pages. I thank the Department of Political Science at UNILAG and Professor Jinadu for their warm hospitality, and the numerous colleagues and students who assisted me with my research and made my experience in the department so rewarding. I thank Pastor Tony Rapu for allowing me to work with his ministry; Pastor Abiona, Pastor Okotie, Brother Tosin, Brother Bernard, and Sister Funmi for teaching so much about their movement; and those countless others who gave their time and energy to help me during my first two years in Lagos. I thank the British Academy for funding my Research Fellowship at SOAS between 1996 and 2000. I am ever grateful to Louis Brenner and J. D. Y. Peel at SOAS, and Karin Barber and Paulo de Moraes Farias at Birmingham for the remarkable opportunity of working with them for three years on the New

Religious Publics and the Media in Nigeria Project. In Ibadan, I cannot thank enough for his extraordinary work my colleague and friend, Dr. Matthews Ojo. I am grateful as well for the remarkable contributions of Dr. Hakeem Danmole and our field assistants, in particular Franklin Ukah. I am grateful to Dr. Yann Lebeau and the staff of the IFRA in Ibadan for their assistance in the late 1990s. In Ibadan since 2006, I must thank my staff at IFRA for their assistance, especially Martin Esukise Mbella, as well as my colleagues Guillaume Thiery and David Enweremadu. I'm grateful to the people at home for keeping the show on the road: Elisabeth, Kenneth, and Double G. I must also thank those who were there from the beginning at Oxford and have suffered with me over the years, encouraging me to continue my research and writing: first, Gavin Williams, whose patience has been tried, but whose faith has never wavered; my dear friend Jocelyn Alexander; Terry Ranger, David Maxwell, Karin Barber, Louis Brenner, Paulo de Moraes Farias, Raufu Mustapha, and many others. I thank my French academic family whose intellectual support over the years has greatly contributed to the realization of this study and whose dear friendship has sustained me: Richard Banégas, Jean-François Bayart, Béatrice Hibou, Peter Geschiere, Achille Mbembe, Roland Marchal, and Janet Roitman. I especially thank Richard Banégas, Béatrice Hibou, and Juan Obarrio for their unwavering friendship and support during the difficult process of writing. My eternal thanks to my spiritual brother for God's money, the new life and a gift beyond debt. I am ever grateful to my family for their patience, love, and support: my parents; my siblings John (thanks for making that bet), Kim, and Fiona; and of course my three saving graces, Chloë, Elise, and Anna, for their mostly cheerful forbearance, their unwavering faith, and their enthusiastic egging on. Thanks also to JM for teaching me the true sense of overcoming. I would like especially to thank J. D. Y. Peel, without whom this endless project would never have been realized. His constant support, faith, and friendship, as well as his careful reading and criticism of my work, have made all the difference.

Introduction

"Time is growing," he added. "And our suffering is growing too. When will our suffering bear fruit? One great thought can alter the future of the world. One revelation. One dream. But who will dream that dream? And make it real?" B. OKRI, *INFINITE RICHES* (LONDON: ORION BOOKS, 1999), 5

Nigerian novelist Ben Okri's poignant questioning is taken up by Pastor M. O. Ojewale in these terms:

This is the eve of a national revival. Call it spiritual awakening or revolution if you please. There are few revolutions in history without bloodshed. But there is one revolutionary—the greatest revolutionary of all time—who did not shed another's blood to establish his Kingdom . . . His was a spiritual revolution and it has changed the course of the history of man. . . .

The warfare we are presently engaged in is the battle of translating the victory of Jesus over the devil into the everyday, natural realities of our personal lives and also of our political, religious, economic and social systems. It is a battle of reclamation: to reclaim from the devil what he illegally holds in his control. . . . It is warfare. But we are on the winning side. This is the time to muster the army—the Lord's army. Here is a clarion call to battle. . . .

We are disadvantaged if we lean on carnal weapons. Prayer—militant, strategic and aggressive prayer—must be our weapon of warfare at this time. It is a spiritual warfare and it needs spiritual weapons. This is a call into the ring to wrestle, to sweat it out with an unseen opponent. For we wrestle not against flesh and blood but against spiritual wickedness, against invisible powers in high places (Ephesians 6:12). . . . Nigeria is indeed poised for a revival of an unprecedented dimension. You and I are active participants in what

God is about to do. Militant, strategic, unceasing and aggressive prayers will hasten the heavenly visitation. The early showers of revival which many of God's servants have prophesied have begun already. Join the Lord's army to bring about rapid changes that we desperately need in all areas of our national life. We are at the dawn of a new era. I can see it in my spirit.[1]

In this *Call to Prayer for Nigeria* written in 1990, Pastor Ojewale claims that the country is on the verge of an unprecedented Christian revival. Nearly two decades later, we can confirm his prediction. Since the early 1970s Pentecostal Christianity has become a growing force across the world, especially in Latin America and Africa. Nigeria has been the site of Pentecostalism's greatest explosion on the African continent, and the movement's extraordinary growth shows no signs of slowing. A marginal current within Nigerian Christianity in the early 1970s, by the turn of the millennium Pentecostal or Born-Again[2] Christianity had become its overwhelmingly dominant form, counting tens of millions of adherents, and powerfully influencing Christian practice and doctrine across all denominations. Pentecostalism constitutes the single most important sociocultural force in southern Nigeria today,[3] and over the past decades has played a central role in the increasing political cleavage and violence along religious lines.[4]

Pastor Ojewale speaks of power and struggle, of revolution, of coming battle, of militancy and strategy, of raising an army to hasten the changes required not only at the level of "everyday, natural realities of our personal lives" but also the "political, religious, economic and social systems." Invisible powers, heavenly visitations, unceasing prayers, prophecies, spiritual visions: we can see that this is no regular army, no ordinary battle. But, while the language of Ojewale's call appears eminently political, we find it difficult to reconcile these invisible and ephemeral forces with more classical political forms of representation and action. Indeed, religious belief is not reducible to political militancy or ideology. And yet, taken in all their irreducibility, the forces of faith that have driven and continue to drive this movement contribute as such, rather than by default, to the historical conditions in which the complex field of political practice and representation is produced.

Pastor Ojewale's revolutionary program is more than a simple utopian form of proselytizing; rather, it is part of an explicit strategic program that responds to and engages with the context of epistemological, normative, and ontological insecurity of life in urban postcolonial Nigeria. The Born-Again movement has as its principal aim a project of individual and collective renewal and regeneration through a process of conversion based on the idiom of new birth. It deliberately positions itself as a response to what are represented as corrupt or ruined religious and political traditions. The project of conversion involves the elaboration of new modes of government of the self and of others, in which practices of faith are fostered by specific disciplines of the body and the mind, emphasizing purity, rectitude, righteousness, and interiority. The idiom of new birth[5] takes on a renewed significance in the light of the uncertainty of the postcolonial present. Not only does it stage the possibility of redemption, it reiterates the promise of hope and the possibility of the new that Arendt identifies as inherent in the very fact of natality.[6] Through a self-conscious engagement with the Nigerian past and the failures of the civilizing mission to redeem its promises, the Born-Again program introduces new and significant ruptures of its own. This engagement, the ruptures and changes it gives rise to and their ambivalent political effects, form the central object of this study.

This study takes religious faith seriously. It attempts to restore intelligibility to religion in its irreducibility, to make sense of the inherent rationality of its disciplines and practices, over and above its social, cultural, or political functions. The first and most challenging question is thus how to clear an analytical space in which we might be able to understand practices and forms of life that are otherwise impossible to recognize from the standpoint of the secular vocabularies instituted in public debates and underwriting social scientific knowledge. A philosophical reframing of the questions at stake in the discourses and practices I encountered and an analytical approach that engages with them nonreductively is thus the first task of this study. The necessity of this was underscored by the dissatisfaction I experienced with social scientific approaches to religion in the light of the evidence itself.

Understanding the explosion of Pentecostalism in Nigeria and its complex political productivity in a nonreductionist way demanded the rejection of a priori understandings of the relationship between the religious and political, and hence the extrication of analysis from the opposition between faith and reason that is still central to many forms of critical inquiry today. Born-Again political rationalities, and the terms in which power, redemption, sovereignty, and other political themes are staged in its practices and professions of faith, stubbornly resist the distinction between sacred and secular we have come to take for granted in Western society and the categories of analysis we deploy to understand them. For example, the reinforcement of a magico-materialist ontology of spiritual power, one of the "unintended" consequences of missionary Christianity, gives rise to a universe where words and things have agency. In this context, the language of faith is truly performative and accords to testimony and prayer a force that is genuinely foundational: to invoke God, to praise Him, to pray to Him, and to testify to His works constitutes both the act of faith—what Paul called the *performativum fidei*[7]—but also, very literally, an *action* on the world. Through prayer and witness, converts do things with words.[8]

However, one of the central arguments of this study is that the inadequacy of dominant approaches to the study of religion and politics to help grasp the Born-Again phenomenon in its irreducibility cannot be explained purely by cultural difference or the by the lack of "fit" between Western theory and non-Western practice. First, many of the practices and discourses deployed by Nigerian Pentecostals, which appear to be the manifestations of historical and cultural particularities, are in fact shared across the world: for example, American Pentecostals pray to exorcise the "spirits of disease" the devil has planted within fetal DNA[9] in the same spirit that Nigerian Born-Agains might touch the television during an evangelical broadcast in order to receive divine healing. Indeed, in its programmatic form, internal rationalities, and general theological and specific doctrinal content, the Pentecostal project of conversion is remarkably uniform across the globe. Second, there are good reasons to suspect that the myth of secularization has run its course today; the global rise of Pentecostalism and indeed the revitalization of religion and spiritual practices in a multitude of forms provide evidence that challenges this myth and demand that we finish with it altogether. The separation of the domain of the political and the religious at either the imaginary or institutional level does not, in and of itself, lead to the opposition between faith and reason that occurs under the sign of "disenchantment," nor does their separation itself lead to secularization. At its outset Christianity's political theology proposed this separation, through the famous formula "Render unto Caesar . . ." This opposition between faith and reason, belief and knowledge, much more than any institutional arrangement, underpins the myth of secularization and appears as *the* hallmark of modernity. Rather than undermining this myth, the majority of analyses examining religion today continue in different ways to give credence to the ongoing and tenacious belief that modernity was fueled by reason, despite the widespread evidence to the contrary.

A critical evaluation of the dominant social scientific approaches to religious or spiritual phenomena in Africa reveals the ongoing salience of the opposition between reason and faith, knowledge and belief. We should hardly be surprised by this, given that it is the epistemological precondition for social scientific knowledge in the first instance. Political science and political economy and their applied fields, such as development studies, through their assumptions and methodologies (the most obvious being rational choice theory and its variants) continue to uphold the myth of a modernist teleology that measures progress and development in terms of the emancipation of reason from "premodern" or irrational modes of cognition and action, and the related expectation that the more "modern" Africans become, the more religious institutions or religious worldviews will recede from the realm of politics. Current religious revival is understood in terms of the failure of modern institutions, forms of organization, and political rationality to take hold, and religious responses appear as simultaneously the *reason for* and the *result of* such failures. This circular argumentation perpetuates a culturalist conception in which "tradition"—unchanging and irrational—is the force that hampers modernization and democracy. The opposition between modern standards of political rationality and religious worldviews is often just a proxy for a culturalist opposition.

A similar logic and set of assumptions underlie many anthropological studies, even if at first view their underlying objective appears to be the restoration, in the light of a history of exclusion and otherness, of alternative or radically different ways of thought and action to their rightful place in the history of humanity. Anthropological analyses of religion in Africa still appear primarily concerned with examining religious practice in terms of the local and ethnographic, under the paradigm of the "domestication of modernity," in which religion is assimilated to culture and its functions of signification and interpretation become the medium for a message about something else, something nonreligious. A lengthy discussion of these approaches follows in chapter 1. I consider that much of this literature constitutes a form of apologetics in which analysts attempt to give alien, inscrutable, and ostensibly irrational ways of thinking and doing a human face and an agency that might restore to them the reason and meaning that, from the point of view of social scientific knowledge, they lack.

While I focus on the specific characteristics of the Born-Again revival in Nigeria, referring to the complex and singular historical conditions within which it has developed and the specificity of its effects, my study is not offered as an ethnography of the movement. The anthropological narrative of the "domestication of modernity" (and its related concept of "alternative modernities") in which Christianity and new spiritual practices are analyzed reveals one of the central analytical aporias common to ethnographic studies. My analysis of the Born-Again deployment in Nigeria helps bring this to light. The premise of modernity's "domestication" depends on tracing, not the ruptures that "conversion to modernity" brings about, but rather the lines of cultural and historical continuity. It tacitly endorses the boundaries or oppositions that the very process of this "conversion" itself puts into place: local versus global, Western versus non-Western, "modernity" versus "tradition." The notion of authenticity is a central analytical tool in the operation of "sorting," whereby specific practices are allocated to one or other of these categories. However, these distinctions or oppositions, and indeed the idea of authenticity itself, are not mere analytical categories or heuristic devices. Rather, they are objectifications created through real struggles, through the play of differences between relations of power and knowledge, which from the colonial period up to the present give rise to highly contested processes and practices of identification. That this system of differentiation continues to be central to modes of political subjectivation in Africa is evident in the current and simultaneous rise of transnational religious identities—Pentecostalism and reformist Islam—and the recrudescence of nativism or identification in terms of autochthony, both of which have this system of distinctions at their heart. Beyond the conflation of analytical categories and objectifications arising from practices and struggles, there is still a tendency in anthropological studies to understand this struggle in normative terms, according to a schema of power and resistance, true and false consciousness. This is largely due, on the one hand, to the ways in which Christianity has been a vector of Western imperialism, and on the other, to the ongoing salience of the trope of authenticity, which still underwrites the ethnographic gesture. Becoming "authentically African" is a political project realized through actual practices, not least of which are the discursive practices of ethnography past and present. This observation should make us fundamentally suspicious of analyses in which authenticity plays an implicit or explicit part.

The Born-Again "break with the past" involves a deliberate engagement with the system of distinctions inherited from the colonial period. The movement finds its central force through a constant, self-conscious mediation between global Pentecostal forms and local practice. Indeed, the transnational character of the movement is central to the imaginaries of community and belonging it fosters, and a critical engagement with local "traditions," histories, and practices constitutes one of the central Born-Again techniques of "making believe." More specifically, the Born-Again program of conversion in Nigeria self-consciously and critically engages with local cultural practices, moral codes, modes of sociability, rituals, forms of authority, and techniques of power, subjecting them to a normative reevaluation, which renders possible and legitimates new practices, and also producing a body of knowledge and truth claims about them that competes with those produced by social science. There is no external scale of truth or meaning according to which these competing claims and representations may be judged. In other words, the Born-Again revival positions itself deliberately as a means for an African access to a *universal* form—a move that directly challenges the objectivist and universalist pretentions of social scientific knowledge. This study takes seriously the struggle for such an access, refusing to read into it any a priori normative or political meaning. Social scientific approaches inevitably imply an a priori notion of the proper field of religion and religious activity—its boundaries, its proper field of authority, what it can know about the world, what it cannot. But what if contemporary religious activities in the continent and beyond are also about struggles over this very process of definition? As a South African Zionist put it: "There is one enormous omission throughout the whole history that has been written by outsiders. The work of the Holy Spirit throughout our history has simply been left out. The events of our history have been recorded as if everything could be accounted for simply by sociology and anthropology. We would like to write our own history from the point of view of the Holy Spirit."[10]

My argument will be made through an examination of the ways in which the Born-Again revival engages with the tradition of Christian practice in Nigeria, as well as with the promises entailed in the civilizing mission, a discussion undertaken in chapter 2. Gil Anidjar argues that we should regard Christianity as the principal agent of European colonialism by recognizing that Christianity has disenchanted its own world by dividing itself into private and public, politics and economics, even religious and secular,[11] echoing Marcel Gauchet's thesis.[12] However, while it is clear that this process of universalization has profound effects and that the colonial encounter is from every point of view a situation of *beginnings,* there is not in Africa a historical isomorphism between the sword of the spirit and that of the flesh. As Mbembe points out, this process occurs not only through coercion, but also through pure seduction.[13] The two central vectors of the civilizing mission were religious and political—Christian mission and the colonial state—but the historical relationship of these two vectors, in terms of their techniques, institutions, imaginaries and aims, was complex and contradictory, at once complicit and antagonistic. This gave rise to a creation and distribution of spaces between the sacred and secular which by no means led to either secularization or disenchantment. More important, the project of mission could only be strategic and programmatic, and the results of this encounter obey the logic of history as event: a logic of struggle, improvisation, chance, bad calculations, missed opportunities, in whose interstices arise new and unexpected forms of practice.[14]

The context in which the Born-Again revival develops provides the conditions of plausibility for the deployment of its program, but the relationship between crisis and religious revival is by no means a causal one, as many materialist or idealist approaches seem to suggest. The genealogy of the movement's rise and the reasons for its success are complex, even if the themes of corruption and insecurity, understood in their broadest senses, appear to be central to its self-positioning. Alongside, or perhaps as an effect of, the universalization of the rationalities and institutions of post-Enlightenment political and economic life can be observed the development of generalized uncertainty, which I believe is not specific to the postcolonial context, even if it is perhaps more acute there. One of the signs of this uncertainty in the West is the renewed salience of ethics, or at least of a yearning for certainty and moral mastery, as well as a politics of difference increasingly staged in terms of moral absolutes, in which the distinction or struggle between good and evil has become crucial. The engagement with the demonic, as Pastor Ojewale's manifesto makes clear, is central to the Pentecostal program of redemption and salvation. The image of the invading army and the paradigm of spiritual warfare are at the heart of the Born-Again project of both individual and collective "overcoming," and underwrite new forms of political subjectivation and violence.

This context of uncertainty, which goes beyond purely material problems of poverty and physical insecurity, is especially palpable in postcolonial Nigeria, where the institutions, modes of thought, and disciplines instituted by colonialism have failed to provide the means for either understanding or mastering the ordeal of the present, opening up lines of flight that have led to a generalized "crisis of governmentality" of increasingly acute proportions. In this context of radical insecurity and its specific contours in Nigeria during the boom-and-bust years of the mid-1970s to the mid-1980s, the Born-Again revival found its initial conditions of plausibility and pertinence and sites of political engagement, a discussion developed in chapter 3. This context was marked by a widening gap between rich and poor as well as the growth of absolute poverty—a chaotic normative and regulatory pluralism where the degree of adherence to acknowledged norms appeared increasingly lax and moral consensus in colonial-created ethnic publics undermined, where old structures and codes underwriting relations of patronage based on structures of kin and ethnicity were breaking down, and where strategies of social mobility through education and patronage were failing. The political context was marked by the increasingly predatory use of power on the part of elites, a growing premium on access to the state but a reduction of opportunities of access, the nation-state's progressive inability to monopolize the moral resources of community and command political loyalty, and the Orwellian disjuncture between the exercise of power and norms of the rational-legal state and juridical citizenship it claimed to serve. From the mid-1980s, new economies of prestige and a slippage in the categories and social representations of power developed, now reoriented toward the ruse, the con, the informal, the criminal, and above all, the occult or supernatural.[15] In particular, the esoteric forms of spiritual power understood to underwrite elite authority came to be seen as destructive and demonic, taking the form, over the 1990s, of a growing public obsession with evil occult powers. These developments all contributed to a "crisis of representation," in a situation of radical uncertainty, where signs and their referents become increasingly unmoored, giving rise to a heightened sense of social insecurity, a fear of fraudulent identities and of strangers, and a growing quest for moral mastery and the ability to control what were seen as untrammeled and dangerous powers. In Nigeria, the trope deployed to evoke these complex developments is that of "corruption," an overcharged term that carries not only a politico-economic meaning, but also an ethical and spiritual dimension. The Born-Again project of redemption responds to the latter in ways that both critically reframe and reinterpret the crisis of the present, and also provide new strategies for coping with its material effects.

The engagement with and the explicit staging of the problem of moral uncertainty and mastery in an uncertain world is central to Pentecostal practices of faith everywhere today. Yet, as Mbembe argues,[16] this engagement relies on realms of experience and modes of cognition that are situated beyond reason, displacing the moral relativism of secular modes of political action and thought. This engagement with the demonic, implying a Manichean division of the moral universe, is one of these forms of displacement. The other can be found in the specific form of individualism expressed through Pentecostal practices of faith, with their emphasis on interiority and individual disciplines or techniques of self-fashioning. These emphasize purity and righteousness, practices that "restore to the act of faith itself the dimension of subjectivity which categories of analysis grounded in the Enlightenment prejudice against religion have hardly been able to engage with."[17] This individualism is by no means that of the secular subject; it finds its expression in an ethics of submission and openness to the miraculous work of the Holy Spirit in everyday life. It is combined with other forms of displacement: in the place of a politics of reasoned deliberation, a politics of affect, motivated by the desire or passion for God; in the place of an agency born from the exercise of human reason, of man "making" his own history, the performative power of prayer and the agency of supernatural forces; in the place of a teleology of progress, or the manifestation of Reason in history, the urgency of the messianic instant. Direct, unmediated revelation from God takes precedence over other forms of evidence, and we see the deployment of forms of veridiction[18] (*véridiction*), or truth-telling, which rely on experiences of interiority: prophecy, dreams, or "seeing in the spirit," as Pastor Ojewale puts it. In other words, as Mbembe argues, "in order to grasp the religious nature of the politics of our time, we need more than before to pay attention to those realms of experience that are situated beyond reason and that are so much a character of the politics of faith and piety today. We have to take into account the shift from the contested politics of reasoned interpretation as one of the hallmarks of modernity to a more avowedly affective politics of truth and revelation—the politics of purity, self-righteousness and interiority."[19] This is increasingly expressed in what I have called the "religions of the subject."[20]

I thus proceed to analyze the Born-Again program of conversion and redemption in terms of a Foucauldian problematic of subjectivation. However, an analysis in terms of subjectivation is pertinent not merely because Born-Again practices of faith focus on interiority and express modes of moral subjectivation whose emphasis is on the relationship that the self develops with the self. The value of this approach is principally methodological: I deploy Foucauldian insights about history, power, government, and subjectivation in order to frame the objects of study in a new way, an approach set out in detail in chapter 1. In focusing on subjectivity, it is not so much the subjective experiences of converts and practitioners I try to bring to light; the sense of subjectivity I employ here has little to do with the problem of subjective consciousness or the individual person. The analysis in terms of subjectivation, which is developed substantially in chapter 4, is employed to understand how Pentecostalism functions as a prescriptive regime. By focusing on Pentecostal regimes of practice—on the programmatic and

strategic aspects as well as their internal rationalities and disciplines—
and their ongoing agonistic interaction with other regimes and traditions, I try to elucidate the various elements that come together to make
a new experience of the world and new practices possible, and the ways
in which such a program can only be strategic and programmatic—as
Foucault says, "it never works."[21] I discuss the ways in which conversion
to the prescriptive regime of Pentecostalism produces new subjects, in
the double sense of being subjected *to* and the subject *of* a practice.
The latter pertains to the relationship of the self to the self through
the deployment of various techniques of the self in processes of self-
fashioning, and the former to modes of "making believe" that constrain or compel, moments in an overall process that is neither entirely
disciplined nor completely autonomous. I thus consider the ways in
which the Born-Again program constitutes the expression of a "political spirituality": "Is not the most general political problem that of
truth? How to link one to the other, the way of distinguishing the true
and the false and the mode of governing the self and others? The will
to found entirely anew, one and the other, one through the other (discover an altogether different division through another mode of self-
governance, to govern oneself altogether differently through another
division) that is what 'political spirituality' is."[22] My aim is to show
how, in a particular concrete case, this "will to found anew" finds its
historical expression and then to analyze its principal political effects.
This is an altogether different project from attempting to show that
religion provides an ideological interpretation of and means of adjustment to changes in the "real."

An examination of these concrete historical effects means telling
the story of the complex changes within the movement, for there is not
one Nigerian Pentecostalism, but many. Throughout this study I trace
the development over a period of thirty years of different moments of
revival, showing the ongoing agonistic interaction between the earlier
"holiness" or "righteousness" moment of the revival in the 1970s and
the rise of the "prosperity" doctrine over the 1980s and 1990s. The
analysis of the significant differences across the doctrinal and institutional Born-Again spectrum constitutes the underlying historical narrative, adding a diachronic and empirical depth to the analysis of the
movement's development and its ongoing political effects.

The problem of collective "political redemption" in the Born-Again
program is expressed through the work to be done on the individual;
thus, my examination of the ways in which it constitutes a form of
"political spirituality" centers on the analysis of the process of con-

version and forces of obedience the movement deploys. The focus of Born-Again conversion is individual conduct, expressed in the trope of personal mastery through a variety of techniques of the self, such as bodily asceticism, fasting, prayer, assiduous Bible study, permanent self-examination, and public witness. Its principal means of propagation occurs through the circulation of narratives of testimony and evangelical witness, increasingly through mass-mediated forms, giving rise to transnational, media-created publics with no sense of place. While various forms of institutionalized accreditation exist, pastoral authority is represented as inhering in a personal call from God; anybody with a vision can start a church, a fellowship, or a mission, and they do. Very significantly, access to knowledge and spiritual power is represented as being free, open, and public, and despite the ongoing bid on the part of pastors to stabilize and institute their charisma and authority, this representation stands in stark opposition to the secrecy and exclusivity that characterize longstanding local regimes of knowledge and power. Central to revival is the staging of the demonic (Ephesians 6:12) and the struggle against "principalities and powers and spiritual wickedness in high places," which from the early phase of revival take the form of a political critique of the abuse of power, practices of corruption, and elite predation that were seen as being responsible for the current state of things. This is done through dramatic showdowns between the power of the Holy Spirit and demonic powers in the form of a variety of "traditional" and other spirits in highly detailed testimonies and practices of healing and deliverance. These testimonies and practices problematized for individuals in a new way the relations among power, wealth, and salvation, as well as representing the past as something that could be both overcome and redeemed. In particular, they enabled new forms of conduct and community that offered individuals ways of extricating themselves from the forms of social debt that Mbembe argues are at the heart of longstanding modes of elite domination and the enormous "social machine" of corruption.[23] At the same time, these accounts, which could be heard in every public space—buses, taxis, markets, taxi-parks—also served to reinforce the growing public obsession about evil powers, functioning as a technique of "making believe."

Beyond the dramatic staging of the dangers of the present moment and the promise of the means to overcome them, the program of conversion and the paradigm of Christian growth deploys other techniques of "making believe" through a process of moral subjectivation. Despite attempts on the part of pastors to monopolize charisma, and

thus institute religious authority, obedience to the Pentecostal program does not occur through submission to the authority of religious specialists or forms of institutionalized orthodoxy. Rather, it takes place through the creation of a verisimilitude, through the perpetual public repetition of testimony to the miraculous power of the Holy Spirit and the staging of the exemplary through radically changed conduct. The Pentecostal program is a prescriptive apparatus that expresses an ethic whose central force does not lie in a code, where the "essential aspect is found in the instances of authority which prescribe this code, impose the learning and respect of it and who sanction the infractions."[24] Rather, it expresses an ethic where the accent is placed on the forms of the relationship that the self elaborates with the self, on the development of a style of life.[25] However, the emphasis on interiority, affectivity, unmediated revelation, and the miraculous reveals a fundamental instability in the effectiveness of techniques of the self, and underlines the inherent difficulty in creating orthodoxy, institutionalized authority, and, indeed, any form of political community. The problem of "signs following" constantly oscillates between two conceptions: one that locates the fruits of conversion as arising from the work of the self on the self through the proper application of Born-Again techniques of personal edification entailing the control of desire, and one that interprets it purely as the intervention of supernatural power, whether as a form of divine grace or spiritual corruption by evil powers. This internal instability, which troubles Pentecostal theology and practice generally, is complicated by the changes brought by the rise of the doctrine of prosperity throughout the 1990s and an increasing emphasis on this-worldly salvation. Conversion promises not only "everlasting life," which in the earlier phase of revival found its expression in an antimaterialist retreat from the world and a messianic eschatology, but also "life more abundant" in the here and now. This promise finds various expressions throughout the different moments of the movement's rise; in particular, the instabilities created through the new emphasis on wealth, in which pastors become multimillionaires through doing "God's work," and a growing inability to distinguish between the powers of the Holy Spirit and those of the devil, reveal the ways in which the problem of radical uncertainty, individual mastery, and sovereignty in postcolonial Nigeria is by no means resolved in the development of the Pentecostal program, but rather appears increasingly exacerbated by it.

Winning Nigeria for Jesus means the projection into collective, public space of a highly political agenda. The image of the invading army, sweeping all unbelievers in its path, expresses the political ambition of replacing a corrupt regime with a new form of righteous authority that presents itself as the unique path to individual and collective salvation. This ambition does not take the form of the creation of a theocracy, where spiritual authority underwritten by institutionalized religion would constitute the basis for political authority. Rather, conversion is represented as a means of creating the ideal citizen, one who will provide a living incarnation of the *nomos* of a pacified and ordered political realm. The democratic access to personal spiritual power, the control and abnegation of personal desires, a new form of "individualism" and the paradigm of Christian obedience all stage the possibility of a pacified and ordered universe, drawing a clear contrast with postcolonial governmentality.

However, beyond this programmatic form, the Born-Again deployment in Africa reveals that God is most definitely not a democrat. The bid to stabilize pastoral authority and the perpetual engagement with the figure of the demonic shows the antidemocratic side of the Pentecostal political engagement. The enemy that rules over us is not only the one that may inhabit the convert's consciousness or body, but also the spiritual forces at large that inhabit others, and give them power over life and death. Underlying the bid to convert the other is the need to *convict* and *overcome* him, to identify within him the demonic that needs to be destroyed for salvation and redemption to occur. The ambivalence and excess of meaning that the "sacred" embodies creates the need to interpret the demonic not only in terms of individual moral failure, but also as part of a global struggle between forces of good and evil. This provides the grounds for the violent assertion of identity through the image of spiritual warfare that extends outward from the individual soul to the entire globe: at the heart of salvation, an ongoing and permanent engagement with the demonic. The representation of global spiritual warfare through the figure of the "invading army" stages the profession of faith as faithfulness to an exclusive prescriptive program, obedience to which is a matter of life and death. While the struggle between Pentecostalism and Islam finds its expression globally, in Nigeria since the 1980s it has taken an extremely violent turn. The prevailing domination of federal politics by the Muslim North since independence provided the grounds for a conflation of Islam, satanic spiritual powers, corruption, and misrule, in which the "enemy" to be convicted and overcome becomes principally the religious other. This battle is not to be feared, but rather anticipated as part of God's plan, engendering a relationship between salvation and terror through which a politics of vengeance becomes itself an ecstatic experience.[26] This last observation leads me to consider the place of the Nigerian Born-Again movement within the global revival of Pentecostalism, as well as the dangers and challenges that this revival poses for the politics of our time. The "re-evangelization" of the West has become one of the ambitions of non-Western Pentecostals everywhere, and Nigerian Pentecostalism is one of its principal vectors. There is a growing engagement by critical thought with the resurgence of religion and a reexamination of the aporias or decline of Western political forms and post-Enlightenment thought[27], which together have created the conditions for what Jean-Luc Nancy has called the possibility of a hyperreligious uprising.[28] One of the aims of this study is to engage with the political and theoretical challenges these developments present.

ONE

Rethinking the Religious and the Political in Africa

If Jesus Is the Answer, What Is the Question?

Over the past twenty years the African continent has witnessed a religious effervescence unprecedented since the colonial period.[1] Can religious revival be understood primarily as a response to material crises? Or should it be thought of as a response to crisis in moral or symbolic regimes? Or some combination of the above? If we suppose that religious revival is a response, or reaction, what sort of criteria may we use to determine the question to which it constitutes an answer? Why is it that solutions to crisis should be sought in the repertory of the religious? Answers to these fundamental questions in the study of religion in Africa are too often influenced by culturalist arguments that express a presupposed ontological link between particular cultures and the propensity for a chaotic spirituality and/or a tendency to interpret the world through the lens of religion. Such approaches interpret particular historical experiences in terms of "culture" and "tradition," so that more or less ahistorical ethnographic forms are understood tacitly or explicitly as social realities rather than as modes of objectifying social practice, modes that are themselves the outcome of complex historical struggles over representation.[2] The problematic of identity in Africa is the prime example of such an approach, whether identity is understood in primordialist or constructivist terms. In the "domestication of modernity" approach, local religious forms are seen as attempts to master the effects of globalization and the transformations it imposes upon local societies.[3] Some of these studies depend upon a reading in which the master narrative of Western progress or imperial hegemony provides the explanatory key to the rise of religious movements and other forms of spirituality, based on an essentialist and ahistorical understanding of behavior. This effervescence is often tacitly or explicitly seen as resulting from the failure of Western institutional models and notions of time and change to impose themselves, opening up the space for the "revenge of paganism."[4] However, even if we reject crude accounts that privilege "the intrinsically religious character of the African"[5] and attempt a finer and more historically nuanced analysis, we cannot answer this question by taking material crisis as our initial object of inquiry, or as the principal object of religious practice, for to do this is to beg the question. If we invoke situations of material crisis—poverty, social exclusion, failure of modernization and development, demise of forms of sociability and itineraries of social mobility, "confusion" engendered by processes of globalization, neo-liberal capitalist relations—in order to explain the rise of religion, then we tacitly see these movements in terms of their functionality: as modes of accumulation, socialization, or political combat, or as languages that translate the real and help to understand it. While religious movements can indeed fulfill these functions, nevertheless, as an *explanation* for both the current religious effervescence and its political signification, they are both circular and inadequate.

Whether religion is understood in terms of a troublesome identity politics or in terms of local attempts to interpret global forces, it is considered as a medium for a message that is about something else, something nonreligious; the religious sphere is not interrogated *as such* for its political significance.[6] These criticisms are by no means new.[7] More than a decade ago, Bayart argued for the rejection of interpretations that privilege a relation of exteriority between the political and the religious, and traced the contours of what he termed the *cité cultuelle* (city of cults), insisting upon a historical reading of the relationship of these domains in Africa.[8] Mbembe before him argued that the religious imaginary does more than simply act as a metaphor for the relations of force or domination in a society, or as a mode of sublimating social aspirations through myths and utopian themes, and placed the accent on the concrete role of the religious and symbolic realm in historical change.[9] Most approaches within social science are based on more or less tacit assumptions of a formalist or functionalist nature about sociopolitical collective and individual needs or imperatives, interpreting the relationship between the spiritual and material from predetermined schemas, of loosely Marxist, Weberian, Durkheimian or other tendencies.[10] Such arguments not only prove to be circular, but even if we accept this circularity, can only provide general keys that fit into every lock. We are still no closer to understanding why religion comes to be seen as a "solution." Taking for an explanation precisely that which requires to be explained, these general keys empty the object of study of its historical particularities, its rare, accidental and fragile form.[11] Born-again Christianity operates in Nigeria within a terribly crowded religious field. What sort of inquiry will enable us to understand why *this* particular form of religious practice develops here and now, and uncover the secret of its remarkable success? What question(s) is Jesus really the answer to?[12]

Studies of the political significance of Christianity in Africa have too often presumed the models of the relation between religion and politics with which social science represents Western society, resolving differences between African expressions of these forms and the Western models in terms of "a combination of a dialectical or evolutionary theory and the idea that the elimination of the religious from the political field marks the formation of a rational, or a potentially rational, type of society in which institutions and practices appear, or begin to appear for what they really are."[13] The meaning of the relationship between the religious and political spheres "is established by reference to a law of historical development or the laws of the dynamics of social structures," whether approaches follow a loosely Marxist or Weberian inspiration.[14] Approaches that give themselves to discerning the laws of social structures and showing how they interact depend on a reifying procedure whereby given objects—religion, modes of production, political structures such as the state or civil society—are taken as realities, as historical agents, and their essential, objective characteristics are determined in concert with the laws of their functioning.[15] This is particularly clear in studies that focus on the institutional relationships between the religious and political spheres.

The "symbolic" comes into play in such analyses as the ensemble of signs through which, once isolated and deciphered, the real can be read and society revealed in its truth. Yet it is both misguided and circular to proceed as if the functionality of these signs with regard to material realities constitutes an *explanation* of these realities. As Claude Lefort reminds us, once we begin with the separation of the "real" from what is "cultural," "symbolic," "juridical," or "ideological," we inevitably rely on an artificial conception, whether we define the real in formalist or materialist terms. When, for example, analysts define the specificity of political activity by subordinating it to functional imperatives, such as ensuring the cohesion of the social whole, making it possible to formulate and achieve objectives, they rely on a definition that is purely formal. They recognize that such functions can only be performed if the agents have internalized the political imperatives behind them. To account for this internalization, they resort to invoking the values, norms, and beliefs that guide behavior in the society in question. But then they assign specific functions to these norms, values, and beliefs, and look for the preconditions of their efficacy within the coherence of the system from which they derive.[16] These approaches forget that the relationship between the political and the religious is an eminently historical one. As Lefort observes: "Political science and political sociology relate to a domain which has been delineated in response to the imperatives of positive knowledge—the imperatives of objectivity and neutrality—and which is, as such, circumscribed and distanced from other domains which are defined as, for example, economic, social, juridical, religious, aesthetic, and so on. I consider such a division to be artificial, but by no means accidental . . . it loses all pertinence when we consider most of the societies revealed to us by anthropologists and historians, that it testifies to the existence of a form of society which appeared in the West and, given the long history of humanity, at a relatively recent date."[17] With certain notable exceptions,[18] studies in political science and political sociology have failed insofar as they have not examined or understood the historicity of the relations between the religious and the political in Africa. Whether religious activities are approached from the angle of an opposition between the state and civil society or through an analysis of the "clash of identities," religious movements are analyzed purely from the point of view of the roles they play as one among a variety of social or political movements or institutions.[19] But these approaches assume the sorts of distinctions that depend not only upon institutional divisions of a formal kind (one of the legacies of colonial rule), but also the assumption that the colonial enterprise created the same sorts of distribution between sacred and secular as in the Western tradition. The evidence shows, on the contrary, that despite colonial efforts to control and circumscribe it, the sphere of the religious perpetually flows into other domains, in particular the political. At the same time, as I have argued in my introduction, such approaches confirm a modernist teleology in which reason is understood to be the motor of history and the hallmark of modernity.

Echoing the terms in which ethnicity has been understood as structuring African politics, analyses of "identity politics" focus on the ways in which different constituencies struggle against one another in a bid to capture the state and occupy the public space, in the context of radical pluralism marked by chronic scarcity and the failure of mechanisms of political regulation. What is missing in these accounts is a genealogy of the formation of identity in the African context and the role of historically formed imaginaries in the constitution of group identity. Despite several decades of anthropological and historical analysis that have deconstructed the "illusion of identity"[20] and shown the ways in which contemporary forms of collective identity owe their conditions of plausibility to struggles that emerged over colonial techniques of identification, ethnographic inscription, labor, health, and practices of missionary evangelization and conversion, political science remains stubbornly impervious to this historicizing tendency.

In the West, the rise of identity politics has been analyzed in terms of the erosion of the territorial nation-state's monopoly over the moral resources of community formation.[21] Contemporary identity politics is represented as the public expression of conflicts over what constitutes "subjective harm," and the lack of any political mechanism on the part of the liberal nation-state for arbitrating these conflicting claims to difference.[22] Analysis focuses on how notions of identification, in particular the conflicts over subjective notions of difference, cannot be extricated from the construction of both empire and the modern nation-state, and their subsequent, but partial, deconstruction in the era of globalization.[23] Others discuss the erosion of the distinction in modern Western nation-states between the public and private sphere, and the questionable pertinence of the notion of civil society.[24] These studies, coupled with other, more philosophical inquiries,[25] bring us to recognize that the concept of identity itself is a historically determined one. It is a child of "modernity," as Rouse's and Chatterjee's work shows,[26] which emerges within imperialist and capitalist discourse and practices, and whose genealogy leads back to early Christian discourses on the self retooled by Enlightenment thought.[27] Talal Asad has made similar arguments concerning the historical emergence of the possibility of the concept of identity: "the politics of consciousness, like the politics of personal identity of which it is part, is an entirely modern Western possibility. The self-conscious selection and integration of new elements into that identity (which many anthropologists refer to as syncretism or hybridity) is central to that possibility. That is to say, the centrality of self-constructive action is due to a specific epistemic structure."[28] The universalization of this epistemic structure through both colonial coercion and seduction does not, however, imply its identical reproduction. Rather, in examining Africa, it is this process of "conversion," the ruptures with the past and the play of differences that emerge from the encounter, their transformations and the new political identifications they give rise to through ongoing struggles, which should be the starting point of studies focusing on identity politics.

Religion, Witchcraft, and the Domestication of Modernity

In anthropological studies over the past two decades, a concern to restore events in their historicity is clearly observable. Nevertheless, certain themes persist and tend to counter this turn. First, there is a tendency to see in new forms of religiosity and spiritual or occult practice the creation and elaboration of a vernacular language that has as its principal function to translate into a form of popular knowledge destabilizing processes, such as globalization, relations of domination, and socioeconomic crises—in short, to see them principally as forms of the "domestication of modernity."[29] Whether religion is seen as symbolic, metaphoric, or metonymic, or even in terms of an imaginary, it is more or less reduced to its function of signification, forgetting that it is, perhaps above all, a site of *action,* invested in and appropriated by believers.

Moreover, these approaches do not help us answer the question of why a *particular* form of religious expression develops or is chosen as opposed to another, or why certain forms, in particular Pentecostalism and Islamist movements, have had such remarkable success in recent decades. The unemployment that hits urban youth, the violence with which they are confronted, their political and economic exclusion, the breakdown of support networks, and the failure of classical strategies for social mobility which have led to changes in the way in which success is now represented and imagined:[30] none of these developments explains why some become born-again, delivering themselves from tradition and waging spiritual warfare, while others reinvent traditions under the sign of authenticity while taking up real arms, some find their place among Islamic reformists or in a new relationship with their sheikh, some join cults of satanic worship, some make "money medicine" or participate in gruesome occult traffic in body parts, while others just stay quietly at home.[31]

Some recent studies link the rise of evangelical revival to processes of globalization, as forms of the "production of locality" in the context of increasingly transnationalized flows. Geschiere and Meyer's edited volume addresses the ways in which "globalisation reinforces the production of cultural difference," implying some sort of causal relationship between the intensification of global flows and a new and pressing need for forms of cultural and political closure. They introduce the notion of identity as an "analytical tool," which refers to people's attempts to "fix the flow" and mark boundaries in "the ongoing flux of globalisation processes."[32] In this collection, Van Binsbergen's study of religious practices in urban Zambia employs an extremely problematic understanding of how the current "globalized" context "resuscitates" past practice: "Who would expect ancestral cults to take place in urban settings? What theory of change and continuity would predict the continued, even increasing practice of ecstatic possession ritual in urban residential areas, often in the trappings of new formally organised cults posing as Christian churches or Islamic brotherhoods?"[33] His use of a highly contestable notion of "virtuality" to account for the relationship between the past referent (village religious practices) and the present activity (cults "posing" as churches) is not designed, as one might imagine, to show how identity formation involves the self-conscious selection and integration of elements from a mythicized past. Rather, this notion appears as a kind of shorthand for false consciousness. The villagers think they are Christians performing "modern" rituals, but since any connection they might have with historical, local practices can only be "virtual," they don't realize that they are actually reconstructing "age-old" village practices. Enter the anthropologist, who can "read" the "dream of the village model" in these highly urban, indeed transnationalized, identities and practices. We should indeed wonder what sort of hidden culturalist assumptions are at work when anthropological studies seem determined to account for the construction of "locality" in terms of long-forgotten local pasts, especially when the marks of the past in the present are understood, tacitly or not, in terms of authenticity.

Clearly, continuity in a phenomenological sense is in the eye of the beholder; yet when it comes to the question of the construction of identity, we are dealing with a situation of historical and epistemological rupture. It is anachronistic to speak of precolonial "identities" in Africa. The colonial incursion introduces this novel epistemological and political possibility; the project of "converting" its subjects had, as we know, complex and far-reaching effects, but perhaps the most far-reaching ones were the new possibilities such an encounter provided

Africans for constituting themselves as subjects. As Asad observes, "given that there was now a possibility of recognising themselves as *authentic,* what part did this new fact play in their constitution?"[34] Mbembe has persuasively argued that the appropriation of this problematic of authenticity by Africans (but also, he might have added, Africanists), and its expression in Marxist and nationalist narratives on African identity, has fundamentally determined how Africans continue to construct their discourses on the self. He sees the recent rise of nativism and the new anti-imperialism as the most recent resurrection of a "corpse which continues to rise after each burial."[35] He locates alternative forms of African subjectivation in two increasingly dominant forms of "instituting imaginaries": those of religion and warfare.[36]

In Meyer's paper on Pentecostalism in Ghana, globalization is held to either provoke or intensify a series of anxieties, such as the danger inherent in commodities from global capitalist networks.[37] She relates the dangerous and animated nature of the "sexy underpants" and other "luxury goods" in Ghana to their status as a commodity that is implicated in, and symbolizes, global networks, which Pentecostal practice defetishizes and renders less dangerous. However, rather than being seen as a local or vernacular response to capitalist incursion, in which the lines of cultural continuity provide the explanatory keys, these practices could just as easily be related to a longstanding tradition within Protestant and, more recently, Pentecostal doctrine against "worldliness." This doctrine has only recently been challenged by changes within Pentecostalism, and the account Meyer gives of the need to defetishize commodities appears wherever Pentecostalism is found. One could also argue as convincingly for an explanation that relates their danger to the monopoly that the local political and business elite have over them, invoking the links made between material and supernatural or occult power in the local popular political imagination. The paradigm of domestication is also central to her monograph on the appropriation of Christian categories among the Ewe in Ghana, in particular the figure of the devil, which ultimately stands for the enchantment of modernity.[38]

Recent work by the Comaroffs and their students has taken on a quasi-paradigmatic status in anthropological understandings of the explosion of new forms of supernatural or occult belief and practice in Africa and elsewhere. In these studies, various elements of a supposedly local repertoire of the imaginary are mobilized in response to such themes of modernity as coming to terms with new forms of desire, suffering, inequality, frustration, and moral perplexity. In this sense, they represent attempts to "pin down seemingly random, ramifying and impersonal forces, to give them visible faces and human motives . . . to demystify modernity and its charms—its perverse inequities, its political pieties, its threats to the viability of known social worlds."[39] In all these analyses, both the emergence and form of these practices are understood primarily as local efforts to "demystify" and "plumb the magicalities of"[40] modernity and contemporary global politico-economic forms. The conditions of labor, consumption, frustration, inequality, and desire that "millennial capitalism," "neo-liberalism," the "New World Order" imposes upon "the marginalized and disempowered," their "contradictions" and "conundrums,"[41] are seen as questions that demand a response. Indeed, "under such conditions," "it is only to be expected that there would be an intensification of efforts to make sense"[42] of these developments. This response takes the form, in Africa (often) and even in the West (very occasionally), of new and often gruesome forms of witchcraft and occult discourse and unorthodox religious practice. Zombies, Satanic cults, money medicine, the neo-Pentecostal doctrine of prosperity are all ways of "solving the mysteries of neo-liberal capitalism."[43] One of the aims of these studies is to demonstrate the "modernity" of witchcraft and discourses on occult or evil supernatural powers, and to show how "their enduring liveliness typifies the process through which local practice retools more general forces, inserting themselves into the diverse cultural configurations, the contested realities, the multiple subjectivities of particular worlds."[44] In these approaches, the accent is placed on ritual as signifying practice, and analysis typically proceeds by identifying those specific symbolic practices that, when enacted, constitute the link between the universal and the particular, and perform a "demystifying" signifying function.

While I agree with the insight that witchcraft and other forms of religious revival are highly contemporary, I also concur with Tonda[45] that the reasons for this are purely historical. The Comaroffs' work also shows that today's figures of occult practice and religious discourse are not atavisms from the distant past. Nonetheless, smuggled into some of these analyses is a tacit understanding that perpetuates the relation of exteriority between Western and African modernities. Approaches such as Van Binsbergen's and Devisch's[46] endorse the historico-cultural figure of the "pagan spirit" introduced by Mbembe in his study of African "indocility," implying the endurance of figures from the past that, according to a binary model conceived in terms of power and resistance, contemporary African practice reaffirms in order to deconstruct the Western Logos, even unconsciously, or despite themselves. In the words of Otayek and Toulabor: "We are in the presence of those pagan spirits, which, even converted to Christianity, the African keeps under his hat in order to, in the words of Achille Mbembe, 'deconstruct' the Western absolute. Drawing strength from its instrumentality—its aptitude for managing daily life by not problematising it in an excessive fashion—paganism 'envelops' Christianity, and without any other form of process, suffocates it in an embrace which closely resembles the kiss of death."[47] As I shall argue in greater detail in following chapters, no properly historical or substantive distinction can be made between "tradition" and "modernity." Contemporary forms of witchcraft or occult practice participate in the same field of social practice as Christianity because, as objects—or, more precisely, as objectifications of thought and practice—they have been produced through the same historical experience. Born in the moment of rupture inaugurated with colonialism and mission, they develop through a complex historical relationship of mutual constitution. Witchcraft and Christianity are not eternal objects, but historical, rare, and particular forms that exist only in and through the relation to other historically situated practices, and which are thus never identical to themselves. Although one thing does lead to another in history, there are no lines of cultural continuity in an objective or material sense; such lines are only analytical abstractions or forms of representation objectified through practices, whether practices of ethnographic inscription or real political struggles.

As Tonda argues, once we do away with the false opposition, "tradition" versus "modernity," we must admit that these "opposing" forms are contemporaneous, and that they are forged through the same historical event: "the historical God of the civilising mission and the *génie sorcier*, as symbolic realities inscribed in the dynamic of history and marked by ambivalence, do not define themselves in Africa in a relation of irreducible exteriority. It is one and the same power that is symbolised by God, *le génie sorcier*, luxury goods and the coalition of the aggressive forces found in the imaginary of 'African modernity.'"[48] Pentecostalism and healing churches are often viewed as a sort of revenge on Western imperialism. For Devisch, these churches represent a response to the Belgian colonial intrusion, the modern state and capitalist consumerism. They attempt to overturn foreign models of modernity and heal the psychological wounds inflicted by occupation and "whitening" undertaken by colonial missions and schools.[49] As Tonda notes, the revenge of "paganism" implies that the "powerful of suffocation of the pagan spirit (*génie sorcier*) finds itself reinforced by a coalition of absolutely redoubtable forces, put on the same level: demons, the Devil, ghosts, non-Christian god and luxury merchandise which symbolise them. . . . The conspiracy for deicide thus has, as at the epoch of Judas, accomplices in God's very entourage: demons, the Devil and merchandise that arrived in Africa in Christ's company."[50] The central question is to see how past and contemporary forms of representation and objectification are produced by these practices, how they mutually constitute one another. Practices are always localized in time and space, and their precise form depends those of neighboring practices. Capitalism and Christianity only "exist" insofar as they are practiced; they are not essences, but relations. As such, they always have a "locality," even if the compression of time and space, the extension of scope of what may be considered "neighboring practice," as effects of processes of globalization, have changed the terms in which we understand the local.

Second, local responses are understood as attempts to master what is purportedly a dangerous, incomprehensible, confusing, fetishized ensemble of practices, processes, and objects. But where did all this confusion, fear, and need for fixed identities or mastery suddenly appear from, and more important, what does globalization really have to do with it?[51] In a continent whose history has been marked by fluid boundaries and the continual integration of strangers, and where intimate spaces are often the most dangerous, where economies have been structured over several centuries through at times extremely brutal forms of economic extraversion, and where radical, violent change has marked the past century and a half, these assertions should raise some eyebrows. Are people really more confused by globalization or neoliberalism than they were by colonialism? What is it precisely about globalization that causes such confusion, and why should such processes create a more intensified need for closure or mastery than earlier processes of colonial incursion, domination, and state formation? Why should the response be found in the register of the supernatural? These are precisely the relationships that need to be explained, not asserted as the principal movers behind current religious or spiritual effervescence. To do this, we need a more precise understanding of the ways in which globalization really affects African societies, beginning with an understanding of the local vectors of global processes, in particular African nation-states and religious forms such as Christianity and Islam. The failure of local forms of political authority to provide stable modes for representing and regulating difference and legitimating social inequality are surely linked to changes in global capitalism and the enormous increase of global flows of goods, people, images and ideas, and there is certainly a growing sense of radical insecurity; but again, we need to shed more light on the exact nature of these links and ways in which new forms of government are being constructed. Such failures may indeed make possible alternate forms of social organization, relations of authority and obedience, relations of productivity and consumption, new imaginaries of power, and forms of political subjectivity. And yet these constitute only the conditions in which new practices may be plausible, not an explanation either of why such forms actually arise, or why they take the form that they do.

Third, analysis depends upon assigning particular procedures, bodies, actions, or discourses a metaphorical or symbolic meaning, such that they are able to represent some other definable event, procedure, activity, or discourse. The problem is who decides what this other definable event, procedure, activity, or discourse is? And according to what criteria? What allows the Comaroffs to assume that these practices are principally modes of interpretation and understanding? Why might they not be, rather, principally forms of political practice, modes of *action* on the world? Would the authors of these discourses and practices recognize themselves in these interpretations? What evidence enables us to assert, for example, that Luise White's case of Tanzanian prostitutes who were accused of drawing blood from their migrant clients to sell to the government agents, abetted by firefighters, can be read as a story of "the extraction of value from African persons and communities, extraction both by distant forces and local accomplices,"[52] that it "centres on commodification of bodies; bodies that have lost their integrity, as it were, bodies made to yield up their parts to a rather literal black market," where "the impact of commodification is often linked to the capacity of money to reduce local resources—people, land, cattle— to alienable form (blood, meat, labor, power) so that their essential value may be siphoned off by forces from distant centres"?[53] How is killing old women because they are witches stealing young unemployed South Africans' jobs a form of "interpretation" and "demystification" of the labor relations imposed by millennial capitalism?[54] For the young men doing the killing, it is a form of political practice whose aim is to liberate themselves from forces that prevent them from finding work. Jean Comaroff argues that occult powers and their victims "personify" the conflicts of modernity and "the ways in which foreign forces invade local worlds, turning ordinary people into monsters and eroding established life-ways—themselves fetishized by a sense of impending loss."[55] Such an argument sounds seductive, but nevertheless, this fetishization of established lifeways and "sense of impending loss" is distinctly absent from the most successful contemporary forms of African religious and cultural practice. The rise of Pentecostalism is extremely instructive on these issues, as we shall see in later chapters. Pentecostalism capitalizes with great success on its promise to make a complete break with the past, understood in terms of local practices and cultural forms, even if the exact nature of this apparent rupture shows above all the extent to which both Christianity and witchcraft continue to forge themselves together in a relationship of historical interdependency and mutual constitution. Islamic movements likewise increasingly place the accent on the construction of a global *umma*, decrying the "innovation" implied in the religious *concubinage*[56] expressed in its local traditions. Today in Africa, a great majority of the population is only too eager and willing to hasten the erosion of established lifeways, and such a politics of nostalgia is a peculiarly Western obsession.

The central problem in analyses that rely upon an interpretation of symbolic, metaphoric, or metonymical discourses and practices is that the relationship relies upon treating practice as a text, and establishing between practice and its interpretation a relationship of intertextuality. Witchcraft and religion—by which I mean the complex unity of cognition and practice—are not texts. I am not denying that witchcraft and religion are, among other things, carriers or producers of meanings, but I am questioning *whose* meanings. To say that religion and witchcraft speak about material processes is one thing. We shall see that religious narrative production is indeed extremely prolific on such questions and directly addresses problems related to the ordeal of everyday life in postcolonial Nigeria. But to assert that religion and other forms of spirituality have these processes as their *object,* and to imply that the precise form they take can be understood from an apprehension of these processes themselves is to assert something altogether different, something for which the evidence is invariably lacking. It must be admitted that terms like commodification, alienation, the extraction of essential value, and so forth are part of *another* story, a narrative that relates to a long history of engaged political critique and analysis, whose salvific and utopian aspects continue to make their own gestures toward an elusive transcendental. The argument that sees religious and spiritual practices principally as local interpretations or resistances to destabilizing global forces operates on tacit assumptions that still consider religion as performing a second-order process of adjustment. In the absence of the knowledge required for mastery, it is insinuated, Africans make do with religion.

Asad brings the political implications of this point home in his discussion of the idea of cultural translation, in which the anthropologist's understanding and representation of another culture is understood as a process of reading signs and determining implicit meanings. He gives as his example Ernest Gellner's study of Berber religious belief and argues that the meanings Gellner assigns to Berber belief are not "the meanings the native listener actually acknowledges in his speech, not even the meanings that the native listener necessarily accepts," but those he or she is "potentially capable of sharing" with "scientific authority" in some "ideal situation." In other words, when native listeners can come to accept the interpretations of the anthropologist, they are in "an ideal situation" in which they would no longer be a native listener, but somebody coming to resemble the anthropologist himself. Translation presumes a lexicon or master discourse in terms of which the translator will render intelligible the text to be understood. Thus the authorial voice, which speaks through the cultural text that is local religious belief, is the anthropologist, who assumes a godlike aura by insisting that religious or supernatural signs signify a truth hidden from those who express and elaborate them. Asad concludes by pointing out that this appropriation of others' meanings is not innocent, that it constitutes a representation that cannot normally be contested by the people to whom it is attributed, and that as a "scientific text" it eventually becomes a privileged element in the potential store of historical memory of the society concerned.'[57] Let us recall the South African Zionist's frustration about the omission of the role played by the Holy Spirit in the making of South African history: Everything cannot simply be explained by anthropology or sociology.[58]

Finally, Jean Comaroff somewhat disingenuously claims that witchcraft as a response to globalization is not merely a local or African phenomenon, and cites American and British cases of satanic abuse to make her case: "But lest we conclude that this is a peculiar, peripheral response, I hope to persuade you that very similar processes occur in ordinary American communities, where actors also try to press a human likeness on dilemmas posed by the so-called 'New World Order.'"[59] It may be argued that a certain commonality as regards local reactions to this new context could be expected, as one could claim this context as globally shared and one in which locality is harder and harder to produce and maintain. Yet what is claimed is more than a phenomenological similarity—it is a similarity at the level of meaning. These practices are all phenomena whose raison d'être and explanation can be found in some sort of global need to "press a human likeness" on dilemmas posed by the "New World Order." But according to what criteria can we establish such a need, and why should it be globally shared? Unless we posit shared epistemological universes, witchcraft beliefs can only signify the same thing in different historical contexts if they are understood as a sign, as a metaphor, or as a text that can be read according to a master lexicon. And yet, I insist, who decides what meanings these discourses and practices, either ritual or everyday, have? In the final analysis, this sort of cultural translation ultimately serves to underline the hegemony of the master narrative that enables us to decipher the truth of these local practices, the secular discourse of social science.

We need to take into account properly historical, empirical questions about the genesis of this type of discourse and its dramatic public presence. LaFontaine, Comaroff, and others who have studied accusations of witchcraft and Satanism in the West have noted that these accusations all originated in what they call "fundamentalist Protestant" circles, were circulated and given public prominence by pastors and evangelicals, who also acted as "expert witnesses" to meetings of other secular experts like social workers and journalists.[60] In Kenya, Daniel Arap Moi, no doubt influenced by his own Pentecostal faith, ordered a parliamentary inquiry into the prevalence and danger of Satanic cults in Kenya. The vast majority of witnesses who gave credence to the danger of this new cult through their detailed and gruesome testimony were born-again Christians.[61] The production and intensification of fears of witchcraft, and arguably of certain types of occult practice, in Nigeria has been directly related to discourses and narratives produced and circulated by Pentecostal pastors and converts. In all these cases, the role of these actors is a very important one, although dismissed by Comaroff as mere "fundamentalist paranoia" (which it clearly wasn't by those involved in making the accusations). The dramatic growth of witchcraft fears and the current form they take are undoubtedly related to the rise of this extremely successful vector of globalization. In the matter of assigning meanings, anthropologists and Pentecostal pastors and converts clearly would not agree. As a globalized form of knowledge and power, a complex, hybrid, supple, and extremely successful mode of organization that elaborates an explicit and globalized program for interpreting the world and governing the self and others, Pentecostalism is by no means a new-age marginal, and we dismiss it as a form of "paranoia" at our peril.

If we look closely, we cannot fail to see a hidden political agenda in accounts that project confusion, loss, and nostalgia onto African practices of modernity. Whence this hidden obsession with authentic identity? Whose obsession is it, really? Mbembe and Mudimbe have traced the genealogy of "authenticity as resistance" to the *odeur du Père*,[62] and have discussed the ways in which Africans and Africanists alike continue to perpetuate it.[63] The model of agency and subjecthood implicit in these studies of occult practice reveals more than just a willingness to recognize the historicity of African societies, to grant them at last their long-denied place in the history of humanity. Underlying these interpretations is a hidden model of agency and consciousness that serves to demystify for *observers* these inscrutable ways of doing and thinking. When faced with "irrational" behaviour, such as religious conversion or witchcraft beliefs, Asad argues, Western social scientists resort to the idea of agency to render such behavior rational and freely chosen. "Everybody has agency; everyone is responsible for the life he or she leads. The doctrine of action has become essential to our recognition of other people's humanity."[64] If we cannot take religious or occult practice at its word, then we can only find its rationality insofar as it performs another action and function. Since no anthropologist is prepared to admit that killing old women is a reasonable or effective way of freeing up the labor market, such actions must be doing something else, something humanly possible. But history teaches us that practice in general, and political action in particular, does not find its logic in being either reasonable or efficacious. Paradoxically, the progressive political impulse behind this advocacy only serves to reinforce a parochial view that fails to take fully into account the radical nature of these practices, their irreducibility, their historical singularity.

Yet what is left out of these studies—that irreducible element of faith that marks the frontier of what it is possible for social science to think, and which analyses circumnavigate, reduce, or ignore—reveals another form of struggle and danger. In many vital respects, religious regimes today not only find themselves, but *position* themselves in competition or confrontation with social scientific forms of knowledge; indeed, they may find themselves in confrontation with certain institutions and practices that social science underwrites through a variety of normative discourses, particularly those of political economy. They constitute, in this sense, distinct regimes for the government of conduct, and lay out a different domain in terms of which the true and the false can be distinguished. For example, the idealistic voluntarism and self-consciously linear and progressive temporality implied in constructs such as development and modernization clash with religious ideas of historical agency and time, even if their interpenetration is more complex than may first appear. The economy of miracles deployed through Born-Again practice develops a complex, conflictive relationship with dominant notions of economic productivity and political agency. This confrontation is explicitly clear in many forms of contemporary revivalism, but the same argument could be made about other forms of occult or spiritual practice. Accounts that speak of religious revival as forms of the "domestication of modernity" or as forms of coping with material crisis talk as if these processes are merely second-order adjustments, ways of making do, African *bricolage* as opposed to Western engineering. And yet in the case of Pentecostalism and Islam, the confrontation between these different regimes of power and knowledge is not a second-order process of adjustment, but rather an extremely salient contemporary political struggle, whose outcome cannot be foreseen, and which in many of its current forms, is literally a matter of life and death.

Religious discourse, practice, and even institutions only render themselves up as an object for social scientific analysis, or submit to such an operation of objectification, with great difficulty. As Barber puts it: "The idea that gods are made by men, not men by gods, is a sociological truism. It belongs very obviously to a detached and critical tradition of thought incompatible with faith in these gods."[65] Bayart has also drawn attention to the centrality of the "dimension of faith" to the study of religious movements, and the difficulty it poses for the social scientist. In Africa, he observes, it is a "dimension no doubt complicated by the straddling and mixing of multiple lines of cultural identification, which Mbembe has wittily called situations of 'religious *concubinage.*' A prodigiously diverse dimension as well, in all its different expressions, from a popular, everyday faith to refined theologies or mystical transports. But a dimension which is irreducible, and which no social scientific analysis will ever manage to fully capture."[66] Any attempt to *reduce* regimes of religious practice, to give an *exhaustive* explanation of them in functional or materialist terms may thus be seen as a sort of battle strategy, akin to wearing down by attrition or siege. That such a strategy purports to tell us the truth about these religious practices, that such an account may be perfectly consistent with its own disciplinary, epistemological, and ontological assumptions, should not blind us to the remainder of this operation. The approaches critically discussed here inevitably imply an a priori notion of the proper field of religion and religious activity, its proper field of authority, action, and knowledge. But the Born-Again program has as one of its central aims the redefinition, by and through practices and professions of faith, of what can be known about the world and what can be done within it.

A properly historical approach rejects the hidden forms of functionalism discussed in the analyses above. It enables us to avoid implying

radical-
ization — a relation of causality between nebulously defined material crises and the rise of new forms of religiosity and spiritual practice. Rather than understanding these "processes" and "forces" (globalization, the crisis of the nation-state, commodification, mass mediation, migration, crises of representation both political and epistemological, new forms of wealth and inequality) as the *object* of religious activities and discourses, I want to see them as contributing to their context of plausibility, as part of the historical conditions that enable their emergence. In this sense I agree with Bayart when he argues for the fertility of a Foucauldian approach in apprehending the historicity of religious movements and their participation in the "complex strategic situation" of colonial and postcolonial governmentality.[67] Such an approach will enable us to maintain these events in the historical dispersion and contingency that is proper to them, and show that the questions to which Jesus is an answer are multiple, contradictory, and above all, produced through the complex interpenetration of multiple struggles and relations. In this study, I will proceed by supposing that religious change is not merely the sign or the effect of change in other domains of human practice, but constitutes rather, in and of itself, a mode of historical and political transformation. I will consider Born-Again Christianity as a specific regime of practice, in and through which particular moral and political subjects are produced. My approach will undertake to evaluate the sorts of political struggles the movement gives rise to, principally through processes of subjectivation, and their effects on the production of politics in postcolonial Nigeria, without resorting to an a priori notion of either religion or politics.

I will thus analyze the Born-Again revival in terms of the Foucauldian problematics of government and subjectivation. Following a loosely Foucauldian approach does not mean endorsing or applying a particular theory, but rather applying a series of principles that serve as an analytical grid. Foucauldian insights about power, history, governance, and the subject do not constitute a theory of these objects, but entail a particular way of unsettling them as objects, a dispersion of false evidences. The two central insights I shall borrow from Foucault are his understanding of history as "event" (*histoire événementielle*) and his analysis of processes of subjectivation, which are closely linked to the ways in which he understands power and the problem of government. While it will be impossible here to render the complexity and depth of Foucault's reflections on power and subjectivation, I will attempt to sketch out the central themes that are of interest to my study, to bring out their pertinence for the study of religion and politics in Africa. The examples cited in my exegeses of these ideas should be taken principally as illustrations of the fertility of such an approach for the study of religious movements in Africa.

History as "Event": Multiplying Causes

Event: we must understand by this not a decision, a treaty, a rule or a battle, but a relation of forces [*un rapport de forces*] which is inversed, a power confiscated, a vocabulary appropriated and turned against its users, a domination which weakens, relaxes its hold, poisons itself, another which makes its masked entry. The forces that are at play in history follow neither a destination nor a mechanic, but rather the hazard of struggle. They do not manifest themselves as successive forms of a primordial intention; nor do they take on the allure of a result. They always appear in the singular uncertainty [*aléa*] of the event. . . .

   To follow the complex path of provenance is to maintain that which has happened in the dispersion which is proper to it: it is to identify the accidents, the minute deviations—or on the contrary, the total reversals—the errors, the misunderstandings, the bad calculations which have given birth to what exists and means for us; it is to discover that at the root of what we know and what we are, there is neither truth nor being, but the exteriority of the accident . . . no one is responsible for an emergence, none may take the glory for it; it always produces itself in the interstices.[68]

This vision of history depends, as Paul Veyne argues,[69] on what he has called Foucault's "philosophy of the relation," which "revolutionizes" history by placing the accent on contingency, struggle, and the almost infinite multiplication of causes: he draws attention to the "rarity" of historical objects, their singularity and instability, their production through practice, via multiple and ongoing relations to other practices. Foucault's genealogical view of history implies a systematic dissociation of identity, which is only "a mask" or "a parody"—"the plural inhabits it, innumerable souls dispute within it," and in each one of these souls "history will not discover a forgotten identity, always ready to be reborn, but a complex system of elements, each in their turn multiple and distinct, over which no power of synthesis dominates."[70] Veyne explains: "Foucault's initial intuition is neither structure, nor rupture, nor discourse: it is rarity, in the Latin sense of the term; human doings [*faits*] are rare, they are not installed in the fullness of reason, there is a void around them for other doings that our wisdom cannot guess; for what is could be otherwise; human doings are arbitrary, in Mauss'

sense; they don't go without saying."[71] A given practice does not have a single or clearly identifiable origin, it "emerges," caught up in this web of multiple forces, and its transformation is perpetual and ongoing. It does not depend upon a preexisting "natural object"—religion, the state—of which it would be one projection; such natural objects are pure abstractions. Instead of an analysis that begins with the object, taken as the end or finality of practice, Veyne suggests we follow Foucault:

> In the place of this philosophy of the object taken as an end or a cause, let us thus substitute a philosophy of the relation and take the problem by the middle, by the practice or the discourse. This practice throws up the objectifications that correspond to it and anchors itself on the realities of the moment, which is to say, on the objectifications of neighbouring practices. To put it more clearly, it actively fills the spaces left by these neighbouring practices, it actualises the possibilities that they prefigure in hollow; if neighbouring practices change, if the limits of these hollows move . . . this practice will actualise these new possibilities and will no longer be the same.[72]

Hence Foucault rejects the idea of the transcendental subject and the necessity of consciousness, intentionality, or a rationality that could be measured against some value of Reason. "There is no need to go through an instance of individual or collective consciousness in order to grasp the site of an articulation of practice."[73] This is why, as Veyne points out, neither ideology nor belief can *explain* practices; if we take them as revealing the signification of practices and inciting conduct through their action on consciousness, we are left to explain the inexplicable, the belief itself, and can only "observe piteously that sometimes people believe, sometimes they don't, and we can't make them believe any old ideology or belief on simple demand, and that, what is more, they are perfectly capable of believing in things which, from the point of view of the belief, are in contradiction with one another, even if they accommodate themselves quite well in practice."[74] If we mean by "ideology" things such as religious doctrines, political ideologies, then we are talking about historical or literary artifacts that are themselves discursive practices. In this sense we should understand the Born-Again movement as a discursive regime, an understanding that requires us to take its internal articulations, doctrines, problematizations and rationalities seriously, rather than only focusing on its concrete expressions through ritual and everyday practices.

So this "rupture of evidence" is the first methodological principle. According to this vision, the dramatic rise of Born-Again Christianity in Nigeria must be seen as having a complex provenance. This study does not aim to undertake its genealogy; such an enterprise would require a much greater scope. Nonetheless, this insight enables us to begin by multiplying the reasons for which Jesus might come to be seen to be the answer in Nigeria today, and to maintain the contingency and the dispersion of these various explanations. The Foucauldian view of history leads us to recognize, for example, that as a category for understanding specific historical change, the concepts of religious syncretism and cultural *bricolage* are analytically empty, only serving as shorthand for processes of historical change more generally. All history is a history of syncretism or *bricolage*.[75] As Veyne puts it, "history is a kaleidoscope, not a nursery, there are no eternal objects—religion, the state—which grow throughout history like ancient trees." One thing does indeed lead to another, and yet we should beware of false continuities, and never forget that what is could have been otherwise. The objects of our practice are rare, fragile, the fruit of chance, and it is in their "unexpected contours and ornamentation [*tarabiscotages*]" that we find "the key to their enigma."[76]

The implication of this position on the primacy of the relation is, as Asad puts it, that we cannot understand the new by tracing the origins of an amalgam.[77] If, for example, we attempt to understand what emerges in the encounter between the Yoruba and mission in terms of the mixing of two distinct systems whose precontact elements will explain the logic of what emerges, we commit the error of endorsing an artificial conception that identifies two religious systems, when history shows us that the objectifications "Yoruba religion" and "missionary Christianity" only emerge through the encounter itself. Tracing the origins of an amalgam means to take the object religion as a natural, ahistorical reality, a form without content, or a form with every content, forgetting that it is only through practices that objectify an ensemble of specific discourses, rituals, and norms as "religion" that this "object" can have any reality. This leads us to recognize that the indigenous Christian practice that emerges from the encounter with mission is something altogether new. Even the local ontology of power and its various rituals, everyday practices, and objects, whose endurance is often seen as the central line of historical continuity, or the proof of the superficiality of Christianity, emerges from this encounter as something altogether different. These new objects—"our traditions" and Nigerian Christianity—were created through a process of objectification, itself the creation of a play of differences that was the outcome of various encounters and struggles: between missionaries and religious specialists and converts, between missionaries and the colonial authorities, between missionaries and local powers, between converts and the market, between converts and the unconverted, between converts and local powers and authorities, between converts and their own past. Hence what we think of as a religious history develops through a multitude of other processes and relations, as the Comaroffs' study of South Africa shows.[78] The ways in which Born-Again Christianity grafts itself onto the historical experience of Christianity in Nigeria thus does not imply the consummation of a chain of events whose logic of internal development would be written into the process from the outset. The Born-Again revival has this history as one of the strands of its provenance, but also finds its historical conditions of possibility in the contingency of the multiple mutations in the complex field of relations that have developed in Nigeria since.

If we follow this method, we needn't ask the question of whether or not people really believe in the reality of miracles, the power of prayer, or the nefarious work of evil spirits; nor do we need to ask what good or evil it does to believe, what function belief may have in this or that social or political process, or whether such and such a belief is rational, and according to which value of Reason. Beliefs are neither true nor false, but only "in the true" of a given historical field: "It's the truth of things which, over the centuries, is strangely constituted. Far from being the most simple realist experience, the truth is the most historical of them all."[79] Finally, we need not examine the content of belief for hidden symbols of the "real" that it might be imagined to either conceal or express. I will thus not attempt to read, for example, a hidden story of capitalist exploitation into the gory and detailed account of Grace Ihere's kidnapping by the evil Queen of the Coast, nor see the devil's underwater computers as a metaphor for the "dangers" of globalization (see appendix for the full text of this testimony). I will not take beliefs for anything more or less than what they are, as a work of the historically constituted imagination, neither true nor false. The point of inquiry is to show how this work of the imagination gives rise to discursive practices that have particular effects on the conduct of the self and on neighboring practices.

Power Relations and Relations of Domination

The second major insight this understanding of history gives us concerning Africa is, as Bayart points out, that it invalidates culturalist explanations, or accounts of identity in terms of authenticity.[80] It makes a nonsense of the opposition between tradition and modernity, understood in terms of a historical reality or as descriptive categories with a determined content, rather than objectifications that arise from practices and participate in struggles and relations of power. It denies any explanatory power to the term "identity" itself, requiring that we investigate the various heterogeneous forces that have gone into constructing what comes to be seen as natural or primordial. This insight is fundamental for the study of ethnicity, as Bayart points out, and as numerous historians and anthropologists have made clear, but the same argument could be made for religion understood as a cultural propensity. It also allows us to see Mbembe's arguments concerning the genealogy of "authenticity as resistance" through Foucauldian lenses, agreeing that the African discourses of nationalism and Marxist liberation do not constitute a reversal of colonial modes of classification and ascription, but rather endorse their principal terms.[81] Such an approach prompts us to consider how "authenticity" as a category of self-representation becomes part of new political and epistemological struggles, and implies the adoption of new categories for situating both the individual and community within new narratives of local and global history and new concepts of time.

It also enables us to conceive the heterogeneity of power in the postcolonial situation, in terms of which it becomes impossible to represent relations of power according to a binary, ontological schema of domination and resistance. Despite what hasty observers have maintained, Foucault rejects the idea of a "system of domination exercised by an element or a group on another, and whose effects, through successive derivations would penetrate the entire social body."[82] His understanding of power is nonsubstantive, nonmaterialist, and entirely relational: "There is no power, but only relations [*rapports*] of power, which are ineluctably born, as effects and conditions, from other processes."[83] The first question Foucault asks, in order to avoid ontological, substantive understandings, is not what power is or where it comes from, but how it is exercised.[84] Distinguishing power relations from "capacities to transform objects" and from "relations of communication," he argues, nonetheless, that these are not separate domains (production, signification, domination), but rather three types of relations that have their own specificity, but are always interwoven, give each other mutual support, and use each other mutually as instruments. He shows how these different relations imply one another, and argues that the degree of coordination among these three types is neither uniform nor constant, and how certain blocs may be formed historically, such as schools, prisons, monasteries, in which the adjustment among these relations is regulated and concerted in a specific articulation. Thus, when it comes to interpretations that view religious or spiritual practices principally as modes of the fabrication of meaning, we can see how a Foucauldian view enables us to understand them in multiple ways, and to see how they also constitute modes of government or modes of productivity.

What makes a power relation singular for Foucault is that it is always a mode of action that does not act directly and immediately on others, but "acts on their action": "it incites, it inducts, it diverts, it facilitates or renders more difficult, it enlarges or limits, it renders more or less probable; at the limit, it constraints or prevents absolutely; but it is always a way of acting on one or many acting subjects, in so far as they act or are susceptible to act."[85] It is neither a relation of violence, nor a relation of consent, such as in the juridical model of the contract, but the "surface of contact where are conjoined the mode of conducting individuals and the mode in which individuals conduct themselves."[86] Foucault locates this singularity in the idea of "government," understood as "conducting of conduct" (*conduire les conduites*) in the double sense of "leading" others by applying forms of coercion that are more or less strict or intense, and of "comporting" oneself in a field of possibilities that is more or less open. Power understood as a relation enables us to see how it is productive, how it does not only deny, repress, prevent, but also enables. Freedom is the precondition for the exercise of power, so that a relation of physical destruction or slavery in which no response is possible is not a power relation for Foucault: "at the very heart of the power relationship, and constantly provoking it, are the recalcitrance of the will and the intransigence of freedom." It is an "agonism": "a relationship which is at the same time reciprocal incitation and struggle, less of a face to face confrontation which paralyzes both sides than a permanent provocation."[87] A confrontational relationship is, in this sense, the frontier where the calculated induction of others' conduct reaches its limits, in which it either reduces the governed to a state of total powerlessness or leads to a reversal, in which those who are being governed become adversaries. "Every strategy of confrontation dreams," Foucault argues, "of becoming a relation [*rapport*] of power, and every relation [*rapport*] of power leans . . . towards becoming a winning strategy."[88]

Government and Governmentality

What Foucault calls a "complex strategic situation" is what other analysts call *le pouvoir* (power in the sense of rule), but his understanding of it is not ontological. "Power [*le pouvoir*] is not an institution, and it is not a structure, it is not a certain force [*puissance*] which some have: it is the name we give to a complex strategic situation in a given society." A certain arrangement of these complex relations can be identified as a particular relation [*rapport*] or exercise of power, but only as long as we consider it as a sort of instant photograph of multiple and continually changing struggles, in and through which this arrangement transforms itself continually.[89] What Foucault calls a complex strategic situation has as its basis relations of power. Power relations, even relations of domination, do not take the form of an ontological opposition between power and resistance, but the form of "multiple struggles in continual transformation," which may, at a given moment, take the form of "a situation, a type of exercise, a certain distribution or economy of power."[90] The utility of such a conception in grasping the heterogeneity of power in the postcolonial context has been well argued by Bayart, particularly in respect to his discussion of the governmentality of the belly.[91] Binary models, in particular those that oppose civil society to the state, or draw lines of distinction between dominants and dominated, between formal and informal, invariably fail to account for the multiple lines that criss-cross these categories. Even Bayart's notion of "straddling" in his *State in Africa* captures with difficulty the complex interpenetration of multiple, simultaneous struggles and logics in which actors and institutions are positioned and position themselves.

In reflecting on what Bayart has identified as the governmentality of the belly in Africa, we must be very careful as to which reading of "governmentality" we employ. As he points out, the term was initially employed in Foucault's research in a highly specific historical sense, to refer to the emergence of a complex strategic situation in the West that has had a certain stability and permanence, and in which power relations find their concentration in the state. Governmentality was the problematic in terms of which Foucault brought the state into the field of analysis of micro-powers, in which he undertook to study medical, penal, and psychiatric institutions.[92] However, from 1979 Foucault extended his understanding beyond the governmental practices of a particular historical arrangement of power relations, to a general analytical frame where power is seen in terms of government as "conducting conduct"—"government of children, government of souls and consciences, government of a household, of a State, or of oneself"[93]—and serves as a "grid of analysis for power relations" in general. In this extended conception, governmentality becomes the strategic field of relations of power, in their mobile, transformable, reversible character, within which are established forms of government, or types of conducting of conduct. More precisely, "since the strategic field is itself nothing more than the play of relations of power amongst themselves," he shows how they imply each other reciprocally, such that governmentality is not a structure, but a "general singularity" whose variables, in their uncertain interaction, arise from particular historical circumstances.[94]

Rather than seeing the governmentality of the belly as a historical form of "the rationality immanent in micro-powers, whatever the level of analysis considered,"[95] or as a certain exercise or economy of power that has a relatively stable and coherent form, I think one might argue that the field of power relations in the postcolonial context is marked by the failure of "a winning strategy" to impose itself. Rather than a relatively enduring arrangement among various relations, a relatively coherent and stable set of mechanisms for conducting others' conduct, perhaps we should see instead the predominance of adversarial relations and strategic struggles, all of which "dream" of becoming a winning strategy, provoking constant and ongoing crises of governmentality. Mbembe speaks of a current context of radical uncertainty in postcolonial Africa. Can we relate this to the permanence in African history of what he has called, somewhat unhappily, a "heretical spirit"?[96] Or could we argue that it is less some sort of historico-metaphysical figure, even taken in a metaphorical sense, than the persistence of multiple, opposed, contradictory relations of power that are the result of a long series of concrete struggles in terms of which African societies have constructed their relations with themselves and with others? Such struggles are revealed in the heterogeneity of the multiple sites in which power relations crystallize in the complex strategic postcolonial situation: state institutions, "traditional" authorities, kinship, ethnicity, religious regimes, capitalist production and consumption, and more diffuse forms related to the acceleration of global flux. Rather than a social imaginary that has order as its fundamental object and norm,[97] we can argue that a social imaginary of disorder is politically and socially productive in the postcolony, and that government becomes a question of managing disorder: variously creating, controlling, inciting, exploiting both disorder and insecurity. The historical form of governmentality that Foucault sees arising in the West does not emerge within the state form in Africa. Nor have the various relations of power within the social body been governmentalized in this particular sense, however much colonial rule relied upon techniques of discipline, classification, coercion, and other biopolitical modes of conducting conduct, and even if we can see the development complex and neo-liberalism as new forms of governmentality which appear in many ways as extensions of colonial governmental practice.[98]

Even if we admit a historical "African governmentality" in the broader Foucauldian sense, such as the "governmentality of the belly," and recognise the historicity of the "imported state,"[99] it appears difficult to identify a specific dominant rationality immanent in the various micro-political sites that would enable relations of domination to stabilize in a durable way, such that their effects would be diffused throughout the social body—indeed, such that they could arise from within the whole of the social nexus[100]—even if we might find such forms of domination at subnational levels. In this sense, neither the national political sphere in general, nor the postcolonial state in particular, is a concentration of a particular governmental relation of power. Even if a form of authoritarian patrimonialism appears as the dominant mode of power's exercise, at the state level the principal mode of "conducting conduct" resides in the prevalence of conflict among competing governmental forms, disorder, and the use of violence.

In studies of colonial rule, the emphasis tends to be placed on the colonial state's disciplinary techniques, programs of territorialization and classification of populations, and the problem of colonial domination. However fruitful such an enterprise may be, it seems that Foucault's fundamental insight about history, and more specifically governmentality, is the recognition of the contingency of any relation of power. If we examine the ways in which colonial power was deployed, and notwithstanding its powers of classification, discipline, and coercion, we must recognize that "any governmentality can only be strategic or programmatic. It never works. But it is with respect to a program that one can say it never works."[101] Here I would complement Bayart's discussion by adding that the central insight we can gain from Foucault's analysis of this form of power concerns how he sees the productivity of this relationship—namely, the continuous formation of the political field itself through the simultaneous existence of forms of power and resistances to these forms. "The political is nothing more or less than that which is born with the resistance to governmentality, the first uprising, the first confrontation."[102]

If we think, then, of the colonial enterprise as a specific instance of governmentality, and focus on its strategic and programmatic nature, the Foucauldian approach enables us to bring to light the ways in which the postcolonial political field emerges through complex struggles over a form of power whose central mode of operation was not merely domination, violence, or economic exploitation, but a mode of conducting men's conduct, of structuring the possible field of actions of the colonized, of making subjects out of them. Such an analysis shows how these processes gave rise to effects that cannot be seen as the outcome of an intentionality, or simply as the fruit of consciousness. If we take the case of the missionary encounter as an example, we can argue that mission was part of an explicit strategic program[103] whose self-representation takes the form of a rational program marked by an ideological voluntarism, clarity as to goals and the instruments required to achieve them, as well as moral certainty and little doubt as to the final outcome. It is thus similar in many ways to the Born-Again movement a century later. The effects of the mission's "strategic program" were far-reaching; their crystallisation into what was presented as a religious discourse concerning salvation drew its logic, as the Comaroffs show, from a series of practices and diverse strategies not exhausted by religious doctrine. Those practices were related to domains such as health, education, productivity, bodily practices such as dress and hygiene, and they employed a variety of different instruments. They were also profoundly implicated in techniques of power and coercion, as well as techniques of classification and distinction, as demonstrated by the cardinal role of missionary ethnography.

And yet, as both Peel's and the Comaroffs' studies of mission show, the actual encounter follows the logic of struggle, of chance, of missed opportunities and bad calculations.[104] If we observe what the Comaroffs have called, unhappily, "the working misunderstandings" of encounter,[105] we can recognize that missionary practice can only be strategic and programmatic. This view leads us to reject the relation of externality so often assumed between regimes of Christianity and indigenous practices of spirituality or power, as discussed above. As we shall see in chapter 2, the indigenous appropriation of Christianity was perfectly consistent with the rationality of an indigenous spiritual practice that was at once instrumental, this-worldly, and concerned with controlling unseen forces, but this should not bring us to assume that conversion was a mere veneer. The indigenous appropriation endorsed the radical changes conversion implied in the ways in which the individual and the group situated themselves with respect to the past and future, as well as to other groups in society, and also the changes in how legitimate authority was established, conduct evaluated, and collective and personal advancement imagined. The result was something radically different from what the missionaries had hoped for, but it marked nonetheless a radical rupture with the past. So viewed, the process of conversion, religious revival, and change takes on an entirely different significance. Conversion is not simply a matter of free will or human agency, nor is it, on the contrary, the outcome of a capitulation. It is not a ruse, a mere veneer, or an instance of a process of the reduction of difference to the same. Rather, it is the fruit of an ongoing struggle occurring within a complex web of contradictory, parallel, juxtaposed forces, at once arising from outside and inside both the society and the self.

Global Pentecostalism, like evangelical mission before it, is a form of "strategic program,"[106] a specific regime of practices that involves determined prescriptions concerning how institutions should be organized, behavior regulated, narrative structured, an order of knowledge and the rules of its verification determined, authority established, spaces laid out, and so forth. As a regime of practice, the Born-Again project of making a complete break with the past through conversion may only be strategic and programmatic. And yet the fact that in real life nothing ever happens as in the program does not mean that such a program is mere utopia, some sort of ideal type or mere ideology. As Foucault argues, that would be to have a pretty thin notion of "the real." The elaboration of such a program both responds to a series of practices or diverse strategies and leads to a whole series of effects in the real: its programs are crystallized in institutions, they inform individuals' conduct, they serve as a grid for the perception and appreciation of things.[107]

Subjectivity and Subjectivation

Alongside Foucault's analysis of power relations and governmentality emerges the problematic of subjectivity and subjectivation, which are the Foucauldian political objects par excellence. What Foucault attempts to bring to light, without resort to any preconceived notion of agency, consciousness, or the subject, are the processes that work, from within and without, to produce that historical singularity which is the subject in the double sense of being subject *to,* and the subject *of* a practice. This latter dimension implies the self in its relation to itself, insofar as it recognizes itself in a code of action and establishes itself not only as the agent, but as the subject of this action. Subjectivation implies not merely the subjected individual, but also the "singularity who affirms itself in the resistance to power."[108]

Foucault's study of moral subjectivation helps elucidate the question of how subjects are historically produced in this active sense. His discussion of what he calls the techniques of the self are central to his analysis of the ways in which the self works upon itself (*le travail de soi sur soi*). According to Foucault, it is as much through what he terms "the techniques of the self" as through the moral codes and obligations of submission that prevail in a society that the individual constitutes himself as moral subject. These techniques of the self, which "allow individuals to perform a certain number of operations on their bodies, their souls, their thoughts, their conduct in such a way as to produce in themselves transformations or modifications, and attain certain states of perfection, happiness, purity, or supernatural power,"[109] are distinct from techniques of production, signification, communication, or domination, even if there exist multiple links among all of them. An analysis of moral subjectivation would involve an examination of moral codes and what sort of means are employed to impose them, as well as a study of "moralities," or the degree to which individuals adhere to such codes, but it also means taking into account the work of the self on the self, in order to show how the self recognizes itself in a code of action, and establishes itself "not only as an agent, but as the moral subject of this action."[110]

All practices are caught up in the intermingled lines of juridiction (power), veridiction (knowledge), and subjectivation. Processes of subjectivation are characterized by the active and free work of the self on the self, and yet this work is itself firmly embedded in relations of power. Even if the work on the self constitutes a separate moment in the overall processes of subjectivation, nevertheless, these practices are not something the individual invents himself. They are schemas he finds in his culture, which are proposed, suggested or imposed by it, by his society and social group.[111] What Foucault calls "prescriptive regimes," such as the Born-Again or missionary projects, involve specific arrangements of these schemas, combining particular doctrinal, institutional, and discursive forms, and lend themselves particularly well to an analysis in terms of subjectivation. In the following chapters, I will bring to light a certain number of interconnections between the work that God's subjects undertake and their insertion in "the world." The work of the self on the self as well as representations of self are realized at the interface of locality and cosmopolitanism; many of the experiences—

indeed, the ordeals in terms of which new religious practices and imaginaries "make sense"—are shared throughout the continent and other parts of the world, as the global success of Pentecostalism testifies. We will observe how today the circulation of religious doctrines and codes; various discursive practices, such as preaching, witness, prayer, and prophecy; objects of material culture; diverse techniques of the self; and elements of lifestyle reflect the relations of power and the strategic games at the heart of processes of globalization and their expression in Nigerian history.

As Deleuze argues, subjectivation "is the production of modes of existence or styles of life." However, it does not imply the reinstatement of the transcendental subject nor does it demand an understanding of "individual subjective experience," about which, in any case, we can know little. As a process, subjectivation is not an interiorization, it has nothing to do with the person or consciousness: "there is no subject, but only a production of subjectivities," no I, only an ensemble of relations.[112] Indeed, it is the rare and singular nature of history as *event* which provides the unstable play between the criss-crossing lines of juridiction, veridiction, and subjectivation through which subjectivities emerge, and yet they appear in a dimension that is opposed to all stratification or codification. A line of subjectivation is "a line of flight: it escapes from the precedent lines [knowledge, power], it extricates itself. The Self is neither a form of knowledge nor power [*ni un savoir, ni un pouvoir*]. It is a process of individuation which applies to groups or persons, which subtracts itself from the relations of forces and constituted knowledge [*savoirs*]: a sort of surplus value."[113] In this sense, it has a normative and political import, insofar as it is "the operation in which individuals or communities constitute themselves as subjects at the margins of constituted knowledges and established powers, even if this means giving rise to new knowledge and inspiring new powers."[114]

The context of Foucault's reflection on the question of subjectivity is in part linked to his experience and observation of the Iranian revolution, in which he poses the question of the Iranians' struggle for "that thing whose possibility we others have forgotten since the Renaissance and the great crises of Christianity: a political spirituality. I can already hear some French laughing, but I know that they are wrong."[115] In his conception of subjectivity, politics, and ethics, we can see the primacy for Foucault of the idea of resistance, "uprising," and various practices that he will call, for the want of a better word, "counter-conducts."[116] Uprising is "the wrenching which interrupts the thread of history" and "which introduces into it the dimension of subjectivity," showing that the exercise of power is always perilous.[117] Spirituality, as a generator of an insurrectional force, is thus linked to his consideration of the problem of ethical and political subjectivity, as is made clear in his analysis of the history of the Christian pastorate, the forms of counter-conduct it gave rise to, and the crises of governmentality they pro-voked.[118] This is the sense of his observation on political spirituality: "Is not the most general political problem that of truth? How to link one to the other, the way of distinguishing the true and the false and the mode of governing the self and others? The will to found both en-tirely anew, the one through the other (discover an altogether different division through another mode of self-governance, to govern oneself altogether differently through another division) that is what 'political spirituality' is."[119]

Taken in a more general philosophical sense, and leaving aside the political import of these observations, I think it is here, in this notion of spirituality, that we can see how Foucault's thought can rejoin that of Deleuze on desire. For Foucault, "the man who rises up is ultimately without explanation."[120] If Foucault has an idea of human nature, it is perhaps this inexplicable quality, this original capacity to act. As Veyne puts it, "man is the actualizing animal": he actualizes the possibilities that neighboring practices have opened up. "This actualisation is what Saint Augustine called love, and turned into a teleology; like Spinoza, Deleuze turns it into nothing of the sort and calls it desire. . . . It is the fact that the mechanisms turn, that the possibilities realise themselves rather than not."[121] This notion shows that there is no human nature, or rather "that this nature is a form without any other content than historical." Why call it desire, the fact that people interest themselves in possible arrangements (*agencements*) and make them function? "Be-cause, it seems to me, affectivity is the mark of our interest in things . . . this desire, like Spinoza's *cupiditas,* is the principle of all other affects. Affectivity, the body, knows more about it than consciousness."[122] The historical work of the imagination and the realization of new possi-bilities through action is not a function, nor the expression of a con-sciousness, but the manifestation in time of this capacity, the fruit of our interest in things. Action, as Arendt argues, is what interferes with the law of mortality, interrupting the inexorable course of daily life: "The life span of man running toward death would inevitably carry everything human to ruin and destruction were it not for the faculty of interrupting it and beginning something new, a faculty which is in-herent in action like an ever-present reminder that men, though they must die, are not born in order to die but in order to begin. . . . Action is, in fact, the one miracle-working faculty of man, as Jesus of Nazareth, whose insights into this faculty can be compared in their originality and unprecedentedness with Socrates' insights into the possibilities of thought, must have known very well when he likened the power to forgive to the more general power of performing miracles, putting both on the same level and within the reach of man."[123]

It is perhaps in its quality as a concentration of both spirituality and desire that the religious has been and continues to be a particular and privileged site for the production of what Castoriadis has called an "instituting imaginary" or, in the words of Lefort and Mbembe, a mode of "governing access to the world" and of acting differently within it. For Mbembe, religious imaginations "knot together in the same network the construction of organising concepts of the world here below and on high with an 'imaginary' of power, of authority, of society, of time, of justice and of dreams, in short, of history and its ultimate truth."[124] And yet, even though it is naïvely peopled by figures taken from human imagination, a religious form cannot simply be reduced to the relations people establish in social life. The sociological truism invoked by Barber earlier—gods are made by men—hides something from our view. This hidden aspect, in the words of Lefort, is that "any movement towards immanence is also a move towards transcendence."[125] What lies behind the elaboration of a relationship with the divine is not something that can be reduced to the relationships men establish in social life. What the religious imagination does in staging a space and time beyond that of social life is a particular way of dramatizing the relations that human beings establish with their humanity, or to put it in the language of philosophy, with Being. What religious and philosophical thought both recognize, albeit in different languages, is that the relationship that human beings establish with the world and with their humanity "cannot be self-contained, that it cannot set its own limits, and it cannot absorb its origins and ends into those limits. Anything that bears the mark of human experience bears the mark of an *ordeal* and the recognition that humanity can only open onto itself by being held in an opening that it did not itself create."[126] This gesture toward an outside brings the ideas of human sovereignty, autonomy, and identity face to face with their own limits. It announces an ontology of becoming, and beyond the transformability and instability of things and values, the possibility of the creation of the new.

In this sense, the importance of spirituality or religious belief is that it expresses and crystallizes the possibility of, as the Born-Agains say, an "overcoming,"[127] and that it manifests itself as a *force*. As Foucault puts it: "What, in the world today, can incite in an individual the desire, the appetite, the capacity and the possibility of an absolute sacrifice? Without us being able to suspect that behind it lies the least ambition or desire for power and profit?" He sees in religious revival "the evidence of the necessity of myth, of a spirituality" in the face of the "intolerable character of certain situations."[128] The irreducible element we have designated as belief or faith is neither an essence nor a substance, nor a function, nor a form of thought that might be opposed to reason, truth, or knowledge, but rather the dimension of subjectivity whose form is affectivity, desire, which finds its expression through the possibility of acting, of beginning anew. The original force of the Born-Again movement is located here, in the deliberate restaging of natality, the possibility of redeeming the past and beginning anew. "The miracle that saves the world, the realm of human affairs, from its normal 'natural' ruin is ultimately the fact of natality, in which the faculty of action is ontologically rooted, those two essential characteristics of human existence. It is, in other words, the birth of new men and the new beginning, the action they are capable of by virtue of being born. Only the full experience of this capacity can bestow upon human affairs faith and hope."[129]

TWO

Rupture, Redemption, and the History of the Present

The Born-Again revival in Nigeria begins in the 1970s, gathering momentum through the 1990s and continuing to grow up until the present. From the outset, the movement self-consciously represents itself as a form of rupture, both individual and collective. I argue that it is this vision and the specific Born-Again program for personal and collective regeneration and renewal that have been responsible for attracting people in such great numbers. As Pastor Ojewale's declaration makes clear, this movement self-consciously positions itself as revolutionary, engaging from the outset in "a battle," spiritual warfare. The idiom of rebirth expresses at the individual level the possibility of "making a complete break with the past"[1] and announces an imminent redemption, staging a stark distinction between the convert's past life and the moment of conversion through which he or she is "born again." Yet the importance of rupture to the Born-Again imaginary is equally evident in the ways in which the community of believers situates itself with respect to the collective past and the world of the present.

The revival irrupts at a particular point in Nigerian history due to a singular conjuncture of events that demonstrates the complexity of its provenance. Present as a religious form in the country since the 1920s, only two decades after the famous Azuza Street awakening in the United States,[2] it nonetheless remained a marginal institutional form for half a century, even if many elements of Pentecostal discourse and practice were set to work in the Aladura movement that sweeps across Yorubaland from the 1930s on. If we take the program at its word, and posit the sudden salience of this form of religious practice in terms of an uprising or a response to a particular historical conjuncture, we need to trace its conditions of plausibility, the multiple elements that contribute to this salience and vitality. As should be clear from our discussion in chapter 1, such conditions are historical. However, this does not mean that they are simply events, in the sense of things occurring at the present moment: the intensification of American Pentecostal evangelism in the late 1960s and 1970s, or a social, political, and economic crisis related to the postwar period and the oil boom, for example. Rather, the complex collection of neighboring practices within whose openings the Born-Again movement finds its insertion, and whose possibilities it actualizes, also involves the conjuncture of a series of traditions of interpretation and action, ways of doing and understanding with which it may engage. In this chapter and the next, we will attempt to see the ways in which this conjuncture gives rise to the movement and makes it plausible and pertinent, while contributing to its remarkable success.

First and foremost, the movement engages with a particular set of Nigerian religious institutions and practices, situating itself in a deliberate way with respect to these different traditions, and representing itself as a specific religious identity. The movement arises as a *religious* form in response to what is seen as a *spiritual* crisis. We need to make the effort of vision to see that such an engagement does not go without saying, and recognize that it is made possible in the first instance by the existence of a local tradition in which Christianity comes to be seen as a distinct identity that should be opposed to other forms of religious identification and as a distinct form of practice that can solve a range of problems, both spiritual and material. I will argue that these are novel possibilities introduced by mission, and reinforced during the colonial and postcolonial period. At the same time, we cannot presuppose what the terms "religious response" and "spiritual crisis" entail. In the following chapters, I will show that these objectifications are filled with a specific content, one that goes beyond a priori notions of the religious or spiritual. They provide us with a crucial insight into the ways in which power and the political field may be understood in postcolonial Nigeria, and also the ways in which this form of Christianity has direct political effects.

Second, in this chapter, I will show that the adversarial position of

Born-Agains toward a specific Christian tradition and toward present and past social practices is determined not only by doctrinal prescriptions, such as evangelism and the necessity of new birth, or global Pentecostalism's self-positioning within a broader Christian tradition, or the need to compete for clients in a competitive religious marketplace, or by the way the new birth is staged in Pentecostal imaginary in terms of a rupture with the past, but also by the ways in which this movement has had to struggle with established Nigerian practices and institutions. If doctrinal prescriptions in particular, and the Born-Again imaginary in general—themselves internally contradictory, as we shall see—propose new codes and interpretive grids for guiding and understanding behavior, we still need to understand why they suddenly appear attractive and plausible at this particular conjuncture in Nigerian history, especially as many of these forms had been present in the country for half a century already. Finally, identifying such an engagement cannot explain why it comes to be represented as a revolutionary form of action on the social, economic, and political realities of the moment nor how, given its important internal divisions, it nonetheless involves the constitution of a community. A whole series of disparate elements combine to make this emergence possible: In this chapter, I shall focus on the Born-Agains' insertion into a Nigerian tradition of Christian practice, and in chapter 3 I will discuss how their engagement with the social, economic, and political conditions in the postcolony gave the early revival its plausibility and pertinence. Here, through a brief discussion of the legacies of mission and a narrative history of the movement's rise, we shall look at how the movement both builds upon and critically reviews the history of Nigerian Christianity and the history of its own rise, to enable it to stage a state of permanent rupture and overcoming.

While the discourse of rupture and rebirth promises something new, its plausibility lies in the way it permits the articulation of "history in the present," inscribing itself within a Nigerian tradition in which Christianity can be expected to solve the problems of the age. Born-Again discourse finds its conditions of plausibility as a form of response to the ordeal of everyday life in postcolonial Nigeria insofar as it is able to project both a vision and the means for rendering this vision plausible and pertinent. But, as Peel argues in his discussion of the creation of modern Ijesha identity, the adoption of new practices and identities presupposes a history that goes beyond the invention of a "mere 'mythical charter' conjured solely out of contemporary interest." It necessitates a history that involves the double senses of a temporal continuity in identity and the mobilization of memory in the recognition of a "possessed past," understood as "history active in the present," which is "a reflexion on a real historical process."[3] Through its engagement with local and distant pasts, the ways in which it builds on the historical role of Christian discourses in transforming Nigerian colonial and postcolonial society, as well as critical reflection on its own history, Born-Again Christianity engages in just this sort of process. At the same time, constant narrative production in which the past is deliberately rescripted in an iconoclastic fashion involves the creation of a collective memory, which itself must be seen as an instrument and objective of the project of government expressed by the Born-Again movement. As Le Goff argues, "Memory is an essential element of what will henceforth be called individual or collective *identity*, the feverish and anxious quest for which is today one of the fundamental activities of individuals and societies. But collective memory is not only a conquest, it is also an instrument and an objective of power."[4] As we shall see in chapter 4, practices of individual remembering are central techniques in the process of subjectivation. At the collective level, the rescripting and control over the past constitute both a strategy in the conquest of the public space and a form of social knowledge in terms of which the present may be evaluated and the future imagined.

The Legacies of Mission

In a decidedly polemical tone, Mudimbe argues that "the missionary was also, paradoxically the best symbol of the colonial enterprise. He devoted himself sincerely to the ideals of colonialism: the expansion of Civilization, the dissemination of Christianity, and the advance of Progress. . . . With equal enthusiasm, he served as an agent of a political empire, a representative of a civilisation and the envoy of God. There is no essential contradiction between these roles. All of them implied the same purpose: the conversion of African minds and space." Mudimbe emphasizes the violence of this purpose when he claims that "the missionary does not enter into dialogue with pagans and 'savages' but must impose the law of God that he incarnates. All of the non-Christian cultures have to undergo a process of reduction to, or—in missionary language—of regeneration in, the norms that the missionary represents. Consequently, 'African conversion' rather than being the positive outcome of a dialogue—unthinkable per se—came to be the sole position the African could take in order to survive as a human being."[5] Here we have a clear, if not entirely accurate, statement of the missionary strategic program. Peel states it somewhat more finely:

The missions thus faced a major cultural task in attempting to bring the Yoruba to a conviction of the uniqueness of the soul's trajectory, as Christian conversion required. One way they tackled it was by seeking to implicate the proposed new personal narrative in a persuasive new collective narrative. In this way an additional use was found for what was already the CMS policy of "Christianity, Civilization and Commerce," that is, the spiritual regeneration of Africa should be linked to, and supported by, secular processes of development. It became a common strategy of missionary argument to invite their Yoruba interlocutors, on the basis of their own recent experiences of historical change, to buy into a new version of how Yoruba history might go, to invite them to rescript their country's history in terms of a unidirectional narrative of social progress—basically a form of what we call modernization theory—which meshes nicely with the Christian narrative of the soul that the missions were urging on the Yoruba as individuals. . . . The missionary strategy or argument, then, was to take up on these indigenous historical assessments and to rewrite them into a new narrative in which Christianity would resolve the problems of the age.[6]

A close examination of mission's form, as undertaken by Peel, shows that the Church Missionary Society in Nigeria expressed a historically particular notion of what it meant to be Christian, and the terms upon which conversion should both proceed and be recognized. Peel rightly argues that evangelicalism, "despite its firm roots in the Protestant Reformation, was the first distinctively post-Enlightenment form of Christianity, in that its experiential base—not the same as its scriptural or theological warrant—was cut off both from any theory of the material world (left to natural philosophy or science) and from any traditional socio-religious order, that is from the orders of knowledge and of society respectively . . . Without the old external supports, evangelicalism had to be self-referentially veridical, grounding itself directly in the believer's own "heartfelt" conviction.[7] Indeed, in the light of this observation, one could agree with de Certeau that for the missionaries, the conversion of Africans was perhaps less a sign of the hegemony of a Christian Logos than the rallying of witnesses to a truth that was less and less certain even to themselves, except perhaps in that private, individual, and circumscribed space of normative self-consciousness:

The metamorphosis of Christianity into ethics and, more broadly, into culture can be located ultimately under the sign of *progress* . . . Messianism, evangelism, cru-

sade: these Christian structures can be reorganised in the enterprise which associates the Enlightenment with their predication, this civilizing mission with the power
of changing nature, and the task of converting the meaning of being and of doing
with the truth of history . . . *De-Christianization reveals in its formality the Christian
practice,* but hereafter that practice is thrown out of the orbit of the *Logos* which
had verified it . . . A social reinterpretation of Christianity is thus inaugurated, which
will flow back over Christian milieus: in them it will develop missionary practices
turned toward the "other" as toward the future witnesses of an uncertain inner
truth; in them it will later provoke the reproduction of the ethics of progress in the
form of the theology of history.[8]

The collective narrative of progress, which was to be translated in
the postindependence period into the catechism of "development"
espoused by the state, is contained from the outset in ways in which
Christianity imposed itself as a moment of historical rupture, in which
conversion implied a conversion to history as the history of progress or
this-worldly redemption. This is perhaps one of mission's most important and enduring legacies, and plays a fundamental role in the plausibility of the Born-Again accounts of the fruits of conversion. In the
case of southwestern Nigeria, the central theme of development was
taken up in the colonial period as a revisited version of the Yoruba notion of *olaju,* transformed as "enlightenment," a process of reinvention
that owes much to the missionary encounter, as Peel argues.[9] It is this
legacy and its subsequent manifestations and failures that the Born-
Again imaginary shall seize upon to address the crisis of the present.
Born-Again iconoclasm, in its rejection of various "traditions," still remains fundamentally indebted to this nineteenth-century evangelical
form of Christian belief as a "religion of the heart,"[10] in which the self
experiences directly in its flesh and soul the message of the Spirit, an
individual conversion process that opens up the possibility of collective redemption.

   These observations pose the question of the exact nature of the object of missionary practice—conversion and collective regeneration—
which Mudimbe raises in such provocative terms. What precisely is involved in the process of original Christian conversion? In their study
of missions among the Tswana, the Comaroffs rightly question the
notion of conversion itself, defined in terms of change in religious allegiance: "how well does it grasp the highly variable, usually gradual,
often implicit, and demonstrably 'syncretic' manner in which the social identities, cultural styles and ritual practices of African peoples
were transformed by the evangelical encounter?"[11] They note that the

missionaries "might have written the history of Tswana civilization as a chronicle of conversions won or lost," and claim that they have shown why the missionary perspective "cannot, and does not, yield a sufficient account of cultural change or spiritual bricolage." They argue that the use of the term *conversion* as a noun "leads, unwittingly, to the reification of religious 'belief,' to its abstraction from the total order of symbols and meanings that compose the taken-for-granted world of any people."[12]

It is true that the missionary reification of "religion" or "religious allegiance" makes little sense as an analytical tool in much of pre-Christian Africa.[13] Peel recognises that "in the traditional cultures of western Africa, 'religion' did not exist as an indigenous category, but was introduced by missionaries and taken up (sometimes reluctantly) by anthropologists to refer to certain cultural and behavioural aspects of the whole community's functioning" and that "in Africa, people only recognize themselves as having 'a religion' when they adopt Islam or Christianity, religions which not only define themselves as such, but construct 'paganism' as their opposition."[14] In his magisterial study of the Yoruba encounter with Christianity, he states that before the encounter, "They had no generic concept of religion as a discrete field of human activity . . . or of particular religions as bounded entities."[15] The Yoruba spoke of "performing the Established Customs"; "the phrase 'country fashion' serves to blur any sharp divisions between the religious and the nonreligious: it implies a shifting and unbounded body of customary practices rather than a definite and integrated 'religion.'"[16] From this point of view, there does indeed appear to be little point in speaking of a change in allegiance from a nonexistent object.

But the central question here is not that the missionary perspective fails to give a proper account of the syncretic process of cultural *bricolage*. The Comaroffs appear to have missed the point that the "missionary perspective" on conversion, insofar as it was an explicit representation or narrative practice, was part of missionary strategy itself. Indeed, the very *idea* of "primary religious allegiance," the possibility of thinking and representing the religious field as a circumscribed domain of activity, as an object of reflection—indeed, the very *possibility* of "religious identity" and the self-conscious inclusion of various elements within it—was produced for indigenous society for the first time through the encounter with mission. The possibility and importance of claiming a distinctive religious identity was fundamentally new, and for the first time opened up the politically novel possibility of making public claims on the ground of particular individual identities, whether religious or ethnic. There is, in this sense, nothing "unwitting" about the missionaries' reification, even if we do not need to assign it to an intentionality. The Comaroffs rightly point out that despite the internal complexity of colonial societies, "they tended to be perceived and represented, from within, in highly dualistic, oppositional terms; terms that solidified the singularity of and the distance between, ruler and ruled, white and black, modernity and tradition, law and custom, European and non-European, capitalism and its anti-thesis, and so on. The objectification of this order of differences was intrinsic to the gesture of colonization itself."[17] Through a deliberate process of rescripting and revalorizing the local past, missionary discourse created a series of oppositions between Christianity and paganism, between opposed orders of doing and seeing. Explicit, though not the outcome of individual intention, yet not "unwitting," this sort of objectifying practice in which religious identity is presented as such for the first time to indigenous practitioners and is opposed to "paganism" is a central, indeed vital, part of missionary strategy, and participates in a general project of an ordering of differences in terms of which the world should now be seen and represented by these pagan others. This ordering of differences is arguably the most significant legacy of mission, one that was taken up with enthusiasm by Africans themselves and subjected to various forms of political reinterpretation, continuing to be central to African modes of self-representation.[18] This process of conversion thus refers to struggle, a play of positions on a field, the contours of which were being determined even as the game unfolded. We can see that the ideas, the new objects and possibilities, produced through this encounter were not neutral, but were caught up in a web of power relations, and that they were themselves instruments of struggle. The "reified" notion of conversion should, in this sense, be taken at the missionaries' word, insofar as it is part of a program for the government of conduct.

Obviously, this process was not accomplished through the simple persuasion of missionary preaching. Rather, what enabled the missions to ultimately succeed was the marriage between this new discourse and the overwhelming material and symbolic power their place in the colonial complex afforded them—a combination of coercion and seduction. We can take the story of mission in Yorubaland as an illustration of this, a similar sort of story being found, as Ayandele relates, in the mission of eastern Nigeria. In southwestern Nigeria, the discourse on personal salvation and the risks of hellfire, powerful in and of itself, was persuasively woven into a narrative about the dangers of the era, and the ways in which mission could help resolve them, putting an end to the terrible internecine wars plaguing Yorubaland since the fall of the Old Oyo empire, in particular the sixteen-year war of attrition triggered in 1878 by the Egba and the Ibadans. Indeed, Ayandele shows how the missionaries deliberately and directly involved themselves in local politics, not only in Yorubaland, but also in eastern Nigeria, calling upon the much-sought-after force they could command to enable their establishment in hostile and dangerous territory, while also directly advising local kings and rulers in their struggles against their rivals. By the end of the nineteenth century, missionaries had managed to convince much of the warring Southwest that they were indeed the principal purveyors of peace: "The white man's religion came to be associated with peace, and it was because of this that the missionary enterprise was zealously patronised by the chiefs."[19] Coupled with the presentation of Christianity as a form of social progress and individual betterment, the role of religious emissaries and spiritual forces in resolving the crises and dangers of the era created a lasting impression in collective memory.

At the same time, the particular ways in which mission found its place in society, the ways in which missions were employed in local political and economic strategies, and the marriage of force and the missionaries' position as religious specialists whose primary business was the things of the spirit would lead to one of the unintended consequences of mission. Rather than bringing converts to a post-Enlightenment view of the social and natural world, missionary activity only served to reinforce the local ontology of power, firmly establishing the notion that individual conversion to the white man's religion could become an effective mode of controlling and subduing untrammeled powers. Christianity was a "power that pass power."[20] The extraordinary capitulation of the Ijebu is an illustration of this conception: the military expedition led against them in 1892, at the instigation of the missionaries, led to the massive conversion of the Ijebu in the next five years. From that point on, the Ijebu, hitherto Christianity's most hostile opponents, would become its greatest advocates.[21] The missionaries themselves were clear as to the salutary effects of the power of the sword: "War is often a means of opening the door for the gospel to enter a country. A sword of steel often goes before a sword of the spirit. The landing of troops here and now may be part of the divine plan for answering our prayers and opening Ijebu and other interior countries to the gospel."[22] Ayandele argues that for many Ijebu, the secret of the white man's power was to be sought in his religion, and their conversion to Christianity was due "partly to the disappointment the Ijebu suffered from their juju. Before the expedition they were buoyed up with the hope that a most powerful deity was fighting on their side, and were reported to have sacrificed 200 men and women to propitiate it. Then there was the question of the 'divine' king who was now superseded by military administrations. Until now it was commonly believed that the Ajuwale was so sacred that to mention his name was to incur disaster.'"[23]

Both Peel and the Comaroffs record countless examples of the missionary despair with the "superficial nature" of African conversion, its "lack of sincerity" or "heartfelt conviction," whose principal signs they took to be the prevalence of "superstition," "idolatry," and the wrongheaded endurance of the ontology of power central to African relations with the supernatural. Indeed, this position is often echoed today in studies of Christianity in Africa, when observers place the accent on the "syncretic" nature of belief, interpreting the religious shopping around, a magical materialist ontology of supernatural power, and the ritual eclecticism of practitioners as a superficial adherence to Christian beliefs. As Peel observes, in the case of the Yoruba, religious practice was centered on a quest for power, and cults rose and fell in popularity as they succeeded or failed to mobilize these "hidden powers." The central religious premise was that "the material, phenomenal world is continuously affected by unseen powers of various kinds and indefinite number."[24] Not only that, he argues that nothing could be more different from missionary religious practice than what he calls here Yoruba "religion." It was "closely integrated with, if not the very articulation of, the Yoruba orders of natural and social knowledge, which means that its validation was realist rather than psychological; its orientation was markedly this-worldly and instrumental; and its ethics strongly backed communal values."[25]

And yet, as Peel shows in his study, one of the most durable and lasting effects of the "conversion to history" effected through the missionary encounter was the powerful sense of individual spirituality that developed among Christians, one that became inextricably linked to the new notions of personal and collective progress and the relationship that should be established with the past. One of the central messages of mission Christianity was the vital importance of individual conscience and sincerity as the signs of true conversion, manifested through the rejection of social practices that the missionaries interpreted directly in terms of their embeddedness in these old cultural forms. Sincerity, in this sense, was both a missionary objectification and aim—not merely a gauge in terms of which missionaries could judge "conversions won and lost," but a category of self-evaluation that converts were incited to use upon themselves in evaluating their own and others' conduct. Individual conscience, the importance of developing an acute notion of personal sin, and the possibility of repentance and future redemption were the powerful messages that fundamentally transformed the ways in which individuals would come to think of the problem of conduct and government.

At the same time, missionary teaching and conversion introduced other important ruptures with respect to precolonial West African cultures and cosmologies, rescripting, through the possibility of immortality and the messianic promise, the individual's relationship with the world, life, and death. Beyond the replacement of a circular cycle of birth, death, and rebirth staged through a permanent commerce between the spiritual and material universe, the missionary message affirmed the sacredness of human life and the primary importance of the aspiration to immortality in the world beyond. This implies not just the vanity of the things of this world, although this is one possible interpretation, but also the notion that individual life on earth is the highest good, insofar as such immortality is a promise that can only be realized through the actions that men undertake while they are in the world: What is offered by grace may be lost through sin.[26] In this sense, it opened up the possibility for the promotion and valuation of individual life over and above the life of the family, the collectivity, or the body politic, a conception that constituted a profound rupture with precolonial moralities and political ethics.[27] At the same time, as ethnographic studies show, while in precolonial spiritual imaginaries and pantheons the figure of the devil and the Manichean division between poles of good and evil was conspicuously absent,[28] missionary discourse and practice, especially through its indictment of paganism, firmly anchored this new division and the figure of the demonic in converts' imaginations, imbuing old powers with an even greater destructive force.

Mission also had unintended effects on structures underwriting elite domination. If, in modern democracies, the site of the sovereign exercise of power is represented as an "empty place," one that cannot be incarnated, and one that no longer makes a gesture to an "outside,"[29] in Africa the "secret origin" of sovereignty is historically designated as an "elsewhere," the world of the invisible and supernatural. The figure of the messianic, as expressed through both the incarnation and the power of the Holy Spirit, reinforced the possibility of the instantaneous action of divine power in everyday life. Indeed, converts took the possibility of the divine miracle and the nefarious power of the devil more seriously than did the missionaries themselves. Through the coalition of material power and the power of the Word, the ongoing sovereignty of an ahistorical invisible realm is reinforced, perpetuating human subjection to supernatural force, underlining the importance of acquiring spiritual means for controlling the material world, as well as the mystical origins of authority. Coupled with a new valuation of individual life over and above that of the community, the missionary message thus opened up lines of flight in which the old forms of political control over the abuse of power became potentially inoperative, making possible new forms of liberation, but at the same time reinforcing the dangerous potentiality of individuals.

Thus, for converts, the acceptance of many of these tenets did not in any way preclude the continued salience of the question of dangerous spiritual powers that must be subdued. Insofar as the missionaries provided the means to tackle these powers, converts were prepared to sacrifice their fetish objects and juju. In this respect, prayer was understood as one of the central modes in which communication with protecting powers could be established, and would prove to be one of the rallying points for subsequent religious revival in the region, as the Aladura (literally, "one who prays") movement of the 1920s and 1930s testifies.[30]

The Comaroffs locate many of the "misunderstandings" they impute to the converts in what they see as the endurance of an indigenous ontology of power. They argue that the converts took "the mission at its word, so to speak, treating literally the implication of its tropes," and made no distinction between symbols and instruments.[31] The Bible, for example, was quite literally an object imbued with spiritual power. But misunderstanding is surely the wrong term here, not least because it implies a shared epistemological universe, which was clearly not the case. Why should we be surprised that converts took the missionaries at their word? Indeed, the contrary would be most extraordinary, not least because it is clear that the Bible and other symbols and tropes were instruments of power from the point of view of indigenous practitioners, objects whose appropriation was a means of furthering their own personal and collective agendas. One could argue that the persistence of "superstition" and the belief that dangerous powers continued to impinge directly upon the everyday doings of individuals, coupled with the willingness of individuals to turn to Christianity in an attempt to control them, reveal a greater investment in the Christian Logos than was shown by the missionaries themselves. Had missionary discourse taken these forces and their own tropes and symbols seriously as real manifestations of the powers of Satan or Christ, the grounds for "misunderstanding" would have been considerably reduced. However, as de Certeau argues, missionary discourse was principally aimed at disseminating an ethics of progress through what had become a predominantly social doctrine, the evangelical zeal and personal conviction of the CMS missionaries notwithstanding.

In any case, for converts, as indeed for the analyst, the "correct understanding" or consciousness of what these symbols were intended to signify is not required to grasp the site of power's operation or its mode of functioning. Such an understanding places the emphasis on both intentionality and consciousness (about which we can know little) and obscures processes of subjectivation by conflating the agent and the subject. At the same time, it forgets that symbols and tropes, just like ritual, are not self-evident or neutral signifying practices, nor do they exist outside the world of practice that objectifies them as such. For the converts, these symbols and tropes were understood in the light of their own ontology of power and their knowledge of the world, and there is little reason to imagine that things could have occurred otherwise. However, such an understanding does not in any way mean a process of reduction to or assimilation within an indigenous cosmology; rather, these new symbols and tropes as well as those that come to be objectified under "our traditions" are forged into something completely different. Misunderstanding, therefore, is a shorthand for the play of differences emerging from the encounter itself, and it is important not to conflate at an analytical level the regime or program according to which these meanings and objectifications are determined with what occurs in the process of encounter, as so many studies of religious belief continue to do today.

The encounter with mission was thus not simply the placing of a Christian veneer on customary practices, nor was it question of merely changing religious practices; rather, it fundamentally changed ways of doing and thinking, in particular, thinking about the self and about time. The encounter was, in every sense, a situation of *beginnings*. That the emerging Christian identity and eschatology was ambivalent, internally contradictory, and full of incongruities from the missionary's or the anthropologist's point of view does not imply that it was a different sort of practice than mission. As Peel's and the Comaroffs' work shows, mission was itself a multiform enterprise, where various different logics, programs, and techniques found their intersection: salvation, spiritual renewal, education, health and hygiene, territorial organization, description and classification of groups, techniques of discipline, violence and coercion, trade and labor relations, to name but a few. Their idea of a syncretic form, or *bricolage,* which supposedly characterizes local response to mission, does not do justice to the nature of these solid and permanent effects, nor to the historical process that brought them into being. The idea of *bricolage* presupposes a pure form against which the mixing, the *bricolage,* may be measured, and the practice of *bricolage* presupposes another type of practice, which we could call, with Lévi-Strauss, "engineering."[32] As Derrida argues, "every discourse is *bricoleur.* The engineer, whom Lévi-Strauss opposes to the *bricoleur,* should be the one to construct the totality of his language, syntax and lexicon. In this sense, the engineer is a myth. A subject who supposedly would be the absolute origin of his own discourse and supposedly would construct it 'out of nothing,' 'out of whole cloth' would be the creator of the verb, the verb itself."[33] Missionary discourse and practice is just as much *bricolage* as is the indigenous appropriation of it. The relations of power may have been uneven, but there is not on one side the *bricoleur,* and on the other the engineer. The use of this term to describe indigenous practice takes missionary power at its word, endorsing a model of interaction that depends upon a classic binary schema of domination and resistance. But as Peel's and Ayandele's work shows, a close look at the encounter reveals not missionaries representing the pole of power, in the face of which converts could only muster tactics of resistance, but rather a long-drawn-out process of struggle in which various relations of power were continuously determined in and through the ongoing process of engagement.

Thus, despite Mudimbe's polemical statement, missionary practice is just as "syncretic," just as *historical* a practice as any other, even if its self-representation takes the form of a rational program marked by an ideological voluntarism, clarity as to goals and the instruments required to achieve them, as well as moral certainty and little doubt as to the final outcome, very much like the Born-Again movement a century later. It is true that this ability to create and articulate such a program and underwrite it by superior material force gave the missionaries a distinctive edge in the struggle that ensued. And yet we must not forget that all actual discourse and practice always follows the logic of making do, making the best of things with what is at hand, while coping with accidents, misunderstandings, missed opportunities, bad calculations. The missionary strategic program is an "event" in Foucault's sense: not a decision or a rule, a battle won or lost, but a relation of forces. As Peel's work shows, the "days of small things"[34] followed this logic, and indigenous practice, quite naturally, was only actualizing the new possibilities that the neighboring missionary practices had opened up. It did not, nor is there any reason to suppose that it should or could have, *become* these neighboring practices themselves. At the same time, the effects of these objectifications were very real, insofar as they fundamentally changed the ways in which the past was conceived and the terms in which individuals could interpret it and act in the present.

The Born-Again revival explicitly and implicitly engages with the tradition inaugurated by mission through a program that takes up its central effects, the objectification and representation of a series of differences: between Christianity and "paganism," between the past and the future. It involves a linear, teleological notion of time in keeping with the notion of the soul's perfectibility; the representation of the present as an ordeal fraught with dangers; the importance of claiming a distinctive religious identity as both the sign and mode of rupture with prevailing norms; the centrality of spiritual empowerment for personal and collective progress; and above all, the possibility of controlling untrammeled powers through individual faith and prayer. These central themes were not all necessarily an explicit part of mission's religious charter from the outset, but as Peel's study of the Yoruba demonstrates so admirably, they were to become central effects of the long process of encounter itself.

The critical reappropriation of the evangelical tradition of mission and its subsequent manifestations is central to the Born-Again project for collective, indeed national regeneration. Through the representation of radical and permanent rupture, Born-Again discourse articulates its revolutionary program of redemption in which the future appears both as the possible overcoming of what has gone before and as the fulfillment of an original promise, in keeping with a long Christian eschatological tradition. However, the Born-Again construction of redemption introduces new ruptures with respect to the missionary tradition. While on the one hand the Born-Again project is concerned with how to guarantee eternal life in the hereafter, it finds its principal force through the staging of a claim for justice and a demand for "life more abundant" in the here and now, both possibilities that are encapsulated in the notion of messianic time and the possibility of the miraculous. One might want to frame these alternatives in a more prosaically political language as demand for development and progress, on the one hand, and the realization of justice or right, on the other—both of which are understood as promises presented through the "civilizing mission" but at the same time ruined through colonial and postcolonial practices. Unlike the theology of history presented through mission and the civilizing project more generally, the messianic and the miraculous encapsulate a sense of time and history fundamentally opposed to the modern teleology of progress whose utopian conception places the end, or the *eschaton,* as perpetually deferred. In the messianic conception of time,[35] the arrival of the messiah may be accomplished "at any instant," in the very heart of history, pulverizing the coherence and continuity of historical time into innumerable messianic instants in which the radically new becomes possible.[36] In a complex argument, which I shall not reproduce here, Agamben shows how messianic time should be understood as the "time of the now." It is not the time of the end and should not be confused with apocalypse; rather, it is the time *before* the end, which is not simply another period of chronological time, but a time that "begins to end," that "contracts itself."[37] It is not a time separate from chronological historical time, which for Paul spans from creation to the messianic event of the resurrection, but rather *the time that remains* within chronological time, between that event and the *parousia,* the full presence of the messiah, and arrival of *eschaton,* or the end. Rather than staging a perpetual deferment of the *eschaton,* messianic time is the incorporation of *parousia* into every instant of chronological time, implying a transformation in the actual experience of time. As Agamben argues, messianic time, unlike chronological time (which is unrepresentable and in whose flow we merely exist passively) presents itself as the *only time we have.*[38] In a certain limited sense, Pentecostalism is more messianic than it is eschatological, even though it takes the kingdom literally, identifying the *parousia* as the thousand-year reign of Christ after the "rapture" and the seven years of tribulation under the rule of Satan and before the *eschaton.*[39] Nonetheless, messianic time is also staged in Pentecostalism as an operational time, as a time *within* the present time. This is evidenced by the experience of faith as a total openness to the presence (*parousia*) of the Holy Spirit; the centrality of miracles; and the fact that the urgency of evangelism and conversion lies not only in preparing believers and the world for *parousia* and the *eschaton,* but also in fulfilling God's plan and *hastening* this fulfilment. For the Born-Agains, the idea of the "end-times" underlines the urgency of the present, as the only time we have left in which to realize the redemption of the past and the possibility of salvation.

As Agamben notes, messianic time is not merely oriented toward the future but also involves a recapitulation of the past, implying a summary judgment of it. The recapitulation of the past is significant because "it is precisely through it that the events of the past acquire their true significance and thus may be saved."[40] Born-Again witnessing to the individual or collective past is a practice that, like Benjamin's anachronism, seizes "hold of a memory as it flashes up at a moment of danger."[41] This practice involves the recognition of the past and enables a critical engagement with the present. But it also implies its redemption in the sense of its fulfillment. "The true image of the past flees by. The past can be seized only as an image which flashes up at the instant when it can be recognized and is never seen again . . . For every image of the past that is not recognized by the present as one of its own threatens to disappear irretrievably."[42] Benjamin's time is messianic: the "image" he speaks about describes a "constellation" in which the relation between past and present is not chronological but dialectical: "It is not that what is past casts its light on what is present, or what is present its light on what is past; rather, image is that wherein what has been comes together in a flash with what is now to form a constellation. For while the relation of the present to the past is purely temporal (continuous), the relationship of what-has-been to the now is dialectical, in leaps and bounds."[43] Born-Again practices of recollecting the past and subjecting it to a summary judgment involve a dialectical exercise—the evils and dangers of the "sins of the fathers" and their expression in local cultural practices should not be seen in terms of a pure rejection, nor should they be understood in terms of a prolongation of the imperial project of mission or the sign of a "false consciousness." Rather, they should be seen as a form of hyper-awareness of the dangers of the present and a recognition of both the urgency and possibility of change and of redemption. As Jewsiewicki puts it: "Time, constructed in the mode of Benjamin's anachronism (as distinct from Deleuze's time), enables subjects to confront other subjects who are their contemporaries, including those who have been recalled from the past by the work of remembering experience."[44]

More specifically, Born-Again accounts of the present and the past take hold of many of the same themes developed under missionary Christianity, all the while laying bare the failure of this tradition to effectively provide both the knowledge and power to guarantee the promise of redemption. Born-Again testimony and witnessing involve a form of staging the immediate and distant past in such a way as to open up the ongoing possibility of redemption (understood as the promise of eternal life, but also in the broadest sense of the alleviation of suffering here and now) at every instant, through demonstrations of how the new birth is both the overcoming of what has gone before and the fulfillment of a promise through the ongoing realization of something new. However, like missionary practice before it, the Born-Again revolutionary project is shot through with the same indeterminacy. It restores the idealistic voluntarism of early missionaries, and yet, notwithstanding its reiteration of the principles of evangelical witness, it engages with the problem of the past in paradoxical ways, giving rise to an ambiguous ethics and opening up a fundamental ambivalence in its political productivity.

The Holiness Revival: "Separate Ye from among Them"

Until the 1970s revival Pentecostal Christianity had been an institutionally marginal current within the Christian population, even if many of its doctrines had strongly influenced indigenous Christianity through the Aladura movement of the 1930s. While numbers are notoriously difficult to obtain, the total Pentecostal population before the 1970s revival was probably under 300,000 in a population of some 75 million, approximately half of whom were Muslim.[45] The Apostolic Church from Britain was the first Pentecostal church present in Nigeria, established in the late 1920s through contact with the future leaders of the Aladura movement in Yorubaland; it played an important role in this movement's formation.[46] The Assemblies of God was established in 1939 in Igboland and still maintains hundreds of congregations throughout the country, particularly in the East. The Four Square Gospel Church and the Apostolic Faith are two other American Pentecostal churches established in the 1940s and flourishing today. The only significant indigenous church originally based on this type of Pentecostalism is the Redeemed Christian Church of God, founded in 1952 by a pastor who had broken away from the Aladura church Cherubim and Seraphim. However, as Matthews Ojo has argued, the particularity of the new movement was its interdenominational nature and relative independence from established Christian institutions, whether Pentecostal or mainstream Protestant.[47] The strongly denominational Pentecostal churches were often initially hostile to the movement, only benefiting indirectly from the revival many years later, and most— with the exception of the Redeemed Christian Church of God, which has gone on to become the largest Born-Again church in Nigeria—have been subsequently far outstripped in membership by churches and ministries founded in the 1980s and 1990s.

The "holiness revival" of the mid-1970s thus began as a broad, interdenominational movement in urban centers, particularly in Lagos. The movement was inspired by the intensification of American Pentecostal evangelism in Nigeria during the late 1960s and early 1970s, giving rise to the creation of a multitude of small prayer and fellowship groups, and breathing new life into interdenominational organizations that had been present in the country since the colonial period. The revival was largely, although not exclusively, carried forward by the youth, and the greater part of early evangelizing and organization occurred in the schools and universities in cities throughout the south of the country. In particular, youth-based interdenominational groups such as the Scripture Union (founded in 1911), the Student Christian Movement (1940), and the Fellowship of Christian Students (1957) played an important role in relaying the messages of revival and Born-Again conversion. The vast majority of the revival's early followers were members of historical Protestant mission churches, in particular the Anglican church.[48]

The most important new church that emerged from the interdenominational revival of the 1970s is without a doubt the Deeper Life Bible Church. Its extraordinary and ongoing success as an organization emerging directly from the early holiness revival, and one that rigidly promoted the strict doctrinal positions of this form of Pentecostalism, demonstrates the ongoing importance of this current, despite the subsequent enthusiasm for the "prosperity" doctrine. Deeper Life's story exemplifies that of many other churches and ministries founded over the next decade, whatever their doctrinal emphasis, with its origins as a small interdenominational bible study group and its emphasis on evangelism.[49]

Deeper Life started in 1973 as a Bible study group of fifteen members, meeting on Monday nights in the sitting room of William F. Kumuyi, a young lecturer in mathematics at the University of Lagos. Kumuyi was a member of the Apostolic Faith church and had been very active in both the Scripture Union and the Lagos Varsity Christian Union at the University of Lagos. By 1975 loudspeakers were set up outside the flat for the group of more than 500 people who gathered in the courtyard outside each Monday. The first retreat was held in 1975, with 1,500 attending. The group continued to grow, and a Thursday-night session for evangelism training was added in the same year. This session was to become, in 1984, the Miracle Revival Hour, in keeping with the church's emphasis on faith healing and deliverance from evil powers. The Deeper Life Bible Church itself was created in 1982, nearly a decade after the first group met. By the time Kumuyi started Sunday

Services and inaugurated the Deeper Life Bible Church, the organization had more than one hundred workers, and its International Bible Teaching College in Gbagada, Lagos, had been in operation for several years. The organization also developed an outreach branch, Deeper Life Christian Ministries, focused on church planting and evangelism. Initially a small, broad-based interdenominational movement like so many others of the 1970s, by the late 1980s Deeper Life was one of the most rapidly growing and strongly denominational churches in the country, with over a thousand churches created in under six years, and a membership of over 200,000. By 1988 Deeper Life church services in its Lagos headquarters attracted over 50,000 worshipers every Sunday, offering simultaneous translation into a dozen local and international languages. The church continued to grow, planting churches in other African countries and in Europe and America, and today it is one of the largest Born-Again churches in Nigeria. In 2001 Deeper Life inaugurated the Deeper Life Conference Centre, a huge complex sprawling over 360 hectares off the Lagos-Ibadan Expressway. Its auditoria have a capacity of 160,000, and the complex features guesthouses, restaurant, exhibition center, library, health and welfare center, satellite connection and communication tower, water and sewage treatment plant, electricity generation, and a bank.

The remarkable rise of the Deeper Life could not be prefigured in the little group that met in Kumuyi's sitting room every Monday in the early 1970s. Indeed, despite the presence of American evangelists during the 1960s and 1970s, there was no, or very little, institutional support or church planting from abroad. Rather, the revival developed through the circulation and proliferation of narratives: stories of conversion and miraculous healing. Aggressive evangelism gave rise to Bible study, fellowship, and prayer groups like Kumuyi's, which sprang up throughout the 1970s in an informal and unstructured fashion, the message passing from mouth to mouth in schools, universities, neighborhoods, and workplaces. The expansion of Kumuyi's own movement during the 1970s occurred in the same informal fashion, at the initiative of engaged converts, even though the group had full-time workers and teams of evangelists. For example, this is how Kumuyi explains the development of Bible study fellowships in Oyo state in the Southwest and Rivers State in the Southeast:

It was informal. Some of the brethren, after hearing about evangelism and bringing other people into the saving knowledge of the Lord Jesus Christ, became concerned for their home states. They came to me with the burden to start Deeper Life Bible studies in their own locations. I would say that was alright, but they should seek employment in those places so that the fellowship would not have to pay them. Thus they went, settled down, and opened their homes up to Bible study. The Bible study materials we had been using in Lagos, which they had filed over the years, were adapted for their individual needs. That was basically how we started most of the first meetings in other states in Nigeria.[50]

The early interdenominational movement placed the accent on becoming born-again and taking up a "new life in Christ, and the message was spread aggressively through personal evangelism. Bible study, witnessing and evangelism, constant prayer, and ongoing self-examination were the methods that would enable converts to guarantee their new life in Christ and profit from its fruits. In the interdenominational prayer groups and fellowships, miracles and "divine healing" (understood in the broad sense of alleviating the causes of suffering, whether physical, financial, spiritual or social) were central elements of religious practice, and some groups even forbade the use of Western medicines.[51] The centrality of the Holy Spirit was evidenced in the "charismatic gifts" of speaking in tongues, faith healing, deliverance from evil spirits, and prophesying. The content of the message stressed the importance of holiness and righteousness, which involved various practices of antimaterialist purification, such as eschewing material goods, retreating from the world, making a rupture with a sinful past, and breaking off relations with nonbelievers. In its first decade, Deeper Life forbade its followers to watch television or drink soft drinks such as Coca-Cola. Women were told not to straighten or perm their hair, and not to wear jewelry or trousers. Strong emphasis was placed on strict personal ethics. Converts gave evidence of their transformation through public confessions (testimony) of past sin and miraculous delivery (from various evil powers, sickness, poverty, hardship); practices of restitution (compensating those who had suffered from the converts' past sinful actions); and strict regimes of bodily discipline (imposed through all-night prayer vigils and long periods of fasting). Through preaching and compulsive and assiduous Bible study, converts were continuously exhorted not to lie, cheat, steal, quarrel, gossip, give or take bribes, drink, smoke, fornicate, beat their spouses, lose their tempers, or deny assistance to other members in need. Strict dress codes were imposed, and limited contact was allowed between the sexes. Marital fidelity was a central tenet, and divorce was not sanctioned. The doctrine was strongly millennial, and signs of Christ's imminent return were commonly sought in national and international events. Converts were exhorted to prepare themselves and live in constant readiness for "the rapture." The second coming of Christ appeared in this vision as the sudden interruption of historical time, a rupture through "rapture," as the doctrine has it. In this account, when Christ returns, Born-Again converts were to be spirited away in the twinkling of an eye (raptured) to join Christ in heaven, while Satan would be left to reign on earth for seven years. True converts were to be both the catalysts and unique beneficiaries of this event. The theme of the "end times" has been and continues to be central to Pentecostalism everywhere, and the emphasis on the imminent return of Christ and the urgency of preparing oneself spiritually for this event, which could arrive at any moment, was particularly strong in the first decade of revival.

The zeal with which young people practiced their new faith was remarkable: indeed, the radical changes that conversion brought about served to set them noticeably apart from prevailing norms and practices. Conversion affected modes of sociability by restructuring relationships of kinship, patronage, gender, age, social class, and ethnicity in sometimes quite radical ways, as well as modes of self-presentation, such as dress and hygiene, attitudes to health and sexuality, attitudes to work, social mobility, accumulation, and debt. Practices of restitution and rituals of self-inflicted humiliation through detailed public testimonies of personal sin or wrongdoing and requests for forgiveness clashed with prevailing notions of honor, status, "face," and public self-presentation.

These practices were coupled with strenuous zeal in evangelism, which served to publicize the experience of rupture enacted through the application of Born-Again doctrinal prescriptions. The distinctiveness of the movement was reinforced by the reception that the early converts had in their own churches. This intensified the sense of renewal contained in the Born-Again message, and also helped create the conditions in which a sense of community would become possible through the shared experience of overcoming adversity. The extremely hostile attitude of the established churches' hierarchies to the new revival and what they considered to be its unorthodox practices, which prompted many followers to leave, or even be forced out of, their congregations, was itself responsible for the creation of new institutions, as Pastor Kumuyi relates:

After the retreats, Deeper Life members would go back to their own churches and evangelise those people who they felt were not born again. . . . They felt the people in the churches were not receiving clear teaching on the new birth; and that their lives did not show clear evidence of the new birth. They also taught them about what they believed was consistent Christian living—holiness, and other practical issues like "do not smoke, do not drink." Now as young people they had zeal, and it was good. . . . But eventually some of them were driven out of the churches. For example, one denomination gave a general type of statement at their headquarters: "Anybody who attends another Bible study outside of the church's, especially Deeper Life Bible study, will be driven out of the church." The brethren who attended the Bible study therefore left that church and went to another church. But the story repeated itself; other churches also drove them out. Eventually my own church sent me out too. . . . I was driven out in 1977, and we just continued the Bible study. . . . In 1982 the pressure was getting high from the people that were being driven out of the various churches. So on November 7, 1982, we started the Sunday worship.[52]

In July 1993, more than a decade after Deeper Life's establishment as a church, a lead article in a Nigerian newsweekly told the story of the withdrawal of the pastoral license of Professor Simeon Onibere for "fanning incendiary passion in the Anglican church . . . and preaching heretical teachings."[53] According to the report, Onibere had begun an evangelical, Born-Again fellowship within the church and criticized the church leadership over a two-year period for "paying overt attention to religious rituals and ceremonies to the neglect of the evangelical crusade," claiming that many church leaders were involved in the Ogboni Fraternity and Freemasons. Onibere quickly gathered a large and committed following. His position on the allegations of the church is made clear in this statement: "I am not founding a church, neither am I engaged in the activity of creating a parallel organisation to rival the Anglican Church . . . I am only seeking a reformation of the existing ecclesiastical systems in the Anglican church which are no longer relevant to our existing reality. . . . the church must realign and live up to its responsibilities, it must accept the new thinking we are propagating. The message that we are sending is that we must be born again."[54]

The struggle for pastoral control over their congregations was central to the attitudes behind the Anglican and other churches' attitude to the new thinking. Even within established Pentecostal churches, it was considered an unacceptable and heretical challenge to orthodox practice. Paradoxically, the rigid attitude of established churches only served to give greater impetus to the movement, and was in many ways responsible for its early institutionalization, as Kumuyi's account testifies. However, by the mid-1990s, after over a decade of accusing the new Born-Again churches of "sheep stealing," many mission-based or orthodox denominations began tolerating Born-Again fellowships and activities. They even at times incorporated "Born-Again interludes" into their traditional liturgies, giving rise to some very incongruous scenes. Thus, in the middle of the typically austere Easter service at the Presbyterian church in Yaba, Lagos, in 1993, the pastor stepped down, a young man came up to the lectern, and three musicians took up an electric guitar, keyboards, and drums, inviting the congregation to follow them in rousing gospel and preaching punctuated by exclamations of "Praise the Lord!" before the regular Presbyterian liturgy continued. The bemused, lukewarm reaction from the congregation indicated that in all likelihood, all of those who had been attracted by the new thinking had already left. By the late 1990s the most traditional of the Aladura churches, such as the Celestial Church of Christ, and the Cherubim and Seraphim, which had been deliberate targets of Born-Again demonization, had begun Born-Again fellowships in many of their congregations, modifying longstanding ritual practices and attempting to incorporate Born-Again doctrine into their preaching.

Perhaps the greatest success story of the revival is the Redeemed Christian Church of God (RCCG).[55] The only early indigenous Pentecostal church that—unlike the mission-based Pentecostal churches—managed to surf on the wave of revival, the RCCG has become the country's largest present-day Born-Again organization, with over two thousand parishes throughout Nigeria, and branches in Africa, Europe, Asia, and the Americas. Founded in 1952 by Pastor Josiah Akindayomi, following his break from the Aladura Cherubim and Seraphim, the RCCG remained, until the mid-1980s, a relatively small and exclusively Yoruba Pentecostal church, with parishes in the historic Yoruba neighborhoods of Lagos and in towns in the Yoruba hinterland. Akindayomi himself was illiterate, and services were conducted exclusively in Yoruba. The church propagated a classic holiness doctrine and drew people from the urban Yoruba lower middle class. Although it emerged from within an already existing institution, its development and expansion followed in many ways the model of the interdenominational fellowships and groups. The appointment in 1981 of Enoch A. Adeboye, lecturer at the University of Lagos, as general overseer fundamentally changed the trajectory of the church. Pastor Adeboye updated the RCCG's image and structure, attracting thousands of young people caught in the wave of ongoing revival. He oversaw the creation in the early 1990s of "model" parishes led by young charismatic pastors in middle- and upper middle-class neighborhoods of Lagos, and the founding of groups such as Christ the Redeemer's Friends Universal, aimed at drawing in elite members of society, as well as the growth of campus fellowships; confirmed converts were encouraged to start local parishes in their neighborhoods, home towns, and throughout the diaspora. In 1991 he inaugurated the Holy Ghost Camp, off the Lagos-Ibadan Expressway, where monthly all-night services were held, attracting thousands of believers. By the late 1990s RCCG services were attended by tens of thousands of worshipers, and annual meetings attracted several million. By the turn of the millennium, the Holy Ghost Camp had developed into a veritable city, on a far greater scale even than Deeper Life's, and monthly services attracted more than half a million worshipers. In 2003 the church opened a private university, offering programs in natural and social sciences and the humanities. Parishes have sprung up in every neighborhood of every southern town and city in Nigeria: some have even made the unverifiable claim that the RCCG has become the largest single property owner in Nigeria.[56] Beyond Nigeria, the church has parishes in more than twenty countries, including the United States and Britain, and is on its way to becoming the largest Pentecostal church in Africa, if it is not already.

And yet, like Kumuyi, Adeboye tells the story of his reform of the church as a perpetual struggle: accused of "worldliness," he had to fight to impose, not the importance of being Born-Again, but the need to "modernize" liturgy and church structure, to temper the rigidity and antiworldliness of doctrine, and to open the church to different social classes and ethnic groups. He told this story in 1993 to one of the older, most conservative parishes within the church, in what appeared to be both a provocation and a justification:

I remember 1975—at that time if you were a Christian [Born-Again] it was considered worldly if you have a car that is bigger than a Volkswagen. The car has to be second-hand to prove that you are holy. I didn't agree with them. My car was a second-hand Dodge Avenger, okay with the brothers and sisters, they thought I was okay. But I had to travel far to preach and had to pray for travel at night. I decided that I must buy a car that can travel in the night. In the early seventies then the robbers were concentrating on cars. I saw one Toyota Crown. No thief will be interested in it. It is cheap to maintain, plenty of room to stretch legs, and there is not a single Toyota Crown in the stolen cars, too cumbersome, warms up too slowly. So I bought it. When the brothers and sisters saw, they said, oh, this young man had such potential, God was going to use him, but he has backslid so soon![57]

In many ways, the early success of both the RCCG and Deeper Life lay in their ability to channel the wave of enthusiasm within a supple yet

powerful structure, which harnessed the informal, democratic force behind the wave of conversions, giving opportunities to individuals who
had heard the personal "call" to express their evangelical zeal within
a network of institutionalized support, over which centralized pastoral control was not yet firmly established. And yet, while Deeper Life
was born from a broad, egalitarian, interdenominational movement,
once it established itself as a church it became very strongly denominational, much like its mission-based predecessors. Control over pastors,
workers, and members was strictly enforced, and church identity was
strongly promoted, although there did exist a definite sense of belonging to a broader Born-Again movement. Up until the late 1980s, Deeper
Life was populated almost exclusively by the poorer members of society. On the whole, church members were literate, but few people above
the status of clerk could be seen in the congregations.

In the first decade or so of revival, the incentives for following the
call were not material. On the contrary, many pastors whose call came
at this phase of the revival represented it as a real hardship, often leaving decent employment for what was seen as a life of privation and social stigma. Both Kumuyi and Adeboye often speak of the hardships of
the early years, and how their decision to leave their career as university lecturer horrified friends and family alike. The holiness doctrine
and what was often termed the fanaticism of new converts marked the
early public perception of the movement. The importance of the Scripture Union movement as an organizational vehicle of this new doctrine
led many to identify the revival almost exclusively with the organization, and the epithet "S.U." came to be used, often in a derisive fashion,
to refer to those who claimed to have been born again. Stigmatized for
their antimaterialism and their constant Bible reading and prayer, students in schools and universities were derided for their rejection of established norms of dress and behavior: "they always looked so poor and
shabby, and instead of studying for exams, they would stay up all night
praying for good results," a colleague of mine at the university said of
the "S.U.s" in his class in the early 1980s. As Ojo observes, members of
the new groups were identified by outsiders in terms of their behavior
and dress styles. They engaged in public witnessing to Born-Again conversion and evangelism, frequent and lengthy prayer, the use of the
terms "Brother" and "Sister," and frequent mention of God and Jesus
Christ in conversation. They dressed in unsophisticated clothing, and
eschewed ornamentation such as jewelry and the wearing of trousers
by women; they often carried a Bible with them, and they maintained

a serious demeanor with infrequent laughter. All these characteristics were seen as identifiers of these new "S.U.s."[58]

Of all of these adversarial relationships, however, the single most important one was that established with the past. The Manichean division in doctrine between the saved and the unbelievers, the Christ-like and the Satanic, finds its translation in both a rejection of and liberation from past practices, of which the new birth is both the sign and the guarantee. As we shall see in chapter 4, the new birth promises liberation from sin and suffering, but the theodicy that emerges is complex and ambivalent. Echoing the missionaries' struggle against idolatry and "paganism," pastors and converts adapted Pentecostal doctrine into a local reading that interpreted many of the causes of suffering in terms of the work of evil, occult powers, explicitly associated with the local past, and viewed many local cultural practices or institutions, regrouped around the term "tradition," as forms of potential pollution by these same powers. This interpretation, essential to the problem of achieving self-mastery and protection in a context of uncertainty, gave rise to the emphasis on deliverance, which was particularly strong in the second decade of revival and reappeared in the late 1990s, crossing doctrinal differences and social classes.

The vigilance with which early converts guarded against pollution by the "forces of evil" in various guises is evidenced by the very large number of deliverances that took place weekly and the extraordinary number of tracts and booklets published locally throughout the 1980s by members who had been delivered and converted from lives spent serving the devil as herbalists, secret cult members, witches, or agents of various water spirits. The most widely circulated of these tracts was Emmanuel Eni's *Delivered from the Powers of Darkness,* published by the Scripture Union in 1987; dozens of others, variously published by evangelical ministries, churches, or itinerant preachers and evangelists, were in circulation throughout the 1980s and 1990s, or could be heard "live" in taxis, buses, and marketplaces.[59] The focus on evil spirits and Satanic forces may be seen as one of the central themes of the early revival, one that would be taken up just as strongly by the second wave, though in somewhat modified terms. Converts and leaders were thus especially opposed to any church that had connections with "traditional" African belief and ritual. The Aladura churches were central targets of attacks by Born-Agains, despite the doctrinal influence of evangelical and Pentecostal Christianity. The Christ Apostolic Church is the only Aladura church accepted by Born-Again Christians, and significantly, it no longer uses the designation "Aladura" for itself. Other Aladura churches, such as the Celestial Church of Christ and the Cherubim and Seraphim, were represented as being satanically inspired, especially because of what was seen as their syncretic ritual activities: the use of candles, soap, and other paraphernalia; their white uniforms and practice of going barefoot; the acceptance by certain churches of traditional social practices, such as polygamy. Directly indexed and demonized by the Born-Agains, of course, were *babalawos* (practitioners of traditional medicine); and adepts of New Age groups or cults; groups such as the Reformed Ogboni Fraternity (a Christianized version of a precolonial Yoruba political institution), the Freemasons, or the Rosicrucians; campus cults; neo-traditional cults, such as Mami Wata; and all forms of traditional religious practice. A highly antagonistic relationship with Islam also developed, exacerbated by Nigeria's postcolonial political history and the rise of radical reformist Islam in the North from the 1970s on.

The early period of revival in the 1970s clearly placed converts in a position of radical rupture with their personal and collective histories and with Nigerian society more broadly. The messianism of this early phase self-consciously represented the movement as the moment immediately preceding the culmination of history. The sectarian impulse of the earlier holiness churches, their antagonistic relations with established denominations, and their emphasis upon the otherworldly nature of salvation have, over the past two decades, given way to a conception in which engagement with the world and the possibility of salvation in this life are regarded as both desirable and necessary.

Salvation Now: Prosperity and the "New Wave"

From the mid-1980s onward a "new wave" of Pentecostalism swept through Lagos and other cities of the South. Initiated simultaneously by several pastors who had been to Pentecostal Bible colleges in the United States, and strongly influenced by the American Faith or Word-Faith movement,[60] this new wave distinguished itself from the older "holiness" wave by preaching to greater or lesser degrees the "doctrine of prosperity" or "faith" gospel. This message does not put into question basic Christian or Pentecostal doctrine, but rather appears as a series of lateral interpretations that imply innovation at the level of practice and the relationship of the believer to the world around him, rather than any deep theological revision. From the retreat from "the world" that characterized the holiness wave, the new wave placed a much greater emphasis on miracles, particularly of prosperity, salvation in the here and now, and "global spiritual warfare." The "new wave" developed throughout the 1970s in the United States and became a growing force in both African and Latin American Pentecostalism from the mid-1980s on (it is often identified under the term "neo-Pentecostalism").[61] In its most explicit forms, the faith or prosperity doctrine has been dubbed "name it and claim it"—a common exhortation in sermons by prosperity preachers everywhere. In this vision, God has guaranteed spiritual and material blessings from the outset; all the convert has to do is name them, and then claim them in the name of Jesus. Furthermore, the material fortunes of believers are represented as being dependent on how much converts give, spiritually but especially materially, to God (or his representatives), who reward him by "prospering" him.[62]

Greater accent was placed on experiential faith, the centrality of the Holy Spirit, and the spiritual gifts of speaking in tongues and miracles. The importance of evil spiritual powers was maintained, and found its expression in the idea of global spiritual warfare and the ongoing accent on personal miracles of deliverance. The second coming of Christ was also part of new wave doctrine, as was strict ethical conduct, but these aspects of belief were increasingly secondary to an emphasis on spiritual gifts and miracles in the here and now. These churches and ministries commonly proclaim, as do many holiness organisations, that they are based on "signs and wonders," and it is not unusual to meet pastors who take credit for numerous miraculous healings, even cases of raising people from the dead. While in the holiness churches the categories of prestige center upon attaining the personal qualities associated with leading a blameless, simple, and Christ-like life, in the prosperity or new wave churches, for the most part, the economy of prestige is based on the acquisition of both spiritual power (expressed in the ability to heal, exorcise, and prophesy) and material success as evidence of God's favor. Salvation became increasingly this-worldly, and the evidence of new life as much material as spiritual. Moral rigor and strict personal ethics were not superseded, yet the notion of transformation was broadened to include the possibility of material change in everyday life. In 1991, during a service at one of the rapidly growing prosperity churches, a guest pastor of the prosperity-inspired Grace and Faith Ministries drew this clear contrast between the old and new waves, underscoring the social prestige attached to conversion and defining the "meaning of the name of Jesus" in no uncertain terms:

It is now fashionable to carry a bible on the streets of Lagos, it is fashionable in the city of Lagos to have B.A. [Born-Again] degree. People with position, people with power, Jesus people are taking over the society, and not the kind with scarf on head, not washed hair, smelling. You see the best people, the most educated, newest car, best dressed. If you are not born again, your mind is old fashioned. The king of kings is speaking through me as an instrument, we shall be the wealthiest people on the face of the earth, that's what God is restoring to the church. Some of you are saving money, N14,000, to get ticket to New York, to wash dish and to live in a carton with no address. The answer to prosperity is not in America, but it is in your nation, your capital is Jesus! God is prosperity, salvation, deliverance, health—that is the meaning of the name of Jesus.[63]

The new wave of converts did indeed incorporate a much higher percentage of educated, upwardly mobile university and school leavers. Christ Chapel was the first of the churches established from this second Born-Again wave to compete for membership in Lagos with the already established churches. Christ Chapel became popular not only because of its relatively relaxed attitude to dress and its emphasis on personal miracles, but because of its youthful and articulate pastor, Tunde Joda, who led highly emotional and charismatic services. Christ Chapel's success from 1985 onward gave rise to several new churches with similar emphases (prosperity; the centrality of the Holy Spirit, speaking in tongues; miracles of healing and monetary reward) as well as highly charismatic and emotional preaching styles. Both the Household of God Fellowship, led by ex–pop star Kris Okotie, and Powerline Bible Church were formed in the late 1980s by disgruntled members of Christ Chapel. Many other churches started from small fellowships, or through internal splits from other new churches already established. In the mid-1990s ironic onlookers dubbed many of the new churches "yuppie churches," in reference to their young, upwardly mobile membership.

Many of the pastors of the first new wave or prosperity churches received their religious training at one of the Bible colleges led by prosperity or faith preachers in the United States. Rhema Bible College, run by Kenneth Hagin in Oklahoma, was one of the more popular. Those unable to travel abroad often enrolled in the correspondence courses offered by such colleges. The cost of these courses became prohibitive for many young, aspiring preachers with the devaluation of the currency in the early 1990s. (In the early 1990s Rhema's three-year course, comprising eighty-five books, plus instruction by correspondence, cost $370, approximately N3,700. The monthly salary of an office clerk at the time was about N500, or $50.) Although the prestige attached to enrollment in one of these courses was high, and the potential for material reward in the future greatly enhanced, most aspirants had to content themselves with attending one of the rapidly proliferating Nigerian Bible schools. Undoubtedly the most popular throughout the 1990s was Benson Idahosa's Bible College in Benin City, which formed part of his multimillion-dollar Miracle Centre. The accent on the training and the ordination of pastors, never particularly strong, nonetheless slackened throughout the 1990s when all that was required to found a church was a "vision" from God.

No longer was the religious landscape one of strictly denominational organizations that attempted to create strong church identity and fidelity, such as Deeper Life. Instead, movement between churches on the part of converts became increasingly frequent, and the organizations themselves took on more diverse forms: interdenominational missions and ministries, house and university fellowships, multiparish megachurches, one-parish "mission" churches with evangelical outreaches, small neighborhood churches whose founders clearly hoped to surf the wave and develop outward from these modest structures. Many ministries no longer invested their money in building a permanent site, but instead rented cinema halls, restaurants, banquet rooms, and hotels. It is with this shift that we see the enormous growth of transnational networks, the privileging of transnational connections and experiences in the operation and symbolism of local organizations, and converts' embrace of the representation of a transnational Born-Again community.

Within the new wave, as in the old, membership in a particular Pentecostal church was not central to one's identity as a member of the Born-Again community. Even today, many Born-Again Christians still belong to the "mainline" denominations, especially the Methodist and Baptist; all the mainline denominations have been profoundly affected by the Born-Again message and styles of worship. Some believers do not attend any one church regularly, preferring to pray and worship in small, informal fellowships. Despite determined efforts on the part of church leaders to create stable and loyal followings, and in contrast to the denominationalism of the old holiness churches and Deeper Life, converts in the 1990s represented church affiliation as relatively unimportant, even though they were very often strongly attached to their current church. A survey of the religious itineraries of over five hundred Born-Agains in 1993 showed that the overwhelming majority were attending their second Born-Again organization, and more than half had already regularly attended two or more. Research undertaken in 1999 showed that this trend had continued and even accelerated, with many believers who converted in the early 1980s having changed organizations three or four times. Churches do have loyal members, however, and loyalty is very often tied to a charismatic leader or aspiring pastor. Since the organizations are notoriously schismatic, members appear to be easily won to new congregations when an aspiring leader breaks away to form his own church. Congregation sizes range from a dozen members in the smallest to several thousand in the most successful, with the notable exception of a dozen or so mega-churches with multiple parishes, such as Benson Idahosa's Church of God Mission, based in Benin City; Living Faith Church International (Winners Chapel), based in Ota; and the Lagos-based Overcomers Assembly.

Alongside these most outspoken proponents of the prosperity gospel, many other middle-sized organizations, such as the Redeemed Evangelical Mission, led by Bishop Mike Okonkwo, the Latter Rain Assembly, led by Tunde Bakare in Lagos, and Wale Oke's Sword of the Spirit Ministries in Ibadan, developed over this period. While inspired by the wave of prosperity and the possibility of salvation in the here and now, and a strong emphasis on personal miracles, they nonetheless preached a more tempered message, somewhere in between the strict antimaterialism and personal discipline of Deeper Life and the crass worldliness of the "name it and claim it" pastors. The RCCG's reform should be seen in the light of this "modernization": while still proposing a doctrine based on holiness and sanctity, the church increasingly placed the emphasis on miracles, charismatic gifts, and personal experiential faith, and deliberately targeted an elite clientele.

Benson Idahosa's mega-church in Benin City was one of the foremost proponents of the prosperity doctrine, despite his early struggles (very much akin to those of Kumuyi and Adeboye) following his conversion in the 1970s. His unashamed attitude to personal wealth and the prosperity of his followers opened up new possibilities for middle- and upper middle-class aspirants, and indeed any others hoping to better their condition in the here and now. One believer explained the attraction of the new wave churches to me in these terms:

When Christ Chapel started [1980], what really drew people in there is that people were tired of these "Sunday, Sunday" churches, packing [carrying] your Bible and don't read it. And then we have to compare with Deeper Life. Most members of

Deeper Life are mostly clerks. People will not want to go to Deeper Life even if it means they are going to hell. Because of their way of dressing, and they have this condemnatory message, like if you don't become Born-Again, you are going to hell, and if you want to confess your sins in the Holy Spirit only, that won't do it, if not with your mouth too. [In reference to Deeper Life's practice of public confession and restitution.] So when these Pentecostals [new wave, or prosperity] came in, they just filled the vacuum created by the Deeper Life people. People were free to wear jeans, people who didn't want to cover their hair could come to the church. They were looking at us as rebellious, but people were seeing results, miracles and so on. I think that those people that came out of Deeper Life came out first because of curiosity, and then maybe they see they are in bondage, don't do this, don't do that. So churches like Christ Chapel brought them out of that place.[64]

In discussions with young adepts of the new wave, all tell the same story, in which the moral rigidity and extreme otherworldliness of Deeper Life and other holiness churches is contrasted to the "needs" of young believers thirsting for spiritual fulfillment and empowerment, dissatisfied with the orthodox denominations, yet nevertheless unwilling to sacrifice freedom and lifestyle, or their aspirations for social mobility and success, for redemption in the next life. For many new converts and youth attracted to the new wave, the moral rigidity, strict control over practice, and antimaterialism of the old and new holiness churches was part of the "old ways," part of a sclerotic tradition that would have to be overcome:

The Scripture Union believe that it is in the Bible, "separate ye from among them." You should separate yourselves in that manner if people, unbelievers, are wearing jeans, then separate yourselves from them. If they are using a kind of slangs, then don't use it with them. The Pentecostals [new wave] believe we should not only move as Christians, but that the solution to development may be, in Nigeria, in Africa, separating ourselves out from the traditional link. They believe that a lot of things keeping us behind is because of tradition. In the church, but also in the society. This tradition and all these dos and don'ts. In the Old Testament, there are a lot of dos and don'ts, but in the New Testament, we are being led by the Spirit. So nobody has to tell you to cover your head, or don't wear jeans, or don't do this or that. The Spirit of God in you should tell you what is right and wrong. But the Pentecostals also believe in faith, miracles, prayers, holiness and all that. The problem is all these traditions, church traditions and African traditions.[65]

When asked to explain why the Born-Again revival met with such a resounding response, pastors and converts, whether adepts of the holiness or prosperity tendencies, invariably tell the same story of spiritual dissatisfaction with the churches they had been attending until then, and the unwillingness of church hierarchies to respond to their "needs": spiritual deadness or lukewarmness, empty ceremonies and ritual, Sunday "social club" atmosphere, no empowerment or spiritual response, corruption and complicity with the dirty politics of influence and big-manism, no "results," no solutions. As we saw above, Onibere presented his struggle in the Anglican church as a bid to make the church relevant to people's needs in this "contemporary situation": "The church, if it must be relevant, must seek its meaning in the activities of the people. That is to say that what is required under this contemporary situation is a *Living Church*. A church is living when it reaches the people. . . . We are faced with the conservatism of a few powerful leaders who have currently monopolised the leadership. . . . The Ogbonis and the Free Masons are in influential positions within the Anglican Church. They are a hindrance to the gospel . . . They want me out of the church because I remain a stumbling block to their evil machinations and plot to unduly politicise the temple of worship.[66]

All those attracted to the "new thinking" from the early 1970s on saw it principally as an answer to problems that their current religious organizations were unable to resolve. The resounding success of both "holiness" and "prosperity" over the space of a decade points not simply to the differences in the needs, aspirations, and frustrations of different social classes, but to a generalized sense of the need for spiritual renewal and moral regeneration, liberation from the past, and deliverance from the dangers and ordeals of the present. The astounding success of the movement over the past twenty-five years has meant that Born-Agains no longer represent themselves as a marginal community existing in a state of exception within the broader Nigerian religious and social landscape. And yet, although Born-Again Christianity has become an increasingly hegemonic social and cultural form, at both an individual and collective level the notion of rupture and difference remains particularly strong, and the community continues to project itself as an exceptional force for regeneration and redemption, in direct struggle with prevailing norms and the dangers they carry.

The Born-Again movement has continued to grow strongly, some twenty-five years after the original revival began, coming to dominate the Christian landscape of southern Nigeria, as research carried out in Ibadan between 1997 and 1999 illustrates. In 1999, in the neighborhood of Agbowo, Ibadan,[67] there were 164 Christian institutions, attended by a total of 24,000 individuals, most but not all of whom came from the area. Seventy-seven percent (126) of these institutions could be classified as belonging to the loose category of Born-Again evangelical, the remainder being divided among Anglicans, Catholics, Baptists, Methodists, Aladura, Jehovah's Witnesses, and other mainline Protestant denominations. At least 60 percent of the Christians attending institutions in the Agbowo area belong to or are associated with these Born-Again organizations.[68] Significantly, the vast majority of these organizations were established over the past fifteen years. Among this group of 126, more than 70 percent had been established in Agbowo since 1990 (87), and more than 40 percent only since 1995 (50). If we examine the dates of the earliest congregations established, we find that, with the exception of the Apostolic Church and the Assemblies of God, no Pentecostal/Born-Again churches existed in Agbowo before 1980.[69]

Interestingly, none of the organizations discussed above proposes a full-blown prosperity doctrine. While all place the emphasis on the Holy Spirit and on miracles, on the spectrum of "holiness–prosperity" attitudes to personal wealth and commerce with "the world," the great majority situate themselves in a sort of middle ground. Indeed, with the dizzying growth of the movement, the opposition between holiness and prosperity, so sharp in the early 1990s, has gradually decreased, especially with the increasing emphasis on miracles adopted by the great majority. The Born-Again community now appears fairly evenly distributed across the whole spectrum, while the extremes of strict antiworldliness and excessive materialism have been outnumbered by the great mass in the middle. Nevertheless, Born-Again Christianity is anything but homogeneous; important doctrinal, organizational, sociological, and material differences mark the broad community of believers. While religious doctrine, as an explicit regime of discursive practice, does provide a general grid for the perception of things and a series of explicit rules for the ways in which relationships with other forms of practice should be established, nonetheless, even at this most explicit level, contradictions are as significant as commonalities. The tension in the doctrinal positions of holiness and prosperity, between this-worldly and otherworldly salvation gives rise to a highly ambivalent eschatology. What is remarkable, however, is the extent to which the original interdenominational impetus present in the early revival has persisted, fostering the imaginary of an overarching community of Born-Agains despite these significant internal differences.

In his address to the first national meeting of the Pentecostal Fellowship in Nigeria (PFN) in 1991, Reverend Dr. Boyejo, general overseer of the Foursquare Gospel Church and president of the PFN, told the story of the Pentecostal rise in these terms:

As individual organisations we have prayed and laboured to hand down a heritage of a full-gospel message. They have sowed the seeds and watered them with their tears. They have been persecuted, ostracized, prosecuted for daring to believe in the total proclamation of the full gospel, different from the tailored or limited gospel of their contemporaries. Today those seeds have germinated and grown into the harvest of the vast multitudes of Pentecostal believers scattered and found in every corner of this great country. For about six decades that message and ministry of the Pentecostal movement has gone as if through a process of metamorphosis developing from the embryo to an adult state, from infant state of immaturity and inexperience that has unfortunately brought along behaviour and practices which were sometimes fanatical, extreme and unbecoming. The Pentecostal people have come of age, shedding childish behaviours and practices. Instead of the cold attitude, hostile stance and downright persecution of the powers that be, even including instigation from some religious leaders of the opposite camp in the past, Pentecostal leaders have now been accepted, appreciated, or at least tolerated by our brethren and leaders from other frontline denominations. The Pentecostal movement was so fragmented in the past decades in such a way that its identification was often confused with cults, groups and organisations that are not holding such fundamental doctrines as the Apostles' Creed, the protestant doctrine of justification by faith as propounded by Martin Luther, the doctrine of sanctification as taught by John Wesley, the sanctity of marriage of one man to one woman, and the fundamental truths of the Holy Scriptures. But for the first time by providential guidance the Pentecostal Fellowship of Nigeria was founded on the 14th day of November 1986 with the main purpose of bringing together into one fellowship all the Pentecostal people throughout Nigeria. That is why we are here, to draw closer to one another, to know more of one another, to hear from one another what God is doing in our nation, to learn from ourselves, to tap of the unlimited and precious resources of grace, wisdom, knowledge and truth deposited in one and the other. We are here to sing together, to clap, and face the future together. I am not afraid now since I know that you are with me and I am with you.[70]

In this story, we have the optimistic reference to a new, powerful, and united community of believers, singing, clapping, and facing the future together, overcoming past fragmentation and confusion. We also read the importance of the idea of difference and rupture through a direct critical engagement with past and current Christian practice, a practice that is "limited" and "tailored," coupled with a story of "persecution" and struggle, in which the world itself reinforces the rupture and difference the Born-Again message proclaims. The coming of age is represented as the moment in which marginality ceases to be imposed from the outside, where "fanatical," "extreme," and "unbecoming" behavior gives way to more "adult" forms, integrated into the world and accepted or tolerated by it. At the same time, differences among members are represented not as an obstacle but as an opportunity, where dialogue may enable members to "tap" the "unlimited and precious resources of grace, wisdom, knowledge and truth deposited in one and the other."

This bid to unite Born-Again believers under an umbrella organization that could represent their interests within the Christian Association of Nigeria and engage in dialogue with the state on questions of importance to the Christian population testifies to the sense in which the community, despite its internal divisions, saw itself as having a national mission to which all should contribute. Nonetheless, in the three days that followed Pastor Boyejo's welcoming address to this inaugural meeting, the discussions among participants centered almost exclusively on the organization's position on holiness and worldliness, much to the frustration of its organizers. Bitter arguments arose over questions such as these: Should women be allowed to enter the church with their hair uncovered? What about those wearing trousers? What was the organization's position on pastoral wealth? Is it Christian to use cinemas and restaurants, where people engage in sinful activity during the day, as temples of worship? What should be the Christian's main concern in these last days, if not evangelizing and preparing for the rapture?

Reflecting upon the movement's developments from the early 1970s to the 1990s, one successful pastor of the holiness tendency in Kano lamented:

We saw in the 1970s people who were really prepared to serve the Lord. The fire was burning in them. They were really prepared to serve the Lord. They were the first generation Christians. The second generation Christians are those who repented in the 80s. The quality of this set of Christians is less than the first generation. They are not committed. They are not dedicated. They are not even trustworthy. They fall into a category of Christians who can defraud their fellow believers and non-believers in business ventures. They tell lies as a matter of course. This second set of Christians need a second touch of God in their lives. The third generation Christians are those who repented in the late 80s and 90s. They are a shade below the second generation Christians. They lack depth, and like the second generation group, need a second touch of God in their lives.[71]

The advent of the new wave and the increasing accent on salvation and prosperity in the here and now called into question the terms in which the movement had positioned itself with respect to Christian traditions, but especially norms prevailing in society more broadly. Under these conditions, how can the rupture that the new birth announces and the project of collective regeneration be realized? The initiation of a critical internal debate that reviews the rise of the Born-Again movement and poses the problem of unity and identity is also one that continuously projects and restages the problem of ongoing renewal. The constant sense of the precariousness and incompletion of salvation that criticisms evoke, the liveliness of the ongoing internal debate, project upon the community the collective dangers that "backsliding" represents at the individual level, and contribute to staging the past as an ongoing challenge and source of danger to be perpetually overcome. This internal debate is an essential part of the process of subjectivation: While conversion and adhesion to the Born-Again program involve being subjected to a series of rules and modes of interpretation, it also means becoming the *subject of* this new conduct. The critical aspects of this debate show that, despite what certain analysts have maintained, conversion does not imply the suspension of judgment.

Deeper Life's members, even if they were fervently waiting for the rapture, also wanted to see "results and miracles" like the young believers flocking into Christ Chapel. Whether the narratives speak of deliverance from the evil powers of witchcraft, the corruption and moral decadence of contemporary society, the necessity of overcoming the rigidity of a tradition of "dos and don'ts" and embracing the freedom of being "led by the Spirit," rejection of the spiritual emptiness and corruption of the orthodox churches, insistence upon the need for a church that is living and responds to the "need of the people," or indeed the trajectory of the Born-Again movement itself and the dangers its development have opened up, the past is permanently present. Present as a form to be broken with, but perpetually called up and brought alive in the proliferation of narratives and stories that speak of its being overcome in various different forms. The story Born-Agains tell of the rise of their movement is a story of iconoclastic rupture: rupture with existing institutions and traditions, even those internal to their own movement, a permanent dynamic of change and renewal. And yet this story is also, and perhaps above all, the story of the fulfillment of a ruined tradition.

The holiness movement's adversarial relations with established Christian structures were largely the effect of these institutions' hostility, reproducing a classical schema of heterodoxy and schism found throughout the history of Christianity. In many ways the situation revisits the dynamics that at the turn of the twentieth century gave birth to the African church movement, in which Nigerian clerics and laymen set out to "indigenize" Nigerian Christianity in the face of missionaries' preponderant control and increasingly racist attitudes.[72] In some ways it mirrors the disputes that arose between the future Aladura leaders and their Pentecostal missionary sponsors over issues of faith healing and cultural practices such as polygamy.[73] Interestingly, this local history is never referred to when pastors and converts speak about the adversity and rejection they suffered at the hands of their churches and other "Christian unbelievers." Rather, the "ruined tradition" that Pentecostal Christianity everywhere claims to restore and fulfill refers to the early Christian church of the apostles, contrasting the long history of Christian institutions to this idealized early model, as is so often the case in revivalist or reformist religious movements. In Nigeria, this reference is an enduring theme, both in the early period of revival and subsequently, and it is frequently evoked as an inspirational model, the acts of the apostles serving as a model for modern evangelism, the vitality of faith and the spirit of sacrifice as examples of discipleship, and the persecution of the early church as a spur to greater commitment and dedication.

This "return to origins" itself involves an imaginary of rupture, staging a time and space beyond local historical trajectories. In this sense, it participates in the production of identities through a process of extraversion that emphasizes the universal over the particular, rather than being a process of Christian inculturation. This gesture involves not only a process of demarcation between local and global pasts, but also the incorporation of this global tradition, through the production of discourses that permanently bring this model and its principal protagonists into the everyday lives of converts, such that an imaginary dialogue may be established with these figures from a distant time and place. Converts refer not only to their intimate relationship with Christ, proper to evangelical doctrine everywhere, but also very commonly speak of the apostles as one would a friend or family member, as people they know well and love: "I'm afraid of dying, I guess. Even if I know where I'm going. But then I remember how wonderful it will be to finally meet Jesus, and Peter and Paul and all the others, to see them and talk with them," one convert explained to me. Through the proliferation of narratives, a dialogue with the early church is initiated. This dialogue is a practice of memory that transcribes local histories into world history, particular into universal, connecting individuals across cultures, times, and spaces.

The rescripting of memory and the initiation of a dialogue with figures from a mythical past constitutes one mode in which Born-Agains stage their project of rupture and overcoming. In the same spirit, the Born-Again engagement with the central concerns of the spiritual needs of "the people" involves a tacit recognition of a longstanding local evangelical tradition inaugurated with mission, in which Christianity can be seen to solve the problems of the age. It is this tradition that the Born-Again revival will restore through its engagement with the local past, the principal source of current dangers, as indeed it was seen by missionaries a century earlier. Traditions of power, traditions of accumulation, traditions of belief are set out in an explicit program that announces their overcoming.

"Be not deceived; God is not mocked: for whatsoever a man soweth, that shall he also reap." (Gal.6:7) What is it that we sow that could be responsible for the unfavourable conditions that prevail in this country presently? Why is the truth relegated to the background or completely obliterated while unrighteousness, ungodliness, and injustice reign supreme? Why do we advertise or publicize mediocrity at the expense of excellence? Why do we rejoice at spiritual elimination? Why should anyone hinder the spread of the Gospel and ban early morning devotion at schools? What is basically wrong with us as a people? Why do we massacre in cold blood our defenceless students at the slightest excuse? Why do we have such a large number of juvenile delinquents? Why is armed robbery a very "profitable" profession in our midst? Why do we have deceit in governments and high places? Why do we have instability in government to the extent that anybody in uniform can occupy the "hot" seat and pronounce himself Head of State even when he has nothing to offer? Why do Christians obey man rather than God when we know that Isa. 10:1 says "Woe unto them that decree unrighteous decrees and that write grievousness which they have prescribed."[74]

This poignant questioning is followed by a response expressing the conviction that it is not simply present-day individual sin that has led to this state of things, but the "sins of the fathers." Born-Again discourse and practice engage with the "history of the present," questioning the social, political, and cultural forms that they see as the historical ground for the present crisis. This questioning focuses not on external interventions, such as colonialism or capitalism, but rather on the local, on the *practices* of local agents: "What is basically wrong with us as a people?" The fierce rejection of all forms of sociocultural practice that are seen as particularly "Nigerian," "traditional," and "local" expresses a form of sociopolitical critique that emphasizes individual agency—it is individual sin and the personal rejection of Christ that opens up the space in which the failure of the nation is manifested. It also stages the Born-Again project of "making a complete break with the past" as the condition for renewal and redemption. And yet the permanent staging of nefarious forces of the past as the sources of current danger to be overcome, their constant objectification through Born-Again narratives and practices, has far-reaching and unintentional effects, giving them a power and reality far beyond that which is proclaimed in the message, creating a fundamental indeterminacy in the assumptions about the world that underwrite the establishment of norms of conduct, their interpretation, and the efficacy of practice, all the while contributing to the possibility of a permanent renewal of the necessity for rupture and struggle.

THREE

Revival and the Postcolonial Crisis of Government

The Born-Again revival irrupts and gains momentum at a particular conjuncture in Nigerian history. As previously discussed, the movement stages itself as an instance of rupture in the personal and collective lives of converts. However, the plausibility and pertinence of its self-positioning as a mode of practice that will solve the problems of the age, as a way of overcoming the ordeal of everyday life, and as a means for personal redemption and national regeneration must be sought not only in an analysis of its multiple points of engagement with traditions of religious practice, but also with its broader socioeconomic and political context.

Understanding the nature of this engagement requires critical reexamination of the ways in which the "political" is framed as an object of study. As discussed earlier, despite ongoing and repeated critiques, a great many analyses of the political field in Africa continue to focus exclusively on classical political forms, in particular the postcolonial state and various other forms of institutional power, often nebulously defined as "civil society." The development of an enormous literature on "failed" or "weak" states, particularly in the realm of conflict studies or development studies, and the use of a binary and materialist model of power (domination/resistance; hegemony/accommodation; state/civil society; formal/informal) continue to inform many studies of the Nigerian political field, and the study of power in Africa more generally.[1] This focus on institutions, in particular the state, not only involves an a priori notion of what is "political," but also invariably leads to analyses that see African modes of government only as pathological variants of an ideal type. The entire developmentalist rhetoric presupposes a set of models in which, through a series of adjustments, institutional, economic, and political deviation may be corrected. The critique of such approaches is extremely well worn, especially in anthropology and French political science. Nonetheless, such models continue to inform the production of knowledge and various practices on Africa.

Seen through a Foucauldian lens, the production of such knowledge and the practices that are both its object and effects should not be considered merely as forms of scientific inquiry about how Africa "really" is, but rather as elements that inform a strategic program of government. What are development, structural adjustment, liberalization, and "good governance," if not forms of "action upon other actions," modes of "conducting the conduct of others"? These apparatuses and the scientific, technical, and moral knowledge that underwrites them, while they cannot be understood as the outcome of an intentionality, nonetheless have effects on the constitution of African political fields. Analyses in terms of "dysfunction" or "failure" obscure the fact that these effects are themselves productive of the political field in a determined way. James Ferguson has made this argument persuasively, concerning the depoliticizing effects of the development apparatus, an "anti-politics machine," in an analysis of Foucauldian inspiration that could be applied to the "state of structural adjustment,"[2] or more recently, privatization, liberalization, and "good governance."[3]

If we reconsider the problem of power relations and their role in the production of the political field without a preconceived notion of properly "political" sites or institutions, we end up with a different picture. If we reject a binary model, in which domination is conceived in terms of the opposition of two poles—power and resistance, state versus society, dominants versus dominated—and an analysis in terms of institutional or group interaction (state/civil society or elite/mass; class, ethnic, and religious identities), we see that the sites that contribute to determining, for example, the lines of solidarity, the social bases of the state and its political and economic rationalities, the various rationalities and techniques employed in the exercise of different types of power, and the systems of differentiation that underlie relations of inequality all have a multiple provenance and are rooted in the ensemble of the social nexus. Such an approach requires us to examine how various forms of power relations, crystallized in different sites of "government" that "superimpose, cross-cut, limit, cancel out, or reinforce one another,"[4] interact in an incessant and unstable mutual play to constitute the political field. We can name a few instances in which power relations crystallize in a nonisomorphic fashion within the complex strategic postcolonial situation, giving rise to multiple and interrelated modes of subjectivation: global or transnational forms, including various institutions related to global capitalism, the development complex, and its associated institutions; the state and its institutions and its associated micro-political forms, such as schools, the military, hospitals; ethnicity and forms of "traditional" authority and its associated imaginaries; family and kinship; various forms of religious institutions and regimes of spiritual practice; but also many more diffuse, unsystematic forms, related to the acceleration of global flux. Dominant concepts of the operation of political power in Nigeria, such as prebendalism or patrimonialism, fail to capture the heterogeneity of power in the postcolonial context. As Bayart puts it, in Africa "the fields of the 'politically thinkable' are composite and at least partially reversible. They consist of ensembles, relatively integrated but nevertheless incomplete, disparate genres of discourse which the competing social actors mix enthusiastically. The baroque style of contemporary political constructions is the result of many different formative processes and borrowing from political repertoires, made possible by cultural heterogeneity and extraversion."[5]

In Nigeria, as elsewhere in Africa, domination at the state level is realized less through the stabilization of a governmental relation of power than through the prevalence of violence and confrontation, giving rise to a situation in which politics may be understood as war by other means.[6] If there is a "winning strategy" in the postcolony, it is one in which the power to kill becomes the ultimate arbiter of conduct.[7] We can identify localized sociohistorical blocs in which relations of domination take the form of "a global structure of power," whose manifestations and consequences we can find in the very fiber of society and which are the result of "at the same time, a strategic situation more or less solidified in a long-term historical confrontation between adversaries."[8] (Here we might want to cite the Hausa-Fulani domination of Northern Nigeria as an example.)[9] The political space of the nation-state is characterized rather by a fundamental instability and the prevalence of confrontational or adversarial relations among instances of domination, as well as the perpetual play between local and global governmental modes, such that political rule appears to be marked by a vested interest in disorder and insecurity. Perhaps this is the sense in which we can understand the radical pluralism that appears to mark the construction of a "public sphere" in postcolonial Nigeria, which is illustrated by the difficulty inherent in the creation of a common "civic culture," the prevalence of violence as a political technique, the perpetual mobilization of competing forms of identification that work against the creation of stable forms of national identity (although such identity is nonetheless a central form of political subjectivation, and is decisive in certain types of struggle), the centrality of "factional struggles" at the heart of authoritarian or centralized state power, and the constant play on the part of individuals between different registers of identity. This radical pluralism is also evidenced in the chaotic juxtaposition and simultaneous deployment of forms of discourse whose underlying epistemological assumptions appear diametrically opposed. Indeed, the postcolonial Nigerian political field is nothing if not baroque.

The Born-Again revival occurs at a turning point in Nigerian sociopolitical and economic history. And yet the sudden changes in the Nigerian political economy, its global insertion during the 1970s, and the multiple effects in the political, social, and economic spheres do not, in and of themselves, explain why this particular form of religious practice suddenly becomes relevant. Rather, we need to observe the ways in which a transnational religious movement, whose original explosion in Nigeria can be linked to the intensification of American evangelism and its transnational character, finds its own, autonomous logic through a process of mediation between global and local. This process of mediation entails the renegotiation of different traditions of social practice and modes of representation that are central to the exercise of power in the postcolony.

Oil Wealth, Corruption, "Corrective" Government, and Misrepresentation

All our people are now caught in this intense craze for money. Money and women. People are terribly mean to each other now. The old trust, the open handshake is gone. There is so much hatred now, a lot of hatred and a lot of bitterness and a lot of greed and a lot of jealousy, in short, a lot of everything that is bad. And the reason is that everyone wants to be rich. So they steal from each other and plunder the nation's coffers and use the people carelessly and shamelessly. . . . And women are amongst the most cruelly and callously used. Women are used as logs are used for the fire.[10]

Beginning in the mid-1970s we can locate a turning point in Nigeria's postcolonial trajectory. Inaugurated by the effects of the civil war and the oil boom, consolidated by the dramatic economic crisis of the early 1980s, and compounded by the disastrous political heritage of the Second Republic, this period initiated a deep popular disaffection with government and fundamentally destabilized many of the mechanisms that had enabled the great majority of Nigerians to confront the ordeal of everyday life.[11] This crisis is not merely institutional, economic, or political, but also involves a "crisis of representation" in which the dominant values, signs, and markers that had underwritten the perception of the material world, guided conduct, and legitimated authority, accumulation, and relations of inequality became increasingly unstable and polysemic. The themes of insecurity, violence, disorder, and uncertainty came to dominate the representation of everyday social experience, and authoritarian military rule became no longer a state of exception, an interregnum, but both literally and symbolically, a "transition without end."[12]

The oil boom of the 1970s intensified the themes of insecurity, violence, and corruption, but it did not introduce them, nor did it mark a fundamental departure from the dominant mode of government in Nigeria. As Ihonvbere and Shaw observe, "the military putsch of January 1966 came to most Nigerians as a welcome relief from the prevailing conditions of insecurity, uncertainty, violence, bitter politics and deepening socio-economic crisis."[13] The military was expected to provide immediate solutions to the various problems facing the country, and its positive reception "reflected a total disenchantment with the uncertainty, violence, corruption and waste that had characterized civilian rule since 1960."[14] The intense factionalism and divisions among political leaders were seen to be the principal motivations behind the military's accession to power.[15] Since independence, the exercise of power had been marked by the use of violence and thuggery, the prevalence of regional struggles inherited from the colonial structuring of the postcolonial polity, and the centrality of factional struggles within these regional blocs, within and between political parties, and within the various instances of the state.[16] State rule was exercised through a relation of power that had as its central object the control over the production and circulation of both material and symbolic resources; its central system of differentiation was drawn from various forms of status inherited from colonial rule (distinctions that simultaneously mobilized "traditional" forms of status with those associated with the modern state); and its main techniques were the use of violence and the mobilization of resources of extraversion.[17]

This predatory and extractive exercise of power was well established during the colonial period,[18] as was the discourse against corruption, by which various local factions attempted to delegitimize their opponents, principally in the eyes of the colonial government.[19] For the postcolonial period, Richard Joseph called this "prebendalism," a term that designates a predatory exercise of power in which public office and privilege are the principal means of extraction and accumulation of both symbolic and material value.[20] The "anticorruption" discourse would become the principal mode of both challenging and assuring the exercise of state power, creating a situation of discursive ambivalence related to the complex and contradictory ways in which extraction and redistribution were represented and which was itself politically productive. The ambivalence of the issue of "corruption" has been analyzed at length, and we shall not revisit these discussions here,[21] but merely note that the modes in which accumulation of wealth and its redistribution were legitimated had their historical roots in local forms of power in which wealth in people was more important than goods, and authority depended upon the ability to maintain a clientele through redistribution.[22] Norms introduced by colonial labor relations, commodification, Christian or Muslim conversion, discipline within colonial institutions, and new forms of state regulation were to complicate and multiply the different registers in terms of which accumulation and inequality could be legitimated, as well as creating new objects or sites to be governed.[23] Contradictory attitudes about legitimate authority and modes of accumulation served to underwrite and incite much of the behavior that was seen as corruption; everybody expected their communal leaders and patrons to redistribute the nation's wealth to the advantage of the community—getting their piece "of the national cake," as the saying had it—but nobody endorsed the notion that "public" or collective goods should be used primarily for personal profit. The equilibrium between extraction, accumulation, and redistribution was a delicate balance, and was mobilized in factional and regional struggles that were only worsened by Nigeria's regional political structure, in which northern domination at the federal level had been written in from the outset and was to endure in various forms throughout the next forty years.

The successive military regimes during and after the civil war presented themselves as forms of "corrective government" whose principal goal was to restore national unity, "remoralize," and bring order to the public sphere and the affairs of state.[24] At the swearing-in ceremony of new military state governors in July 1975, replacing those who had served under the Gowon regime, the new military head of state Brigadier Murtala Muhammed, announced that the former governors had been removed because of allegations of graft and misuse of public funds, and widespread public dissatisfaction with their ostentatious living, flagrant abuse of office, and acts depriving people of their rights and property. Other allegations against them included "perversion of time-honored government procedures, nepotism and favoritism, desecration of traditional rulers. All these gave the impression that the states were being run as private estates."[25] During his short-lived regime, Murtala embarked on "a massive shake-up and clean up—dismissal, retirement, suspension, demotion of hundreds of thousands of leaders and workers—commissioners, professors, cleaners, judges, soldiers, policemen, clerks, chief executives, in fact all categories of workers—in the public services and parastatals for indolence, indiscipline, corruption, lateness to work, inefficiency, irresponsibility, mismanagement and other offences. Of course, there was a lot of witch-hunting."[26] This last remark is indeed telling, and while the regime was too short-lived for us to be able to judge the effects such a program may have had, the assassination of Murtala itself shows that factional politics and violence continued to be determinate in the exercise of power.

At the national level, the "public sphere" was an eminently contested and morally empty space.[27] MacGaffey's characterization of Zairian social structure as a spider web seems extraordinarily apt in designating the limits of such a space as a domain that theoretically enables the questioning of right and power, and the formation of opinion that may be seen as having a certain representativeness.[28] We should locate the national "public sphere" in the center of the "spider web," a "zone where 'existence' prevails, from which one slips into more or less vast areas of non-existence. In the zone of existence people are able to live in accordance with modern standards, having an income that gives them access to housing, schools, markets, hospitals and football stadiums. Politically, this is the true nation to which the regime feels itself more or less responsible."[29] In postcolonial Nigeria, the social categories that are most successful in representing themselves within this space are "the membership of the higher echelons of the state apparatus; career politicians, senior civil servants, senior army officers, and managers of state economic enterprises."[30] In light of this we can better appreciate General Obasanjo's characterization of the new Shagari "democracy" of 1979 as "Contractocracy"—"a government of contractors, for contractors and by contractors."[31] Pluralism in Nigeria does not mean, as theorists of liberal democracy explain it, a plurality of interests meeting in a public sphere whose underlying cohesion is determined by a principle of citizenship captured by the ideology of juridical equality and symbolic force of "the nation." Rather, it means a plurality of "citizenships," each with its own internal moral economy, invented history, symbolic form, model of power and authority, and institutional expression, all interacting in the context of an authoritarian power whose control over public goods and accumulation is constantly under the pressure of their claims and whose legitimacy is challenged by their alternate visions.[32] With the increasing concentration of state power at the federal level from the civil war on, the national official public sphere became not less but more synonymous with state power, and did not denote an intermediate space of negotiation.

Forms of "civic public" did develop at a regional or intra-ethnic level, as Barber has demonstrated in her study of Yoruba popular culture.[33] From the 1940s to the 1970s, she traces the growth of a "Yoruba public sphere" characterized as "an active, public-spirited, civic-minded collectivity convened around the idea of 'progress' and 'enlightenment'" through education, and willing, at least at one level, to overlook religious, class, ethnic, and local affiliations (although at another level mobilizing them). In her account, this new public was made possible in the early colonial period by new disciplines of time and space introduced by church, school, organized sport, and the press. Popular music and theater used an amalgam of moral idioms, drawn simultaneously from "traditional," Christian, and Islamic sources, to generate a kind of ecumenical common sense whose project was a conservative progressivism, and "enlightenment" (*olaju*)[34] that did not sacrifice traditional hierarchies and indeed recuperated many longstanding values and practices under the guise of "our tradition."[35] Her analysis of popular culture complements Peel's account of the ways in which mission, colonial government, and Islam combined in a process of subjectivation from which a pan-Yoruba identity emerged, which could be mobilized against the conflictual affiliations associated with warring city-states, contributing to the rise of Yoruba nationalism and providing a model of government that would be deployed in struggles at the national level.[36]

The sudden advent of the petro-naira from 1970 greatly increased the premium on power, exacerbated the predatory nature of its exercise, reinforced the power of the central state, profoundly dislocated the social relations that had hitherto formed the nexus of social solidarity, and further unsettled the registers determining "truth" and "falsity," "seeing" and "believing." The 1970s saw the development of what Michael Watts has called a "mineral monoculture"; by 1980, 95.3 percent of total export revenues were derived from oil. This had a triple effect in creating new international linkages; as Watts says, it brought the "internationalisation" of the state, a new regime of capital accumulation based on rents, and a process of state centralization, growth, and enhanced autonomy.[37] The centralization of state power, which had begun during the civil war, was reinforced in 1973, when the creation of fourteen new states from the original four regions increased regional state dependency on the federal state with respect to revenue allocation. This also greatly increased the bureaucratic structures of the state, such that capital expenditures increased by 800 percent in real terms between 1973 and 1980.[38]

The creation of a veritable rentier state in the space of a few years dramatically increased not only the material, but also the symbolic importance of access to resources of extraversion, and valorized the conspicuous consumption of foreign goods. With the growth of the state sector, and with the naira stronger than the dollar, a massive spending spree ensued. Nigeria throughout the 1970s was a land of opportunity, with huge contracts to be made, an influx of foreign investment and expertise,[39] and a market flooded with commodities. "The proliferation of everything from stallions to stereos, a world apparently awash in money, produced a sort of commodity fetishism, what one commentator called Nigerian cargo cultism."[40] Construction throughout the 1970s grew by 20 percent a year; combined with the new opportunities linked to the trickling down of wealth, it encouraged rural labor to flood into sprawling, chaotic cities in the total absence of any urban planning. Neglect of investment coupled with rural-urban migration rendered the agricultural sector increasingly sluggish, leading to massive food imports and expensive schemes that created land speculation; it also dramatically redistributed the local balance of power in many rural communities in favor of speculators and large-scale farmers with connections to the regional and federal states.[41]

The successive military regimes failed utterly to channel this new wealth in a productive fashion: poorly planned and mismanaged programs and investments, corruption, inflation, an overvalued exchange rate, and an escalation of external debt due to chaotic and unregulated federal and state borrowing all meant that "the good ship oil prosperity was as a consequence already heading for the reefs of austerity and cutbacks even in its halcyon period" of the late 1970s.[42] By the early 1980s severe austerity measures were announced.[43] The Third Plan, covering the period of 1975–80, declared the purported goals of self-reliance, egalitarianism, justice, equal opportunity, unity, freedom, and democracy. Yet the period of the Third Plan, which had ten times more investment than in the Second Plan, "was plagued with corruption, waste, indiscipline, mismanagement and drift. Massive reviews did not help the situation as the cost of living shot up and unemployment figures rose. Food, clothing, and other basic needs gradually became luxuries for the poor."[44] As Watts argues, oil revenues may have "lubricated" the return to civilian rule in 1979, yet at the same time they permitted substantial continuity in the membership of the political elite, dominated since independence by the northern power bloc, as well as their predatory practices, even if some alliances had changed. The Second Republic of Shehu Shagari, elected in 1979, became notorious for its profligacy and irresponsibility, political infighting, and factionalism.[45]

This sudden influx of money and commodities had profound effects on the social conditions legitimating accumulation, status, and wealth. The rules and values that had hitherto helped legitimate and reproduce relations of inequality under an export system relying on agricultural surpluses, in which wealth was strongly associated with work and authority tied to the ability to develop kin-based networks of labor and patronage, were undermined by the overwhelming influx of petronairas. As Barber points out, the problem was not only the size of the petro-naira tide, but the fact that its production involved only a small number of Nigerians, and that those who received the wealth were not seen to have produced it by work. It was a situation in which "gigantic sums of cash seem to have appeared as if from nowhere, being appropriated by those who contributed virtually nothing to its production, and in the process personally enriching a few Nigerians on a colossal scale."[46] Apter notes that there was a sudden expansion of the middle class, in particular businessmen, contractors, middlemen, and entrepreneurs, which created "a credibility crisis within the status system as the old hierarchy was overwhelmed"[47] and as the norms underpinning status were increasingly undermined. This nouveau riche class invaded the margins of the elite, creating a growing anxiety in their ranks. While a certain amount of wealth trickled down through patronage networks, and while standards of living in the middle class did improve, nonetheless, the central effect of the oil boom was to dramatically widen the gap between rich and poor, resulting in the growth of absolute rural and urban poverty.[48] Popular disgust with government was increasingly widespread; already in 1971, Gutkind notes the radicalization of popular discourse among workers in Ibadan against "the rich," politicians, and "moneybags," in comparison with attitudes canvassed in the mid-1960s.[49] While in the 1960s workers still professed faith in their patrons and the state, a decade later disaffection, disgust, and increasingly radical political positions were being expressed at a popular level.

In 1981 international oil prices crashed, Nigerian oil production fell by two-thirds, and the Second Republic woke up to the hangover of the century: the party sponsored by the boom was well and truly over. As Watts puts it, "the ship of state ran aground with particular devastation" with the combination of the oil crash and the "discovery" of a massive external debt.[50] The economic crisis of the early 1980s, coupled with what Ihonvbere and Shaw have termed "the visible rape of the country under the civilians,"[51] inaugurated a fifteen-year period of successive military rule, austerity, unfinanced structural adjustment, increasing division, growing authoritarianism and state violence, the almost total collapse of state services, the dramatic impoverishment of the middle class, the descent into absolute poverty of the great majority, and the resounding failure of traditional strategies of social mobility and success.[52] The dramatic failure of successive governments to deliver on their promises of development and prosperity flew in the face of Nigerians' strong sense of belonging to a great and wealthy nation with a manifest destiny. The demise or collapse of state services such as health and education, the chronic and debilitating hopelessness of basic Nigerian infrastructure (electricity, roads, communications, water), the incompetency and graft that characterized every government office or state enterprise, the increasingly desperate struggle to cope with the chaos of everyday urban life all contributed to a growing sense that the country had dramatically lost its way. From the mid-1980s on the "SAPped[53] generation" dreamed of one thing: "checking out" of the country and seeking their fortunes in the West. Throughout the 1990s the fundamental dynamics underlying this exercise of power did not change, but only grew increasingly predatory and violent.[54] The "transition without end" of the Babangida regime, continued through the "Big Scam" of the annulled 1993 elections and the seizure of power by the military dictator Sani Abacha, reinforced the sense in which Nigerian government had become a permanent state of exception.[55]

We can argue that in Nigeria from the mid-1970s on, the principal mode of power's exercise revealed a growing instability in the terms in which the "real" was represented, a perpetual disjuncture between the sign and its referent. Apter recounts how the changes in the 1970s gave rise to a social anxiety about fraud and fraudulent identities, and the growing sense that wealth and status were being obtained by fraudulent means. In particular, fraud concerning university diplomas, which had formerly been one of the main modes of social mobility in the middle class, presaged the advent, a decade later, of the "419" confidence tricksters.[56] He argues that these anxieties point to a slippage in the registers of truth and falsity in the determination of social identities: "if seeing was believing during the oil boom, being seen could also mean passing and deceiving."[57] At the same time, the commodification of other forms of political authority, such as chieftaincy titles, giving rise to a spate of "naira" chiefs, and the growing influence of political "godfathers," mafias, and "moneybags" upon whose patronage political officeholders were entirely dependent created a deepening crisis of legitimacy and the impossibility of grounding authority in collectively held values. More profoundly, this situation relates to a more general crisis of representation, which was to worsen over the next two decades, as Apter's analysis of the rise of confidence tricksters and the "Big Scam" of the 1993 election shows. However, we must recognize the political productivity of these developments, and see them as contributing to changes in how people govern themselves and others: Government was not a question of managing relations among groups *in spite of* crisis and disorder; rather, crisis and disorder were one of its instruments as well as its central effects.

The enduring phenomenon of "corrective" government in Nigeria provides an excellent illustration of this. While successive military regimes may indeed have had serious intentions and programs for righting the ship of state, the logics inherent in the exercise of power, at the regional and state level, but also within the military itself, meant that the results obtained were exactly the opposite. As in many forms of authoritarian rule, in postcolonial Nigeria there is a perpetual, almost Orwellian, disjuncture or opposition between the terms in which the objects of power's exercise are represented and the objects it actually creates through this exercise. Attempts by the postcolonial state to moralize the political economy, to link power with virtue and thus legitimate its exercise, reveal not the officially stated ambitions extolled in the press—a just society, a thriving economy, prosperity for all, and other such cant—but the dissimulation, the "unreality" (*le simulacre*) that Mbembe places at the heart of postcolonial relations of power.[58] While continuing to plunder shamelessly the coffers of the state, living lavishly, and publicly displaying their power in a manner that reflects well Mbembe's characterization of the state in terms of excess and obscenity, various leaders with the aid of the national press attempted to impose "morality" and "discipline" by fiat. Murtala's shakeup in 1976, Shagari's "Ethical Revolution" during Nigeria's Second Republic, General Buhari's "War against Indiscipline" in 1984, and Babangida's "Mass Mobilisation of Self Reliance, Social Justice and Economic Recovery" (MAMSER) in 1987 are all examples of the outrageous sort of "doublespeak" that those exercising power have used throughout Nigeria's political history. As used by the state, the discourse on corruption and indiscipline has as its principal effect not the creation of a true civic culture and national consensus around the public good, nor the rationalization of economic and political forces and their increasingly close adjustment for the creation of political order and economic growth, but rather the exclusion of rivals and the consolidation of control, which is based on a vested interest in chaos and a perpetual blurring of registers of truth and falsity.

When groups or individuals refuse to participate in this "dissimulation," when their claims go beyond what can be silenced by state rhetoric or bribery, violence and the threat of violence are the ultimate arbiters of conduct. The extravagance and violence of the exercise of state power, its arbitrary interventionism, and its deployment of the various signs and cultural repertoires that are the marks of its rootedness within the social nexus create both the epistemological instability of representations within the public sphere and their normative polyvalence. This dissimulation or pretence (*le simulacre*) that distinguishes postcolonial rule finds its dissemination in the national press and television, even though the Nigerian press is one of the freest in Africa.[59] As Oluyinka Esan shows, popular responses to news and information programs characterize them as "lies," "a nauseating business."[60] But, as Mbembe makes clear, it is not as though people *believe* in the pretence; the question of belief is separate from that of power's exercise. The exercise of state power produces relations of "domesticity" or complicity insofar as it deploys techniques of subjectivation in which individuals are caught up in power's web, subjected to, but also active subjects of, a whole range of social practices and forms of knowledge upon which its exercise depends.

One of the central epistemological registers used to represent power in Nigeria is the idiom of the supernatural. However, beyond simply functioning as a register in which power may be understood, recourse to supernatural means should also be seen as a *technique* or *practice* of power, a form of sociopolitical action on the world. Dixon shows that with the economic collapse from 1982, common people began to see their relationships with the "big men" of their community in different terms. In his study of the Yoruba, he notes that those who had expanded their businesses and benefited in the years of plenty were seen as having selfishly abandoned their clients when the crunch hit. *Ase* (the power successful Yoruba men possess), understood in supernatural terms and associated with the possession of *oogun* ("medicine" or juju), came to be associated in the 1970s with "naira power" as more and more capital flooded into the economy at the peak of the oil boom.[61] For many, this type of power was a source of admiration and real assistance as networks expanded. Those excluded from this new wealth began to see these big men as not having acquired their wealth through legitimate means by the standards of Yoruba norms—hard work and individual struggle. Rather, they appeared to have come by their fortunes through a *"coup de chance"* or a *"coup de gueule"* (by chance or by force) in the words of Pius Nkashama observing Zaire.[62] As the economy began to collapse and urban austerity was put into effect, clients abandoned by their patrons, urban workers, servants, clerks, and the new army of unemployed middle-class people all began to vilify the big men in the most extreme terms. The most scathing criticism was reserved for those at the top—the politicians and business elite—but changed attitudes to the exercise of power were registered at every level. *Ase,* the spiritual power that elite and even moderately successful people were presumed to possess, was recast in imagery that emphasized its evil, destructive, corrupt, and occult nature.[63]

The association with and evocation by the state of the repertoires of occult or supernatural power have served to reinforce this imaginary and have contributed to the insecurity and confusion that is at the heart of its exercise. Here we can see evidence of the juxtaposition of various discursive registers that constitute the baroque Nigerian public sphere and the ongoing difficulty of securing a clear relationship between signs and their objects. The developmentalist state pays lip service to its Western model; official public discourse remains secular and rational, in particular in the official media. And yet the outrageous excess of personal accumulation, the extravagance of elite lifestyles, the arbitrary uses of terror and violence, all of these immediately refer to the idiom of occult powers and witchcraft. This idiom of the "belly" and "eating," employed in popular parlance to refer to accumulation, access to the state, and social expectations of redistribution ("you chop, I chop"), also evokes the relationship between eating and the world of occult forces, in particular, witchcraft.[64] As Peter Geschiere argues, in Africa "the problem of power has reached unprecedented proportions. . . . [T]he association between power and eating (and thus witchcraft) serves to express a profound anxiety, but at the same time an obsession *vis à vis* power, and its new forms."[65] In Nigeria, power is itself the evidence of strong spiritual connections; all "big men" that have "eaten well" are understood to have links to secret and occult forms of power whose normative value is determined through social practice. Over the 1980s and 1990s such elite practices were increasingly exposed and staged in such a way as to emphasize their destructive and debasing nature, as this Born-Again testimony illustrates:

Satan will eat so deep into the hearts of men that they will never be satisfied. They will forget who they are, their parents, homes and above all, their religion. Many wealthy business tycoons without any financial embarrassment whatsoever, who lived in cities and in fully air-conditioned mansions, ride luxurious cars and wear jewelries worth thousands of naira, would be so debased and bewitched by satan that they will come down to a little village of about six houses to a witchdoctor, kneel down or prostrate before his idols and seek for more power. Oh what a calamity! This dirty trickster of a doctor would prepare concoctions from deadly dirty materials including dead human flesh and bones, give them to eat, and will charge them heavily for this evil power. Sorry to say, most of these so affected always die mysterious deaths. As their wealth came, so it would also go.[66]

The state, with its references to Nigerian "culture," its use of evocative symbols and language, reinforces these connections and their increasingly negative valuation. As Apter's study of the event shows, the symbol for many Nigerians of this predatory "occult power" was the Festival of African Culture (FESTAC) held in Lagos in 1977.[67] For the Born-Agains, this event is unanimously designated as the turning point in the spiritual and material demise of the nation, the sign of a satanic power at work. From the mid-1980s on, the political realm and power in general are recast predominantly in terms that emphasize their occult, destructive, arbitrary, and amoral nature. In this sense, the term "corruption" comes to be overloaded with an excess of symbolic force, implying not a deviation from a certain model, but rather the death and decomposition of social worlds in the absence of a promise of renewal.

The decade of boom and bust thus introduced a series of changes in the relations of power underlying modes of government with which the Born-Again revival would productively engage with great success. Categories of status and prestige became tied to what might be termed an economy of "miracles," in which wealth and accumulation seemed to have become unmoored from the social conditions of their production, appearing as if by magic. This development destabilized the system of distinctions inherited from the ordering of differences during the colonial period that had hitherto underwritten the exercise of state power: both "traditional" forms of status, such as chieftaincy, and those associated with the modern state, such as education and diplomas, were undermined by their sudden commodification. Old hierarchies were further destabilized by their failure to exercise their socially productive roles: the old system of kin-based or ethnic patronage failed to curb the growing perception of inequality created by the dramatic widening of the gap between rich and poor, and following the crash, the system of patronage began to collapse under the weight of austerity. The status associated with education was eroded first by the inflation of diplomas, the delinking of competence and qualification from wealth and social mobility, then in the 1980s by the collapse of educational systems and the sudden devaluation of diplomas in a rapidly shrinking employment market. These developments slowly gave rise to new economies of prestige and a slippage in the categories and social representations of power, now reoriented toward the ruse, the con, the informal, the criminal, and above all, the occult or supernatural.[68]

The destabilization of local economies of value according to which inequality could be regulated and legitimated fundamentally undermined the consensus that had developed from the colonial period in what could be called "ethnic" public spheres, as studied by Peel and Barber in the case of the Yoruba. In this regard, the institutions that had been at the forefront of the development of such a consensus, in particular mission-derived Christian churches, independent churches, and Islamic modernizing movements, were also put into question. Another related effect was the new premium attached to symbolic and material resources of extraversion and international connections and commodities, coupled with the increasing monopoly of these resources in the hands of the minority with direct connections to the state. These developments all contributed to what we have termed a crisis of representation, in which signs and their referents became increasingly unmoored, giving rise to a heightened sense of social insecurity, a growing quest for moral mastery and the ability to control what were seen as untrammeled and dangerous powers.

Sites of the Born-Again Engagement: Rupture and Reworking

Fear and lack of confidence in the future are becoming the common currency of the day. Job seekers have no future to look up to—at least not from the system. We no longer trust *anything* or *anyone*. Those we trusted have mortgaged us and held us to ransom for foreign loans which we did not benefit from. . . . Everything—absolutely everything—is on the decline and on the verge of collapse. What more is still promising? What is it that is not declining? Is it education, health, agriculture, industry, politics, religion, marriage, or the family? No jobs, no money, no food, no clothing, no personal dignity. Any hope for tomorrow?[69]

This passage written by M. Ojewale in the early 1990s captures the Born-Again sense of rupture with the past. As discussed in chapter 2, the first site of engagement for the Born-Again movement was the tradition of Nigerian Christian practice. In the decade of crisis, the adversarial relations that developed between the revival and mainline and independent churches and the project of rupture also reflect a critique of the implication of these institutions in the state of decline. Born-Again conversion came to be seen to be a plausible and pertinent renewal of a tradition in which Christian practice could be seen to solve the problems of the age. If, at the most general level, Pentecostal doctrine, with its rigid division of the moral universe between acts that are Christ-like and those that are the works of Satan, provided a ready-made conceptual framework for reorganizing a chaotic moral field, the attraction of these new forms of knowledge and practice, their plausibility and pertinence, lay in the ways these general precepts, taken from biblical Scripture and American Pentecostal literature, were interpreted and set to work by pastors and converts in the light of their everyday experiences.

The local appropriation and setting to work of discourses on "development" and "modernization" in the sort of "public sphere" Barber examines as developing among the Yoruba relied upon the system of distinctions, discourses, and institutional forms inherited from the colonial state, the missions, and the independent churches. It points to the central role of Christianity in developing the grounds not only for the deployment and local appropriation of such discourses, but also for many of the institutional forms associated with the colonial complex. Indeed, Bayart has made the point that the independent churches, such as the Aladura, generally considered as prime examples of the revenge of "African culture" on processes of Christian "acculturation," also demonstrate important continuities with the missions and early twentieth-century popular Christianity. "In the final analysis, perhaps the independent churches were less the vectors of a radical 'incultura-tion'[70] of the Bible than they were agents for the implantation of a bu-reaucratic form of religious organisation in the sub-continent."[71] Re-reading Peel's study of the Aladura churches among the Yoruba, one can concede this point without too much difficulty.

Yet despite the self-conscious use of the language of liberal devel-opmentalism, the moral consensus underpinning discourses on de-velopment or enlightenment was not secular, nor did it depend on the distinction between public and private, in which religion moves from the realm of (public) "social fact" to that of (private) "opinion." Rather, these discourses were underwritten by a supernatural refer-ent that was seen as the ultimate enabler and arbiter of individual and collective success or failure in everyday affairs. By a curious sleight of hand, the centrality of what must be called properly religious activ-ity gets written out of a lot of the history of the sort of civic activity that Barber analyzes. Peel cites the centrality of prayer, for example, as an integral part of any collective meeting of these voluntary bodies or important individual decision or ordeal, such as school examina-tions, interviews, and business trips. As Chatterjee has argued,[72] reli-gion is, in its most general sense, at the heart of the construction of the sort of civic public described by Barber—an argument also developed in Lonsdale's discussion of the construction of civic virtue among the Kikuyu in his remarkable study of Kenya.[73] The development of this sort of public sphere did not, of course, preclude other modes of po-litical subjectivation; nonetheless, a broad consensus over the forms of social knowledge and norms underwriting civic behavior went a long way in creating a relative degree of political cohesion and social stability.[74]

In Barber's account, until the mid-1980s religious and sub-ethnic di-versity was tolerated, and this toleration appeared to be based on a con-sensus over definitions of good and evil—definitions that were clearly not secular and, one might add, that owed a great deal to processes of Christian acculturation, despite what might be seen as a relatively high degree of ecumenism. At the same time, she shows how a sense of continuity with the past was constructed through the self-conscious "recuperation" and integration of "our tradition." In the wake of the crisis in the 1980s we witness the breakdown of this consensus, a grow-ing sense of moral chaos, and the dramatic increase of religious intol-erance, conflict, and violence—primarily among Christians and Mus-lims, but also on the part of both Born-Again Christianity and Islam against what they saw as "traditional" and "occult" practices. Religious conflict was not limited to the north of the country, although it was much more intense and violent there than elsewhere.[75] More surprising was its expression in Yorubaland, as this population, divided more or less equally between Christianity and Islam, has long been presented in the literature as the icon of African ecumenism; although the famous "live and let live" attitude has no doubt been exaggerated, growing intolerance from the late 1980s on certainly represented an important rupture with the past.[76] From the mid-1980s the country saw the rise of "secret cults" involved in racketeering, threats to staff, and even ritual murder in institutions of higher education,[77] along with the beginning of intensified fears of witchcraft and urban rumors about occult power—an example is the missing genitals scare, in which dozens of people were lynched after having been accused of spiriting others' genitals away through casual contact—as well as the proliferation of public and publicized representations of the workings of occult powers in various forms of popular and electronic media. These new forms of occult practice appeared unmoored from the relations of social inequality and functions of social control expressed through witchcraft, in which victims and accusers were connected through ties of kinship, ethnicity, or prior social knowledge. As Smith points out in his study, people became increasingly concerned by the lack of social rootedness and by the apparently arbitrary nature of new and often gruesome forms of occult ritual practice.[78] At the same time, as Barber shows, such stories of untrammeled occult forces were not accompanied by any moral messages that would enable the elaboration of "correct" behavior and modes of self-protection, as in the past, but only staged violent figures of divine retribution.[79]

The religious institutions so important in the dissemination of an ethics of progress and "enlightenment" were thus seen as increasingly disarmed in the face of the crisis: in the case of Christianity, at least, their prevailing modes of worship, institutional organization, and forms of knowledge appeared to offer little in the way of solutions for the reestablishment of moral mastery and the control of untrammeled powers, nor were they able to legitimate the new forms of wealth and sudden commodity fetishism brought on by the oil boom. 'Moreover, the old institutions were increasingly associated in one way or another with the governmentality of the belly: mission-based and orthodox denominations were seen as reproducing within their institutions the same sorts of relations as produced by state power[80] As Onibere accused: "The Ogbonis and the Freemasons are in influential positions within the Anglican Church. They are a hindrance to the gospel. They want me out of the church because I remain a stumbling bloc[k] to their evil machinations and plot to unduly politicise temple of worship."[81] The failure of orthodox denominations to provide either spiritual or material solutions to the growing crisis, their opposition to the "new thinking," and their implication in the dirty politics of state and "big manism" were to provide the grounds for their desertion during both the holiness and the prosperity moments of revival. The Aladuras were rejected for many of the same reasons. In both cases, these institutions were seen as being in league with dangerous powers, understood either tacitly or explicitly in occult and satanic terms, an appreciation that speaks to the inability of these institutions to address the problems of the age, as the tradition had it. The charismatic interdenominational and egalitarian holiness revival of the 1970s thus emerges as a position of direct rejection of dominant forms of Christian knowledge and practice, as well as both new and old distinctions underlying relations of power, social norms, and practices.

Among the flood of foreign experts arriving in Lagos throughout the early 1970s were American Born-Again evangelists.[82] Their preaching and the dissemination of literature were rapidly taken up by the already existing interdenominational, groups such as the Scripture Union. Evangelical witnessing and testimony obeyed the narrative imperative central to the propagation of this global religious form, and the revival grew through the proliferation of new narratives, stories that were both signs and instruments of an explosion of religious imagination. The appropriation and circulation of the holiness doctrine in the urban South, particularly in Lagos, provided what appeared to be a ready-made critique of, and response to, these developments within the established churches and broader society more generally. Through an adaptation of global Pentecostal teachings and a local biblical hermeneutics, the growing holiness movement directly opposed dominant forms of the exercise of power and many of the social relations upon which it depended. The extremity of their antimaterialism and their messianic bracketing of the here and now placed converts in fundamental opposition to an exercise that had material wealth and immediate consumption as its objects. Strict reinterpretations proscribing the consumption of foreign goods and images, coupled with a rejection of local forms of ritual and material culture, produced the image of a sort of conservative modernism in direct contrast to the cargo-cultism of the decade. There was an implicit political import in this stance: in the first decade of holiness revival, there was a self-conscious embracing of the idea that "many that are first shall be last; and the last first" (Mark

10:31), as well as frequent references to the camel, the rich man, and the needle's eye (Matthew 19: 24).

The injunction to break with unbelievers involved the rejection on the part of the new converts—as members of social groups excluded from the new wealth (youth, women, and the lower classes)—not only of the new forms of prestige associated with the boom, but also of old hierarchies and differentiations, such as kin, generation, ethnicity, and even gender, upon which dominant relations of power, forms of social solidarity, and strategies for upward mobility had rested. At the same time, discourse and confessional practice focused on "correcting" negative forms of social behavior that suddenly appeared rampant: dishonesty, jealousy, greed, selfishness, violence, bribery, and all nature of bodily excesses were decried in preaching and witnessing. Born-Again converts managed to project this new image beyond their communities and into the public sphere. Capitalizing on the moral uncertainly engendered by the boom and bust, converts presented themselves as a new sort of citizen: honest, hardworking, trustworthy, and incorruptible. No doubt greatly exaggerated, nonetheless, until the early 1990s the qualities associated with Born-Again conversion had the effect of creating a new sort of social capital. Interpersonal relations beyond the community were thus also mediated by the new expectations for social practice that conversion implied: employers of all confessions recounted how they actively sought out Born-Again recruits, and lecturers complained that Born-Again female students could not be pressured into exchanging sexual favors for passing grades.

Although the new wave of the mid-1980s, inspired by faith and prosperity doctrine, was to break with the antimaterialism of the 1970s, the context of the dramatic economic crisis and the failure of the old strategies of social mobility rendered particularly pertinent the ways in which doctrine rearticulated the problem of wealth and social mobility. In the prosperity congregations from the mid-1980s, the symbols of prestige—fine clothes, nice cars, foreign goods—valued during the boom years were common currency. By embracing the symbols of prestige associated with consumption, education, and upward mobility, and by colonizing aspects of popular culture, such as highlife music, video film, and television, the new wave was not rejecting "naira power" but reinventing the rules of its use, reworking the dominant categories of distinction and the codes and knowledge that underwrote them. The power to succeed and prosper was presented as being given to those living exemplary Born-Again lives through the spiritual power of Jesus, and material gains were to be distributed according to His rules. Those who aspired to riches and social status were taught that only through adherence to Born-Again doctrine, prayer, hard work, and generosity in giving (of time as well as money) would they likewise "be prospered." Those who failed to live a "true life in Christ" were depicted as gaining wealth through contact, consciously or not, with evil forces, and were likewise to be ruined by them. In many senses, prosperity doctrine provided not only a new interpretation of the "economy of miracles" introduced by the boom, but also the means for those in the struggling middle classes and even the elite to legitimate their aspirations for wealth and success, or to "whitewash" status and wealth already acquired. This reworking and the ambivalence it gives rise to over the 1990s are the subject of chapter 5.

The revival was primarily fueled by the enthusiasm of the youth and of women, the two social categories most affected by both the boom and the economic downturn. Resolutely trans-ethnic and egalitarian, converts re-created the bonds of social solidarity and reconstructed networks of social support. Calling each other "brother" and "sister," members appeared to put aside the usually pronounced respect for social status found in Nigerian culture. Even in the prosperity movement, this tendency was marked: as one believer from Christ Chapel put it, "Maybe I'm a banker, and this brother is a clerk, and because of emotions and everything involved, I can meet him, maybe he talks to me any how, but I can take it."[83] Particularly for the youth throughout the 1970s, this held great attraction, enabling them to develop a sense of individual self-worth outside the new categories of material success and allowing them to compete with people who no were longer considered superior simply by virtue of age or wealth. For many ambitious young people struggling to get ahead despite the difficulties of urban life, the institution of the extended family, and the social expectations placed upon them, their inscription in cycles of debt and obligation were increasingly experienced as an unbearable burden. Intergenerational conflicts over values and practices were resolved or at least alleviated by the ways in which churches and fellowships presented themselves as the "new family," which, coupled with the exhortation to break with unbelievers, helped attenuate severe crises of conscience.

Marriage strategies changed, as conversion came to be seen as a way of finding a reliable and serious spouse, and the social bond of marriage came to be mediated by the approbation and critical eye, not of the extended family, but of the pastor and fellow believers. One of my close Yoruba friends had developed a relationship with a young man in her church, who asked her to marry him. Her family was strongly opposed to the union, as the young man was not Yoruba but Urhobo and her family had their own candidate. She suffered considerably from her parents' attitude, praying for nights on end that the marriage might go forward. Through the mediation of her pastor, the intervention of members of the congregation, and her own insistence that it was God's will for her, she finally convinced the family to give her their blessing. Another significant attraction for women was the proscription of adultery and divorce. Furthermore, churches stressed the nuclear and not the extended family. Although in doctrine the woman was presented as subordinate to the authority of her husband in the home, it was made clear that the husband had an obligation to respect her and treat her with consideration. Husbands were enjoined to treat their wives like partners, involving them in daily decisions, and helping to take responsibility for child rearing, even domestic chores. Children were presented as "gifts from God," and it was often stressed that blame for failing to reproduce does not fall on the woman, with the story of Elizabeth (Luke 1:36) being offered as proof that the Lord works miracles and that His time is the best. Many young couples were also drawn by the fact that wedding ceremonies in Born-Again churches were not the fantastic extravaganzas one finds typically in Lagos, and both parties were encouraged to keep their material expectations modest.[84] As one young woman put it: "The brother I'm waiting for can come in a leggedes-benz [on foot] as long as he's a true child of God." Finally, within the church the choice of a spouse was left to the individual, and was not the outcome of negotiations of the part of family members. This excerpt from a cartoon strip in a Born-Again magazine illustrates this point:

MAMA NGOZI: Papa Ngozi wants to give Ngozi out in marriage to a very rich man who has promised us so many gifts. Your friend said no, she is born again.
CHI: P-R-A-I-S-E GOD Mama, those days are gone. People marry because they love and more so born again Christians because it's God's perfect will these days.[85]

These developments constituted an opportunity to escape or renegotiate old forms of social obligation, particularly given the pressures placed on networks of kinship from the sudden rise of rural-urban migration from the 1970s, and to replace them with ties based on fundamentally different premises. Transethnic solidarity was also strongly encouraged, particularly through the positive attitude of the movement toward interethnic marriage, which likewise downplayed the importance of ethnic obligation and patronage, and created the basis for a broad Born-Again public. Relations of reciprocity were developed in the setting-up of a kind of rudimentary social security, especially in the holiness tendency. Members organized into small neighborhood prayer groups not only encouraged each other spiritually, but re-created the relations of reciprocity previously expressed through kinship. However, one did not see the reproduction of kin-based forms of sociability, debt, and obligation within congregations; instead, the model appeared to be based on elective affinity or friendship, leaving considerably more leeway for individual expression and freedom. Many churches set up nurseries and kindergartens, provided "medical services" (usually faith healing) at "faith clinics," and offered counseling services on financial, marital, and other matters. Missions and churches also engaged in sponsoring individuals in a variety of educational and business endeavors, related most often to the running and propagation of the organization and its assets—transportation, building, publishing, petty crafts and trade, Bible college administration. There was a conscious pride in these "self-help" activities, which were presented as demonstrating the ability of these communities to develop alternatives to social services that the state was no longer providing.

In the place of status as determined through the old hierarchies, the early Born-Again revival proposed an economy of prestige in which the possession of spiritual power was associated with the virtues of sanctity and devotion. This was expressed by the avoidance of negative social behavior and a rejection or reworking of the signs and codes underwriting the exercise of a variety of power relations expressed through social institutions and forms such as family, kin, class, ethnicity, generation, and gender. Indeed, the ability to eschew negative forms of social behavior and break longstanding social ties, as evidence of a new life was presented as merely the external effect of a new spiritual power, the "infilling of the Holy Spirit." In the prosperity movement, while the manifestations of the Holy Spirit also took more worldly, immediate forms, nonetheless, as in the holiness tendency, the "power in the blood of Jesus" attained through conversion centered on the themes of protection and deliverance from evil forces. This message was presented in such a way as to emphasize the moral agency of the convert, providing individuals with a sense of protection from the dangers and ordeals of everyday life, as well as moral mastery.

The most striking aspect of both these moments of revival was the extent to which access to this form of power and the knowledge that accompanied it was presented as egalitarian and public. The egalitarian distribution of power of the Holy Spirit and the "gifts of the Spirit," as manifested in the miracles of healing and the alleviation of suffering, the openness and accessibility of knowledge offered to converts through preaching, and the exhortation to constant individual study of Scripture and a vast quantity of literature and recorded messages, represented a striking departure from the model of pastoral power exercised in other Christian institutions. More generally and very significantly, it also clashed with the dominant relationship between knowledge and power, in which the exercise of power depended upon access to secret and esoteric forms of knowledge. Indeed, this connection between secrecy and power, inherent in practices of witchcraft and the forms of social prestige and authority attached to religious specialists such as the *babalawo,* and implied in the status and power associated with the big man, had only been exacerbated during the oil-boom years: the inexplicable origin of new wealth immediately evoked the possession of a new and powerful form of secret knowledge. This open access to both power and knowledge—indeed, the active encouragement of individual empowerment—and the relatively weak and informal modes of institutionalization represented by house fellowships, interdenominational groups, and prayer meetings all gave new meaning to the power of the laity.

One of the most powerful forms of discursive rescripting of relations of power undertaken by the Born-Again movement throughout the late 1970s and 1980s was the merging through new narrative production of global Pentecostal doctrine with a local ontology of power, something that mission or orthodox Christianity had failed to do. This gave plausibility to new practices of deliverance that are part of Pentecostal orthodoxy everywhere, and the Born-Again articulation of the problem of spiritual pollution and affliction involved a fascinating mediation of global and local. American Pentecostals are completely at home using the Internet to discuss how demons enter the body and how to make sure deliverance is complete, or praying during the early stages of cell division in fetal development in order to exorcise the evil spirits of previous generations that might be lodged within the fetal DNA.[86] Nigerian Born-Agains identified immediately with the way that one of the central oppositions in the colonial and postcolonial ordering of difference—"modernity" and "tradition," "science" and "superstition"— found untroubled marriage in this new form of global modernity. These connections gave local appropriations an intellectual legitimacy and prestige, a kind of global guarantee, reinforced by the international reception and diffusion of Nigerian Born-Again narratives and media

productions, which also strengthened their sense of transnational belonging and purpose. Central to evangelical witnessing and testimony,
these stories, together with more everyday accounts of miraculous healing and prosperity, were to constitute the movement's most powerful
discursive forms.

This imaginative reworking involved a vivid critique of the dominant political economy and exercise of power, attempting to re-moor
floating signs and uncertain identities within a restructured moral order. This question of the resolution of the "crisis of representation" by
Born-Again discourse and practice is extremely complex, and will be
addressed in chapters 4 and 5. Here I will draw attention to the political
fertility of these accounts in rendering plausible the Born-Again project
of redemption in a context of crisis, as techniques of "making believe,"
but also as new forms of social knowledge. These stories should not
be read as simple metaphors for more material realities, such as commodification, capitalist exploitation, or military authoritarianism, or as
vernacular attempts to understand the mysteries behind new forms of
power and wealth, although they did involve new modes of interpretation. They should be seen as forms of knowledge about the world in
terms of which the convert and the unbeliever may contemplate both
the promises and dangers of different modes of self-conduct. Evangelical witnessing is a modern technique of the self: it involves "giving an
account of oneself"[87] and also constitutes a form of *praemeditatio malo-
rum,* the Stoic practice of anticipating future evil so as to forestall its
realization.[88] The stories identify realities that had been created as objectifications through forms of deadly and secret political practice, and
represent modes in which the government of others is effectuated. By
being made public, these stories would not only "unmask" the workings of such powers and promise protection from them, but paradoxically, intensify an existing anxiety about evil occult powers and their
presentation by cultural entrepreneurs in various public forums, such
as the popular press and the video industry, throughout the 1990s.[89]
They have given rise to a widespread genre reproduced and circulated
throughout Africa and the diaspora. Not mere cautionary tales, they
are a most fertile form of religious imagination through which a new
geography of the divine finds its expression and a mode in which the
themes of redemption and resurrection in a world of corruption and
desolation acquire a graphic force.

Ephesians 6:12 encapsulates Pentecostal teachings on the true enemy of the Born-Again Christian: "For we wrestle not against flesh and
blood, but against principalities, against powers, against the rulers of

the darkness of this world, against spiritual wickedness in high places." This is one of the most often quoted biblical passages in Born-Again circles and has been reworked in highly imaginative ways to depict the struggle for redemption, both individual and collective. It contains the central theme of some of the most widely circulated booklets and testimonies, bearing titles such as *Delivered from the Powers of Darkness, Former Satan Deputy in the World Turned Follower of Christ,* and *Redeemed from the Clutches of Satan: Former Head of Seven Secret Cults Now an Evangelist,* and describing in detail the works of "the Evil One" in Nigeria.[90] All of these testimonies, the great majority dating in published form from the mid- to late 1980s, make reference to practices over which Satan and his "government" exercise control, and which seek to destroy Born-Again Christians.[91] The testimonies generally follow a pattern in which an individual is initiated into the echelons of the satanic hierarchy, portrayed in terms of a "government" with "ministers" and a large "army of soldiers" or, as Eto puts it, "a military kingdom" of "millions of evil spirits who oppress, suppress and posses human beings."[92] As one of Satan's agents, the person receives great wealth or power, and usually moves up the hierarchy to become "second in command to Lucifer," or one of his righthand men or women. The individual uses satanic powers to bring economic ruin to non-Christians or "weak" Born-Agains, to cause disasters such as road accidents and sudden deaths, to perform crimes such as armed robbery, or to obtain great wealth or political office. At a certain point, the individual hears the Word, is delivered, and becomes converted, and uses the power in the name of Jesus to ward off enemies in the spirit world, and eventually defeat them. Very often, satanic activities involve initiation into secret cults, which may be "traditional" (various shrines, cults), "neo-traditional" (Mami Wata), of colonial origin (Freemasons, Reformed Ogboni Fraternity, Rosicrucians, Osugbo Guild), relating to Islam ("Arabic Societies"), and/or international (various esoteric groups from the Asian subcontinent).

In his booklet *The Works of the Devil,* Emmanuel Eni clarifies Ephesians 6:12 in this way:

The devil is an excellent administrator. He is the champion of the division of labour. He knows how to organise things in an evil way so as to finally achieve his goal. . . . in Satan's governmental hierarchy, the four mentioned in the above Scriptures are: (a) the "principalities," (b) the "powers," (c) "the rulers of the darkness of this world," (d) the 'spiritual wickedness in high places." . . . The "principalities" are the "Cabinet members" or the "Federal Ministers" of Satan. They are directly responsible to, and take orders from their "Prime Minister" or "President"—the devil.[93]

At her "pinnacle of satanic power," Evangelist Victoria Eto tells us in her testimony *How I Served Satan until Jesus Christ Delivered Me* how she decided to become "head of state":

I consulted my invisible colleagues and they advised me to get in touch with Lucifer himself. I was referred to a Muslim contact for seven days. For seven nights I recited the incantation and slept in the nude. On the seventh night Lucifer came. Looking very fierce and scowling he asked, "What do you want?"

"Power"

"What for?"

"Political power."

"You have it."

"Yes, but can I become the President of Nigeria?"

He was silent for some time.

"It is possible but very expensive"

"I will pay"[94]

In Eni's testimony he, like Grace Ihere,[95] spends a considerable amount of time under the sea with the "Queen of the Coast," the head of Mami Wata spirits in the Lagos area, with whom he makes a satanic covenant. While there, this is what he finds:

I went into the scientific laboratory to see what was happening. I saw psychiatrists and scientists all working very seriously. The work of these scientists is design beautiful things like flashy cars, etc., latest weapons and to know the mystery of this world. . . . I moved into the designing room and there I saw many samples of cloth, perfume, and assorted types of cosmetics. All these things according to Lucifer are to distract men's attention from the Almighty God. I also saw different designs of electronics, computers and alarms. THERE WAS ALSO A T.V. FROM WHERE THEY KNEW THOSE WHO ARE BORN AGAIN CHRISTIANS IN THE WORLD. THERE YOU WILL SEE AND DIFFERENTIATE THOSE WHO ARE CHURCH GOERS AND THOSE WHO ARE REAL CHRISTIANS.[96]

He concludes this chapter of his testimony by stating; "I was not yet qualified to meet with Lucifer but only to be his agent. All the same I was satisfied that I now had powers and could face, challenge and destroy things at will." The story resolves itself by his Born-Again conversion and a showdown on the spiritual plane between him and his erstwhile satanic masters. He vanquishes them with the "name and the blood of Jesus," noting that "the name of Jesus or the Blood of Jesus in the mouth of the believer sends out fire . . . THE NAME OF THE LORD IS A STRONG TOWER, the righteous runneth into it and is safe (Proverbs 18:10)."[97]

In Balogun's testimony, he begins his life as a Muslim, and as early as third form at school, he is initiated into witchcraft by the mother of a schoolmate, who seals the pact by giving him *akara* (beancakes) fried in human blood. He becomes a wizard and begins to night-fly, and by the time he is in fifth form receives increased powers and a mission "to suck blood, deform people, cause accidents on commercial vehicles and kill outright." The only people impervious to such attacks are the Born-Again Christians: "The Born-Again Christians have got some divine powers encircling them that no demonic power can penetrate through."[98] He subsequently joins seven different secret cults and becomes wealthy, and finally is granted an audience with Satan himself.

Satan as we all should know has an established kingdom and government . . . he has a lot of soldiers who have specific functions to perform. There are the familiar spirits, the superior and servant spirits and finally the major and sub-princes. Satan has an unseen power which takes full control of one's heart and dwells there. From this abode he brings all sort of demonic thinkings into the brains of his victims who in turn reciprocate and carry out the action. He has the power of inducing a man and influencing him to doing thousand and one evil acts.[99]

His meeting with Satan turns sour when he carelessly mentions the word "Jesus." Satan roars in fury, and sends him on a mission to attack a Born-Again church and bring him "thirty or forty human hearts." His mission fails when he approaches the singing congregation during their night vigil and sees that "from nowhere an iron fence had surrounded the church." He turns into a snake, but is unable to scale the fence, which is covered in some slippery substance that causes him to fall off. Dawn arrives and Satan is furious, and sacks him on the spot.[100] He loses all the wealth he had gained as a well-known traditional healer, and becomes a vagabond. Finally he meets a pastor who brings him to Jesus, and after several satanic temptations, gets his deliverance, and is Born-Again. The conversion story concludes with an exhortation to renounce demonic activities:

DENOUNCE OCCULTIC MEMBERSHIP! They are not able to hurt you. Be a Born-Again Christian and Jesus will support you . . . Let alcoholism be your forbidden practice and avoid being conferred with chieftaincy honours. If you are already one of these so called chiefs, renounce the title today, for at the end is hell fire. If you are one of those people who use demonic power black soap to get wealth, throw away that soap today. If you are a wizard or a witch . . . renounce your membership today.

You will vomit out the demonic power you swallowed as I did mine after my deliverance. Mine was vomited before an audience of more than 2,000 people. Yours can be so.[101]

The book ends with fifteen pages of exhortations to conversion, advice for young converts and church leaders, and a series of prayers to be repeated upon conversion and for various occasions and particular purposes.

Dagunduro, an auto mechanic who notes on the cover of his book that he has a diploma in "Auto Engineering," relates in his testimony his initiation into (among other cults) the "Arab Cubic Cult," described as "a cult and a secret society through which the members become excessively rich through sorcery and necromancy. The members are Alhajis and Sherriffs [sic] who bring one human being each every year for their ritual murders and sacrifices." According to his gruesome account, kidnapped victims would be brought to the cult house, and if "their god" commanded they be killed, "they would say Muslim prayers over his body, say 'bisimilai' three times over him, and slaughter him with a sharp knife like a he-goat!" following which the victims were skinned and their skins used as prayer mats. However, victims could be rejected by "their god," in which event "they hit him with a medicinal band on his head to take away his human consciousness from him and turn him to a mechanical robot that would be used there for ever to count money or arrange the moneys that they make there with sorcery." He describes the wealth of the cult's members in these terms: "The money in their cult house is never rationed. You can cart away as many thousands as you can carry every day! Money in their store is as plentiful as waste paper in the public disposal ground of a metropolis."[102]

These narratives directly address many of the sources of insecurity and anxiety, and the social and political forms that were seen as being responsible for them. They project powerful redemptive messages in which conversion empowers the individual in his personal life, providing him with a new form of "power that pass power," which promises not only protection and salvation but also the strength to do battle with powers and principalities, "raising up an army for God in the Land." The critique of governmentality of the belly in these testimonies directly links the questions of the abuse of power and of obscenely excessive "eating" with the problem of both historical affliction and future redemption. In the account below, we see the question of historical rupture implied in making a complete break with the past in terms of a history of affliction in which the continent is held in the grip of an evil spirit, a sort of primordial racial curse, an account whose origins can be found in the missionary use of the biblical story of the curse of Ham.[103] However ambivalent such a portrayal may be, we must avoid interpreting it in the light of an account of the African subject as victim, in terms of which history is a form of "stuttering," the eternal return of subjection and dehumanization, and the impossibility of participating in a form of the universal.[104] This view of history and the self's possibilities is in opposition to the Born-Again vision, however ambiguous and contradictory it may ultimately prove to be.

Nimrod, he was a hunter . . . and there's a hunting spirit that has come all the way down from Nimrod. Now notice that Nimrod was a man who dealt a lot into sorcery, he was into all kinds of things. And most of the continent of Africa, you notice, are the people of the descendants of Ham, and the things that you find in the life of Nimrod, you find all over the continent. . . . The man was actually possessed of a leopard spirit, a hunting spirit . . . many African leaders seem to have something in common with the leopard. A lot of them love leopard skin, either as part of the decoration of their houses or as part of their regalia. If you look at their hats, certain of these leaders somehow derive powers from the spirit of the leopard. . . . Now, these hunting spirits affect the political life of this continent. You notice that hunters actually steal the life of the animals, and when you look at the way corruption goes on in this continent, you will see that it is a derivative of this hunting spirit. What does a man want to do when he steals 8 billion dollars, 10 billion dollars? Even if he lived five lives he will not be able to spend 10 billion dollars. He probably will be able to spend maybe 2 or 3 million, but when a man steals 13, 14 billion dollars, then he's richer than the nation itself which he's ruling, then you begin to understand that there is something in it. When you notice that virtually every civil servant wants to steal from you because he is in a position where he has to help you, and if he does not sign the paper, he does not pass the file on, then whatever you want cannot be done. Then you understand that something is at work. It's not necessarily poverty only, there's a spirit behind it.[105]

The preacher here articulates the disgust and despair Nigerians feel when faced with the excesses of elite predation and violence. This excess is not simply on the material level, but signals an excess of meaning—"something at work"—that is concealed and must be brought to light, and which constantly overflows any secular political discourse that purports to circumscribe or explain it.

The "sins of the Fathers"[106] are most often represented in terms of "traditional" religious practices—shrines, masquerades, covenants—but this *religious* otherness represents a danger to Pentecostalism as the only true religion. Religious Others, in particular Muslims, are typically demonized in Born-Again discourse; however, this demonization of the past is not about the contemporary threat that "traditional" religion poses in terms of religious competition, but rather involves witnessing to a history that failed to provide the moral grounding for a good society in the present. Here we find the theme of "making a complete break with the past" employed in its most political sense. Local relations of power as shaped and deployed in the complex strategic situation of postcolonial govenmentality are not presented in nostalgic terms; there is no sense of "impending loss" for the "erosion of established lifeways."[107] Rather, they appear as forms of subjectivity that must be broken with at all costs: "The spirit of sin from the ancestors can enter subsequent generations. Worshipping of traditional idols, masqurades [sic], family shrines and other family traditions can be passed down to other generation. Ancestral sinful practices of blood covenant with evil spirits may tie their children's children to that spirit. Generation can be affected with the curses and sin of their forefathers unless there is true and genuine repentance and turning to God for forgiveness."[108] The preacher recounting the story of Nimrod, quoted earlier, expands his account of the spiritual affliction affecting the nation. He begins by speaking about the various rites, such as naming ceremonies, puberty rites, and circumcision, going on to explain how such rites are specified by the "spirits of the land," with the purpose of bringing people under control. These "territorial spirits" affect the minds of the people living in the land:

There are certain people who are prone to violence, there are certain that love money a lot; if you want to check up if a man is dead, you could just chuck money round his ears and if he doesn't wake up, then he's dead. And there are certain people, they are never straightforward, you could never rely on them, if you relied on them, you would break and pierce your heart. And then there are some others who manipulate everything. . . . There are others that are violent, if there is an argument, it ends with blows. Then there are those that, by this hour, they are drunk. There are certain parts of this country that if you went now, the men would be gathered in places just lounging around and drinking, the women would be in the farms. The women would come back and pound the yams and the men would have the audacity to eat. It affects people, this is the way territorial spirits operate. . . . Now you look at certain parts of the country, people have a disposition to lie, and I mean they lie by the second. Now if you had them on a church committee, whenever there's going to be a scandal, notice they will be at the end of it. They will trade gossips between these ones and the other ones, they are the people who know who and who, what is doing what. Now you know, there are certain types of deliverances that may not, I'm using the word may, that may not come through, unless you deal with the thing that is on the land, the particular powers that hold the people.[109]

What the convert must be delivered from is the history that makes these practices commonplace. Here we find expressed the idea that all moral orders have their spiritual counterparts, that there is no real distinction to be made between the natural and supernatural. Clearly, if things have come to such a pass, it is because the wrong sort of spiritual-moral order has held sway. In their engagement with local forms of knowledge and practice, Born-Again narratives develop an on-going critical debate about government, one that indicts the immorality and violence at the heart of power's exercise. It is, in part at least, through this "intellectual response to social process, [this] contest of moral knowledge"[110] that we may understand the political import of the movement.

However, the political implications of this engagement go beyond the simple indictment of exploitation, injustice, and violence. The apprehension of these realities constitutes an *ordeal,* an experience of the intolerable that cannot just remain a bare and senseless fact, but demands a move from the plane of immanence to that of transcendence. It signals in many respects an experience of the limit, as do so many experiences in the postcolony today, which marks the realm of what the political domain is or has become, and what political rationality is capable of expressing or bringing into being. It demands another way of living together, another mode of governing the self and others, signaling that in its current forms, those practiced and those proposed or imposed from outside, the political realm takes on a dimension it nonetheless cannot integrate, which perpetually overflows it. This is "the dimension of an ontology or an ethology [*ethologie*] of being-together [*l'être-ensemble*] articulated upon the absolute excess of meaning and the passion for meaning of which, after all, the word 'sacred" was only ever the designation."[111]

I have proposed the idea that the religious imaginary, beyond its specific manifestations, is not just another form of social imaginary, but performs an original function through the ways in which it stages and gives meaning to human existence. This function cannot be reduced to a mechanism or part of an assumed whole, as in a functionalist reading, but should be understood in the sense that the religious imaginary not only consolidates the ordering of the world, but also brings into being new worlds: it is, in the words of Castoriadis, a form of instituting imaginary.[112] Born-Again Christianity is a force not merely as a result of successful competition within the religious field, by providing spiritual and material benefits others did not. Its radical success in conversion has as much to do with its reconceptualization of the moral and political order, representing a vision of citizenship in which the moral government of the self is linked to the power to influence the conduct of others. Through its project of rupture and renewal, it sets itself the political mission of healing the land, quoting Isaiah 58:12: "And they that shall be with thee shall build the old waste places; thou shalt raise up the foundations of many generations, and thou shalt be called the repairer of the breach." Kehinde Osinowo, when asked why he had started his organization Christians for the Regeneration of the Nation, explained that "without spiritual change, no program will have its effect. The sin of the nation is based on the sin of the individual . . . we shall restore Nigeria to moral probity, godliness and prosperity."[113] The individualism expressed in this vision is clearly not that of the modern secular subject, but nonetheless involves a strong rearticulation of missionary messages in which individual conduct and conscience was the cornerstone of sociopolitical redemption. At the same time, repairing the breach involves not only convicting or overcoming the past, but also building up the old waste places and thus redeeming them. This reconstruction is couched in terms of spirituality, but also implies material changes and projects, through the creation of what are self-consciously represented as modern functional spaces and institutions, forms of worship and self-presentation, forms of sociability and family structures. It involves the creation of new networks and the provision of effective forms of social security and services, as well as new attitudes to wealth, labor, and debt that find their expression in the creation of new entrepreneurial structures and modes of accumulation. The projection of these material changes into the public sphere through various forms of mass mediation provides a challenge to the postcolonial state, not only indicting its failure to bring "development," but proposing an alternate mode for achieving it.

The complete break with the past through conversion not only entails the redemption of the past, but also announces, as the Born-Agains say, the "new creation"[114] and a new era, the coming of the Kingdom. What does the idea of living in the "end times" mean in the Nigerian Born-Again context? The double sense of living in a period of tribulation and the ecstatic possibilities of the rapture give an added force to the critical engagement with the dangers of the present moment and the urgency of change. When I arrived at Lagos airport from London on 29 October 1992, the first question I was asked by the friend meeting me, a young lawyer at a big commercial bank, was "Did you think the world was going to end yesterday?" I was totally perplexed, but soon learned that the leader of a Korean church, Mission for the Coming Days, had announced, with much global publicity, the second coming of Christ and the rapture of the true believers to take place on 28 October.[115] Nigerian newspapers reported that thousands of people had failed to come to work, preferring to stay at home in preparation, many having bade farewell to friends and family members, colleagues and neighbors, in the days before. Over the next few days, as I moved about the city meeting friends and reacquainting myself with the chaos of Lagos, everybody seemed to be discussing the prophecy. Stories abounded, and it was the occasion for impassioned comments and reflections—the necessity of conversion, the power of the Holy Spirit, the nature of sin, the works of the devil, the place of prophecy, the dangers of false prophets—as well as what seemed a renewed zeal on the part of many to reexamine their own lives as Christians in the light of this close brush with eternity. In the Pentecostal church I attended that Sunday, the pastor put the failed prophecy to good use, preaching on "Are you ready for the rapture?" Over the next few weeks I discovered that there had been a sudden increase in Born-Again conversions in the weeks before the fateful date. The "dispensationalist"[116] reading of history, preaching the urgency of living in the end-times and preparing oneself spiritually and ethically for the imminent rapture, is a central theme in global Pentecostalism,[117] one that most Nigerian churches and missions also, at least formally, subscribe to. The degree to which Nigerian Born-Agains take this possibility to heart varies considerably across the doctrinal spectrum; nonetheless, the messianic figure is present in both the otherworldly and this-worldly emphases of the Born-Again program. It stages both the dangers and promises of the present in an idiom that presents change not only as urgent, but also as immanent in the present moment. It makes for an experience of the present whose qualities have been altered by the presence of the Holy Spirit and the possibility of miracles, in which the present becomes not only the *only time we have* to realize the potentialities that may be released by faith, but also a time in which the messianic presence is already there, in which these potentialities and the future they announce may be accomplished at any moment. As Pentecostals say of this struggle, "be of good cheer, we are on the winning side."

The reworking of the various social relationships in the first decades of revival through the adaptation of global Pentecostal doctrine to the ordeal of everyday life was made both powerful and plausible, not so much because of the actual results obtained with respect to the promises of the alleviation of suffering and protection from the vicissitudes of urban life, although many significant material and symbolic advantages could be gained from conversion. Rather, one of the central reasons for its plausibility was the way it renegotiated the relationship between global and local, universal and particular, in the context of the boom-and-bust years. Taking up the central ordering of differences inherited from the colonial period, this religious imagination reworked the self's relation to the various modes of subjectivation that had emerged from this order and had become increasingly problematic, through a rewriting of many of the codes and forms of knowledge by which power was exercised over individuals and groups. The pertinence of this reworking lay in how it opened up the possibility, not simply of understanding the world, creating moral order out of confusion, making sense of confusing new forms of wealth and power, but also for acting differently within it. However, such a project did not by any means undo this ordering, in terms of which power was underwritten by forms of global knowledge, mediated through a complex series of local relationships. Rather, as a transnational religious form, it renewed the promise of an earlier evangelical tradition, harnessing new global linkages and flows, and reworking old categories, giving rise to an interstitial space, captured by the idiom of the "end times." It breaks with many dominant accounts of African subjecthood, deploying a form of instituting imaginary in terms of which the subject's liberation from affliction becomes thinkable. However, the staging of this possibility in a programmatic and strategic fashion in such a way as to render it both plausible and pertinent, emphasizing the revolutionary potential of the Born-Again message and program, does not, as we shall see, guarantee the forms it will take.

FOUR

God's Subjects

The success of the Born-Again revival is not merely related to how it provided opportunities for agents to reinterpret their experiences and act differently in the world. Rather, its expansion and growth are also the result of a series of techniques employed both in the propagation of this religious form and in the process of subjectivation proper to the Born-Again program of governing the self and others. Global Pentecostalism, like evangelical mission before it, is a form of "strategic program" (*programmation stratégique*)[1]—a specific regime of practices that involves determined prescriptions concerning how institutions should be organized, behavior regulated, narrative structured, an order of knowledge and the rules of its verification determined, authority established, spaces laid out, and so forth. As we shall see, becoming born-again is considerably more complex than a simple decision by free agents or the disciplining of God's subjects through pastoral power. The project of "making a complete break with the past" through conversion may only be strategic and programmatic. Even though in "real life" nothing ever happens as in the program, nonetheless, we should not conclude that such a program is mere utopia, some sort of "ideal type" or mere ideology. As Foucault argues, that would be to have a pretty thin notion of "the real." The elaboration of such a program both responds to a series of practices or diverse strategies and leads to a whole series of effects in the real: its programs are crystallized in institutions, they inform individuals' conduct, they serve as a grid for the perception and appreciation of things.[2]

The success of the Born-Again project of conversion is related to the ways in which conversion as a process involves a mode of subjectivation, in which the individual is both subjected to this regime and becomes the active subject of the new practices and modes of interpreting the world they involve. I will examine the ways in which this particular regime of practices works upon individuals such that not only do they announce a particular "truth" about the world, but also they recognize themselves in it, becoming not only the agent, but the subject of these new modes of seeing and doing. I will look at the ways in which the process of the work of the self on the self, through a variety of techniques of the self proposed or imposed through the Born-Again conversion process, has as its effect a new sort of self-knowledge. That new self-knowledge has as its object protection, self-mastery, and spiritual empowerment, and it is explicitly linked to the creation of a certain style of life. One of the central themes elaborated in the Born-Again prescriptive regime is the problem of desire and its objects. Indeed, desire in general is what prompts the moral questioning of the self. In the encounter of the individual's own desire and that of another, the person must ask him- or herself the question of how to act and what to do. It is in the space of this relationship between the subject, the subject's own desire, and that of others—in the individual's relationship to the various rules and codes that are proposed or imposed as modes of directing conduct—that an ethic emerges. Born-Again practices of the self involve acts and experiences of faith whose focus is on interiority, enacting in various forms processes of self-examination and "giving an account of oneself."[3] These accounts focus primarily on the self's own trajectory along the road to salvation and self-recognition, and thus constitute one of the principal techniques of subjectivation and modes in which obedience is created.

Agency, Power, and Moral Subjectivation

To understand precisely what we mean by processes of subjectivation, we need to make a clear distinction between the notion of the agent and that of the subject. Too often these two terms are merged and agency treated as if it had a clear and universal meaning, when in fact both notions are objectifications that are highly culturally specific and historically fashioned. In the Western tradition, deriving from Kant and Enlightenment thought, bolstered by the Protestant doctrine of individual responsibility, agency is typically understood as the principle of effectivity, which implies an acting subject understood as the seat of consciousness. In this conception, the subject appears as a universal, transcendent form that depends upon a metaphysical understanding of consciousness. Agency is assimilated to the struggle for self-constitution, expressing the relationship between consciousness, free will and reason. Foucault's concern with the subject is precisely to bring to light the historical particularity of the mode of subjectivation that characterizes Western modernity, in terms of which the subject is compelled to tell the truth about him- or herself and establish a particular relationship with the self. It is also the account of a particular mode of problematizing the world, in which Kant asks the historically novel question: "What is this world, this precise moment in which we are living, and who should we become?" thus bringing to light a particular epistemic structure.[4]

Yet even if we put aside the Kantian concept of the transcendental subject, or its Hegelian version as consciousness, in its most quotidian and psychological sense as awareness, intent, the giving of meaning to experiences, consciousness is inadequate to account for agency. One does not have to be a full-blown Freudian to see that instinctive reaction, the body and the unconscious, work, in their different ways, more pervasively and continuously than consciousness does. In his seminal article on techniques of the body, Marcel Mauss writes: "I think there are necessarily biological means of entering into 'communion with God.'"[5] His discussion not only resituates ritual with respect to a tradition that sees it primarily in terms of symbolic action to be interpreted, but also implies that particular mental states may be a function of taught or untaught bodies. The specific role played by desire, instinct, and the body is historically and culturally determined: an agent can only act within a field of possible actions, where the possible is always determined by the historical constitution of the thinkable and doable. Within a given historical field, the agent's action is always caught up in relationships that both precede the self-conscious subject and go beyond it, because action is always action in relation to others. The relations that have gone before the subject determine its very constitution, desires, bodily capacities, ways of seeing and doing. At the same time, intentionality or consciousness in no way circumscribes either the meaning or the effects actions may have once they leave the realm of individual intention. These precisions show that consciousness is a dependent concept, a historical objectification, not a transcendental reality. Within the contemporary Western epistemological field, the instability of the relationship between consciousness and agency is also revealed in the ways in which we ascribe agency to instances that cannot be seen as having a consciousness (groups, legal entities, companies, and so forth).[6] Such a view also shows that we do not have to rely upon an idea of consciousness to identify the site of power's operation. Subjectivity, as noted earlier, is not a form of knowledge, a power, an essence, or a function, but rather a relationship—between the self and the world, between the self and the self—whose content is historical, "rare," and fragile. Subjectivation implies that the individual is always worked upon by a historically specific series of relations of power and knowledge that determine the possible field of his or her actions, prompting or imposing certain conducts and the recognition of a certain truth about the self and about the world. At the same time, this process implies the active engagement of the subject, such that the subject recognizes him- or herself as not only the agent, but also the moral subject of his or her own action.

Rather than adherence to a particular group or institution, the Born-Again evangelical program has as its principal object the transformation and control of individual conduct and the creation of a particular type of moral subject: it is a form of "prescriptive apparatus."[7] A study of processes of moral subjectivation involved in the process of becoming Born-Again entails an examination of how the Born-Again program expresses an ethic,[8] as well as the values and rules it proposes, their level of internal coherence and explicitness, and the means employed to impose them. At the same time, an ethic also includes the study of moralities, "the real behaviour of individuals in their relation to the rules and values which are proposed," and "how, and with what margin of variation and transgression individuals or groups conduct themselves with reference to this code."[9] But in studying an ethic, we also need to take into account an additional aspect, which finds its expression through the application of techniques of the self, and which concerns the manner in which the self must conduct itself, recognize itself in a code of action, and constitute itself, in a self-reflexive relationship that is more than simply self-consciousness: "not only as an agent, but as the *moral subject* of this action."[10]

Conversion, becoming Born-Again, is not simply a free act of will, a sign of agency, even if "deciding for Jesus" is presented in terms that appear to emphasize individual intentionality and will as well as personal empowerment. Becoming Born-Again is an event of rupture, but *being* Born-Again is an ongoing existential project, not a state acquired once and for all, a process that is never fully achieved and always runs of the risk of being compromised. The centrality of the notion of "backsliding" and the perpetual possibility of "losing one's salvation," as well as the pedagogical and prescriptive structure of preaching and teaching, stress the notion of growth and development of the Born-Again subject. It is a process that must be learned, in which the intellectual apprehension of moral doctrines is combined with gradual acquisition and enactment of a series of bodily techniques (fasting, speaking in tongues), narrative forms (testimony, prayer, song), and aesthetics (dress, comportment). Through this process the convert gradually learns, with heart, soul, and body, how to experience the truth of revelation and the power of the Holy Spirit. In this process, the subject is fashioned toward a certain religious experience, caught up in the webs of the lines of juridiction, veridiction, and subjectivation that this regime elaborates through its agonistic relations with neighboring practices, in particular those of Nigeria.

In the elaboration of this new personal ethic, we can also observe significant differences between the early phase of the revival, with its accent on a retreat from the world, the imminent return of Christ, and the promise of salvation in the next, and the later wave, following which salvation becomes increasingly centered on this-worldly achievement and success. If the moral codes and values are fairly standardized across doctrinal differences, important distinctions need to be made in terms of how the individual finds him- or herself subjected to these codes: the extent to which various forms of coercion or sanction are deployed, but particularly the modes of subjectivation. Asad argues that it is not mere symbols that impart true Christian disposition, but power: "Long before Foucault, Augustine knew that power could be both productive and repressive, power—*potens*[11]—is at once torment and ability."[12] For Augustine, it is the effects of power that impart Christian disposition: "power, the effect of an entire network of motivated practices, assumes a religious form because of the end to which it is directed, for human events are the instruments of God. It was not the mind that moved spontaneously to religious truth, but power that created the conditions for experiencing that truth."[13]

Pastoral Power, Institutional Authority, and the Born-Again Community

While the rules and values the believer's conduct is supposed to express are laid out through endless preaching and exhortation, and while they are explicit, they are nonetheless relatively simple and not the fruit of a complex theological elaboration. Their truth does not impose itself through formal codification, systems of sanctions, strong institutional forms, or a powerful or hierarchical ecclesiastic authority with secular powers over the population. Even within the most strongly institutionalized organizations, the denominational holiness churches such as Deeper Life or the Redeemed Christian Church of God (RCCG), the extension of the organization occurred on a fairly informal basis. There are no standardized or institutionalized processes of accreditation of religious authority, even if within certain churches or ministries, such as Deeper Life, RCCG, or Idahosa's Church of God Mission, internal training and accreditation is dispensed and closely controlled. There are no standardized or restrictive modes for acquiring scriptural knowledge or spiritual power. Of fifty pastors canvassed in 1993, only three actually had diplomas from a Bible college. The great majority had followed part-time "training" sessions in a church or ministry for periods from one week to six months. Invariably, pastors described their "call" as arising from a personal revelation through personal communication (dream, vision, voice) with God, sometimes seconded by support from within their church or ministry, but sometimes as a mark of opposition to it. Even in some of the older, more bureaucratic Pentecostal churches, leadership is determined not according to standardized practices of promotion or collegial decision but rather by the direction of the Holy Spirit. This is the case with the Gospel Pentecostal Assembly, founded in 1959: "if there occurs a need to fill a vacant position in the church it would be on the Holy Ghost's direction after seeking the face of the Lord and not on the basis of hierarchy."[14] This tendency has been increasing marked over the 1990s: individuals with minimal training decide to start a church or ministry on the strength of a mere call, and institutions are increasingly schismatic.

There is a large degree of independence among leaders, but they have a high degree of dependence, in terms of both their authority and their financial success, on their followers. This is demonstrated by the marked tendency of believers to move from one church or organization to another. With the exception of denominational holiness churches, such as Deeper Life and RCCG in its early years, pastors have little real control over their congregations. Even Deeper Life abandoned its cell system in the 1980s; in the cell system, each member was affected to a particular group, surveyed by a supervisor who was responsible for observing members' conduct and who reported to a superior authority in a pyramid structure leading to the head pastor. Nonetheless, individual churches and pastors do attempt to impose institutional fidelity and their own interpretation of the message. When you arrive in a Born-Again church for the first time, irrespective of its doctrinal emphasis or the social class of members, either an usher will take you up to the front row of seats reserved for newcomers, or following the praise and worship sessions that open every Born-Again service, a call will be made from the pulpit for newcomers to come forward and be seated in front. Following the service, newcomers will generally be invited to share a soft drink and give their personal information, or at least, counselors or "helpers" will come and ask for their names, addresses, and contacts. In some organizations, information cards have been prepared in advance; in others the procedure is more informal. It is not uncommon to be visited by one or several members of the church after this first time, either helpers, or evangelists, or even assistant pastors at times, depending on the size of the church and also the perception of the importance of the potential convert.[15] For those who have decided to take the altar call during the service, which generally comes after the sermon and sessions of speaking in tongues, they are either led away by counselors or ushers before the end of the service to a separate room, or they are met afterward and arrangements are made for members or the pastor or assistant pastor to visit them and begin to prepare them for the long process of becoming Born-Again.

In the beginning, when you join Glory Tabernacle, you have to go through some teachings for newly Born-Again, to help them grow spiritually, and to know the doctrines of the church. Like house fellowships, where we use handouts on Christian growth, also Bible study, fellowship at home. It's compulsory to go through the teaching before joining any of the teams; ushers, women's groups, men's groups, choir, visitation [where new members are contacted and followed], counselling— when you have a problem you go to them and they will pray, advise you using certain Bible passages; documentation and publications. You can join at the most two teams. Of course we also have children's groups, Sunday school.[16]

And yet, despite these efforts, the interdenominational and charismatic form of the early revival and its persistence as an underlying imaginary has continued, leading to a great variety of institutional forms, very few of which seem to follow the bureaucratic model of the denominational mission churches. Over the past fifteen years, church planting has become the fruit of internal schism within individual organizations, and conflicts among institutions are commonplace. The authority and fortunes of pastors rise and fall. They are subject to close and critical scrutiny on the part of converts. Particularly in prosperity churches, pastors whose lifestyles appear too far removed from the norms of Born-Again conduct may suddenly find their churches deserted. With the rise of the new wave, "legalism" of all sorts became the subject of attack, and attempts to impose ecclesiastical authority within the movement are often resisted. The difficulty of attaining institutional authority was expressed by a leader of a campus fellowship: "All work is both mandatory and voluntary. Mandatory as we counsel all members to be in an activity group and on the other, it is voluntary, because we cannot force them."[17] The egalitarian access to spiritual power and knowledge that is at the cornerstone of the message means that those who attempt to impose their authority by monopolizing spiritual or scriptural authority may find believers leaving for other establishments, as this pastor's remarks illustrate:

I found out that there were so many so-called preachers who were indoctrinating people with things they considered biblical, but they were not. Because of their lack of knowledge. So I spoke against those things. So I wasn't so popular amongst such people. Like house fellowships. I was the first to speak against it. I explained to them that it is not that there is anything wrong with the house, but they must be supervised. There must be a kind of authority structure. That God will hold them responsible if there is false doctrine being held in such a meeting. Not that any group of young people will just start up a thing and call it a fellowship. They start teaching things they did not understand. So I had to go back to the Scriptures and bring examples. . . . Nobody had done that here before. Everybody just mind his business. If that guy don't know what he is saying, well, that's his problem. So a lot of people left after that.[18]

An over-arching imaginary of the community of the "saved" has nonetheless persisted at a certain level, despite increasing competition, divergent attitudes to salvation and correct practice, and internal strife. This is in part related to the sense in which the Born-Again imaginary is transnational and "delocalized" from the outset. Two related tendencies already present in these egalitarian and interdenominational groups of the early years became accentuated with the arrival of the new wave throughout the 1980s and intensified throughout the decade of the 1990s: first, a process of delocalization of the diffusion of the Born-Again moral code and message; and second, a gradual desystematization of the rules and values originally imposed, giving rise to juxtapositions, contradictions, and, increasingly, occasions for escaping the strictures of the code. This last issue is above all related to changes in the processes of moral subjectivation that occur with the this-worldly orientation of the new wave, but is also connected to the development and intensification of the principal technique of diffusion, that of the proliferation and circulation of narratives.

Part of the power of both missionary and Pentecostal Christianity is that new Christian subjects are realized through narrative, understood as discursive practice. At a collective level, as Mbembe argues, the production of new discourse is a sign of the religious imagination at work, the mode through which "new geographies of the divine" are put in place: "In the post-colony, the creation of a new geography of the divine is carried out through the proliferation of stories [*récits*]. Stories of the postcolonial event, narrative propositions which themselves seek to become institutionalised and transform themselves into traditions. But what do these propositions interpret, if not an idea of the human person and his limits, an image of time and the beyond of time [*l'au-delà de la durée*], of power and its ends, of order, of death and its opposite (eternity)."[19] The Pentecostal evangelical program for conversion has at its heart a narrative imperative. Whether in the form of interpretations of the sacred text, discourses such as sermons, prophecies, testimonies, prayers, or songs, its propagation and mode of self-invention proceed through the proliferation and multiplication of stories. Peel argues that narrative is a preeminently political discourse, in that it offers the possibility for the subject to achieve a sense of agency: "Narrative empowers because it enables its possessor to integrate his memories, experiences, and aspirations in a schema of long-term action."[20] But the question is more complex than the simple expression of historical agency and the new possibilities offered to the individual for developing a schema of action, even if the role of individual imagination and the manifestation of a "political spirituality" is also at the heart of the movement's success. Discursive practices of representation and self-representation are central to processes of subjectivation, and control over discursive production and practice, the rules of its ordering and structure, is a fundamental issue of government as "conducting conduct," as well as of the creation of obedience to the Born-Again prescriptive regime.

The Born-Again movement in Nigeria involves a perpetual process of mediation between a global religious form and universal sacred text, on the one hand, and, on the other, the forms of its appropriation in local practices and discourses. Beyond its specific local institutional manifestations, doctrinal emphases, and the particular content of narrative, the project of Born-Again conversion and evangelism corresponds to a series of broad doctrinal principles, general styles of worship, models of pastoral and institutional power, narrative forms and techniques of proliferation, all of which have become remarkably uniform the world over, despite the marked absence of any overarching institutional authority or confessional unity. The mediatization of the message is a central technique of Pentecostalism everywhere, which lies at the heart of its transnational character and its evangelical expansionist project, and has played a vital role in the movement's success in Nigeria.[21]

The central form of the circulation of narratives remains individual word of mouth. Nonetheless, since the early 1990s, nearly all ministries or missions in Nigeria have become producers of some form of print and/or audio and video production. More and more services, rallies, revivals, and assemblies are videotaped as well as audiotaped. The tapes are sold to members, distributed to various shops, circulated to inter-denominational groups, or simply passed from hand to hand. Born-Again weeklies or monthlies appear and circulate for a period, sometimes breaking off production, or being replaced by new editions. A huge quantity of Nigerian as well as foreign booklets and tracts can be found in the numerous private Christian bookshops; such publications are also sold by itinerant sellers at large assemblies and stocked in church or ministry bookshops. Videos of local revivals, rallies, and plays, as well as many Born-Again films or religious broadcasts from the United States and other countries, can be rented from a growing number of Born-Again video rental outfits. Those individuals wealthy enough to have satellite television can watch and record foreign evangelical programs, but even a television with a regular aerial will enable Born-Again viewers to tune into a variety of local televangelists, especially on beleaguered state networks.

While religious doctrine and ritual proper (Bible study, sermons or pastoral teaching, prayer guides, testimonies of miracles, deliverance from evil spirits, and healing) make up a significant part of these media discourses and images, they are by no means the entirety of what is available. A dizzying quantity of discourses on subjects including history, politics, development, economics, family life, sexual behavior, professional conduct, dress codes, culture, and lifestyles can be found in the form of books,[22] tracts, articles, lectures, discussion groups, sermons, taped or televised messages, testimonies, music, public rallies, plays in theaters or video movies, radio broadcasts, public preaching, and street evangelism. Born-Again organizations expend enormous resources on the dissemination of messages in forms that excite and inspire, bringing technologies of modern media to bear on the issues and idioms central to popular urban culture. In the West, in particular the United States, televangelism and the intense mediatization of the

Pentecostal message seem somehow in keeping with the totalizing grip of the media on popular culture. But mediatization has particular significance in cultures where the media still represent "islands of modernity" in a sea of local "artisanal' culture.[23]

The use of the media allows for the multiplication of narrative forms, and the delocalization of messages. Sermons preached to local congregations are videotaped or audiotaped, and then circulated not only among members of the given church or ministry, but among Born-Agains and their unconverted friends, relatives and neighbors; the tapes may also be taken by missionaries to different parts of the country and even the world. Taped sermons are often transcribed and published in a variety of magazines, tracts, and leaflets with an equally wide circulation. The organizational structures of many ministries developed over the 1990s with local parishes or branches, as well as associated groups, such as youth, women's, or professional associations. Such associated groups, which are often interdenominational in membership, also ensure the circulation of discourses dissociated from a specific social place or institutional locus. The growth of religious complexes, such as ministry headquarters or prayer camps, in what was previously socially empty space—bush land, reclaimed swamp, industrial urban areas, or spaces unclaimed or "colonized" by a determinate social group, such as cinemas, national stadiums, and sports grounds—reinforces the delocalization of identity and community.

The media are not simply a tool for the dissemination of representations and messages; over the 1990s, they became increasingly central to the imagined form of the community and tended to reinforce the processes of delocalization associated with their transnational form and the diffuse nature of the propagation of messages. At the same time, the media allow for the development of an internal debate among members, involving the evolution of a Born-Again "public opinion," but also the continual staging of the variety of antagonistic relations that traverse the community and mark its relations with the rest of society. Rather than dramatic cleavages, we see the development of mobile and transitory points of resistance, changing distinctions and regroupings among various tendencies, remodeling and redetermining them. Born-Again "communities of sentiment" are formed through Bible study and through reading, watching, and discussing sermons, tracts, magazines, and videos—interchanges that entail articulations and discussion not only of models of "correct" behavior and new regimes of personal and collective discipline, but also of new attitudes toward consumption, dress styles, aesthetics, and ways of speaking and moving. In the prosperity or new wave churches, these articulations are made with reference, often self-conscious, to a global Pentecostal community and its perceived modes of worship, models of behavior, styles, and culture.

I remember attending a birthday party thrown by a group of Born-Again friends in a small Lagos flat in the early 1990s. Someone had brought an amplifier and speaker, although the space was easily small enough for those preaching to be heard without them. A young woman led the praise and worship, speaking with an odd American accent. My friend with whom I had come started to giggle, and when I asked him what was funny, he told me that the nearest the girl had been to the United States was Ikeja (where the airport is). My friend was forced to retire outside so as not to disturb the praying group when the girl started to preach in Yoruba with an American accent. Rather than being evidence for the "Americanization" of local culture, this anecdote points to the way in which these new forms of social behavior also express categories of prestige and models for social interaction that draw their power—not simply among members, but in the eyes of broader Nigerian society as well—from global images of wealth and success. Part of the Born-Again movement's success in Nigeria is related to the community's ability not only to give regular people access to these global repertoires, but also to use this in its self-representations to an outside that has not yet been saved—an outside that constitutes a potential threat, but also a challenge. Increasingly intense competition in the religious field means that "resources of externality" are more and more essential for success. While they constitute expressions of lifestyles that are connected to the categories of prestige at large in urban culture, they still have their own internal logic, and may be seen not merely as identifiers with regard to an outside that should be saved, but also as forms of distinction within the Born-Again community. A friend of mine explained to me how to tell the difference between "Wordites" and "spiris" on campus in terms of their dress codes: "Wordites" emphasized studying Scripture, or the "Word", while 'spiris" placed the accent rather on the emotive experiences of faith, such as prayer or the infilling of the Holy Spirit. New modes of self-expression are constantly being devised as part of an ongoing process of revision and remodeling of the self via various bodily techniques, ways of moving, dressing, and speaking, which themselves express a process of constant mediation between global and local forms.

The mediatization of the message has an effect on the nature of institutional structures themselves. The case of Bethel Church in Lagos provides a striking example of how the media penetrate even the intimate space of the congregation. It also demonstrates how new places are built from spaces without creating localized social formations, underscoring the diffuse and unsystematic nature of the Born-Again identity and the ways in which it re-creates forms of sociability based less on neighborliness and sociocultural affinities than on a shared imaginary without a proper sense of place. Bethel Church, one of the more successful prosperity churches in Lagos, is an impressive complex developed in the late 1980s on recovered swampland along the Leki Peninsula, about ten miles from Victoria Island (where the rich and powerful live) and at least half an hour by car (on a Sunday) from the Lagos mainland. In 1990, proudly presenting itself as the only air-conditioned Born-Again church in Lagos, it boasted a large and beautifully decorated central church surrounded by well-appointed offices worthy of any of the offshore banks that could be found in neighboring Victoria Island. The church had a fleet of new buses, which it sent out early on Sunday mornings to various parts of Lagos to bring the faithful to worship. The services were extremely high-tech, even by prosperity church standards, featuring closed-circuit televisions dotted throughout the congregation, which numbered about three or four hundred people. What I remarked immediately upon entering was the incongruity of these televisions in a space that, while large, still appeared relatively intimate in comparison with the many other new "converted warehouse" churches that hold congregations of several thousand. One could see the pastor on the raised stage from all points within the church; clearly the televisions were not there to ensure everyone could see as well as hear the message. But people watched them. The congregation was socially mixed, consisting of people from all areas of Lagos, different social classes, different ethnic groups. Many were young and fairly middle-class, but there were also middle-aged businessmen who arrived in Mercedes, their beautifully groomed wives on their arms. I spoke with a couple of older market women in traditional attire, and shared a pew with a young man in a worn suit who told me he was a vulcanizer. In this example of the mediation of the message, the performance staged by the preacher on his closed-circuit televisions takes to an extreme the tendency for the church to become less the site for the formation of "local' communities, and more and more a stage for a performance whose audience is elsewhere. One could almost say that at Bethel, the physical audience was already only virtually present.

If we compare these organizations with other older, more established churches, among mainstream or orthodox denominations, the Aladura churches, and even earlier holiness churches, we find striking differences in how congregations are set up as communities, and how they identify themselves as co-religionists. As André Corten argues with reference to Pentecostalism in Latin America, "through the media, transversal relations [among churches] are formed. The community of the church still exists as a reference, but is transformed from a place of praise and cohesion to a 'show place' [lieu de spectacle] where deliverance and divine healing are staged. In this staging of a 'show,' there is a change of imaginary [imaginaire]."[24] This change of imaginary involves the ways in which Pentecostalism inserts itself into a situation of urban crisis, where "local' identities and social relationships in the sense of "neighborhoods" are harder and harder to maintain and reproduce.[25] As discussed earlier, this is in part due to the ways in which identities are imposed and manipulated by the Nigerian state. It is also related to economic crisis and the strains placed on local networks and social relationships' increased rural-urban migration; and, perhaps most important, the ways in which the global images, ideas, commodity forms, and technologies have been absorbed by local culture. But this form of community is also due to the nature of subjectivation and the experience of faith itself. The expansion and increasingly heterogeneous nature of the Born-Again movement gives rise, through processes of mediatization and the constant negotiation between global and local forms, to a Born-Again moral community with no definite "sense of place."[26] However, this imaginary of belonging is not only the result of these local factors, it is proper to Pentecostalism everywhere. At the same time, while the experience of conversion is represented as a conscious "choice," the Born-Again movement does not give rise to a decisive identity within the Christian community per se. Indeed, Born-Agains refer to themselves most often simply as "Christians"—of course, with the tacit or even explicit understanding that they are the only true holders of the faith. More than the development of a religious identity, the Born-Again program of individual and collective redemption, through the process of conversion and transformation, attempts to reconstitute the experience of the world.

Acts of Faith: Moral Subjectivation and Techniques of the Self

Conversion participates in the constitution of worlds: that which arrives for the first time. But the act of conversion also participates in the deconstruction of worlds. To convert the other is to incite him to abandon that which he believed before. . . . Theoretically, the passage from one belief to another should lead to the submission of the convert to the institution and the authority in charge of proclaiming the new belief. In reality, every conversion has always been, at least tacitly, a sorting operation. In this sense, it has always necessitated on the part of the convert the active exercise of his judgement.[27]

The ways in which pastoral authority is instituted and legitimated, the interdenominational and delocalized imaginary of belonging, the increasingly diffuse and unsystematic nature of the messages, the dispersion of the sites of its articulation all pose the question of the authority and institution in charge of proclaiming the new belief and ensuring submission to it. Unlike many other Christian traditions or institutions, the Born-Again program is a prescriptive apparatus that expresses an ethic whose central and dynamic element lies in its forms of subjectivation and techniques of the self. Of course, one cannot really separate the codes and values from the forms of subjectivation, nor is subjectivation removed from relations of power and knowledge. Nonetheless, the Born-Again ethic does not rely on a model whose importance lies in a code—the code's systematicity, its richness, its ability to adjust itself to every possible case and cover all domains of behavior. In such an ethic, the "essential aspect is found in the instances of authority which prescribe this code, impose the learning and respect of it and who sanction the infractions. In these conditions, subjectivation occurs for the most part in a quasi-juridical form, where the moral subject refers himself to a law or a series of laws to which he must submit or expose himself to punishment."[28] Rather, despite a certain degree of juxtaposition and composition among different Christian traditions, in which a tradition more oriented toward the code does find its expression—as attempts to impose pastoral authority and techniques of pastoral control demonstrate—for the most part the Born-Again program expresses an ethic where the accent is placed on the forms of the relationship that the self elaborates with the self.[29] As we shall see, despite doctrinal prescriptions, forms of discursive ordering and public sanction that constrain and compel, subjectivation occurs principally through acts of faith that depend very largely on experiences of interiority and the techniques of the self.

The Born-Again program of conversion and salvation stages personal empowerment through an ethics of submission. The entire Born-Again program is centered on the question of rupture and change, perpetual overcoming; it employs a language of will, intentionality, self-help, self-mastery and personal empowerment. And yet, the individual is acknowledged as being fundamentally powerless, at God's mercy, dependent entirely upon His grace: "we must crucify self and allow the Spirit of God to possess and control us."[30] This form of submission does not involve submission to the laws of an authority, whether secular, ecclesiastical, or even that of God (in his wrathful, law-giving, Old Testament sense), nor does orthodoxy, underwritten by ecclesiastical or institutional power, prescribe or impose the exact terms of this submission. The notion of the "crucifixion of self," a total openness and submission to the power of the Holy Spirit, the imperative nature of the "call," all these themes are expressed endlessly by preachers and converts in describing what it means to take Jesus Christ as one's personal savior. The submission figured here reflects, quite imperfectly to be sure, that outlined by the Pauline "messianic life." Agamben's remarkable study of Paul[31] gives us the elements of what is entailed in the "messianic life." His first observation is that the messianic vocation, or call, stages the Christian paradigm of strength through "weakness," in which those things which are weak and insignificant will prevail over those which the world considers to be strong and important (Matt. 19:29–30, Matt. 20:16, 1 Cor. 1:27–28).[32] Being called is also being "seized upon" and then "straining" to answer the call (Phil. 3:12–13) and depends upon the notion of grace—as when Christ spoke to Paul in a vision and said, "[M]y grace is sufficient unto thee: for my strength is made perfect in weakness" (2 Cor. 12:9–10).[33]

The second issue, which the expression the "slave of the Messiah" and "the call" as a vocation implies for Paul, is the neutralization of the various divisions of the law and social distinctions at the time he was writing (slave/citizen, Jew/non-Jew, man/woman). Weber distinguishes between a purely religious notion of the call to salvation, which he qualifies by its eschatological indifference to worldly activities, and the secular vocation as a profession.[34] However, Agamben argues that in Paul, these two are joined within the notion of the messianic call, which under messianic time involves the "revocation of every vocation,"[35] as in 1 Corinthians 7:17–24: "But as God hath distributed to every man, as the Lord hath called every one, so let him walk. And so ordain I in all communities [ekklēsías]. Is any man called being circumcised? Let him not remove the mark of circumcision. Is any called with a foreskin? Let him not be circumcised! Circumcision is nothing, the foreskin is nothing . . . Let every man abide in the same calling wherein he was called. Art thou called being a slave? Care not for it: but if thou mayest be free, *use it rather.* For he that is called in the Lord being a slave is the Lord's freeman: likewise also he that is called, being free, is slave of the Messiah." Or again, as in verses 29–32.[36] In his careful analysis of these texts, Agamben shows how "the messianic vocation is not a right, nor does it furnish an identity; rather, it is a generic potentiality that can be used without ever being owned. To be messianic, to live in the Messiah, signifies the expropriation of each and every juridical-factical property (circumcised-uncircumcised, slave-free, man-woman) . . . this expropriation does not, however, found a new identity; the 'new creature' is none other than the use and the messianic vocation of the old,"[37] as exemplified in the expression "use it rather."

We have seen the importance of this second aspect in chapter 3, the ways in which the revival stages the rupture, with distinctions underlying modes of government and the exercise of power in the postcolony, through its messianism, asceticism, and antimaterialism, and its egalitarian bracketing of various forms of social distinction. Born-Agains do not replace the old distinctions and hierarchies with new ones; rather, through their forms of address and actions, they behave as if they *were not*, reiterating the experience of 1 Corinthians 7, when "time is short," a time when "circumcision is nothing, the foreskin is nothing" and when what is, is "as not"[38] (when those weeping may be as not weeping, those buying as not possessing). In doing so, they render them inoperative. They are brothers and sisters in Christ; as the young man quoted in chapter 3 said, "Maybe I'm a banker, and this brother is a clerk, and because of emotions and everything involved, I can meet him, maybe he talks to me anyhow, but I can take it."[39] Distinctions based on ethnicity, age, status, and gender are to be lived in such a way as to liberate the subject from their previous strictures. This sense of the call may also be seen in the ways in which the vocation of being Born-Again is deployed not only to the realm of religious activity, but to everything the convert does in his professional and social life. The relative unimportance of institutional affiliation; the instability of pastoral authority; the egalitarian access to spiritual power and biblical knowledge; the transnational, dispersed, and diffuse sense of belonging; the schisms and internal differences—these also point to the inherent lack of content in a Born-Again "identity." Being Born-Again does not mean belonging to this or that institution, or projecting a specific, clearly identifiable public persona. The exemplarity staged by changed conduct is, in theory at least, simply the application of Christian principles to all aspects of daily life.

How is the experience of empowerment through weakness, through openness and submission to the Holy Spirit, realized? What is the role of the subject's own judgment and work of self-fashioning in these processes? Here the first sense of the "messianic vocation" takes on its full significance. I argue that the particularity of Born-Again modes of sub-jectivation lies in the ways in which they are effected through what I will call "acts of faith" and the "word of faith." Both are techniques of self-fashioning and modes through which the subject is constrained by a power that goes beyond the self, enabling the experience of the rebirth as well as the enactment of and obedience to the new norms and modes of conduct Born-Again doctrine prescribes. Their specificity lies in the forms of veridiction they employ, and how they articulate the relationship between the subject and truth. I shall argue that they present, in their programmatic form, modes of veridiction distinct not only from many of those at work within Nigerian society, but also from those of the secular traditions of Western modernity. These modes of subjectivation do not fundamentally break with a long Christian tradi-tion of spirituality, but they do introduce some innovations and de-partures, particularly in the ways in which they are deployed in the Nigerian context.

In the Western tradition, both philosophy and religion are con-cerned with the problem of "truth": what can be known about the world and the self and how it can be known. What Foucault designates schematically as "spirituality" distinguishes itself from "philosophy,"[40] that "form of thought" which, at least since Descartes, takes as its prem-ise the primacy of the self-conscious subject such as it is, as the grounds for determining the access to knowledge and truth. The philosophi-cal subject may or may not be able to access knowledge and truth, but the conditions and limits of this access are not something that can be modified by any work the subject may do on himself. The fundamental premise of "spirituality" in the Christian tradition is, on the contrary, that the subject, such as he is, is not capable of truth—it is never given fully to him—which means there can be no truth without a conversion or transformation of the subject, who must put his being at stake in order to achieve it. As such, "spirituality" designates "the inquiry, the practice, the experience through which the subject operates on himself the necessary transformations for gaining access to the truth. We can call 'spirituality' then the ensemble of these inquiries, practices and experiences which can be purifications, asceticism, renunciations, con-versions of seeing, modifications of existence, etc., which constitute, for the subject rather than for knowledge, for the very being of the sub-ject, the price to pay in order to have access to the truth."[41] At the same time, the object or effect of this conversion is not merely access to the truth—truth is not only something that is given to the subject as a form of recompense, as it were—but rather, by a sort of circular return, this truth illuminates the subject, it is that which brings beatitude or tranquillity of spirit, which accomplishes the subject, which transfigures him. This conversion or transformation can take different forms. Foucault schematically sets out two major ones in the Christian tradition. The first is that of "love," or *eros*, which tears the subject from himself, his current condition and status, whether through a movement of the ascension of the subject himself, or through a truth that appears to him and illuminates him.[42] The second is that of "work," or *askêsis*, which involves a long labor, an active work of the self on the self, a progressive transformation of the self, which the subject is responsible for.[43]

Pentecostalism employs variably both these modes of conversion or transformation; indeed, the techniques of the self we will discuss below all demonstrate aspects of both "love" and "work." However, its modes of subjectivation represent a departure from the Catholic tradition Foucault studied, with his analysis of pastoral power and confession as a form of truth-telling whose importance as a mode of subjectivation is less in the content of what is said than in the act of speaking the truth itself and recognizing oneself in this truth. It is also fundamentally different from the modes of veridiction employed in the model of the juridical subject and the politics of truth which characterize the relationships between power and knowledge in the secular Western tradition.[44] But these modes also represent a departure from those that develop out of various local traditions of veridiction, in particular, those that are most commonly seen in terms of the persistence and endurance of longstanding, even precolonial, modes of knowing the world and mastering it, which we might want to characterize as "magico-juridical."[45] In what follows I will bring together both the methodological insights of the Foucauldian problematic of subjectivation and the ways in which the Born-Again subject is realized through "acts of faith," a combination of the experience of faith in terms of "love" and a labor of self-fashioning: acts that, in their programmatic form, should bring about the effects of truth, which is the "new creation."

The first point essential to the idea of "acts of faith" is to understand how they are performative. Faith is performative insofar as it is entirely experiential, immune to the predicate "in."[46] It does not denote a "belief in," but rather performs a *being-in* belief. Both Agamben and Arendt draw our attention to the ways in which the experience of faith is like the experience of love: "Love does not allow for copulative predication, it never has a quality or an essence as its object. 'I love beautiful-brunette-tender-Mary' not 'I love Mary because she is beautiful, brunette and tender,' in the sense of her possessing such and such an attribute. . . . Love has no reason, and that is why, in Paul, it is tightly interwoven with faith."[47] Faith, once again like love, is also performative in terms of its powers of revelation: "love, although it is one of the rarest occurrences in human lives, indeed possesses an unequalled power of self-revelation and an unequalled clarity of vision for the discovery of *who*, precisely because it is unconcerned to the point of total unworldliness with *what* the loved person may be, with his qualities and shortcomings no less than with his achievements, failings and transgressions."[48] However, unlike being in love, which might be understood as an almost passive experience, faith is an experience realized in action, as in James 2:17: "Even so faith, if it hath not works, is dead, being alone." In the Born-Again articulation, the performative power of the act of faith is not merely that articulated through the work on the self, but is also, and perhaps above all, expressed in the double articulation between the miracle and the "word of faith." But the first act, or "miracle," of faith is the act of conversion itself. As Deeper Life pastor Kumuyi puts it, "Needless to mention, the miracle of conversion is, by all parameters, incomparably greater than every other miracle, even the raising of the dead."[49]

The act of conversion, "giving one's life to Christ" and "accepting Christ as one's personal Lord and savior," is presented as the moment of rupture that marks the end of the old and the beginning of the new. If we examine the ways in which the experience of conversion is described as having been lived, we see that the individual invariably presents this spiritual moment as an intensely powerful and private dialogue of the self with the self, yet one in which the individual recognizes him- or herself as being in the grip of a power that goes beyond the individual, a power that reveals itself in an imperious fashion, demanding that one cede or capitulate. Converts commonly relate how they heard the "voice" of God speaking to them, how they had a vision or a dream, or were overwhelmed by a sudden physical feeling of spiritual presence, or how they were compelled by extreme experiences of fear or desire brought on by a personal trial or illness. The experience is invariably solitary, and tends to be linked to moments of self-reflection or reckoning. Beyond personal trial or trauma, converts often explain how the revelation came upon them after reading a particular biblical text or hearing a preached message. The altar call is a standard liturgical practice in all Pentecostal services, generally coming after the sermon, where individuals are urged by the pastor to come and give their lives to Jesus and repeat a profession of repentance and faith. Yet more than half the converts whose testimonies I collected had experienced this private "moment" of conversion and revelation outside the context of Born-Again institutional forms, whether churches or fellowships. This moment very often came after the altar call for those who had taken one, and always after their exposure to the message in one form or another. The importance of a moment of decision, which converts are incited to witness to publicly, and the feeling of compulsion often attached to it are signs that the convert is already caught up in the desire for change, for empowerment and supernatural intervention in his life. The ordeal of everyday life and a spiritual tradition that underwrites the quest for supernatural solutions to everyday problems give this desire both poignancy and pertinence.

I was born again in 1978, but I can't really say I was saved, even though I had always gone to church. I really got saved when TREM was founded [The Redeemed Evangelical Mission] and I went to a program. A Ghanaian pastor preached at the revival and I found I was speaking in tongues. That was when I really felt the power of God.[50]

In around 1987 I joined the Focus Fellowship of the Celestial Church on campus [Aladura], where they were teaching some Born-Again doctrines. My conversion was with that fellowship, in 1987, but I have to say it wasn't a true Born-Again conversion, since I was still attending Celestial Church, and you know they have many doctrines that aren't really Christian. My daughter also became a member of the fellowship later on, but then she started going to Glory Tabernacle [Born-Again church] at times. My daughter quarreled with her father, who was a Celestial member, she tried to convince him to come out of that church, but her father replied who was she to tell him what to do. They started persecuting us, the people in Celestial Church started persecuting us, because of the Pentecostal teachings. That is why my daughter fell sick, and I knew they were going to do more. Finally, she grew even sicker and she died. As she was dying, she said, "I have to go, it is for the salvation of the family." She died in 1996. I saw that God has a purpose in taking my daughter. So although I was Born-Again earlier, that is when I really understood what a real Christian is. Especially my husband. The very same month, my husband got Born-Again. Now he goes to church five times a week and he also sings in the choir at special programs.[51]

I got converted at the Redeemed Headquarters in February, 1975. I had no problem at the time, I was well-paid, so I didn't see any real need of going to church. But my junior sister persuaded me to go with her. I went, as it was close to the house. But during the service, I felt like objects were moving inside me and something was pouring onto me. I attended some more services, and two weeks later I answered the altar call. I got the baptism of the Holy Spirit in September, 1975 [physical "infilling" of the Holy Spirit manifested by speaking in tongues.].[52]

I had friends who were believers, who were trying to get me to listen to what they had to say. I had the layman's point of view, that there was God and that there was Jesus Christ, but it was a generalized thing. It was not personal, I did not appropriate my faith personally. When you appropriate Christ through the blood of propitiation, it requires a certain amount of commitment. I wasn't ready to do that, so I just carry on as a nominal Christian, enjoy the rituals and the emotions. But by 1983, in November, on the 6th, to be precise, I went to listen to the preaching of a friend of mine. It was like a flood that reached its peak. Things that other people, friends of mine, together with that young man, had said, just came to me. I remember I went back to my hotel room at about 2 am, and all these things were in my head. Then by supernatural intervention, I began to hear the voice of Jesus talking to me. He started talking to me about a lot of things. I tried to defend my lifestyle, why I felt the things I was doing were okay. [Before becoming one of the better known pastors in Lagos, Okotie was a very popular musician and owned a record company.] We went on for a long time, almost twelve hours. By 2 pm or so the next day, He had persuaded me, He gave me so many examples of things He had done in my life, that I did not realize [recounts story of being suddenly healed from serious illness, where he prayed to God and promised to serve Him if he was cured]. Some more things happened that afternoon, and by the night I was converted.[53]

Most converts can date their conversion to the month and the year, and very often to the day, even years after its occurrence. The highly personal and mystical aspect of the "revelation" that often accompanies conversion is repeated in the great majority of the hundreds of conversion testimonies I collected. The experience of compulsion is common, and converts often relate how they struggled against the manifestation of a divine call. In the early days of the holiness revival, the social stigma and privation attached to becoming a pastor led many to describe in their testimonies how, when their "call' came, they "argued" with God about it, begging Him not to ask them for this "sacrifice." Yet even many years later, when conversion had become much more associated with this-worldly salvation, self-help, and prosperity, the call is still represented as a risk and a burden. Doing "God's work" may be lucrative, but it is nevertheless presented as a form of self-sacrifice and personal risk, even when one's affairs are not prospering: "I was a business woman and I was also involved in the Ministry. I discovered I was encountering different barriers and problems in getting contracts.

People who helped me before were no longer helping me. Then God told me that if I continue with my business, then I will not have time for God. I didn't find it funny at all, so I asked God, "How will I feed?" God told me, "I who called you am able to hold you and I will supply." So I turned all I had into the gospel."[54] One young woman told me how she really enjoyed going to services at Glory Tabernacle in Ibadan, but always left just before the altar call, since she was afraid of "getting converted." She was the mistress of a very rich military officer, and told me how she was afraid of having to give up her current lifestyle, all the gifts and good things he gave her. Like the problem of "spiritual pollution," the power of the Holy Spirit and the Word is conceived in an ontological sense, as an almost physical force under whose grip the subject falls and is in some ways powerless to resist. It is here, I think, that we may locate the agonistic relation between an outside, which works upon the individual, soliciting in him an openness and a desire, and the inside of the self, which suddenly receives and appropriates this call through a private communication of the self with the self.

As noted earlier, becoming Born-Again is a moment of rupture, but being Born-Again is a learned process, expressed in the notion of Christian growth, where "baby Christians" develop and become "strong in the spirit." In this process, various ritual practices and techniques of the self are deployed, which combine elements of the transformations involved in spirituality as discussed above, "work" and "love": being caught up in a power that exceeds the self, a form of affectivity that grips both the heart and the body, as well as determined work of self-transformation. A multitude of messages, contained in preaching, teaching, and a whole range of literature that converts are pushed to consume, instruct the individual on the correct application of various forms of ritual practice and spiritual exercises. Prayer manuals provide converts with prayers to use for specific occasions and to various purposes, such as fasting (for how long, to what ends) or the interpretation of dreams (examining them for signs of demonic spiritual activity, using prayers according to whether one dreamed of water or eating or whatever else), and advise converts at what times to pray, what to say, and in what positions. Speaking in tongues, generally thought to be the spontaneous, ecstatic sign of the Holy Spirit, can also be learned. Ways of moving, dressing, and addressing are set out in a variety of forms, which themselves indicate the relative importance in believers' practice of "work" and "love," as the above-mentioned distinction between "Wordites" and "spiris" indicates.

Prayer—"unceasing" and "fervent" as the Born-Again prescription has it—is a central technique of the self, in which, through a personal communication or discussion with God, the convert articulates both desires and fears, plenitude and lack, and is brought to envision an imagined future. Prayers are used to invoke both divine protection and empowerment, and the fervency of Born-Again prayer creates in the subject an emotional, almost ecstatic state. Indeed, in public services and in private practices, prayer is the discursive form that directly precedes glossolalia, or speaking in tongues, a trancelike state in which the individual experiences the "infilling of the Holy Spirit." Prayer is a constant part of Born-Again daily life; any event, no matter how mundane or trivial, is prayed about. Most churches or ministries issue daily prayer guides, in which a biblical verse is cited along with a specific theme and purposes of prayer. All-night prayer is a regular part of Born-Again practice, and typically takes the form of night-long vigils in the church or fellowship, yet it may also be practiced by the convert in private, particularly when facing an important trial or event. My flatmates at the University of Lagos, two young women working on a UNICEF project, spent every Friday night praying together until dawn. The subjects of their prayers touched upon every aspect of their daily lives: family, work, love relationships, health, money. Through her prayers, the convert is perpetually brought to evaluate the efficacy of prayer, and question herself as to what aspects of her life or conduct may hasten or block a divine response. But at the same time, prayer is one of the principal ways in which the "word of faith" finds its performative power; it is both a supplication and a witness. Speaking in tongues, represented as the physical presence of the Holy Spirit and the ultimate sign of divine empowerment, is described by converts as an ecstatic state of self-abandon and mystical communion in which one physically feels the power in one's body. As I discovered from my afternoon spent with Pastor Tony Rapu from the RCCG, it is nonetheless a technique of the body, which converts can be taught to acquire.[55] Intervening in services and revivals as part of standard liturgical practice, tongues are solicited by the pastor who "spontaneously" leads the congregation. Ritual in this sense is as much about correct performance and well-taught bodies as it is about expressing meanings.

Constant study of Scripture and a perpetual quest for understanding also constitute a central part of the work of the self on the self: Converts are given biblical instruction in fellowships and services; however, daily study of the Word is considered the first responsibility, or work, that the convert must undertake for his transformation. In individual study, the convert reads the Word to find a sign for its relevance to his personal situation. "God gave me an understanding of Jeremiah 17:5.[56] I used to trust man for my needs and it had become a part of me. In fact, I could not trust God for so many things. In 1996, people I trusted disappointed me. When I came across Jeremiah 17:5, it dawned on me that I had been carrying a curse on me for trusting man. I repented and asked God for forgiveness. Then I began to trust God and doors began to open in several ways. When one door closed, seven would open for me. Praise God!"[57] We can see in this account the marriage of revelation and transformation involved in such study. Matters of trust and credit are associated with the very being of subject: "it had become a part of me." The sudden revelation of the meaning of the scriptural text, the act of repentance, and the renewal of trust changed the life of the believer. Scripture is an authoritative form of knowledge whose study and deciphering provides the basis for the regulation of conduct and the acquisition of spiritual power and authority. The application of biblical precepts in one's everyday life through a constant individual biblical hermeneutics requires an ongoing process of self-scrutiny and evaluation. At the same time, the act of reading the Word has the performative power of revelation.

The central Born-Again technique of the self, the one that best demonstrates the ways in which the subject's openness and submission to spiritual power and his or her own work of self-transformation creates its effects of truth, is that of testimony or witness. Testimony and witnessing is part of the evangelical obligation that falls upon all converts. At every service or fellowship meeting, individuals testify to the signs of God's work in their lives. It is a central technique of evangelism, and indeed, the principal mode of creating obedience and collective belonging. Born-Again publications reserve many pages for converts' testimonies, and sermons and "teaching" are peppered with stories of individual miracles. Sometimes the testimonies are highly dramatic, with the convert having suddenly received incredible wealth or opportunities, or having been saved from life-threatening and incurable illnesses, violent crimes, witchcraft attacks, or the "outer limit" of perdition as figured in covenants with Satan and his minions. Others, in fact the great majority, are very banal and everyday. How God saved me from slipping on the soap in the shower; how Jesus made the water come out of the pump clear and not dirty, even though my bucket was first in line and the water is always dirty at first; how I passed my exam when I was sure to have failed. Anything that happens to an individual may be seen as the sign of God's grace and power in his or her life. Converts are urged to witness to this grace and power at every occasion. Through the ongoing repetition of testimony to conversion or personal miracles, the signs of change may be read, evaluated, and developed in an ongoing way. Adherence to moral rules and codes; techniques such as prayer or fasting; modes of dressing and carrying the body; "giving" to God and "working" for God are all the fruit of active work, whose purpose is to bring, in return, God's power to work in directing the events of one's life and to assure the personal ability to continue "overcoming" and to adhere to these codes. One friend of mine explained: "When I got Born-Again, I thought there was no way I was going to manage to give up smoking and sex, going out to night clubs and all those things. I thought I wouldn't last a week. The first couple of months were hard, but after about three months, the desire for those things just went away. It's easy now."[58]

And yet, notwithstanding the reality and the absolutely singular nature of the private religious experience, testimonies all follow a standard narrative structure. In the case of conversion, this involves drawing a stark distinction between past and present lives, often marking the rupture between the old and the new through examples of the miraculous intervention of the divine in everyday existence: healing, prosperity, success in jobs, exams, marriage, birth of a long-awaited child. Many individuals self-consciously blacken their pasts, inventing or exaggerating sins and ill-deeds, crises or lack in their "old lives," in contrast to the new.

I was living a rough life. Even when I was in school, I was bad, I was in charge of the school bad boys. I'll tell them what to do and how to do it. That was not all, I was also disobedient to my parents, wayward and so on. Like when we plan to go and stone our principal because of something. We did it and they put us in prison. I came back to regret it. It was during my exam times, I used to go to the bush to read and it was there I begin to pray for a good result and when the result came, I was very surprised to clear them. I used to smoke before, to the extent that some people will come and tell my dad that I smoke, that I was smoking Indian hemp. There was this time I was very ill and they did all these medical tests, traditional even, there was no result. So my father took me to an Apostolic church. In the church they start to pray for me and then the preacher told me if I die and I don't confess my sins I'm going to hell, but if I do I'll go to heaven. I said God, I don't want to go to hell. So there I confess my sins, and I asked my Mum to go get me a Bible, I want to start reading. And when I read and read and read and read, I say, "God, forgive me." One day, one of the preachers was preaching and preaching, suddenly he said "You! You! You better repent because you are going to die!" I shouted, I said, "I'll repent!" I was crying. So they took me out of the hall, and then and there I gave my life to Christ. That was in 1984.[59]

Pastors also use this as a technique of "witnessing." In 1999 I heard one of the most famous pastors in Nigeria preach to a revival meeting and claim that he'd spent time in prison for armed robbery before his conversion. I had investigated his life story seven years earlier, and am certain the man, a university lecturer, had never been a convicted criminal. The standardization of this form and the compulsion to mark a break between the past and the moment of change involves a staging of memory "as a miracle which would restore lost truth."[60] And witnessing to this memory may be seen as constant reminder of the danger of losing the self, of the uncertainty of the trajectory of the soul, which may slide backward as well as progress forward. In many respects, the rupture with the past and the renewal promised by conversion is one which must be constantly and forever renewed, through repeated acts of faith. And yet the structuring of narrative also stages the experience of rupture such that each individual event of conversion or each personal miracle becomes interchangeable with every other, the sign of a general form, an eternal repetition of the same story. This proliferation of narrative concerning both conversion and its fruits is the sign of a certain exercise of power; indeed, it is one of its techniques. Evangelical witnessing is a modern technique of the self insofar as it involves "giving an account of oneself," both to oneself and to others. As Judith Butler argues, giving an account of oneself involves "norms that facilitate my telling about myself but that I do not author and render me substituable at the very moment that I seek to establish the history of my singularity. This last dispossession in language is intensified by the fact that I give an account of myself to someone, so that the narrative structure of my account is superseded by the structure of address in which it takes place."[61] Yet, despite this particular form of staging, which compels the subject and constrains his telling, despite the violence done to memory through its rescripting via the narrative form of witnessing, this constant seeking of God's work in one's everyday life takes the form of an ongoing self-scrutiny and self-evaluation, and constitutes the central form in terms of which the work of the self on the self may be organized and developed in an ongoing way.

The relative emphasis on the importance of the work of self-fashioning—self-scrutiny, constant study and biblical hermeneutics, fasting, prayer, suffering, laboring, "waiting on the Lord"—and the experience of self-transformation through "love"—the illumination of the self by a power and revelation of truth from without—changes over the development of the revival. In the first decade or so of the revival, faith and prayer were accompanied by the close study of Scriptures and strict retreat from the world and its temptations. Public repentance and practices of restitution, in which the convert compensated those he or she had wronged in the past, and a constant and ongoing scrutiny of conduct for signs of sin or moral laxity were developed and policed by pastors and co-religionists to ensure the convert's adequate preparation and constant readiness for the "rapture." The rupture was made evident by changes in conduct and appearance, marking the group off from the rest of society. Yet alongside this work of self-discipline and the discipline of others was the notion that the power of God could do anything, as long as one's faith was strong enough. The miraculous intervention of God in individual lives was at the center of testimony and evangelical witness. Indeed, miracles were considered a necessary evangelical tool, an important technique for leading unbelievers to Christ. Kumuyi himself acknowledges the ambivalence of this practice, laying claim to a form of indulgent cultural understanding worthy of any nineteenth-century missionary:

The stories of miracles documented here may unseat some sincere minds. I blame them not. Some may feel that miracles are not for today. Others may think all the church should care for is the salvation of souls. But in Africa and amongst the black people of the globe, hard-core Gospel teaching may not give the desired result. The Gospel must be preached with "signs following." The proof and evidence of the love of God pave the path of the Gospel in Africa. It prepares the heart of the people for the word of God. God, in the growth of Deeper Life, has strategically and prudently used miracles to make all come to him (John 3.26)[62] in Deeper Life. Needless to mention, the miracle of conversion is, by all parameters, incomparably greater than every other miracle, even the raising of the dead."[63]

The combination of these two modes was thus present from the outset, since alongside the exhortation to constant work of the self on the self through study, fasting, prayer, and testimony, there developed the notion on the part of many converts that prayer and other techniques of the self were a form of practice that might "capture" divine power, opening the door miraculously to all sorts of mysteries and abilities one previously did not have. Students tell of how the S.U. would pray all night before exams rather than studying their textbooks, under the impression that God would miraculously impart in them the knowledge found in the books they hadn't opened. The entire question of deliverance rituals and divine healing by the laying on of hands reinforced this tendency. This gave rise to an economy of miracles in which personal work and dedication was suspended upon the grace of God or could be undone by the workings of evil powers, which might inhabit an individual without his or her awareness. In the early years, this ambivalence was less marked, since the teleology of the moral subject was oriented toward otherworldly salvation and a self-conscious rejection of the various objects of desire that characterized the cargo-cultism of dominant forms of distinction, as well as of many of the social relationships that underwrote the entire system of distinction and inequality. However, with the arrival of the prosperity gospel, making a complete break with the past through work and the refashioning and control of desire was to become increasingly problematic.

And yet, as well as the centrality of personal miracles of prosperity and healing, the new wave with its emphasis on this world did develop a discourse on self-fashioning through study, reflection, and awareness of the self, with the object of bringing individual and collective salvation into the world. A Born-Again version of American self-help psychology, in which positive thinking and personal empowerment are associated with the development of both spiritual and secular knowledge, also was central to the message of the new wave, reiterating the messianic "use it rather." This tension between internal work and external power has thus been central throughout the movement's history, whatever the doctrinal emphasis. In the account that follows, the early holiness attitude to techniques of "capturing" divine power through pure faith and prayer are called into question, and the work of self-improvement is depicted as central to gaining the fruits of conversion and the manifestation of divine power.

Pentecostal churches are now becoming aware of the fact that if you are a child of God, you need to exercise yourself intellectually in the things of God. Before they shied away from it, they only want to say John 3:16.[64] But if you talk about technology, I'll see you tomorrow, if you talk about anything, I'll see you tomorrow, without knowing that things will change. They're now becoming intellectually aware that even though we are Christians, we still need these areas to improve on earth. So spiritual intellectual awareness, social intellectual awareness, finance intellectual awareness that you must have to worship God. Because before, if you don't have money, and you go to God "Oh God, oh God, give me money" and you are asked to pray for ten hours. A sister was telling me that she told her small boy about five years old, "Let us pray for food." He said, "I'm not going to pray again. How long

will it take God before hearing us?" . . . You need intellectual awareness. You know
when you want to go for exams tomorrow and you don't know two plus two equals
four. How would you pass but you know two plus two equals four? Your prayer
must be that God should help it stay in your brain. But if you have brain problem
and you read and forget, then you will pray to God, God, give me the wisdom to
understand and remember what I am reading. It is in the Bible. James 2:17.[65] But
they thought that He'll give you wisdom in the mathematics you've not studied.
No! Neither will God give you wisdom in the Scriptures you've not studied. It is the
same principle.[66]

This tension also reveals another, related to the ways in which acts
of faith appear to take the form of a reiteration of a local ontology and
practices of spiritual power. Many analysts are quick to see in these representations the signs of the "revenge of paganism." However, as I have
argued, contemporary spiritual practices have been forged together
within a single complex in which it becomes impossible to distinguish
or oppose these forms at an analytical level. Even with respect to the
new modes of spiritual practice born from the colonial encounter, these
representations involve a new rupture. Indeed, they provide evidence
for the performative power of the "word of faith" as it is practiced in
Pentecostalism everywhere. Across the doctrinal spectrum, the "power
in the word," particularly the name of Jesus, has properly performative force of its own. Shouting the word "Jesus" or biblical citations in
a moment of danger is a means of protection or deliverance. Indeed,
practices of healing and deliverance are exclusively performed through
the use of prayers and exhortations. The laying on of hands is a possible addition, but not necessary. The extensive use of stickers on cars
and homes with epithets such as "Covered in the blood of Jesus," "Jesus
protected," or "Angels on guard" is a technique used to ward off attacks
from armed robbers, to say nothing of more spiritual threats such as
witches and "hidden enemies." The central technique of proliferation
of the message through media is also seen to be imbued with a potentially dangerous or salvific power. The mediatized message has a kind
of supernatural force that has a profound effect on the self.[67]

I always ask my children not to watch Yoruba plays on television. For example, there
was one with a wicked man who had satanic connections. This can be very dangerous, especially for children, as they don't have the maturity to defend themselves
against it. The spirits invoked in the things can affect the Christian, they can be
victim of demonic attack, and some can even be initiated through television. Likewise programs on Islam. The Bible says, when you hear the word, it will affect you,

there is power in the word. So hearing these programs, it can affect someone any-how, psychologically, or through spiritual attacks. You should avoid such things, the words will be affecting you.[68]

Many early Born-Again tracts, such as the ones mentioned in chapter 3, detailed the ways in which the devil and his agents watch the activities of born-again Christians on televisions in their underwater lairs, and control their satanic agents in the world by use of computers. The majority of Born-Again organizations expect their members to restrict their viewing of television to programs that are edifying for Christians, although very few proscribe television viewing altogether. Even Deeper Life, which for several years forbade its members to watch television, now produces videos and has a well-produced website. In the wrong hands, the media and media technology present a powerful tool for evil. The recent video boom, which has close relations to the Born-Again staging of demonic powers, now produces films staging gory showdowns between occult forces, yet without the moral messages on the wages of sin, repentance, and redemption proper to their Born-Again cousins.[69] The director of Mount Zion Productions told me how in casting roles for their Born-Again video productions, they are very careful to chose only "confirmed" and "mature" believers whose faith is strong to play witches, juju men, secret cult members, and other satanic characters. Demonic attacks through the roles played in the films are a real threat to those whose Christian life is not strong enough.[70]

I often heard references made to those who were healed by touching the television, or who were moved to conversion after watching a broadcast. Below is an example of the rediffusion via the media (a taped message) of an indirect experience of the miracle of the mediatized word:

I always share this testimony everywhere I go. This happened some years back. I was preaching on television in Benin City and a man watched my program. As he watched, this man, according to his testimony, he has been sick for five years and had been on his sick bed at home. When I was done preaching I said—now you see, I didn't even know he was there—I said, "get out of that bed in the name of Jesus. Do what you couldn't do before." He believed me. He jumped out of his bed. His relative grabbed him and said, "No, you can't do that." Listen to me, your relatives will love you to death. They will love you and kill you. They said, "You can't do that. For five years you've been on the bed, you can't. Oh Uncle, stay on the bed." And he said, "thank you, I've listened to you for five years and it didn't help me. I like what that man just said." He said, "Get me some water, I want to take a shower."

For five years they were dry-cleaning him on the bed. He got up, staggered to the bathroom, took a shower, a good shower, after five years. He said, "Put my food on the table." He got down and ate his food on the dining table for the first time in five years. And you know what he did next? He got out of the house, he walked to the T.V. station and he said, "I want the manager." And they took him to someone there. And he said, "You know, I don't know that man that just preached, but I want you to let him know that it works."[71]

The message conveyed in this testimony is not simply one of the powers of televangelism. It also relates changes in the ways in which supernatural power can manifest itself and create new relationships based on different social premises. The miracle occurs in a "virtual' relationship between the preacher and the sick man. Though they are total strangers, the sick man immediately identifies the preacher's televised message as a personal, intimate call. His extended family, who have been caring and ministering to him for five years—feeding and "dry-cleaning" him on his bed—are depicted as the obstacles to his healing, salvation, and personal success. They may love him, but it is a dangerous love, one that thwarts and ultimately kills. Here, the reference to witchcraft is more than implicit. The space of intimacy is thus displaced, and the story finishes with the recognition by the healed to the healer, not through person-to-person contact (although we must imagine that such a contact subsequently took place), but rather via the television station manager.

The representation of power in these accounts and in the problematization of Born-Again subjectivation portrays it as a substance that inhabits an individual, often provoking physical reactions and directing his will. The power of the Holy Spirit and the nefarious powers of the devil are both at large in the world and present within the subject. Indeed, we could say that the central work of the self on the self, which is never truly achieved, is a permanent deciphering of the line between the self and the world and the powers that inhabit it, and an attempt to interpret and control these forces and their effects through various techniques. The project of the crucifixion of self through the submission to the Word of God and the Holy Spirit sits uneasily with the possibility of being seized upon by evil and occult powers. Mbembe argues that conversion, in reality, "always has a hybrid, composite, heteroclite and baroque character" and that 'the erosion of old references and 'traditional' ways of doing which always goes hand in hand with the rewriting of fragments of new memories and a redistribution of custom."[72] Conversion is an event in the Foucauldian sense: "the plural inhabits it, innumerable souls dispute within it." At the same time, this agency of words and spirits is central to Pentecostalism everywhere, and arises from within a global religious episteme in which the agency of evil spirits and of God are very real.

This efficacy of the word and the agency of spiritual power called up in testimonies and the experience of miracles of healing, deliverance, and prosperity is not merely the reenactment of "traditional" modes of spiritual practice under a new religious garb. One of the signs of this is in the ways in which Born-Agains refuse all techniques that might be understood in terms of "fetishism" or "magic": they admit no intermediary substances, which might incarnate the power of God, nothing that may come between the word of faith and its effective action. No anointed oils or holy water, no "anointed" soaps or handkerchiefs, nothing except the word, whose power, however, may be reinforced by brandishing the Bible itself. During rituals of divine healing and deliverance in Born-Again churches and ministries, only the laying on of hands, in one of which might be held the Bible, can accompany the fervent prayers and commands that call the demons and spirits causing affliction to leave the body. The deliverance results very often in the "extraction" of objects or substances from the body: objects such as locks, stones, or rings that are "taken" from the body, as well as foul substances vomited up. They are displayed, as are the various "fetishes" and juju the converted bring to churches as part of the accomplishment of their conversion, as simple objects whose "demonic" power has been neutralized. Indeed, the public experience of demonstrating the neutralization of such powers is an ecstatic experience in itself, as Balogun's testimony, discussed in chapter 3, illustrates: "You will vomit out the demonic power you swallowed as I did mine after my deliverance. Mine was vomited before an audience of more than 2,000 people." The power of the word is compared exultantly to the "old powers" and their objects, which nonetheless still have their dangerous efficacy.

Beyond the ways in which rituals of healing and deliverance are staged in a self-conscious opposition to local practices, this rupture with longstanding spiritual practices is also evidenced by the ways in which Pentecostalism attempts to restore the original Christian experience of faith, of conversion as the *performativum fidei* (act of faith), which is expressed in the word of faith: in the declaration "Jesus Messiah," or as the Born-Agains put it, "declaring for Jesus," "professing Jesus Christ." Indeed, every Born-Again practice of the self, every act of faith is at once a profession and a witness, performing, through its very enunciation, a *being-in* belief that transforms the believer, empowering him or her and giving access to another experience of the world.

Notwithstanding the importance of witnessing in public, as well as public rituals of repentance and forgiveness, the effects of truth that are produced through witnessing and testimony do not principally depend upon recognition, as in Butler's theory of subject-formation,[73] but rather on experiences of interiority in which revelation and judgment are almost indiscernible. It is in the personal space of affectivity and reflection, in the elaboration of a dialogue with the self, and in ecstatic bodily experiences that the signs of God's presence in the convert's life are sought, expressed, and verified. The centrality of the subject's own work and affect in the acquisition of a spiritual state and the ways in which it affects his or her self-conduct demonstrates a rupture from the attitudes and practices decried by the missionaries, whose early converts seemed so impervious to "heartfelt" conviction.[74] The Born-Again ethic of submission and openness to the power of God through the work on the self, and its principal mode of veridiction are stated very clearly here, in the explanation offered by a convert whom I questioned about how one could tell the difference between the power of the Holy Spirit and the operation of other spiritual powers in the life of the believer:

A religious man is serving God. . . . If he is not looking to God, then he is serving the devil. For instance, you're looking for children, and you go to the *babalawo* or witch to give you. In a real sense, you believe that he can do it because you feel he's superior, a superior being can do something for you, based on the fact that you have to bribe him. It's very logical. You have to look at Christianity and witchcraft, and you have to draw the line. That's where you need to know the Word in quote. I went to a revival, and there's a man who's speaking in tongues, and he was possessed by a demon. How do we solve that? We solve that by saying that they speak in the tongues the spirit gives them. In the church, we have a lot of people and it's not the Holy Spirit giving them utterance. One has to test the spirit, and if it is of God, it will confess that Jesus is Lord and that He's our only savior. People believe in miracles, and people use miracles to further their own ends, for making money. If a miracle is going to operate through you, the Spirit must be willing, not you. This might be where you come into witchcraft. Because you are willing, but not the Holy Spirit. Just to keep up your image. You might easily fall into witchcraft in all the prosperity churches, because some people mostly emphasize power. You can't seek power without seeking the giver of power. You might end up getting power from a different source. Most people go into witchcraft because they needed power. What really matters is maintaining a balance between studying the Word and the Spirit. There are a lot of Born-Agains who don't speak by the inspiration of the Holy Spirit. The only way you may know is by a witness, a personal witness in your spirit. You need the spirit of discernment.[75]

Here, the meaning of witness takes on its full significance. Witness, of which testimony, prayer, and praise are but specific examples, refers to a different and more foundational status of the word, one that goes beyond representation and the relationship between signifier and signified, beyond the denotative relationship between language and the world to the experience itself, rendering inoperative the distinctions between consciousness, reason, affect, and the body. Agamben cites Paul in Romans 10:6–10: "But the justice which is of faith sayeth this: 'say not in thine heart, " 'Who shall ascend into Heaven"?' that is, to bring Christ down from above: Or " 'Who shall descend into the abyss"?' that is, to bring Christ again from the dead.' But what sayeth it? 'the word is near thee, even in thy heart and in thy mouth,' that is the word of faith which we proclaim. That if thou shalt confess with thy mouth Lord Jesus and shalt believe in thine heart that God hath raised him from the dead, thou shalt be saved. For with the heart man believeth unto righteousness; and with the mouth confession is made unto salvation." He goes on to explain that the word of faith is "an experience of the word's being near, held in the harmony between mouth and heart. . . . The belief in the heart is neither a holding true, nor the description of an interior state, but a justification; only the professing of the mouth accomplishes salvation."[76] Further on, in verse 11 we read: "For whosoever shall call upon the Lord shall be saved." The power in the name of Jesus, which Born-Agains shout as a means of spiritual protection, takes on an entirely different light if we see it in terms of the word of faith. It no longer represents simply a form of magical practice, it enacts the experience of faith itself and its transformative effects. The messiah is near, in the "harmony between heart and mouth"; professing Jesus and witnessing in the Spirit take the form of a revelation: "Each revelation is always and above all a revelation of language itself, an experience of the pure event of the word that exceeds every signification."[77] Witnessing and declaring Jesus do not have a denotative or constative function, they refer to a reality they themselves produce and reveal. This reality is the world of faith: "not a world of existences and essences, but of indivisible events, in which I do not judge, nor do I believe that the snow is white and the sun is warm, but I am transported and displaced in the snow-being-white and the sun-being-warm. . . . a world in which

I do not believe that Jesus, such-and-such a man, is the Messiah, only begotten son of God, begotten and not created, cosubstantial in the Father. I only believe Jesus Messiah: I am carried away and enraptured in him, in such a way that 'I do not live, but the Messiah lives in me.' Gal. 2:20." As Agamben argues, comparing the performative effects of language in the Old Covenant and the New: "there are two ways of going beyond the denotative function of language toward the experience of the event. The first, according to the oath paradigm, attempts to use it as a means to ground contract and obligation. For the other, however, the experience of the pure word opens it up to gratuitousness and use. The latter is the expression of the subject's freedom ('our freedom which we have in the Messiah' Gal. 2:3); the former is the expression of his subjection to a codified system of norms and articles of faith." As the young believer cited in chapter 2 put it: "In the Old Testament, there are a lot of dos and don'ts, but in the New Testament, we are being led by the Spirit. So nobody has to tell you to cover your head, or don't wear jeans, or don't do this or that. The Spirit of God in you should tell you what is right and wrong." The acts of faith, the combined effects of "work" and "love"—"maintaining a balance between studying the Word and the Spirit"—bring about their effects of truth, the "new creature," through their very performance, eliciting the circular return of truth upon the subject, which illuminates and transforms him and his experience of the world.[78]

In their programmatic form then, Born-Again modes of subjectivation give rise to new processes of individuation that place the accent on the individual's subjective experiences and work of self-fashioning, in which submission to codes and doctrines is articulated within the tension of the messianic "suspension of the law." This entails the possibility of overcoming various forms of distinction and old forms of power and knowledge, as well as the redemptive promise of the messianic life, in which the "new creation" is none other than the use and the messianic vocation of the old, thus opening up the possibility of the subject's freedom. As we shall see, this ethics is fundamentally unstable and ambiguous: the space opened up for gratuitousness and use threatens to overwhelm the stabilization of rules and norms. Perhaps we can understand the Born-Again line of subjectivation in Deleuze's notion of a "line of flight," something that escapes and subtracts itself from the precedent lines of knowledge and power.[79] Realized through the acts of faith, the operation of giving oneself to Christ and receiving Christ as one's savior gives rise to a surplus, a "new creation" that is less an identity than a new experience of the world.

However, as Deleuze goes on to say, while subjectivation is the "operation in which individuals or communities constitute themselves as subjects at the margins of constituted knowledges and established powers," this also means giving rise to new knowledge and inspiring new powers.[80] The urgency to which the Born-Again revival responded was that of postcolonial radical insecurity, the permanent disjuncture between signs and their objects, the unreliability of human relations, the impossibility of securing the grounds for certitude in a world of falsification, violence, and arbitrariness. If the central thrust of Born-Again modes of subjectivation is the ways in which the individual acts of faith open up the world to the believer for gratuitousness and use, how may obedience to the codes and doctrinal prescriptions become instituted and stabilized? How is it possible to know what sort of power is at work both within the self and within the world? Who is authorized to decide, and according to what criteria? Beyond the acts of faith themselves and their effects on the individual, it remains to be seen how the new birth enables the creation of a new collective ethic and the establishment of a community—the "new family," as Born-Agains say. If the *telos* of conversion, which is not merely "everlasting life" but also "life more abundant," is to be realized through a program of individual self-mastery through submission to the power of the Holy Spirit, how may it find its collective expression? How does this program respond to the urgency of providing intersubjectivity with new and stable forms of expression, in which acts of promising and forgiveness, which depend upon the presence of others, may provide the guarantees that make living together possible? What sort of politics does this work of self-fashioning give rise to? The ways in which the community of faith is established lead to clashes with religious others with similar ambitions for the revolution of individual conduct and collective government. In the account given here, we can see a dangerous opposition of the discourse on the work of Christian self-fashioning and the self-government of religious others:

Being Born-Again is the way out of Nigeria's problems. All our past leaders have not been Christians, they have all been Muslims or other non-Christians. If they had been true Christians, things would have taken for the better. Christianity teaches you both getting to know God and completely overhauling yourself towards this direction. It reshapes your life and totally makes you want to be a 100% faithful in your dealings with the Almighty Father and your fellow. Your romance with the Evil one or the devil and his antics, is totally discouraged or wiped off. You're made to repent totally away from your evil ways. You're made to renounce all evil ways totally and never go back to them again. This is not the same with Islam. There is a place in the Koran which tells, which spells out, the rituals that should be done once someone commits a sin. Once these rituals are done, then the person is sin-free. This is bad, it encourages believers of Islam to sin and know how to get off their sins without any repentance.[81]

If spirituality is the mode in which the subject undergoes a transformation of his or her being in order to access a truth that will, in return, illuminate and transfigure him or her, how does the political "will to found anew" the divisions of true and false in the ways in which men govern themselves and others find its concrete political expression? In many ways, Pentecostalism expresses a negative political theology, whether one understands this term in its sense of a theology of sovereignty or as a theology of community. With its emphasis on individual salvation, interiority, and affectivity, coupled with its incipient messianism, it has great difficulty in either founding an authority that commands obedience and may embody divine will, or creating the foundations of a political community. As we shall see, this indeterminacy facilitates the staging of new powers. On the one hand, there is a growing bid for pastoral monopoly over spiritual authority with increasingly theocratic tendencies. On the other, there is an engagement with the demonic that, rather than resolving the problem of radical insecurity and founding a new politics of living together, gives rise to a politics of settling scores and vengeance. It is perhaps this indeterminacy that makes it both so successful in our current world and so potentially dangerous.

FIVE

Born-Again Ethics and the Spirits of the Political Economy

HUMAN PARTS FOUND AT ASO ROCK IN ABACHA'S JUJU SHRINE

[T]he world has continued to be inundated with a string of atrocities committed by the maximum ruler all in the bid to perpetuate himself in power. While the ripples created by the discoveries of the staggering sums of money allegedly carted off by Abacha and his cronies are still reverberating, another shocking find was made last week at the Aso Rock villa [presidential residence in Abuja]. . . . This time, there are heaps of objects suspected to be the carcasses of the various fetish sacrifices which the late Head of State was known to have affinity for while in office. . . . Some, the hoofs of rams, black pots, small gourds, unburnt candles of many colours, including effigies and a miniature coffin. . . . Some hairs that certainly do not belong to any known animal, some things that looked like human finger and toe nails; skeletal dentures that bear semblance to human beings including some skull which we could not identify the origin.[1]

TWO MAN-EATING CROCODILES FOUND IN ASO ROCK—GORY DETAILS OF HOW ABACHA FED THEM WITH HUMAN FLESH

The death of General Sani Abacha has made many Nigerians to have a rethink about the possibility of anything. General Sani Abacha whose demise exposed one of the greatest records of man's inhumanity to man, was another Head of State [with Idi Amin, Kamuzu Banda, Mobutu] who watched over the execution of his innocent countrymen in cold blood. Another Abacha wonder emanating from Aso Rock last week was the shocking discovery of an artificial

river constructed by the late Head of State, where he nurtured two giant crocodiles which he fed with human flesh from time to time. It was gathered that the
secretly concealed "river" in the very expansive Aso Rock villa was stumbled on by
a Lagos-based spiritualist who was charged with the responsibility of cleansing the
Villa spiritually to detonate Abacha's legion of charms. . . . "Shocked by the development," a source obliged, "the spiritualist quickly alerted the new Head of State,
General Abdulsalam Abubakar, who instantly ordered the killing of the crocodiles.
On a search into the man-made river, remnants of human parts like bones were
retrieved from the bed of the Abacha river" the source narrated. . . . Late General
Abacha, whose thirst for blood became public knowledge when human parts were
discovered in his special rooms (shrines) a couple of weeks ago, was said to have
deliberately nurtured the crocodiles to perpetuate his own secret jungle justice. . . .
TC [Today's Choice] was hinted that the mysterious disappearance of people all over
the country may not be unconnected with the periodic rituals at the man-made
"Abacha river," because it became apparent that the crocodiles could hardly eat any
other thing than human flesh. . . . apart from the fact that the crocodiles were used
for vindictive purposes, the two demonic creatures were also believed to be serving
a ritual purpose of sort.[2]

Nigerian dictator Sani Abacha's sordid death in the arms of foreign
prostitutes on 8 June 1998 brought to an end one of the bloodiest and
most corrupt regimes in Nigerian political history. His death opened
the floodgates to wild speculation in the popular press, and at the same
time revealed the extent to which his rule had taken the rape of the
economy and state violence to levels unheard of even during Ibrahim
Babangida's extremely predatory regime. Alongside stories of his macabre juju shrines, man-eating crocodiles, and outrageous consumption
of women and luxury goods, the reality of his regime's extraordinary
pillage rapidly emerged: in five years, over a billion dollars siphoned
from the Nigerian economy and placed in accounts around the world;
entire rooms stacked from floor to ceiling with foreign exchange notes;
his wife Maryam stopped at the airport with thirty-eight suitcases
stuffed with cash.[3] These revelations were made against the backdrop of
an economy in tatters; shocking levels of poverty and unemployment;
chronic scarcity; total administrative breakdown; unprecedented state
violence (including the murder of Ogoni leader and writer Ken Saro
Wiwa); endless petrol shortages (in one of the world's largest oil producers); unprecedented levels of criminality, insecurity, and violence
among groups and against the state; and a new pariah status within
the international community. When he seized power following the
June 1993 electoral holdup, Abacha, in a repetition of the eternal text,

had announced he would rid the country of corruption. Even by Nigerian standards, one indeed had to have "a rethink about the possibility of anything." The simulacrum appeared to have reached its paroxysm.

The problem of corruption and illicit gain relates directly to the relationship between the web of debt and obligation that historically structures forms of predatory extraction, accumulation, and domination. The bases for challenging legitimate authority depend to a large extent on the perceived relationship between the source of power and wealth, and the social and political uses to which it is put. The failure to honor various obligations arising from different structures of sociability (kin, ethnicity, gender, friendship)—indeed, the very desire to liberate oneself from the cycle of debt and obligation—becomes increasingly suspect at precisely the moment when these various structures appear to be breaking down. The overall structure of elite domination and accumulation depends on a historical experience and exploitation of the relative instability between signs and their objects, an instability that is expressed through the idiom of invisible secret powers and practices of witchcraft and witch-finding. This instability is gravely exacerbated by the changes in the Nigerian political economy from the 1970s onward. But the problem of corruption and the illicit or transgressive also relates, more generally, to the historical structuring of desire, and the various modes of its realization or frustration.

Mbembe has recently proposed an analysis of what he has termed the "moral economy of corruption," relating contemporary African political economies to the ways in which sovereignty, domination, and accumulation have, over the long period of African history, been forged in a relationship that emphasizes the libidinal and suicidal, or at least destructive, nature of power's exercise.[4] From the period of the slave trade African "elites" have invariably maintained a relationship to the "act of corrupting and being corrupted" that was not merely expressive of a relationship between power and its object (domination and its morals) but was eminently socio-erotic, based on the calculation of enjoyment [le calcul des jouissances]. Colonial rule reinforced this tendency toward a libidinal investment in objects that were all the more desired as they were scarce, and instrumentalized to its profit this investment, which had characterized the exercise of power since the slave trade.[5] Without endorsing Mbembe's Lyotardian and Lacanian flights or historical overgeneralizations, we can agree that the historical exercise of power has given rise to a certain aesthetics of violence and excess, and that intense desires for material objects and wealth and the frustration of these desires appear to increasingly mark the moral economy of accumulation and power at work in the postcolony. The circumstances of Abacha's death and the nature of his rule provide an eloquent illustration of Mbembe's point: In the case of Abacha and his shrines and crocodiles, the link between "occultism," human sacrifice, libidinal excess, and theft could not be clearer.

Certainly, power's exercise in contemporary Nigeria is not one whose general operation follows a Western bio-political model, in which, with the birth of pastoral power, modern Europe passes from a power defined in terms of the capacity to "put to death and to let live" (the model of sovereignty under the monarchy) to one defined by the capacity to "give life and to let die."[6] I am not sure that one can endorse, for all that, Mbembe's characterization of the postcolonial exercise of power in terms of "necropolitics."[7] However, I agree with him when he argues that in its excess of violence and phantasmagorical projections, what he terms the "accursed share" of colonial rule has its logic in a sacrificial reason by which the indigene is transformed into an animal, a process that also involves the dehumanization of the colonizer. Mbembe sees this relationship as anchoring the roots of colonialism in an experience of death without reserves.[8] Through a contradictory process of "injury" and "healing," in terms of which the body is at once "stripped, enchained, forced to work, beaten, deported, put to death" and "healed, educated, dressed, fed and remunerated,"[9] this hybrid regime "concentrates the attributes of logic (reason), fantasy (the arbitrary) and cruelty. This administration of terror passes through a certain staging of true and false, a certain rationing of prebends and gratifications, the production of things at once moving, captivating and always spectacular," creating an emotional economy and a phantasmal apparatus whose cornerstone is the idea that "there is no limit to wealth and property, and thus desire."[10]

The problem of sovereignty in the exercise of colonial and postcolonial domination leads us to ask how its site is represented. If, in modern democracies, the site of the sovereign exercise of power is represented as an "empty place," one that cannot be incarnated and that no longer makes a gesture to an "outside,"[11] this is not the case in postcolonial Africa. Rather, as both Tonda and Mbembe point out, the "secret origin" of sovereignty in Africa is designated as an "elsewhere" and symbolized in the world of the invisible and supernatural. Since the colonial period, this world is indifferently symbolized by the power of God and by a formidable coalition of demonic forces, fashioned in the encounter between Christ, the witch, and the witch finder—a pantheon of pagan spirits, merchandise, writing, technology, and violence.[12] According to Mbembe, the rule of the elite has historically expressed a symbolic economy that has profound effects on the ways of thinking, acting, and living in the societies they dominate and pillage. "One of the pillars of this metaphysics of existence is the preponderant place accorded to the communicative state between the human being on the one hand and objects, nature and invisible forces on the other."[13] The division between a visible and occult world "accords supremacy to the domains of the invisible, secret origin of all sovereignty, and makes the human person perpetually the plaything of realities which are out of his reach. This absence of individual autonomy finds its most manifest expression in an economy of subordination whose forms have not ceased to vary and relay one another, to the extent that they now constitute what we must designate as the structure of servitude and auto-destruction."[14]

Domination does not historically occur only through control over productive labor, nor does accumulation depend principally on the extraction of surplus value through labor's overexploitation.[15] Forms of colonial subjectivation reveal the hybrid nature of colonial regimes; sovereignty is expressed as much by the power to kill and let live as it is in the power to make live and let die. Control over and conspicuous consumption of scare goods or goods of prestige—Western commodities and knowledge, women, children, and allies—are historically at the heart of local modes of domination, and Africans' investment in this hybrid economy was essential to colonial rule. As Mbembe points out, at its origin, "leaning upon the existence of a cult of fetishes whose essence was properly materialist and ceremonial (amulets, necklaces, pendants, costumes, charms, ornaments) a mercantilist ideology develops as a *power over life* (necromancy, invocation of spirits, witchcraft) and the figure of abundance."[16] "Wealth in people" implies the centrality of notions of social obligation and debt and the virtues of a redistributive economy that are central to longstanding modes of African accumulation and sociability, and yet such logics also refer to the possibility for power to accumulate persons through their (partial, at least) transformation into objects or commodities. As Mbembe puts it, corruption as both license and transgression functions over the long term as "an enormous social machine,"

in which as much at the summit as at the bottom of society, the relationship between goods of consumption and goods of prestige (women, children and allies) is conjugated in terms of a model of the penetration of merchandise into the soul of the subject. Why, under these conditions, should we be surprised that power ends up taking the form of a "dog-man" for whom theft is the same as the gift and that the relationship to people is reduced to a block of debts, as in the "ancestral" system? Why should we be surprised under these conditions that everything, even social violence, is formed in this relation of owed/debtor? Or again, trapped in the snares of the fetish, that we are unable to stop thinking that our death, like our destiny, arrives from outside?[17]

This cycle informs the nature of relationships of power at the micro-level of everyday sociability as well as at the macro-level of the insertion of African countries into the global economy. It stages the relationship between Africa and the world as one of debt for the theft of identity whose loss must be compensated. As Mbembe puts it, "this debt takes the double form of a debt of procreation (development) and of hospitality (immigration)."[18] In these articulations, the site of sovereignty is designated as an "elsewhere": a capricious power that subjects both individuals and groups and upon whose good or bad faith the future depends. Such an articulation fundamentally limits the possibilities of freedom, self-determination, and self-mastery. He cites as an example of subjection to this metaphysics of existence the ways in which the exercise of power and elite domination occur in a perpetual present. This entails, on the one hand, the inability to employ general strategies for remembering the past as other than a "history of sorcery" and enchantment, thus constructing forms of collective memory and patrimony that might structure the public space in such as way as to reappropriate the site of sovereignty. On the other hand, there is the total disdain for the very idea of the future, a characterization that resonates powerfully with the Nigerian context of the 1990s:

Everywhere dominates the perception in terms of which money, power and life are regulated by a law of chance. Immense fortunes are made from one day to the next, without the factors that have contributed to them being in any way apparent. Others disappear at the same rhythm without any visible cause. Nothing being certain, and everything being possible, one takes risks with money, as with bodies, power and life. Both time and death are reduced to a huge game of chance. On the one hand, a strong sense of the volatility and frivolity of money and fortune imposes itself, and on the other, a conception of time and value based on the instant.[19]

This description captures the contingency, the absolute uncertainty that had come to mark just about every relation, transaction, object, or value in Nigeria over the past twenty years.

Coupled with the extreme volatility and unpredictability of everyday life, and the development of increasingly criminalized and occult

forms of accumulation over the 1990s, we can observe a growing public obsession with unseen evil powers, which find its expression in dramatic public and publicized accounts, which stage new forms of wealth,
desire, and frustration in increasingly violent terms. The idiom of occult powers bursts into the Nigerian public sphere in an unprecedented
way in the early 1990s, increasing in intensity throughout the decade.
Although it was always part of popular discourse, from this period on
we see increasing references to a broad range of invisible and occult
forces in various public forums: from the mid-1990s the popular press
becomes rife with such stories, and even the national media increasingly report stories of occult practice, money medicine, transformations
of people into animals, and ritual murder. Press surveys undertaken on
six national dailies during an eight-month period between 1991 and
1992, and then again in 1998, showed a startling rise in reporting on
religious questions more generally. Apart from reports on secret cult activities in institutions of higher learning, no stories of money medicine,
the activities of witches or wizards, or other occult powers were found
in the national press in the period between 1991 and 1992. Altogether,
articles pertaining to religion more generally numbered fewer than five
hundred. In the eight-month period in 1998, the national press regularly reported on such topics, and the number of articles pertaining to
religion more generally numbered more than eight thousand. Popular
rumors circulated of occult powers, Mami Wata spirits, and other predatory invisible forces, giving rise to urban panics. Recent ethnographic
monographs tend to focus on local forms of witchcraft practice, which
are usually more or less tacitly understood to be longstanding and culturally highly specific.[20] And yet the representations projected in these
public forums are culturally unspecific, mixing various types and forms
under the category of "evil powers." Powders, charms, wizards, witches,
ancestor spirits, *orisa, obanje,* juju, Ifa, voodoo, Mami Wata, other water
or marine spirits, snakes, owls, vultures, crocodiles, cats, and other animals, but also a whole pantheon of biblical demons, as well as the occa-
sional reference to Indian and Egyptian deities; apparently, there is no
end to evil. Occult supernatural power is associated with the growing
criminality of the political economy: power, accumulation, and domination increasingly take the form of enchantment, exacerbating the instability between signs and their objects, the uncertainty of economic
and social value and the modes of its creation.

I have argued that the central force of the Born-Again program lay in
the ways it articulated the problem of subjection, radical uncertainty,
and corruption, as well as the elaboration of strategies for overcoming

the ordeal of life in the postcolony. The ordeal is not merely one of material hardship or the place of the individual or group in a long history of suffering and subjection; rather, it concerns the problem of regulating modes of conduct in a social, economic, and political universe marked by transgression and license, and the instability of signs and their referents. The relationship among salvation, wealth, and power has always been central to the Born-Again imaginary, as has the theme of corruption and its overcoming through the "new creation." Whether through an ethics of renunciation of the world and its pleasures, or through the deliberate affirmation and claiming of prosperity and success in the here and now, the question of desire and the relationship of the self to enjoyment and death are at the heart of the Born-Again ethic.

Born-Again processes of subjectivation rearticulate the relationships among accumulation, work, debt, and domination. The new individualism the movement gives rise to represents in many ways a revolutionary departure from the forms of social control and the cycle of debt and obligation that constitute these historical forms of subjection. However, the question of autonomy as it is articulated in Born-Again doctrine and practice is highly ambivalent. Processes of subjectivation stage the control and the channeling of desire as central to the problem of salvation and propose techniques of the self in terms of which such mastery may be obtained, liberation from debt and bondage guaranteed, yet this work is constantly interrupted by the action of supernatural forces beyond the self. The Born-Again imaginary, in elaborating a complex and contradictory economy of miracles, inscribes itself within occult forms of accumulation and power. The instantaneous production of value through the performance of miracles in many ways appears to mirror modes of the production of wealth and domination in the Nigerian political economy, a situation exacerbated by the shift from antimaterialism and the struggle against worldliness to the emphasis on salvation in the here and now. This economy of miracles both destabilizes pastoral authority and obedience to Born-Again prescriptions and renders the bid for pastoral charisma and institutionalized authority all the more acute. While Born-Again discourse and practice enables a rescripting of social debt, emancipating individuals from old forms of social control and obligation, it nonetheless fails to create the basis for a distinct identity or new modes of sociability in which trust and promises may find their guarantees. Its contradictory articulation of sovereignty appears to uphold, though in an ambivalent way, a long-standing moral economy of corruption and domination. The critical position of the Born-Again program with respect to a collective "history as sorcery," in which the past is represented in terms of subjection to untrammeled desire and infinite debt, reveals its instability. Through doing "God's work," the Born-Again project both questions this history and participates in its ongoing elaboration.

God's Work: Debt and Social Obligation

Born-Agains often use the term "doing God's work"[21] to refer to the activities they undertake in pursuit of their salvation. This term "work" is polysemic, and in its religious sense, it includes not only the work of evangelism and various activities undertaken within their church or ministry, but also tithing and giving. Of course, the principal workers in God's vineyard are pastors and evangelists; nonetheless, any activity can be couched in terms of "doing God's work," insofar as there is a self-conscious association between one's Born-Again faith and ways in which one practices both one's religious life and one's secular profession or other daily activities. At the same time, the term is used to refer to the fruits of conversion and divine miracles, which are spoken of as the signs of "God's work" in the life of the believer. Doing God's work also entails enacting His prescriptions concerning personal conduct and relations with others. It is through doing God's work that the messianic promise of "life" and "justice" may be realized. These promises are understood as "life more abundant," which takes the form of freedom from various forms of suffering and lack, and also as the reestablishment of trust and security in social relations and the creation of more just and equitable forms of community, as staged in the early model of the "fellowship."

From structures of family and ethnicity, age groups, and other longstanding forms of sociability and affectivity, the relationship among individual wealth, social obligation, and debt has been rescripted in Born-Again teachings, such that the individual is urged to transfer all of his or her social debts to God, who has "paid" for the convert's sins through the sacrifice of His Son. In this articulation, salvation and its fruits are a purely individual affair. "Blessings," financial or otherwise, are deliberately and explicitly detached from a redistributive economy based on kinship and ethnicity, particularly if one's extended family are not Born-Again. They are also explicitly opposed to the various financial obligations associated with these forms of sociability and distinction: spending on weddings or naming ceremonies, payment of bride price, costs of funerals and various "traditional" festivals and activities. Themes of a Protestant ethic from another era can be found in the countless sermons and teachings on the problem of "giving to the Lord" and "doing God's work" in order to "reap one's rewards," particularly in the teachings of churches that have continued to place an emphasis on holiness or living an exemplary life.

The central themes of these teachings focus on the importance of "work": a long labor of freeing oneself from sin; separating oneself from unbelievers; showing diligence, positive thinking, and determination; and giving cheerfully to both the gospel and those less fortunate.[22] "Separation from unbelievers" means not so much rejecting friends and family out of hand (not least because the first obligation of the convert is to evangelize and bring others to "the love of Christ") as separating oneself from the sorts of conduct practiced by the "unbeliever." Debt of all kinds is considered sinful: "God hates debt generally. That is why He gave his verdict on debt: 'Owe no man anything,' Romans 8:13. Literally, this verse discourages us from owing any man anything. By this we should not put ourselves under bondage of anyone. We shall be free of slavery of any man. God hates borrowing to meet our needs."[23] Debt is typically identified in sermons and teaching as being the result of "being yoked with unbelievers," failing to pay tithes, or desiring wealth for its own sake; laziness, carelessness, or inability to plan wisely and follow a budget; demonic oppression and curses; and especially lack of discipline: "Indiscipline is the instant gratification, desire or the lust which lurks in all of us and whispers, 'that is pretty, get it'; or 'that is a bargain; grab it'. Indiscipline leads us to do many things in excess. It leads to greed, covetousness, and pride. Indiscipline leads us to hold many worthless ceremonies. They would overspend on occasions like marriage, birthday, burial ceremony, annual festival etc."[24] Giving is essential—giving to the church through tithes and offerings, but also to the poor and needy. Nowhere is it ever stated that one's first obligation is to give to one's extended family: poor and needy are understood in a socially unspecific way. Giving must be done willingly and cheerfully and out of the sight of men.

Perhaps you have said, "If I don't give my offering through my church, I won't receive any credit for it." What sort of credit are you looking for? Do you want credit so that men will know that you have given it? If you are seeking credit with your church merely in order to have the praise and approval of men, then you are making a big mistake. Listen to the warnings of Matthew 6:1–2: "Take heed that you do not do your alms before men, to be seen of them: otherwise ye have no reward of your Father which is in heaven. Therefore when thou doest thine alms, do not sound a trumpet before thee, as the hypocrites do in the synagogues and in the streets, that they may have the glory of men."[25]

These models of conduct are in marked contrast to the modes of sociability prevalent in the postcolony, and distinct from Mbembe's characterizations. Even the most blatantly prosperity-oriented churches, such as Overcomers or Winner's Chapel (Bishop David Oyedepo), teach that prosperity depends on knowledge and application. As Oyedepo writes, "Wealth in the kingdom does not answer to prayers, nor does it have respect for fasting, it only answers to qualitative covenant exercises."[26] The great majority of ministries and fellowships continue to spread messages of self-overcoming through work, discipline, control of desire, prayer, and "waiting" on the Lord: "Jesus saw the dangers of prosperity and of material things. Possession of wealth constitutes two things in Christianity. 1. It is an acid test. Can you, as a rich man, bear it worthily in humility and service to God and your neighbour? A rich man should use his wealth in such a way as to show clearly his love for God and his neighbour. 2. It is a responsibility. A rich man should be judged by how he got his wealth, and what he is doing with it."[27] While failure to prosper can have as its causes curses and demonic oppression, deliverance is presented as a potential complement to the ethical work of the self on the self, and is not represented as standing in for it. And yet, without faith, none of this work can have any effect. Demonic oppression and failure to prosper generally is above all a failure of faith, as this exhortation to renounce the "superstitions and traditions of men" implies:

Do not believe in superstitions and traditions of men. This is a sin, it is a form of bondage. You cannot grow and prosper in sin and bondage. If your father or your husband tells you pregnant woman that you cannot come to night vigil because the demon is waiting to drive your baby out and replace it with demonic baby, that is a lie. You shall come to night vigil covered in the blood of Jesus, no demon can come near you. If people from your place come and say, don't eat that thing, you will bring wahala [trouble] on us, don't mind them. Eating anything cannot affect you. You are in a new family now, it will make you strong. When I was preaching in Ondo in the 1970s, the people there, they don't eat bush rodent. They would bring it to my house, I was frying it, eating it. I invited my Ministers one day to eat with me, they said, "the day we will eat this thing we will die! We are in another world eating our elders!" Who is your elder? WHO?! JESUS!! If you believe this superstition, it is a sin. The two brothers ate with me, and nothing happened. Now Ondo people are eating rodent, and nothing is happening. It has even become costly.[28]

In this rearticulation, the cycle of obligation and debt becomes increasingly unmoored from determined social relations, enabling the individual to break the links underwriting the prevailing forms of the longstanding metaphysics of subjection and an economy of subordination identified by Mbembe. Nonetheless, the mediation of the relationship between work and repayment, debt and obligation, by the capricious intervention of divine power creates the opportunity for the relay of this imaginary through new variations in the relationship between individual autonomy and supernatural sovereignty. In particular, the rise of the prosperity movement and the emphasis on miracles, increasingly realized through pastoral charisma, give the Born-Again moral economy an increasingly occult form. The holiness tendency still exists, and Deeper Life and RCCG remain the largest churches in the country, if not the continent. Yet the emphasis on salvation in the next world, which was so important in the first decade, has given way to an emphasis on salvation in the here and now and the performance of miracles. This shift in the teleology of conversion has implied a shift in the teleology of processes of moral subjectivation and the work of the self on the self, and opens up the space in which the prescriptive power of the Born-Again program begins to lose its "revolutionary" force. The degree to which converts conducted themselves with a strict respect for Born-Again values and codes weakened, and from the early 1990s it was increasingly possible to be "Born-Again from the waist up,"[29] applying in an ad hoc manner many of the moral prescriptions at the heart of the message. Increasingly, becoming Born-Again would be seen as a mode of tapping into spiritual power for one's personal protection and social mobility, rather than a means of radical ethical change through new modes of self-fashioning.

God's Money: New Forms of Accumulation and Prestige

IDAHOSA'S BURIAL EXTRAVAGANZA

- *N 1 million[30] casket flown in from US*
- *Buried in N 10 million all-marble tomb mausoleum*

The life and times of the late flamboyant Archbishop of Church of God Mission International Incorporated, Most Reverend Benson Andrew Idahosa, were characterized by glitz and glamor. His death and burial were no different. While alive, the renowned televangelist attracted people in multitudes. No less turned out to bid him a final farewell last weekend. The ancient city of Benin went agog for the grand burial of Idahosa which was tagged "Coronation to Eternal Glory." The great event—the like never witnessed in Benin for many years—began on Friday, April 3 at *Ogbe Stadium* with a Christian wake-keeping. The main bowl of the stadium could not contain the surging crowd, roughly estimated at thirty thousand people, as thousands were forced to observe the proceedings from outside the stadium. In the mammoth crowd there were top government officials, prominent ministers of God and other eminent Nigerians from various fields. . . . The arrival of the casket bearing the remains of the late man of God at exactly 10:10 a.m. caused a stir at the venue as everybody, including top government officials, bishops and other eminent citizens present struggled to catch a glimpse of the breath-taking casket. . . . The tomb where the highly respected and widely travelled archbishop was interred at his *Miracle Centre* was another attraction. Its construction cost was put around N 10 million [$120,000] and was designed by Architect A. N. Aweku of the University of Benin. . . . Engineer Mike Ugwu, who supervised the project, revealed that the tomb was made of specially ordered marble and Arabian tiles. To honour the late Archbishop were his associates from all walks of life including Bishops from Britain, United States, Ghana, and other West African States. Lt. Gen. J. T. Useni, honourable minister of the Federal Capital Territory, led the powerful Federal Government delegation, which also included the External Affairs Minister, Chief Tom Ikimi and the Chief of Naval Staff, Admiral Mike Akhigbe.[31]

Archbishop Benson Idahosa[32] is generally acknowledged as the pastor who brought the prosperity and faith gospel to Nigeria. With the assistance of the well-known American Pentecostal pastor Gordon Lindsay, he established what would become the first multibillion-naira Born-Again complex. At the time of his death, he had become a national figure, and media reporting of his early demise rivaled that of the pope's visit to Nigeria at the same time. President of the Pentecostal Fellowship of Nigeria, which under his tutelage had gone from a relatively marginal association to a dominant force within the Christian Association of Nigeria, in the years before his death he spoke out on issues of national concern, in particular the detention of political prisoners by the Abacha regime. Based in Benin City, he was reputed to have powerful influence in the politics of Bendel state during the late 1980s and in Edo state when it was carved out of Bendel in 1991. In this account of his funeral, found in a popular tabloid, material wealth abounds. The funeral cortège is described in lavish detail: the fleet of BMWs, Mercedes, and 4x4 vehicles preceding the six-door gold limousine carrying the deceased's wife Margaret. The inventory of Archbishop Benson Idahosa's empire, Church of God Mission International, Inc., enumerated in the article is no less impressive: the enormous Miracle Centre includes a stadium, a hospital, a private university, luxury guest residences, and a bank.[33] The Idahosa family also owns a huge shopping complex, and luxury villas in Nigeria, London, and the United States, as well as a fleet of luxury cars. Wealth "in people" follows: more than 30,000 mourners overflow the stadium, recalling the multitudes he attracted while still alive. He was described as "highly respected" and a "powerful man of God" who had traveled to numerous countries and had close ties to the most famous global Pentecostal leaders, and his wake was attended by many famous Pentecostal leaders from Britain, the United States, and across Africa, and a high-level delegation from Abacha's government.

Also in attendance at the wake and funeral were Nigeria's most powerful Born-Again prosperity pastors. In another article on the same page we read:

BURIAL FALLOUT: PASTORS IN FASHION CONTEST AT IDAHOSA'S FUNERAL
The fashion show of the pastors began on Friday evening at Ogbe Stadium, with the added display of exotic cars, most of which were in the siren-blasting entourage. Pastor Ayo Oritsejafor was no doubt at the burial to prove a lot of points. Dressed in new white cupion lace agbada with a matching pair of white slip-ons, he had a punk hair-cut on with expensive jewelleries to complement the outfit. The next day he stepped out in a well-tailored Italy delivered purple blazer, purple trouser, with a striking purple shoe, gracefully like a Saudi prince. . . . Bishop Elomobar became a jester of sorts. He took along different caps, which he changed about thrice. . . . Bishop David Oyedepo was a good match. He chose for Friday a new purple blazer, on a black pair of trousers and matching black Mauri shoes. On Saturday, he refused to be edged out of the show, stepping elegantly out in an orange suit (obviously new) with a matching pair of orange shoes.[34]

A distinct tone of irony seems to mark this extravagant language, which, were it intended, might refer to the increasingly ambivalent public status of these pastors. Associated with other figures of prestige and success in the popular press—political leaders, sports and music stars—from the late 1990s on these ultra-rich pastors inspired the same mixed feelings of admiration, fascination, and suspicion. Conspicuous consumption and flamboyant lifestyles went hand in hand with extravagant titles, such as "Archbishop," "Bishop," and "Reverend Doctor." At the same time the popular press has taken to publishing cover stories on a variety of scandals linked to leading Born-Again pastors, involving sex, money, fraud, schism, and dissension: "Idahosa in Messy Land Scandal: Oba of Benin Named"; "Pastor Anwuzia Again!

Wife Attacks Mistress"; "Oduyemi's Bethel Church Collapsing: Salaries, Nepa Bills Unpaid, Members Leave in Droves."[35] A whiff of scandal surrounded Idahosa's death: within days of the event, the papers were full of speculation about his successor, expected to be one of his righthand pastors and leading elders. To the surprise and consternation of many, it was finally his wife Margaret, better known for her commercial activities than for knowledge of the Holy Scripture, who officially took over the leadership. Clearly, the relationship among spiritual leadership, the community of the faithful, and private wealth had changed considerably throughout the preceding decade.

The advent of the doctrine of prosperity and the Word-Faith movement provided the discursive and symbolic platform on which to integrate the Born-Again experience of redemption with social mobility, conspicuous consumption, and the legitimation of wealth in a time of scarcity. As the revival progressed, leadership became the province of academics, as well as small-scale businessmen and the growing ranks of unemployed graduates. Their experience of the violence and hardship of urban life was tempered by their relatively privileged positions, and their opportunities for creating international linkages of their own through contact with Pentecostals from the United States and Europe helped to shift the Born-Again discourse from its association with the poor and the downtrodden. The stress on the retreat from "the world" was reduced, and wealth was increasingly understood as being the heritage of the true believer. Older holiness churches began adjusting their doctrinal emphasis and targeting new congregations. The Redeemed Christian Church of God is a case in point. From its poor Yoruba origins, it has experienced dizzying growth in the past two decades since Pastor Adeboye took over. While RCCG doctrine remains clearly on the holiness side of the spectrum, a new emphasis was placed on miracles. Throughout the late 1980s and 1990s Adeboye developed new, so-called "model" parishes in middle- and upper-class neighborhoods, with an educated, upper middle-class, ethnically mixed membership. These congregations fast outstripped the older, poorer "classical" parishes in influence. Born-Again strategies to gain access to the middle and upper classes included fellowship breakfasts at the five-star Eko Le Meridien Hotel and the inauguration of groups like the Christ the Redeemer's Friends Universal, a fellowship organization of the RCCG that requires potential members to have a postsecondary degree or diploma and that publishes a monthly magazine recounting the conversion stories and received miracles of leading businessmen, military officers, politicians, and civil servants. RCCG pastor Adeboye put it like this:

[The elite] need to see that Jesus Christ is not just for the poor alone, but for the rich, the accomplished, for those who have made it in life. And the Lord said, they will listen to me, knowing that, at least, I have a Ph.D. in mathematics. They will also listen to me because they know that fools don't get Ph.D. in mathematics. The main aim of Christ the Redeemer's Friends Universal is to make a forum available to the people who are high in society to mix together in the love of God. . . . I am sure we are also fully aware that the greatest darkness in any nation is always at the top. And if we can bring the light of Jesus Christ to the top, once all is well at the top, it will soon be well downstairs.[36]

Assistant pastorships seem to have become "prebendalized" in the same way public office has. Mrs. A. Williams, the director general of the Federal Ministry of Transport and Communications, became Born-Again in 1987 and attended the RCCG. A mere four years later, she became an assistant pastor, and the church had a solution to its transportation problems.

Following the new wave, throughout the 1990s literally tens of thousands of new churches sprang up across the urban South, with the greatest concentration found in Lagos. The prosperity churches ranged from small groups held in the compounds of private homes to huge multibillion-naira empires with thousands of parishes throughout Nigeria, Africa, and the world. Suddenly the possibility of achieving private wealth through God's work seemed within reach. Many pastors now possessed fleets of luxury cars; presided over marble-tiled, air-conditioned churches, with the latest sound systems and Windows XP on the office computers; and produced weekly televangelism shows where miracles and divine healing were staged. David Oyedepo is a bishop[37] and founder of Living Faith Outreach Worldwide, more popularly known as Winners Chapel. Reputedly one of Lagos' richest prosperity pastors, he bought an airplane in 1995. Scriptural citations were invariably invoked to justify these new acquisitions and wealth. When Pastor Kris Okotie bought his wife a new BMW automobile in 1992 to complement his own new Mercedes, he quoted James 1:17: "Every good gift and every perfect gift is from above, and cometh down from the Father of lights."

"Doing God's work" became a serious career option for many aspiring youth who were locked out of the classical networks and itineraries of social mobility and success. In this sense, founding a church "and "doing God's work" became a means of access not only to a new form of personal accumulation, but to a world of transnational connections, images, and imaginaries. In a marked departure from mainline Protestant and older Pentecostal churches, the model of church organization came increasingly to resemble that of small (or large) private enterprise, and an internal economy developed based on shared faith and new networks. Church activities proper were joined by subsidiary revenue-generating activities: the sale of media productions for the most part, but in the largest ministries, Bible colleges, private universities, banks, medical clinics, and on-line subscriptions. Approximately 80 percent of the churches and ministries founded throughout the late 1980s and 1990s have become de facto the private property of their founder-leaders. Ever since a landmark legal decision in 1998 in favor of a claim by the family of a deceased religious leader in Lagos against his followers who were living in properties amassed by the leader, they are now apparently de jure also.[38] In the light of this, we can better appreciate the logic behind Margaret Idahosa's new calling. That Idahosa's empire should stay in the family at his death and that pastor-founders should have strict control over church finances demonstrate the extent to which God's money and the private wealth of His anointed have become interchangeable. Many founder-pastors of smaller churches and fellowships run small private businesses on the side, such as publishing, travel agencies, small commerce and shops, advertising in the multitude of Born-Again magazines: "Jesus is our Lord—Catering is our Business." In the early 1990s a businessman's fellowship began producing an annual Christian Business Directory, which lists Born-Again churches and businesses in Lagos, enabling the discerning convert to chose commercial partners or service providers while still "walking with Christ." Similarly, professional fellowships grew up, with the purported aim of creating new Born-Again "best practices" in the professional world, but above all serving to create new networks within professional bodies. These include the Christian Lawyers Association, Christian Bankers Association, and a variety of Christian businessmen's associations on the model of the transnational Full Gospel Businessman's Fellowship. Here again we can see how Born-Again identity may be understood less in terms of institutional affiliation and more in terms of "vocation," through the application of Born-Again principles to every aspect of life.

The prosperity doctrine in its most explicit "name it and claim it" form was largely confined to Idahosa's empire and a relatively small group of churches in Lagos. Nonetheless, the success of these churches and the influence of the faith doctrine and the charismatic third wave of global Pentecostalism[39] encouraged other pastors to redouble their emphasis on miracles, creating a rush on churches and the multiplication of special evangelical rallies and revivals, which themselves became important opportunities for making money. Mega-rallies and revivals held by various powerful "anointed" men of God invariably promised miraculous healing, deliverance, and success, attracting millions of people from all social classes. My research assistant and I attended a special revival service at Glory Tabernacle in Ibadan in 1998, a church situated closer to the holiness than the prosperity end of the doctrinal spectrum.[40] During the service, preached by a well-known Lagos pastor invited especially for the occasion, pledges of more than 11 million naira (over $140,000) were made. Over the next three days nearly 7 million naira was actually handed over by those who had pledged, filling huge cardboard boxes. My assistant recognized one of his lecturers, who pledged 5,000 naira, while his monthly salary could not exceed 7,000. Apparently, by prearrangement, the guest preacher went home with 60 percent of the total takings. While transnational linkages are important, revenues are almost exclusively generated locally, even if the largest churches, such as RCCG, Church of God Mission/Winners Chapel, and Deeper Life now preside over global networks, new sorts of multinational enterprise.[41]

With the arrival of the prosperity gospel, money has become incontestably the most significant object in the creation of a common language, seen both as the mode of organizing churches and as the means of entering into contact with God. It is the symbolic object that links par excellence the struggle for the public space and individual communication with the sacred.[42] While tithes were central to the messages of the earlier holiness revival and Pentecostal doctrine generally, the relationship between salvation and money changed radically. Greater emphasis was placed on the necessity of paying 10 percent of one's monthly income for "God's work," and a direct relationship between giving and receiving blessings was increasingly made clear: as Idahosa's ministry motif put it, "Pay your tithe and receive your miracle." Exhortations to make "seed" offerings, in which the convert "seeds" a sum of money into the "work" of the gospel and can expect a "hundredfold return" became increasingly widespread. Through these developments, the very character of the divine changed, as this Overcomers pastor preached: "Your capital is Jesus. God is prosperity, salvation, deliver-

CHAPTER 5

ance and health. That is the meaning of the name of Jesus." During this sermon, the congregation also heard:

Life is not just "Jesus come and take me to heaven." Life consists of you and your possessions. Maybe some people here don't even tithe, come my friend, you are born to mammon. Give that ten percent! Divine change will happen in your life. The landlord will stop harassing you about your apartment, the chairman will give you a promotion, the clothes on your body will be the best ones. How many don't tithe? Stand up *now*! Who is the person who last month made 1 million Naira, who made 500,000 Naira, and has not paid their tithe? If you don't want to be poor for the rest of your life, pay your tithe now! [The pastor repeated this six times, but nobody stood.] We are living in the day of vengeance, you will come to me on your knees. Here in the church, there are not up to twenty people who pay their tithes [out of a congregation of about sixty].

. . . Idahosa is the light in a dark continent. Assemblies were there, Redeemed was there in the 1970s, but with Idahosa, the light begins to dawn. These pastors, they can think what they like about him, but they are jealous. There is nothing they can do to him.[43]

During the request for "seed offerings," the pastor called individuals to bring their "gifts" up to the altar, rather than using the standard practice of placing their money in a discreet and concealed fashion into a basket passed around, or remitting sealed envelopes. The pastor called out denominations, beginning with: "Who will give 200 Naira [$15] for the Lord?" and ending with, "Who can give 20 Naira? Don't be ashamed," urging people to come forward to applause. We can see with the rise of these charismatic "miracle" workers an attempt to impose pastoral control and develop an economy of power and prestige in which divine power and secular power become interchangeable and mutually supportive. This implies a significant shift from the days when a "call" meant privation and social stigma. While the movement continued to take up the themes of corruption and sin, in both their religious and politico-economic senses, the setting to work of the Born-Again discourse against corruption and the abuse of power and wealth became increasingly fraught with contradictions.

Spiritual Power and Occult Economies

Pastors may lose their legitimacy for sinful and "un-Christian behavior," but accusations against particularly successful leaders may also

claim that their power is from "another" source. As a worker in Idahosa's church remarked: "so many people think that the Archbishop is
just a magician, but they are wrong. The man simply inspires people,
he understands how to rouse the potent tool of faith in people for them
to use in achieving whatever they desire."[44] A video released in 1998,
entitled *Aworo* (Crowd Puller),[45] recounts the recourse to demonic activities and the use of charms by a Pentecostal pastor in order to draw
large crowds to his church and fill his private coffers. Tabloid newspapers publish testimonies of "occultic" experts and "wizards" who claim
to have given special powers to Pentecostal pastors to enable them to
perform miracles and draw in crowds.[46] In 1996 a huge scandal blew
up concerning a church in Bendel state where human skulls had been
found buried in the courtyard, prompting Idahosa, as leader of the Pentecostal Fellowship of Nigeria, to take out a two-page ad in the *Guardian*
newspaper defending the Pentecostals. The controversy over Pastor T. B.
Joshua, who claims to have cured hundreds of people miraculously
from cancer and AIDS in his Synagogue church, is a case in point. In
1998 an article in *The Week* newsweekly recounted the visit of a BBC
film crew to investigate the claims of miraculous healing coming from
the church: "From the countries of Austria, Italy, Holland, America,
France many people continue to troop out of the Synagogue with such
incredible testimonies. But a very big question remains to be answered.
Who is T. B. Joshua? Where is his power coming from? From God, or
the gods?" T. B. Joshua himself claimed his detractors were jealous,
and that "by their fruits ye shall know them."[47] Several prominent pastors have spoken out against Joshua, claiming that he is a "sorcerer"
and that his power is satanic. In July 2001 at a "summit" in Oyedepo's
Winners Chapel in Ota, leading Pentecostal pastors from Nigeria and
abroad gathered to condemn Joshua as an agent of Satan. Joshua's fame
has even created international controversy in global Pentecostal circles,
with well-known American pastors and institutions disputing the nature of his power.[48]

The attack by an enraged crowd on a branch of Overcomers church
in the southeastern city of Owerri in 1996 shows the confusion that has
developed between the itineraries of accumulation and success of certain pastors and the trajectories of a new generation of young ultra-rich
"businessmen." These businessmen are popularly understood as having achieved their wealth not only through criminal means (advance
fee fraud, abuse of confidence, drug dealing, fraudulent speculation,
corruption of various sorts) but also through ritual human sacrifice,
macabre trafficking in human body parts, contacts with secret societies

and cults, and pacts with powerful witches and other diabolical spirits. In Owerri, the drama began with the broadcasting on state television of the report of a man arrested for the murder of a child. The images showed the man holding the child's severed head for viewers to see, and the report ended with an appeal by the police for the identification of the child. The next day, the child's body was found in the grounds of a hotel owned by an extremely wealthy businessman where the arrested man worked. Very quickly things got out of hand. A huge crowd gathered and burned down the hotel and a series of other hotels and businesses belonging to other wealthy Owerri businessmen. The attacks continued on the next day, following rumors of other macabre "discoveries": a roasted human body found in one of the properties of a young Owerri millionaire, and in the compound of the Pentecostal church of which he was a member (a local branch of Overcomers), human skulls and a pot of "pepper soup with human flesh." The millionaire's house and business were torched, as well as the Overcomers church, its pastor's house and several other Pentecostal churches. Before the Nigerian army intervened to restore order to the city, more than twenty-five buildings and dozens of vehicles had been burned. As Daniel Smith shows in his analysis of these events, the riots in Owerri were presented as a form of religious purification. The destruction of goods and property was viewed as a popular revolt against an association of evils: child abduction, ritual murder, and instant wealth.[49]

Obsession with falsification and fraud gathered momentum throughout the 1980s and 1990s. Advance fee fraud and a range of confidence tricks involving forgery and impersonation, covered under the article 419 of the criminal code, developed with the deregulation of the banking and foreign exchange system under Babangida's Structural Adjustment Programme from the late 1980s. As Apter argues, "419" became the symbol of a "world-as-misrepresentation"[50] in terms of economic, social, and political practice, as well as the second or third source of foreign exchange in the country throughout the 1990s (after oil, and either before or after narcotics trafficking).[51] Pentecostal pastors were not exempt from these new forms of criminality. Idahosa advocated the trial and jailing of some three hundred pastors involved in a fraudulent "money doubling" investment scam in Benin City in 1993, and in 2001 a certain Bible-quoting Pastor Samuel Power duped thousands of individuals into investing in a fraudulent pyramid scheme, making off with over 2.5 million naira ($19,000).[52] Alongside the problem of falsified identities, the uncertain origins of wealth and its increasingly socially unproductive nature gave rise to a public obsession with invisible and dangerous occult forces and evil ritual practice. The problem of falsification, the origins and value of wealth, and the use and abuse of power were central themes of stories of "money medicine" that abounded throughout the 1990s, relating actual practices in which human blood and body parts were trafficked in macabre rituals for the creation of instant wealth. While many of these stories no doubt arise from the fertile imaginaries of popular urban rumor, nonetheless, the police and the press documented a growing number of cases over this period. On the Ikorodu road in Lagos in April 1998, I witnessed the mutilated body of a dead woman whose breasts had been cut off: the explanation offered by those travelling with me was that this was a case of money medicine.[53] In January 1998, the front cover of *Fame* showed grisly pictures of a woman, and the cover of *Today's Choice*, in the following month, displayed a man's body; both were victims whose eyes had been gouged out for the purposes of "money medicine."

The Nigerian video boom of the 1990s was largely consecrated to staging these activities and those of a wide variety of evil occult forces.[54] While its origins are linked to Born-Again circles, and while many of its idioms draw upon Born-Again accounts of satanic activities and their staging in video productions, the video boom in the South has developed beyond a religious genre, and many productions no longer promote a clear evangelical message. One of the biggest blockbusters of the decade, *Blood Money I* and *II*, tells the story of "Mike" and his involvement in the "vulture cult," involving human sacrifice, the transformation of men into vultures, and the transformation of children into chickens who vomit money. *Egba Orun* (The Necklace), a Yoruba movie, takes up the story of a woman who uses her own daughter in a similar money-making ritual. *Sacred* is described in the tabloid press as exploring "the theme of voodooism where one Chief Austin through diabolical means strips his apprentices of their good fortunes using a bewitched cat."[55] The popularity of such films, some of which are shown on state and private television and in old theaters that have been converted to video projection cinemas, goes far beyond the urban viewing public. Even people who do not have access to television or VCRs are aware of the latest releases and their plots. Urban rumor takes up the themes of these films, and the films themselves are inspired by stories already in circulation. For example, stories about the "vulture cult" abounded between 1998 and 2000; one of my friends told me a version in which two men had joined up to make money and had ended up being stuck in their vulture form.

For the most part, these films are not understood as allegories or fanciful representations, but rather as accounts of real-life events. More-over, like their predecessors in the live theater and the Born-Again film industry, the producers believe that they are imparting an important moral message. In an interview, the producer of *Sacred* tells *Today's Choice*: "Arts must not be for sheer entertainment, it must be responsi-ble and must have corrective tendency on the society, pointing out the evils therein. . . . Such people like Chief Austin exist, in every society in the country, whose evil powers subvert fortunes of their apprentices, tenants etc. *Sacred* is a true life story, and not a figment of someone's imagination. It's a reality. Go to every society, you see it in one form or another. The victims of such misfortune are still alive, if any con-troversy surfaces, I can produce concrete evidence."[56] In these films, as in the various stories circulating in the press and urban rumors, the overriding theme is excessive riches obtained from evil occult power— riches that are seen as antisocial, destructive, and ultimately unprofit-able. The protagonists are depicted as greedy and selfish individualists who refuse to share their wealth, sacrificing family ties (literally sacri-ficing family members) and normal social relations to further their dia-bolical and insatiable lust for power and money. At the same time, the stories engage in an increasingly vocal condemnation of elite practices through the demonization of occult and secret power and the acquisi-tion of illicit and excessive wealth. And as the events in Owerri show, certain forms of Born-Again practice are seen as inscribed within this occult economy.

The success of these prosperity pastors and the multiplication of new churches and ministries had profound effects on both the public per-ception of the Born-Again movement and the imaginary of salvation. The Born-Agains who succeed, or those who want to launder or purify already-obtained wealth, now display their "election" and transforma-tion through material wealth and conspicuous consumption. In this case, how can they be distinguished from others who have succeeded through "sin" and connections with occult powers? The same may be asked concerning the powerful men of God. The direct relationship es-tablished between God's power, whose vessels they claim to be, and their power to attract crowds, heal the sick, and bestow miraculous wealth and success becomes increasingly ambivalent, especially as the conduct of many of these pastors and converts who appear to incarnate this new form of salvation is far from exemplary. With the growing dis-parity between the social prestige, status, and wealth of pastors, on the one hand, and the fortunes of their congregations, on the other, the theodicy in terms of which sin is understood as being responsible for affliction in the here and now becomes increasingly unstable.

The verse "by their fruits ye shall know them"[57] is perpetually repeated by Born-Agains, as the mode in which both the reality of miracles and the conduct of others may be evaluated and spiritual authority grounded, linking the experience of faith to the normative prescriptions of doctrine. As we have seen, it locates the site of this truth-telling and discernment between true and false in the subject's capacity for perception and the exercise of the "spirit of discernment," a faculty in which both revelation and judgment are merged. This mode of veridiction increasingly frames the question of *what* is to be governed in an ambivalent way, such that the object of governance oscillates between the self and the world of unseen and chaotic powers. The problem of verifying the "signs following" thus hangs between a conception that locates the fruits of conversion as arising from the work of the self on the self, and one that interprets it purely as the intervention of supernatural power, as a sign of grace as evidenced in personal miracles, or else as the sign of spiritual corruption by evil powers.

If salvation is considered possible and desirable in the here and now, if pastoral or institutional authority is always unstable and never fully instituted (notwithstanding the powerful modes in which narrative may be structured and diffused), if the ultimate arbiter lies in the individual perception of the nature of spiritual power, and if we should know "them" by their "fruits," what sort of criteria of discernment should be used when the "fruits" become power, wealth, and success in the here and now? This contradiction is only deepened by the increasing emphasis on financial miracles and pastoral anointing and power, as well as struggles against this power, the fragmentation of the community, and the dispersion of the message. When one examines the various teachings, whether oriented toward holiness and the rapture, or toward prosperity in the here and now, the techniques to be applied and the conduct according to which Born-Agains are exhorted to live their lives are invariably at odds with the message of instant wealth and gratification. In Born-Again discourse, wealth, social mobility, health—in short, the satisfaction of worldly desires—constitute the weapon the devil uses to lure souls from the straight and narrow path. These are desires that lead to jealousy, hatred, greed, exploitation, bondage, and antisocial and immoral behavior. If the devil works miracles, it is only through an ethics of submission and obedience, in the form of a control over desire and the rejection of its various objects, that the distinction between the manifestation of spiritual power that saves and the power that brings death may be made. Yet increasingly, salvation is likewise expressed via the realization of these same desires. The prosperity gospel in its most extreme forms reduces the work of the self to the simple ritual act of conversion and the giving of money for "God's work"; the fruits of conversion having been prepared in advance, all the believer has to do is to "name them and claim them." Supernatural power becomes the preserve of those who are able to harness it for the performance of miracles of prosperity and success, creating a circular economy in which enchantment and debt reappear in the relationship between pastoral charisma and converts' obedience. Pastoral power becomes a form of enchantment, and mirrors in many ways the exercise of power on the part of the political elite. The long-standing phantasmal apparatus and emotional economy in which there is no limit to prosperity (and thus to desire) finds its clear rearticulation within the prosperity gospel, such that Idahosa or others may be seen as "magicians" who will enable people to "achieve whatever they desire." The "potent tool of faith" is increasingly dislocated from the work of self-fashioning, and the autonomy of the individual suspended on the performance of the thaumaturge. And yet, this development was implicit from the outset of the revival through the emphasis on miracles.

Miracles: Between Grace and Works

Corten refers to Hobbes's discussion of miracles to analyze how miracles themselves compel obedience and create forms of subjection to power. He argues convincingly that within Pentecostalism, miracles manufacture obedience through the staging of a verisimilitude by repetition of testimony: obedience is "constructed through this infinitely repeatable discourse"[58] and not, as Hobbes argued, through the power of the sovereign to pronounce and guarantee their reality.[59] Hobbes's argument makes the distinction between private conscience and public reason, and submits the former to the latter in the matter of determining the "real." We can see in the case of both Nigerian and global Pentecostalism the difficulty inherent in such processes of veridiction for anchoring the authoritative knowledge essential for the stabilization of the Born-Again ethic. If this destabilization occurs through the agonistic relations that Born-Again practice establishes with prevailing forms of knowledge and techniques of power in the postcolony, at the same time, this instability was already present in its internal articulations. The centrality of testimony about miracles to the performance of individual faith reveals the ongoing tension between "love" and "work," and gives rise to lines of flight.

The Pentecostal model for the relationship between the "law" (or doctrinal prescriptions and moral codes) and "faith" is the one established in the New Covenant between Christ and those who proclaim Him: "this cup is the New Covenant in my blood" (1 Cor. 11:25). In the Old Covenant between Moses and God, the promise between God and the people of Israel took the form of a contract, which was dependent upon their careful following of His commandments, any infraction being punished by His wrath and vengeance. Here we see the importance of the pact that establishes a relationship between God and his people in which faithfulness on both sides takes the form of an exchange. In the New Covenant, however, it is faith, not observance of the law, that guarantees salvation, as outlined in Romans 3:20–25, 28: "Therefore by the deeds of the law there shall no flesh be declared righteous in his sight: for by the laws is the knowledge of sin. For all have sinned and all have come short of the glory of God; being declared righteous without any cost by his grace through the redemption that is in Christ Jesus; whom God hath set forth to be a propitiation through faith in his blood, to demonstrate his righteousness for the passing over of sins, through the forbearance of God. . . . Therefore we conclude that a man is declared righteous by faith without the deeds of the law." The central element in these verses is "being declared righteous without any cost by his grace through the redemption that is Christ Jesus." The original debt in "for all have sinned" is one from which the sinner can never fully extricate him- or herself except by the gift of grace.[60] "Being declared righteous without any cost" refers to the ways in which divine grace takes the form of a gift or service without counter-service: what Derrida calls "the impossible gift."[61] Verse 31 shows, however, that justification by faith does not overturn the law, but rather fulfills it: "Do we then make void the law through faith? God forbid: yea, we fulfil it." Agamben argues that in the Pauline messianic doctrine, it is not so much a matter of excluding works in favor of faith, but of coming to terms with the aporia that emerges from this rupture: the promise of grace "exceeds any claim that could supposedly ground itself in it. . . . gratuitousness does not provide the grounds for obligatory service. Instead, it manifests itself as an irreducible excess with regard to obligatory service. Grace does not provide the foundation for exchange and social obligations; it makes for their interruption."[62] Throughout the history of Christianity, the debate about the role of grace in relation to works and faith has been central. While the Pauline doctrine presents grace as the "impossible gift," impervious to outlay or expenditure, the historical church admits a relative form of grace, in order to justify the persistence of sin and reestablish the link between faith and obedience to doctrine and rules of conduct, thus reinserting grace into an economy of exchange. In the Born-Again imaginary, whether miracles are represented as being based on God's grace as His means of bringing unbelievers to Him, or as a reward for a sin-free life, or indeed, as the result of having contributed financially to His work, the miracle is nonetheless reinserted into a circular economy of desire and its gratification. In the prosperity articulation, the "impossible gift" takes the economic form of exchange: the payment of debt by the convert in a circular economy through actual monetary payment and the giving of time and labor to the new religious community and its leaders. Even when the relationship between labor and value that is created by the miracle is associated with present sacrifice and discipline as the guarantee for a future salvation, the miracle is not understood as a gift. It is not seen as an absolute form of value that is "heterogeneous to outlay or investment," but as part of an "economy of retribution, or equal exchange."[63] As Pastor Kumuyi points out, the miracle is supposed to function as a sign of power, as a technique of making believe, as a means to an end. And yet, this articulation obscures the nature of the miracle and its constitutive powers. The time of the miracle is always the messianic *now:* a miracle by definition breaks into history, snapping the thread of time and causality; it is a *mystery.* It cannot be reinserted into an economy of exchange in such a way as to stabilize either obedience or autonomy without some external institution or authority that can serve to incarnate or dispense it, as in Hobbes's model.

Grace as evidenced through the performance of miracles works both to shore up pastoral charisma and authority, and also to undo them. Despite the influence of a small group of pastors, with the new-wave multiplication of institutions and the dispersion of sites for the enunciation of the message, we are not generally in the presence of individuals whose charisma commands obedience. Rather, there is an ongoing democratization of spiritual power, which pushes pastors seeking a clientele to make ever more ambitious claims to miraculous exploits: telling fantastic stories of healing from paralysis, blindness, cancer, or AIDS, and even resurrection from the dead, in many cases providing medical certificates to prove the reality of these miracles.[64] Here we have a case of mixed epistemological registers that shows the extent to which various forms of knowledge and power are combined in the attempt to create the basis for the authority to determine the "real." Yet rather than demonstrating the authoritative nature of pastoral power, this recourse to medical expertise reveals instead its precarious nature. Outspoken pastor Tunde Bakare of the Latter Rain Assembly claims that while there is no Christianity without miracles, "they are not to be employed to advertise ourselves and to make a name for ourselves. All the miracles Jesus did most of the times, he would say, go and tell nobody about it. There is no miracle-worker except the Holy Spirit and whenever a person becomes a miracle-worker, then I suspect his source of power."[65] The Nigerian federal state through the Nigerian Broadcasting Commission intervened in 2004 to ban "unverifiable miracles" on Nigerian state television, accusing televangelists of defrauding the public, and thereby giving Hobbes's advice an unlikely twenty-first-century application. The ban gave rise to much debate about the role of the state in determining which miracles could be considered true and which false, especially as no criteria were proposed by the NBC in terms of which such decisions might be made. While state broadcasting services were disgruntled at the anticipated losses of considerable revenue, and some ministries directly indicted sought to challenge the ban in court,[66] the great majority of pastors and the Born-Again population were not bothered by the ban, as neither the state nor pastors could be seen as incarnating the sovereign authority who might pronounce on their truth or falsity. As one Born-Again evangelist put it: "I know that anything that has original also has fake. The ban has its advantages and disadvantages. With or without the ban, people must be saved. If the miracles are real, it will be good to encourage people, if fake, then God will disgrace the miracle performers. The ban is a way to control things. People now see miracle as the easiest way to reach God. If you go to this place, you will receive miracles. Nobody tries to know if the miracle is coming from God or not. The ban is good so people will seek God instead of miracles."[67] The problem of the "world-as-misrepresentation,"[68] of a metaphysics of existence based on untrammeled power and desire, is by no means resolved in the development of the Born-Again program; indeed, it appears exacerbated by it.

All these "whassupians,"[69] these prosperity people, they are not serious Christians. Now we see many rich people in the church today. Maybe you want to see the pastor, there are many people waiting to see him. But maybe somebody with a car, they'll just drive up and push you out the way, because they think they have the right, they just treat you like a small boy, because we're so impatient in this country.

We must have everything now, we don't want to suffer. They worship money, but the white man [missionary] doesn't worship money, it's people he serves. The white man is patient, but the black man can't wait, it's in his blood to worship money, to be impatient, this is the problem we have in Africa. The black man doesn't want to suffer for the Lord, but the white man will suffer, he will go to the village, eat food that the black man can never eat, even a place you must trek ten miles before you can see car, the black man can never do this, he wants things to be fine. The problem with us is that among those who call themselves Christians, only ten percent are really born-again through Christ. Many are tainted with occultic sciences, they have this belief you can talk to God in the air. It's not God you are talking to. They think they can have money and miracles just by talking to the air. The old gods still have power, Lucifer, when he was cast down from heaven, still had power. Satan will do something for you immediately when you ask, to prove he has power, but with God, we must have patience and be diligent.[70]

The ambivalence and excess of meaning that the supernatural embodies also interrupts the institution of a Born-Again ethic of community and the new forms of egalitarian social exchange that were practiced in the early interdenominational groups. The rejection of the codes, rules, and rituals underlying longstanding forms of sociability, "the traditions of men," in favor of the "new family" enables the convert to extricate him- or herself from old forms of social reciprocity and obligation. And yet the communities established through the experience of conversion do not foster a strong sense of belonging or identity; identification is diffuse and transnationalized, religious itineraries are marked by multiple affiliations, and relationships of reciprocity are relatively loose and impersonal. The reconstitution of social relationships through the community of the saved, through collective experiences of prayer, worship, testimony, new professional networks, and other new forms of sociability, such as fellowships and associations, is also offset by the violence with which the program of conversion restructures the relationship among social obligation, affectivity and debt, as the story of the mediated TV healing miracle related in chapter 4 shows: "your family will love you and kill you." Indeed, central to many testimonies are the various personal trials and difficulties converts had to overcome at the hands of family members, employers, neighbors, and friends in the face of their new faith and changed lifestyles. Yet the new form of "individualism" is nonetheless experienced as an opportunity and form of liberation by the great majority of converts. As I have argued, it is one of the possibilities that have made the Born-Again project both pertinent and plausible for individuals facing the ordeal of urban life.

It expresses a quest for new forms of subjectivity, an attempt to liberate the self from forms of power that tie the self to the self in immediate, everyday life.

However, the experience of liberation and individual autonomy nonetheless engages with the relations of power and domination prevalent in Nigeria, underwriting relations of subjection and exacerbating uncertainty about strangers and others in general. Because there is no authoritative way to identify the source of supernatural power, converts cannot be sure that they or their neighbors are free from satanic influence. Hence arises the need to exorcise personal experiences of satanic affliction through public rituals of deliverance, and to interpret such experiences in terms not only of individual moral failure, but of the dangers posed by "enemies." The struggle to secure certainty, to institute the bases for new forms of social exchange and trust, is thus permanently interrupted by the omnipresent possibility of evil powers, and the exhortation to "love thy neighbor as thyself" is overcome by the necessity of discerning, convicting, and overcoming the evil the neighbor may be harboring with or without his or her knowledge.

The problem of discernment and the impossibility of securing the authoritative knowledge that could provide the grounds for trust and security in social relations are evidenced by the ever-present testimony of spiritual warfare against the legions of evil spirits that block access to success, health, wealth, and salvation. In many accounts these evil spirits are represented as being capable of acting against the individual even if he or she is living a spotless life. In earlier testimonies, Born-Agains were protected automatically: "Born-Again Christians have divine powers surrounding them which no demonic power can pierce."[71] Testimonies and sermons from the mid-1990s speak of dangerous contacts with and "initiations" by evil powers that converts may have contracted without their knowledge: through dreams, food, material objects, television, anodyne physical contact with strangers in public places, or "pacts" made by family members, even several generations removed, through "traditional" rituals and practice. It is interesting to note that since the mid-1990s, much less emphasis has been placed on the inherent dangers of luxury objects and wealth. A whole clutch of books and teachings warn the convert about the devil's traps and explain various techniques for identifying and protecting oneself from them: for example, techniques for the interpretation of dreams; means for discerning the presence of various types of evil spirits depending on whether one has dreamed of water, food, or sexual relations; the prayers to be said in each case; bodily positions to take while praying; and the means for casting out these spirits and preventing their return.[72] In one booklet, *Satanic Immigration Officers,* we can read about the multitude of evil spirits (more than fifty thousand of them!) that attack individuals and block the flow of prosperity and miracles in his or her life. In a delightful rendering of the corruption experienced at borders, the author explains how "evil officers" stop the individual at "spiritual roadblocks" and ask him or her, "wetin you dey carry?" in order to seize it from him.[73] In these circumstances, deliverance assumes a new significance, and the growing recourse to it shows that the relationship between the application of techniques of the self and the experience of divine power is increasingly problematic. The network of motivated practices and techniques of the self by which the presence of God is to be manifested appears increasingly ineffective, and divine power shows itself to be more and more ambivalent and capricious. At the level of individual practice, the language in which the Evil One who threatens the convert's salvation and prosperity is "convicted" and "destroyed" also demonstrates the violence at the heart of this engagement. In this prayer guide the convert is given prayers to "castigate the conspirators":[74]

Father I thank you because sinners will not go unpunished.

1. Let all rumour mongers be ruined. Ez. 7:26
2. It is my turn to enjoy, let all opponents keep quiet. Eccl. 3:13
3. Let all the rebels in my dwelling place and office dwell in dry places. Ps. 68:6
4. Hunger killed the forty men that conspired against Paul, let all conspirators die of hunger. Acts 23:13
5. Ahitophel hanged himself, let all conspirators hang themselves. 2 Sam. 17:23
6. Make slave of anyone that wants to rob me of my vision. Gen. 50:18
7. All the conspirators in my extended family, be scattered in Jesus' name. I Sam. 7:10

This struggle also shows how the engagement with the demonic becomes itself an ecstatic experience, central to the performative power of faith, as revealed in endless triumphant testimonies to the miraculous protective powers of God.

The Born-Again program thus cannot be seen as developing an unambiguous critical response or form of "counter-conduct" to postcolonial modes of accumulation and domination. But at the same time, it does not simply reproduce old structures of subjection and enchantment, or provide evidence for the "revenge of paganisim." In his magisterial study of divine healing in colonial and postcolonial Gabon and Congo, Tonda offers a powerful argument that shows how the "great division"—that ethnocentric and culturalist distinction which opposes the civilizing mission and the *"génie sorcier"*[75] (spirit of witchcraft)— constitutes a form of theodicy in which the Christian God is removed from the historical structuring of African misfortune. In the "revenge of paganism" accounts,[76] the answer to the question "Whom do converts believe in and obey in the sites of divine healing and why?" is given as "the *Génie Sorcier* of paganism who has enrolled by force the Devil's legions. God has nothing to do with this affair."[77] In Tonda's account, contemporary Christian effervescence is the result of the setting to work of "God's capital" under the domination of what he terms the "Modern Sovereign."[78] Here "capital' is symbolized indifferently by the "spirit of Christ, money, science, technology, witchcraft, the colonial and neo-colonial state." Tonda's rich and compelling account shows how the colonial encounter gave rise to the production of new forms of practice and imaginary significations in which the *"Genie du Blanc"* and the *"Genie Sorcier"* coalesce through a relationship of forces. Tonda's central concern is to develop a sociology of domination, showing through his analysis how "the power at work in divine healing" constitutes a form of subjection to the "Modern Sovereign" through an obedience to pastoral authority established through the performance of miracles of healing.[79] And yet it is precisely the instability of this authority that enables us to read processes of subjectivation as more ambivalent than in his account, which to my mind overemphasizes the powers of subjection to pastoral authority and ultimately to an "ethnocentric God" who will civilize the fallen black man through conversion. Tonda asks the same question as Mbembe: "What in the world today allows the 'overcoming of the African man'?"[80] For Tonda, the meaning of this question is fundamentally negative, for he intends it to signify the destruction of social worlds and the direct participation of the civilizing mission and the Christian God in a history of affliction. For Tonda, the demonization of the witch and the occult in Christian practice involves the devalorization of autochthonous spirits, part of a process of their conversion and submission. The "God that counts" is "the God of the people that count: money, merchandise, and who read."

The demonization of the past and of "autochthonous" spirits in whatever form they take today is central to the message of conversion and overcoming, as is the deconstruction of old forms of sociability and solidarity. It involves a real violence done to memory, a violence that participates in a political project of reordering the present and imagining the future. But at the same time, these forms themselves have been profoundly structured by colonial and postcolonial relations of power. The famous "group solidarity" based on kinship and infinite debt figures in many African accounts of the self as a form of bondage, and has participated in no small way in the history of African auto-subjection. If history is a memory that flashes up in a moment of danger,[81] what is the danger to which a politics of memory as nostalgia and loss responds? And what are those that it ignores? If the desperate search to give a new account of oneself seems increasingly urgent in Africa today, this nostalgia is nonetheless tainted with the bad faith of nativism and the desire for an authenticity that refuses the possibility of African access to a universal. This discourse arises from the perpetual contrast drawn between African modes of being and doing and those of its "Other," a contrast that "enables the subject to inhabit several worlds and to place him- or herself on two sides of the same image simultaneously."[82] It takes on a distinct form in terms of which the African subject writes himself as a victim of history and in which the recourse to a discourse of African authenticity, rather than being a form of African emancipation, entails the endorsement of the objectifications that make up the field of colonial representation of African societies. That the loss of the self and its travesty by colonial violence is lived as a form of affliction is certain, but so it is that today, the relations this form of domination have created are experienced by many as an unbearable burden. The various programs of government that have been introduced to Africa from the outside—from the colonial dispensation and the civilizing mission of Christianity to the development complex and global capitalism—have had overwhelming effects on the exercise of African sovereignty, such that the site of sovereignty is designated as an "elsewhere." This is evident at the national level, where the conditions imposed by Bretton Woods make a nonsense of the notion of a sovereign state;[83] at the village level, where local state offices are popularly referred to as the "white man's country";[84] and in the reinforcement of supremacy of the world of the supernatural. And yet, we should not ask how such "contamination" may be undone, because as Mudimbe so clearly argues, such a project is mere utopia.[85] The question is to understand the ways in which, within a historical ordering whose effects are solid and expressed throughout the social body, the African attempt to gain access to a universal and achieve a form of sovereignty as expressed through the Born-Again program may be more than simply a new relay for these forms of subjection. It may also be seen as an "event" of deconstruction or reinvention, "a power confiscated, a vocabulary appropriated and turned against its users, a domination which weakens, relaxes its hold, poisons itself, another which makes its masked entry,"[86] remembering that "the forces which are at play in history follow neither a destination nor a mechanic, but rather the hazard of struggle."[87]

Nigerian Pentecostals attempt to redeem the promises made and ruined through colonial missionary practice. This project entails an engagement with the past and present that resolutely refuses the discourse of authenticity in the forms in which it has structured African accounts of the self and of historical affliction. But at the same time, the results are highly ambivalent: the story of God's money and the occult economies with which it engages and that it itself creates can be read as a tale of exploitation, domination, and enchantment, just as it can be seen as one of liberation from bondage and debt. As Mbembe argues, Christianity establishes a new relationship between the world of paganism and the world of the promise of redemption, a set of ideas that "because of their ability to enchant, can be defined as magico-poetic." Conversion to revealed truth entails "the abolition of a dissolute existence (tradition and custom)" and "a genuine work on the self (*travail sur soi*), the erasure of any distinct and separate identity, the abolition of difference, and the adherence to the project of a universal humanity."[88] Such an adherence necessarily involves violence, but it may be seen as a violence that responds to another violence, an agonistic relation of struggle. Its political effects are nothing if not contradictory.

The Born-Again ethic and processes of subjectivation in Nigeria are fundamentally ambivalent. They are articulated within the "solidified structure of relations" that make up the Nigerian present, yet within this general framework, the ways in which the various relationships between the individual and his or her desires and the structures of economic exploitation and political domination are played out are multiple and contradictory. Born-Again practices of power and of the self shore up an occult economy of instant gratification and violence and at the same time provide the means for undermining and overcoming it. Indeed, we can argue that rather than merely revitalizing witchcraft— understood in its older ethnographic form as the response to excessive individualism and the subversion of "communal values"—what Pentecostalism does, in staging dramatic showdowns between the power of the Holy Spirit and demonic powers, is to create new objectifications that problematize for individuals the very question of the real and the thinkable, the past, present, and future, making them objects of reflection and individual discernment. This objectifying practice, it should be pointed out, is by no means unique to Nigerian Pentecostalism, for a similar process of questioning the forms and structures of a Western experience of modernity occurs within the Pentecostal discourse in Europe and America. This is not to deny that its effects in Nigeria are both unique and violent.

The proposition of Born-Again Christianity entails the revitalization of the fetish of the past, of "history as sorcery," not merely as a means to assure the domination of its own project, but also as the possibility of an overcoming. When Dr. Beko Ransome-Kuti, a leading human rights and prodemocracy activist incarcerated by Abacha, says, "The fellow was the devil incarnate. A devil cannot do worse than what he has done. A devil cannot do worse,"[89] are we to read this characterization of his rule as yet another ruse of the Modern Sovereign? Distinctions of good and evil, pure and impure, just and unjust are not written only in a predetermined script whose morality mirrors that of Nietzsche's slave. Both the Holy Spirit and the possibility of the resurrection of the dead are, as Mbembe argues, "powers of enchantment and symbolisation" that are used as an inexhaustible resource. "They are powers that enable the believer to think of his or her existence not in a purely politico-instrumental way, but as an artistic gesture and an aesthetic project open as much to action as to meditation and contemplation."[90] This observation in no way entails removing the Christian God from the experience of African affliction or subjection. Born-Again processes of subjectivation participate in the same forms of falsification, arising from the same epistemological and ontological instability as do the spirits of the postcolonial political economy. They are also at times nightmarish in the possibilities of violence they may sanction. The message of the new birth and "making a complete break with the past" involves a promise of redemption, but it also reminds us, as Jesus says in Luke 12:51–53, "Suppose ye that I am come to give peace on earth? I tell you Nay; but rather division. For henceforth there shall be five in one house divided, three against two, and two against three. The father shall be divided against the son, and the son against the father; the mother against the daughter; and the daughter against the mother; the mother in law against her daughter in law, and the daughter in law against her mother in law."

SIX

The Politics of Conviction

In February 1993, five months before the annulled presidential elections, at the second biennial meeting of the Pentecostal Fellowship of Nigeria (PFN), Pastor. E. A. Adeboye, general overseer of the Redeemed Christian Church of God and president of the PFN, made this speech, which he entitled "Who Is on the Lord's Side?":

In Nigeria we can become a fantastic force for good. What kind of force? A fantastic force for good for this nation. . . . Brethren, God expects us to reach a situation whereby we will decree that there will be no rain in Nigeria. And until we call for it again there will be no rain. The Almighty God wants us in a situation where we will say, alright, because the government could not do what it was asked to do, from hence forth we ask the supernatural power of God to paralyse the electricity and power generators, they will not work because the current will not flow. . . . It is written in Proverbs 29:2 "when the righteous are in authority, the people rejoice." And how are we going to get someone who is righteous in authority? Don't let anybody deceive you, thieves will never vote for a policeman. Never. Thieves will always vote for thieves, robbers vote for robbers, in other words, only the righteous will vote for the righteous. So how are we ever going to put the righteous in authority? It is by winning the masses to Jesus Christ. Nobody can bribe him to vote for the wrong man. . . . We can become the force of change not by loving politicians, but by winning souls. If we do what God wants us to do, i.e. if we can get at least eighty percent of the people in Nigeria born again, you can be sure a Christian will be the president. You do not even need to spend a kobo to get them; you won't even need to be a rich man before you become president, because the people will say you are the one they want and you must be there. . . .

The plan of God is not limited to Nigeria alone. Very soon, there will be an extension when PFN will become P.F.A, i.e. Pentecostal Fellowship of Africa. We will take over the whole of Africa. And that is not the end of the whole vision. The Almighty God wants PFN to become number one in the gospel for the world, and other nations of the world will say, what is happening? We thought Nigeria was finished, but all of a sudden it has become leader of the world. Because I want you to know, brethren, when the spiritual climate is right, things will happen in the economy. . . . I remember the time when one pound sterling was almost equal to one Naira. Today, what is the situation? And the politicians are telling you there is no hope. God has promised, it is not going to come from the promises of politicians who said we will do a mighty thing and they didn't build mighty things when they were there. They spoilt the thing . . .

Brethren, may I tell you that the strategy we are going to use to win Nigeria has to be the strategy of an invading army. When an army wants to take over a nation, they have certain characteristics, they don't make noise, like so many of us are doing. Look at those who are really doing substantial work in Nigeria today. They have started building churches, house fellowships are spreading, they are winning people all over the place . . . people who are working while others are sleeping and they take over the essential things, they don't just go and kidnap the president. They take over the media, the radio, the television stations, they convince the rich people, the businessmen, they get the students, they get backings, because when they take over it is the market women and the students they will tell "come and demonstrate it if you are in support." If you want to take over Nigeria you better win the students, win the market women, the media, the broadcasters, the rich, the poor and the press. Glory be to God, I am sure they are here today. By the time they leave, they will be born again.

He elaborates on the theme of God's army thus:

Everybody must take orders from the commander-in-chief. No arguments, no debates. I told you last time you came, I said, God is not a democrat. . . . I want PFN to become an invading army. I don't want it to become a social club. I want to see a PFN by the grace of God that when the devil hears "P" he will begin to shake. That cannot happen if we go about it democratically. Because when God has spoken and we say this is the way we shall go, someone will say, let us vote. I can tell you, whenever you go to vote, the majority will vote for the devil. . . . How am I going to discipline the people who are present founders [of churches]? How am I going to make them soldiers of the cross, how am I going to make them obey orders, unless there are some people on the Lord's side? . . . When I became the General Overseer of the Redeemed Christian Church of God, we had almost the same problem as we are having with the PFN now. Everybody doing what he thinks is right in his own sight. Ask somebody to go on transfer, they will tell you "let me go and pray about it." Or they may even resign, or take the church away. Then all of a sudden the Holy Spirit moved. He did something that I am praying He will do among the Pentecostals. All of a sudden, we held a meeting, we reached an agreement that from now on, once the General Overseer has spoken, the pastors will see to it that it comes to pass.[1]

The speech reiterates the program of conversion as a totalizing project in which individual conduct opens up the space for the political salvation or damnation of the nation. The pastor directly associates just political rule, economic prosperity, and even global power and domination to the project of individual conversion and "making a complete break with the past." He refers to the miraculous power of God and His capacity to directly intervene in the quotidian political life of the nation through the prayers and exhortations of those who are "on his side." We see references to the "invading army" cited by Ojewale at the beginning of this study and to the Born-Again strategy for colonizing the public space through the media and the conversion of the masses. He also alludes to the transnational nature of the community and places the institutional representation of the Pentecostals, through the Pentecostal Fellowship of Nigeria, as having a historic role to play in the religious and political future of the nation. The speech also makes allusion to the divisions and factionalism that mark the Born-Again community and the inherent difficulty of obtaining obedience and discipline, and reveals the ongoing ambition on the part of leaders and their institutions to incarnate the sovereign power of divine authority, making it clear that "God is not a democrat." It contains an endorsement of the authoritarian principle at the heart of military rule through its reference to pastoral authority that may not be questioned and to the proper conduct of "soldiers of the cross."

The other central theme raised in this speech is the relationship between authority and righteousness: "When the righteous are in authority, the people rejoice, but when the wicked beareth rule, the people mourn." This recalls the critique of authority and the exercise of power central to the Born-Again discourse and the ways in which it presents itself as a claim for justice and the alleviation of suffering. A nation of "thieves" will always vote for the devil: through the individual sin and faithlessness of the people and "spiritual wickedness in high places," politics has become a realm of bondage, corruption, and falsification. The staging of the secular political realm as satanic is not peculiar to

Nigerian Pentecostalism, though it takes on a particular significance in the light of postcolonial history. However, the creation of righteous authority through individual conversion brings this claim for collective justice up against the aporias we have identified in earlier chapters. I have argued that while the program of conversion creates the grounds for a new form of individual autonomy, it also reveals an inherent difficulty in instituting new forms of either political sovereignty or community. The messianism and individualism of Born-Again practices of faith, the centrality of grace and miracles, all perform an ongoing interruption of processes of institutionalization that might secure the connection between righteousness and authority, between a new mode of self-government and the government of others, a new ontology or ethology of being-together. In the light of this inherent indeterminacy, this connection can only be established in one of two ways: the institution of a sovereign power by which conduct may be controlled and policed, or the embodiment of sovereignty in a community within which the identity of those promising and keeping promises may be verified. In either case, the engagement with the demonic at the heart of salvation—an engagement that is by no means particular to Nigerian Pentecostalism—takes on a central role in determining the nature of Born-Again political theology as it is played out in Nigerian practice. Born-Again political spirituality develops a negative political theology, but also opens lines of flight through which the program may be put to work in strategies of domination and exploitation and a politics of exclusion and even vengeance.

Born-Again Political Theology

Winning Nigeria (Africa, the world) for Jesus means the projection into the national space of a highly political agenda. The image of the "invading army," sweeping all unbelievers in its path, expresses the political ambition of replacing a "corrupt" regime with a new form of "corrective government" that sets itself up as the unique path to individual and collective salvation. In its programmatic form, the Born-Again project does not refer to a revolution to create a new institutional order, found a new constitution, or elaborate new laws. Rather, it represents itself as providing the conditions for the redemption of the religious and political traditions which were both promised in colonial and postcolonial rule, and ruined through it. In Pastor Adeboye's speech, it is through the conversion of individuals that this ambition may be realized, not through some radical change to the political system itself: "If we do what God wants us to do, i.e. if we can get at least eighty percent of the people in Nigeria born again, you can be sure a Christian will be the president. You do not even need to spend a kobo to get them; you won't even need to be a rich man before you become president, because the people will say you are the one they want and you must be there."

In this articulation, the invading army refers to the urgency of evangelism in the end-times, thus connecting the project of Nigeria's political redemption to a broader global Pentecostal program. Pentecostalism's zeal in evangelism is related to its approach to the "end-times," whereby conversion is seen as a means to both obtain life more abundant in the here and now and participate in the coming of the messiah—the *parousia* or the full presence of God. The *parousia* cannot occur until all nations have heard the word of God. For Pentecostals *parousia* is both immanent, through the presence of the Holy Spirit in every believer, and imminent in the end-times: the coming of the messiah is not to be feared, held back, or deferred, but exalted and hastened. Alongside Christ's exhortation to preach the gospel to all nations, a major scriptural warrant for this position is the enigmatic 2 Thessalonians 2:3–9, which outlines the events preceding the "day of the Lord":

Let no man deceive you in any way. Because it will not be unless the apostasy shall have come first, and the man of lawlessness, the son of destruction is revealed. He who opposes and exalts himself above every so-called god and object of worship. As a result, he seats himself in the sanctuary of God and declares himself to be God. . . . You know what it is that is now holding him back [*to katechon*], so that he will be revealed when his time comes. For the mystery of lawlessness is already at work, but only until the one now holding him back [*ho katechon*] is removed. Then the lawless one will be revealed, whom the Lord will abolish with the breath of his mouth, rendering him inoperative by the manifestation of his presence [*parousia*]. The presence [*parousia*] of the former is according to the working of Satan in every power.[2]

For Pentecostals, the "lawless one," whom they read as Satan and his demonic hosts, is already at work in the world. The enigma in this text lies in the identity of "the one holding him back"— the arresting force or *katechon*—who is not specifically identified by Paul. Among Pentecostals, the *katechon* is interpreted as the Holy Spirit, the only force capable of holding back the "lawlessness" of the current age, a force embodied in every Born-Again Christian. The "church," understood as the body of the Born-Again believers, constitutes this arresting force until the rapture, the point at which the *katechon* will be removed. Since the Holy Spirit dwells in each believer, when the body of believers are raptured to meet Christ and His saints in the air (*parousia*), the Antichrist will be revealed and the tribulation will begin, which will end with the destruction of Satan by the breath of the Lord and His eternal presence (*pleroma*). Coupled with the central Pentecostal text that characterizes all forms of power in Satanic terms (Ephesians 6:12), in which the believer is exhorted to "put on the whole armor of God" to struggle against "the rulers of the darkness of this age," we see how the invading army should function as the "arresting force" against "lawlessness." At the same time, it also is implied that this work of "arresting" lawlessness or wickedness is a necessary step "so that he will be revealed when his time comes." Thus the spread of the gospel is also an actualization of God's plan and a means to enable the moment of the rapture and *parousia*. It places the experience of Pentecostal faith and truth as having a historical role to play with respect to God's identification of the Antichrist and the final revelation of the "working of Satan in every power." Following these verses, Paul says in 2:13: "we are obligated to give thanks always to God for you, brethren beloved of the Lord, because God hath from the beginning chosen you to salvation through sanctification of the Spirit and the belief of the truth." Let us recall Pastor Ojewale's manifesto cited in the introduction: the Born-Again revolution involves "the battle of translating the victory of Jesus over the devil into the everyday, natural realities of our personal lives and also of our political, religious, economic and social systems." Pentecostals depict this battle for global conversion and the struggle against Satan and the demonic not only as urgent, but also as central to God's plan for salvation. It is a victory already achieved, or more precisely, a possibility immanent in the present time, in a state of messianic potentiality, but one that must still be actualized through the work of faith. This historic struggle with the demonic must also be seen as central to the ecstatic experience of conversion and salvation itself.

Pentecostalism takes an ambivalent form of negative political theology, in contrast to those interpretations of the 2 Thessalonians text that see the *katechon* in terms of secular power or institutions, according to a representative model of divine sovereignty.[3] Political theology, as opposed to classical political philosophy, presumes that humanity is not self-sufficient, whether in terms of its innate or of its acquired capacities, and that an immanent rational framework for the founding of human collective life is impossible. It is principally concerned with the question of the embodiment of divine sovereignty, in one of three forms: first, representation, in which the sovereign is God's representative; second, "dual sovereignty," which strictly distinguishes between spiritual or worldly sovereignty; and lastly, theocracy, in which divine sovereignty is instituted directly on earth in an unmediated form.[4] At the same time, it refers to two potentially contradictory meanings, if we consider the concept of "the political." The political implies a horizontal aspect, as expressed in the notion of the *polis*, community, the public sphere, or more generally, the social, as well as vertical dimension that refers to the structure and organization of the commanding, sovereign power within the social sphere.[5] Thus in political theology we can also find two aspects: a theology of sovereignty and a theology of community. The political theorist Carl Schmitt subscribes to a representative model in the vertical understanding of the term, and uses 2 Thessalonians 2 as a foundation for a Christian doctrine of state power. This represents a culmination of an ancient tradition going back to Tertullian (and reinforced by Augustine), which saw the Roman empire as the power that delays or restrains the end of time.[6] For Schmitt, the Christian empire was the historical power, the *katechon*, which could delay the coming of the Antichrist: "the belief in an arresting force that can stave off the end of the world is the only link leading from the eschatological paralysis of every human action to such a great historical agency."[7] The Pauline dictum "all power comes from God" provides the basis of Schmitt's vertical concept of the political, in which sovereignty is the affair of the highest authority and ultimate decision, the declaration of the state of exception that founds the law. As Agamben points out, every theory of the state that sees it as a power destined to block or delay catastrophe can be seen as a secularization of this interpretation of 2 Thessalonians 2. The Jewish theologian Jacob Taubes characterizes Schmitt's interpretation of the *katechon* as that of "someone who thinks apocalyptically from above . . . who struggles so that chaos doesn't rise to the top, so that the state remains."[8]

Pentecostal theology subscribes, though in an ambivalent way, to the notion that Satan works through secular powers and that the rule of man over man cannot represent the messiah. In its Pauline form, the messianic cannot legitimate real, existing political orders but can only make them irrelevant and ultimately replace them, as in 1 Corinthians 15:24: "then cometh the end, when he shall have delivered up the kingdom to God and the Father, when he will render inoperative all rule, all authority and power." But at the same time, the *katechon* may be seen as the embodiment of the sovereign power of God as incarnated horizontally in the "body of Christ," or the community of the saved, through the presence of the Holy Spirit in every individual. With respect to the state, the notion of chaos coming from above rather than rising from below is central to contemporary Jewish political theology (for obvious historical reasons), in which divine sovereignty is embodied in a people. Pentecostal theology does not provide any theological warrant for a theory of state power under any of the three figures. Even if it does distinguish in principle between temporal and spiritual powers, spiritual power is not seen in representative terms (as in the "dual representation" approach). At the same time, this distinction is never entirely clear, because of the omnipresence of supernatural powers. The power of God, and indeed of Satan—the two *parousia* in the verses quoted—are understood as being potentially embodied within each and every individual and at large in the world, through either the Holy Spirit or a host of demonic spirits or forces. Thus, with respect to institutions per se, Pentecostalism still remains attached to the anti-institutional model of the "body of Christ" as embodied in the form of the fellowship. As I have argued throughout this study, religious authority may not in principle be monopolized by an individual simply by virtue of his or her institutional position—as pastor, evangelist, or leader—but rather should be determined by the ethical state of the individual and the presence of the Holy Spirit as evidenced through acts of faith and work. Conversely, any institutionalized form or forum cannot be taken as representative of the community of believers writ large. Indeed, Pentecostalism perhaps more than other forms of Protestantism provides the contemporary archetype of Christianity as "a community without an institution,"[9] but a community of a new type, proper to the forms of diffuse, individualized, and nonisomorphic forms of connectedness in our globalized world. Thus, with respect to structures of political authority or forms of collective association or action, the decisive factor remains the spiritual state of the individual. In this light we can better appreciate how Pastor Adeboye projects the realization of righteous authority through the existing Nigerian political system. Through the conversion of the great majority of the population, the promise of democracy should be realized from both the bottom up and the top down: in the presence of the Holy Spirit, there will be no more thieves to vote for thieves. This is the notion of faith in action under messianic time—the Pauline vocation expressed in the command to "use it rather"—through which may be fulfilled the latent promises of justice and development figured in the notion of just rule. Naturally, this vision has little to do with what actually happens, nor with what Adeboye goes on to say about disciplining the soldiers of the cross, even if it does reveal the underlying theology that animates the Born-Again political imaginary.

For Pentecostals, political structures in and of themselves are neither more nor less legitimate; the decisive factor appears to be the extent to which they permit or prevent the spread of the gospel and the exercise of faith. It could be argued that Pentecostals have a contemporary a priori preference for the institutional forms of democratic political life, insofar as they guarantee the freedoms required for the project of evangelism and conversion, but at the same time, the movement is opposed to the humanist assumptions of democracy, and thus is fundamentally ambivalent with regard to the neo-liberal state. In this respect, contemporary Pentecostalism at large admits as much the possibility of chaos "from above"—in the form of the "lawlessness" of the liberal state and liberal humanism, considering that the community of the saved must counter it "from below"—as the possibility of chaos "from below" in the form of rampant "immorality" (homosexuality, alcohol and drug abuse, fornication, adultery), hedonism, atheism, and disregard for the sacredness of human life (the abortion debate), which should be legislated against, or at least be central to public political debate. We can see this manifested in the conservative political positions of American Pentecostals.

"God Is Not a Democrat"

In the Nigerian context, the situation is very different, particularly as regards the extreme and pervasive character of "lawlessness" or "wickedness" to which the Born-Agains see themselves as responding. The colonial regime and the authoritarian military governments and "democratic" interregnums that succeeded it are a particular instantiation of a "state of exception"[10] based upon a permanent disjuncture between representation and its objects, between the objects to be governed and objects created through governance, and the plurality of norms and rules informing conduct. This experience of "lawlessness" in Nigeria is one of the overwhelming indeterminacy of all things, such that it becomes impossible to distinguish the real from the fake, the truth from the lie, the rule from its exception or suspension, a situation in which norms and the law become in many respects unformulable. This applies as much to the realm of goods and services, as it does to the realm of social interaction and of course to the state and the political sphere. The lawless arbitrariness of a state where policeman are thieves, legislators are criminal predators, and the common man has no hope for any form of redress renders overwhelming the urge to move from the plane of immanence to transcendence in the quest for certainty and understanding. The radical excess of signification produced in this situation provides the historical conditions for domination in terms of exception, and the possibility of power to take the form of enchantment. In staging, as does the paradigm of "development," the promise of future political and economic emancipation, such an order places the political present in a continual state of suspension or exception, in terms of which the achievement of peace, justice, and the guarantee of life may be deferred until the "war" (against indiscipline, corruption, misrule, disorder, underdevelopment) is over. Through this process of deferment, power is free to exercise itself in a perpetual present, and the realm of the political, in which struggles for justice and liberation should find their concrete expression, becomes a mere simulacrum in which the merging of violence and the law suspends life upon the free play of untrammeled desires and infinite debt.

Both the "chaos from above" and the "chaos from below" are addressed in the Born-Again attitudes to the political realm proper. Here again, we can distinguish considerable differences between the early period of revival and its development over the 1990s. In the early years of revival, the realm of politics and political power was invariably represented in terms that emphasized its dangerous and corrupting nature, as shown by the tracts discussed in chapter 3. Indeed, the political realm was figured, perhaps more than any other, as a space of death. The problem was also articulated in terms of the evil and dangerous nature of desire—for power, goods, prestige—and debt, implying that the various social relationships that constitute the nexus of power will ensnare the believer in their webs and inevitably lead him or her, as if through a process of enchantment, to sin and its wages as death. It was only through rupture from these norms and social forms that enchantment might be broken. In the first decade of revival particularly, Born-Again respect for constituted secular authority did not show itself primarily through an acceptance of government as it was; rather, modes of public conduct served to highlight the corruption and flagrant disregard by those in power for the norms and rules publicly professed. In the first and second decades of revival, converts struggled against the prevailing disregard for the official norms associated with administrative structures, state institutions, and political practice. The public adherence to civic practice—refusing to bribe or to peddle influence—and personal standards of honesty and probity gave them a distinct social prestige. The movement thus created a public presence and legitimacy that inhered not so much in the charisma of its leaders and followers as in staging a new exemplarity, at least at the level of civic virtue. It is in this sense that Adeboye presents conversion as a means of creating the ideal citizen, one who will provide a living incarnation of the *nomos* of an ordered political realm.

However, beyond this programmatic form, the Born-Again deployment within Nigerian traditions of political practice reveals that God is most definitely not a democrat, despite the potential force of the Born-Again political critique, as Adeboye makes clear in his bid to unite the community of Born-Agains within the Pentecostal Fellowship of Nigeria. The model of "democracy through conversion" may be projected at the national level, however, the community of the saved must be led by divine authority, embodied in leaders of churches and organizations and legitimated by the word of the Holy Ghost. Among the leaders of the community of the saved, the devil is apparently at large, and not everybody is on the "Lord's side." Adeboye refers to the eternal problem of instituting spiritual authority within the Born-Again community. Within churches and the community at large, the Holy Spirit speaks to each and every one, such that "Everybody [is] doing what he thinks is right in his own sight."

The Born-Again conception of sovereignty fails to institute the distinction between power and right, or to put it in religious terms, between grace and works or the law. In the Western democratic tradition, the original political fiction in which authority and the power of decision are separated both conceptually and institutionally enables the representation of democratic power as secular, insofar is it is designated by an "empty place," which makes no gesture toward a transcendental, and which neither the pole of the state nor that of the "popular" can incarnate.[11] The destruction of the representation of power as standing above society, as "possessing an absolute legitimacy, either because it derives from God or because it represents a supreme wisdom or justice which can be embodied," means that power, to be legitimate, must "conform to right, but it does not control the principle of right. Democracy does away with the judge, but also relates justice to the existence of a public space—a space which is so constituted that everyone is encouraged to speak and to listen without being subject to the authority of another, that everyone is encouraged to *will* the power that he has been given. This space, which is always indeterminate, has the virtue . . . of allowing the questioning of right to spread."[12] The representation of the distinction between power and right does not mean that democratic societies are free from domination, or that the state does not concentrate a form of tutelary power, as Foucault has shown. The democratic paradox, which lies in the fact that the place of power is an empty place that cannot be appropriated, also means that domination tends increasingly to detach itself from any visible representative. The Born-Again community of believers constitutes a form of public space in which everybody is encouraged to "will the power" he has been given, and in which each individual may exercise his or her own "spirit of discernment" concerning the problem of right, or of correct conduct. Nonetheless, the creation of a collective ethic is continually interrupted by the perpetual move from immanence to transcendence in the individual experience of faith, and the conflation of personal spiritual power and the power over others, giving rise to a politics of conviction and vengeance.

The centrality of divine grace in the form of the miracle to processes of veridiction interrupts the dialectic that could enable the distinction between power and right to stabilize along the vertical axes of sovereignty. The functioning (to a greater or lesser degree) of the distinction between power and right in democratic societies does not imply that this representation of legitimate power is not founded on an original fiction, which the state of exception reveals. The rule of law in liberal democracy has both a normative, juridical element and an anomic meta-juridical element without which there can be no instantiation of the former. For Schmitt, it is the state of exception, a space both within and outside the juridical sphere, which founds the law. Both Benjamin, in his critique of Schmitt, and Agamben show that this anomic element that grounds the law and the political order to be pure violence.[13] Such violence is never merely a means to an end, as the framing of it in the state of exception claims, but rather it appears as pure manifestation, in terms of which the link between life and norm is broken. Agamben argues that as long as these two elements are correlated, yet conceptually, temporally, and subjectively distinct (for example, the contrast in medieval Europe between spiritual and temporal power), "their dialectic—though founded on a fiction—can nevertheless function in some way."[14] But when they tend to coincide in a single instance, when they are bound together and blurred—when the state of exception becomes the rule, or when there is a conflation of spiritual and temporal authority within religion—then both the political system and religion find themselves in a dangerous state of crisis. As both Taubes and Agamben argue, the dialectic between these two experiences of the world, between the juridical and the anomic, is absolutely essential.[15]

The miracle is to theology as the state of exception is to the law.[16] Like the force behind the law that founds and guarantees the law, divine power is not means, but pure manifestation, pure violence. Obedience to the norm depends upon the constant repetition of faith through testifying to the reality of miracles, which appear as both the sign of faith and its grounds. In the Born-Again articulation, it is the miracle that provides the dialectical link between normative prescriptions and salvation or "abundant life." As the figure of ultimate sovereignty and historical agency, the power of God through the Holy Spirit takes the form of a pure manifestation, rather than simply a means whose end is salvation. If we recall the modes of making a distinction between true and false power, true and false miracles, between the vessel and the thaumaturge, we can see that the staging of divine power so as to link power to right cannot conceal the fact that, between God's laws and everlasting life, there is no substantial articulation other than that achieved through the mysterious and pure manifestation of God's grace or vengeance. This manifestation of God's power through miracles may be presented in terms of means to an end, but we have seen that this force cannot be contained by the regime that it underwrites.

The miracle could perform its dialectical function only insofar as its promise was clearly figured as a means to an end, as a sign of the promise, but not its realization. When miracles are staged as a technique of "making believe" and salvation is evidenced not only by signs of miraculous grace but also by a new style of life that enacts the rupture with the prevailing "lawlessness," the miracle can be seen to take the form of a means to an end, and so enables the distinction to function after a fashion. The precariousness of this distinction is nonetheless revealed by the impossibility of claiming authoritative knowledge in the matter of discernment. Only through the perpetual public repetition of an uncertain inner truth and its incarnation as an exclusive form of exemplary conduct, which must be perpetually verified through collective and institutional techniques, can pastoral power take on a limited sovereign force, and this only within the limited purview of discrete congregations. When, however, the evidence of faith and obedience becomes associated with the realization of worldly desires and ambitions mediated through miracles in an economy of monetary exchange, this distinction breaks down almost completely, leaving only the arbitrary figure of supernatural power, increasingly appropriated and monopolized by pastors. In this staging of miracles, the problem of discernment reveals the ambivalence of the power that performs the miracle and the ongoing conflation between the law and faith. With these developments, the possession of spiritual power becomes increasingly associated with thaumaturgy of a violent or arbitrary kind, as implied by Adeboye's reference in his speech to "decreeing" power cuts and drought. The promise of grace and the act of forgiveness central to the messianic vocation take the form of staged events in which pastors "promise" miracles, and turn a blind eye to the actual conduct of those receiving them and to the sources of the wealth used by grateful converts to repay God's "vessel." This gives rise to a situation of anomie, in which is exposed the inefficacy of techniques of the self, as well as the arbitrary nature of the decision that declares the reality of the miracle and the illegitimacy of its authority.

The Politics of Conviction

An examination of the Born-Again participation in politics and the public sphere illustrates the ways in which Born-Again political spirituality increasingly gives rise to the two related tendencies we have discussed. On the one hand, there is the development of authoritarian forms of pastoral power, through the attempt to monopolize spiritual power and thus incarnate the righteous authority that the secular realm cannot hope to achieve and that contributes to the ongoing fragmentation of the community. On the other hand, there is a process of *conviction*, in its double sense—identifying the demonic within the unconverted other and overcoming it through conversion. This process both inhibits the creation and institutionalization, from the inside, of a coherent community, or *ekklesia*, within which trust may be established, yet also encourages the creation of a precarious collective identity, impelled from the outside through the clash with a formidable religious other. In the national space of Nigeria and in the light of its political history, this other is of course Islam. Here we see the development of an exclusive politics of identity based upon the notion of conviction and, increasingly, on a politics of vengeance, or settling of scores. Islam has a privileged position with respect to a broader politics of conviction, insofar as the project of conversion runs up against Islam's own project; one can convict Muslims in the first sense, but not necessarily convert them. Pastor Adeboye's speech contains a direct reference to this politics of conviction. Without specifying the "enemy," it nonetheless contains a perfectly clear message about the nature of the "wickedness" of those who have ruled: it implicitly refers to northern political hegemony and condemns what is understood as Islam's competing theocratic and imperialist program for government in a way that listeners could not mistake. While Adeboye did not explicitly index Islam in his speech, nonetheless, in the context of the meeting, this reference was clear to listeners—especially because during closed-door sessions at this meeting, a central theme was the problem of "Islamization" and "evil" Islamic rule in the context of the upcoming elections. There is a certain reticence to making direct indictments of Islam in official public forums, but in closed forums and in individual discussions, such indictments are very common. In the context of a broader Born-Again discourse and imaginary, implicit references of this nature are clearly understood in these terms.

For Born-Agains, Islam's competing theocratic project violently excludes the possibility of national conversion. The past that must be broken with, which includes northern political hegemony, plays a central role in this condemnation, one that is made all the more acute by the ways in which Islam presents its own project of rupture with local traditions. Beyond their increasingly conflictual relations, I will suggest that Nigerian radical reformist Islam, which developed over the same period as the Born-Again revival and among the same social classes, has, in its interaction with postcolonial government and the Nigerian past, many points in common with the Born-Again project. Through their internal articulations and their actual engagement with the state, these religious forms express the relationship between the religious and the political in very different terms, and they evolved within different traditions and local political contexts. Nonetheless, both projects are inspired by a "quest for justice," and they both address the problem of government of the self and others in terms of a challenge to dominant modes of political subjectivation through a politics of piety or righteousness. Nonetheless, their political theologies are radically different and their theocratic ambitions mutually exclusive.

From the strict rejection of participation in political activities or seeking of political office, from the early 1990s pastors have increasingly used their status as spiritual authorities and the wealth thus acquired not only as a means of access to the state and channels of accumulation, but also as means of political influence. The effectiveness of using one's position, status, and wealth was demonstrated by Archbishop Benson Idahosa, during the politics of transition in the early 1990s. Idahosa was a major power broker in the politics of Edo state, and a press report in the Concord newspaper illustrates that it was not only the Born-Agains who were aware of his influence. In 1992 Rev. Peter Obadan ran as deputy governor with the former federal permanent secretary John Oyegun in the Edo state gubernatorial elections, beating the favored Lucky Igbinedion. According to the Concord newspaper: "one reason a lot of people adduced for their victory was the Idahosa factor. The argument was that the Archbishop of the Church of God Mission must have used his enormous influence among his followers to tilt support for Obadan, who is not just a pastor in his church, but also a special advisor to the Archbishop. Already, tongues are wagging that Idahosa now literally rules the state simply by teleguiding Pastor Obadan, who frequently goes to his spiritual leader for crucial consultations."[17] Obadan denied the charge, but defended his "double calling" by saying, "What is wrong in a pastor being a deputy governor, governor, or even the President? The fact that you are a man of God means that you will be fair in dealing with the people. It means you will be firm. It also means you will not steal, you will resist the urge to be unjust."[18] Unsurprisingly, the government of Edo state during this short period did not demonstrate the least change in governmental practice.

The secretary of the Lagos state chapter of the PFN, Pastor D. Ladele, recognized the Born-Again aversion to political activity but claimed, in 1991, that the current situation warranted a change of attitude: "Many Christians believe it is wrong to want to be in politics. But we are teaching them in our sermons, in our lectures that if we don't take active part by helping to choose the right person, you will see that it is the enemy that is coming to rule us again. The Americans, before you can become their President, the church leaders will come, they will agree that this is their man, and they will use the church pulpit to tell all their members. So if we have to do that to get the next President; we *will* do it. Because the suffering is enough."[19] And yet despite this call for greater Born-Again participation in the political affairs of the nation, between 1991and 1993, in the run-up to the national elections, I heard no pastors preaching for civic participation or endorsing any political candidates. No Born-Again spokesmen publicly pronounced an opinion on the annulment of the elections, although many privately expressed their disgust with the political state of affairs. The Born-Again community appeared politically apathetic in the face of yet another military takeover, and despite isolated calls by Idahosa (who took over the presidency of the PFN in 1996) for Abacha to show clemency to political prisoners or to release them, there was very little noticeable interest in criticizing his rule beyond national prayer meetings. The Born-Again community made no attempt to create an alternate political platform in the form of political parties, even if candidates at different levels of government increasingly used the affiliation with Born-Again identity as a means of creating a potential political constituency or attempting to legitimate their tenure. Governor Ada George, elected governor of Rivers state in 1991, publicly claimed his Born-Again identity and instituted prayers in the state assembly. The most significant political appeal to the Born-Again constituency was that of Olusegun Obasanjo in his campaign for the presidency in 1999. As discussed in chapter 5, Abacha was presented by both the Born-Again community and popular opinion as the incarnation of evil power. Even prominent American Pentecostals took up this qualification, as an article in *Charisma,* one of the most widely circulated publications of the Word-Faith movement, testifies:

There is no question that the devil was working during the regime of Sani Abacha, the iron-fisted dictator who ruled Nigeria from 1993 until his sudden death in 1998. A Muslim who had aligned himself with military thugs, Islamic radicals and occult sorcerers, Abacha was steering the country toward another war. It is widely known that he asked Islamic clerics to perform occult rituals in the capital to keep him in power. But Christians say God heard the prayers of the church and sent a miracle. It came in the form of Olusegun Obasanjo, a military leader and born-again Christian who had been jailed by Abacha for treason. Like a character from an Old Testament drama, Obasanjo was suddenly plucked from his prison cell and placed in the presidency after a free election in early 1999.[20]

The author of this article credits Pastor Adeboye of the RCCG with having both announced and hastened Abacha's demise. "An invisible spiritual battle raged during Abacha's last days. While he had asked spiritists to bury fetishes, charms and live animals on the property at Aso Rock, Christians were fasting. Meanwhile, Adeboye, the head of the RCCG, prophesied on June 6, 1998, that God was about to bring a 'new dawn' to Nigeria. Abacha died of a heart attack three days later."[21] Regardless of the sincerity of his individual conviction, Obasanjo's response to the problem of corruption has quite naturally made no impact on the logics of power and the enormous social machine discussed in chapter 5. After eight years of "democratic" rule under his presidency, Nigeria is still plagued by the politics of predation, violence, and radical insecurity. His direct role, in April 2007, in orchestrating one of the country's most unfree, unfair, and illegitimate elections in its history speaks volumes. Indeed, his endorsement by powerful pastors such as Adeboye, Oyedepo, Oritsejafor, Okonkwo, and others has only served to underline the links between this new form of authority and the governmentality of the belly.

Abacha's rule was criticized by Born-Agains not only for its intensification of the suffering and injustice experienced by ordinary Nigerians, but also, employing the language of evil powers and spiritual warfare, for its challenge to the Born-Again program of conversion presented by those who appeared determined to claim the nation for Islam. In global Pentecostalism the framing of the question of conversion in terms of spiritual warfare against wickedness in "high places" and the demonization of Islam takes on particular significance in the light of Nigeria's postcolonial political history. Echoing Ojewale, one pastor elaborates on this state of warfare:

Clearly, we will have to contend and conflict with wicked spirits in heavenly places and rulers of the darkness of this world and wrest their control over entire cities, region, nations and continents to enable us to do our job of preaching the gospel to all nations of the world. The Holy Spirit has recently been calling the Church (the body of Christ) to prepare for unprecedented warfare through many Christian leaders. The 1990s will *definitely* witness the most intence spiritual warfare the Church has ever been involved in over its entire 2,000 year history. There is no de-militarised zone. *You* will have to fight. Be of good cheer our Lord has already given us the victory.[22]

The enemy that rules over us is not only the one that may inhabit the convert's consciousness or body, but also the spiritual forces at large that inhabit others and give them power over life and death. Evangelism and the "new birth" are presented as the gift of Christ through which the other may find protection from these powers and salvation from their bondage, but they also translate the struggle within the self to a struggle on a collective level. The perpetual transposition of this individual engagement with the demonic at the heart of salvation into the public sphere through testimony gives rise to a politics of exclusion and conviction, expressed in the idiom of global spiritual warfare through the figure of the invading army. The devil must be "terrorized and defeated for redemptive time to become a time of exultation, exhilaration and transfiguration."[23]

These internal articulations, which enable Born-Again Christianity to figure any form of difference in terms of a struggle against evil principalities and wicked powers, and which facilitate its extraordinary political plasticity[24] and inherently schismatic character, take on a particular significance in the light of Nigerian political history. While the struggle between Born-Again Christianity and Islam also finds its expression globally, in Nigeria since the 1970s it has taken an extremely dangerous turn. The experience of military and civilian rule and the prevailing northern domination of federal politics, whether military or civilian, provided the grounds for a conflation of Islam, satanic spiritual powers, corruption, and misrule. This situation was gravely exacerbated by the growth during the late 1970s of radical reformist movements within Nigerian Islam, and the conviction of Christians of all denominations that the various power mafias in the North were determined to Islamize the Nigerian state. The simultaneous rise of the Born-Again movement and radical Islamic reformism should not be seen as coincidental. While initially concerned with the revitalization or restoration of their respective religious traditions, and largely inspired by the intensification of transnational relations, both movements arise from within the same social classes, are products of postcolonial educational institutions, and seek to create moral and political renewal and order from the chaos of the oil-boom years through religious revival. Their competing projects were bound to clash, and constant provocation from both sides has meant that the bid for converts and for political representation has taken increasingly violent forms. In a country whose population is roughly divided between Christians and Muslims, both the Born-Again and Islamic reformist activity has gravely exacerbated the already existing North-South political divide.

In a parallel development to Born-Again campus Christianity of the 1970s as studied by Ojo,[25] the radical reformist movements in northern Islam developed largely within the northern universities, spreading more broadly throughout the North during the early 1990s. The various movements that, from the 1970s on, contested the monopoly of sacred and legal questions by the dominant Sufi brotherhoods—the Qâdiriyya and the Tijaniyya—had their roots in the development under British indirect rule of a new *ulama* born from the northern "conservative revolution." This was a slow modernization of Islamic institutions undertaken by Ahmadu Bello, the sardauna of Sokoto and first premier of the Northern Region, and continued in the immediate postcolonial period.[26] These reforms sought an end to the political and religious authority of the Sufi sheikhs and emirs, aiming to replace what were seen as "obsolete" forms of authority with a modern state administration that would bring about far-reaching judicial reforms and social change and consolidate the power blocs that were to dominate northern and indeed national politics for most of the postindependence period.[27] Succeeding generations of Muslim reformers sought to establish transnational links, in particular with Medina and Mecca as well as other centers of Muslim reform in Egypt and Pakistan, showing that transnational connections and the global circulation of discourses and individuals are likewise a central aspect of reformism.[28] Bello supported the founding in 1962 by Abubakar Gumi, later grand qadi of the Northern Region, of the Jama'atu Nasril Islam (JNI), whose purpose was to coordinate Muslim activities in the country and to speak for Muslims at the national level. Highly active in building mosques, publishing reformist literature, and encouraging conversion, the JNI sought above all to popularize correct Islamic practice.[29]

Gumi was also directly involved in the formation of the most popular of the reform movements of the 1970s, founded by Ismail Idriss in 1978, the Jama'at izalat al bid a wa iqamat al-sunna (Movement for the Suppression of Innovations and for the Restoration of the 'Sunna), called Yan Izala (People of Izala) in Hausa. Yan Izala, inspired by Saudi Wahhabism, undertook a crusade to purify Nigerian Islam of "innovation," and railed against Sufi practices such as the recitation of litanies (dhikr), the association of names of Sufi leaders with those of the Prophet (shirk), and the veneration of sheikhs or Sufi saints. However, like the Born-Agains, Izala was not directly politically engaged, but was principally concerned with the reform of individual conduct. Gumi and Idriss's support was drawn from the Western educated section of Hausa society associated with colonial and postcolonial bureaucracy and institutions, much like their Born-Again brethren in the southern campuses. Gumi and his followers were regarded with suspicion by traditional religious elites because of what was seen as their "Western" lifestyles.[30]

The development of Islamic reformism from the late 1970s to the 1990s demonstrates the factionalism and internal divisions within northern Islam more than it shows a broad religious consensus. Indeed, the schismatic nature of these movements mirrors in many ways the growing splits within the Born-Again movement over the same period. Two main groups emerged, one under Saudian Wahhabi influence, the Da'wa (The Call), and the other inspired by Shi'a Islam with ties to Iran, the Umma. Da'wa, concentrating on the removal of "innovations" and attempting to reform certain "unorthodox" practices, managed to impose an Islamic order on the campus of Bayero University in the mid-1970s, leading to the closing of bars and the banning of alcohol; even though there was no formal obligation, the veiling of women became the rule.[31] The opposing group, Umma, known for its radical intellectualist stance and sometimes called the Radical Brothers, or Yan Shi'a, under the fiery leadership of Sheikh Ibrahim al-Zakzaki, had a much more Islamist orientation, taking the Iranian revolution as its paradigm, criticizing the northern ruling elite, and agitating for the creation of an Islamic state. In the 1980s both Da'wa and Umma split into other dissenting groups, more or less politicized and radical with respect to the role of Shari'ah and the establishment of a Muslim state.[32] Until the late 1980s these groups remained largely circumscribed within the campuses of the northern universities. They became central religico-political actors only in the 1990s, their more violent activities being severely repressed by both the Babangida and Abacha regimes. In the 1990s, among younger generations of Muslim radicals, the Iranian model once again grew attractive, not least because it was perceived as a model for resistance against U.S. imperialism and Westernization. The theme of the neo-colonial aspects of Nigeria's political system complemented the attempt to rid Islam of its syncretic elements, expressing the desire to break with past practices and to restore a ruined tradition, inscribing Nigerian Islam within a pure or original Islamic form, inspired variously by Wahhabism, Shi'ism or increasingly, the early nineteenth-century Sokoto model of jihad under Usman Dan Fodio.[33]

Larkin argues that Gumi epitomized a new, "modern" and cosmopolitan Muslim subject who offered a new way of being Muslim that rescripted the relationship between Western education and un-Islamic lifestyles, calling upon a "universal" tradition expressed in transnational Islam to accuse traditional mallams of perverting Islam through syncretism. With its emphasis on individual conduct and "lifestyle," and in a way that echoed the Born-Again political acquiescence or compromise, Izala was content to support the consolidation of northern Nigeria's conservative political status. He also notes the entirely new and increasingly extensive use by Gumi and various other northern reformers of private and public media to transmit messages, in English, Arabic, and Hausa, including the circulation of cassettes and the production of televised programs.[34] In Yorubaland, the borrowing of Born-Again styles of public presentation by Muslims has been noteworthy. Indeed, in Ibadan in April 1998, I saw posters announcing a Muslim "rally" in which people were urged to "come and meet Allah." While the use of media had been shared to some extent by Yoruba Muslims, as Barber's studies of the late colonial and early postcolonial period show, the use of modern media marked a totally new mode of the production of Islamic religious authority in the North.

Umar argues that Izala and the other reformist groups proposed the creation of a more rationalist and intellectualist Muslim, promoting knowledge of Islam through individual reading of the core texts of Islam—the Qur'an and Hadith—not through the intercession of a sheikh.[35] This dependence on individual textual study and the pedagogical nature of the reformist program mirrors the Born-Again emphasis on Scripture and personal edification through study and reflection. As in the Born-Again interdenominational movements, such a shift in Islam undermined the charismatic authority of sheikhs, implying a redefinition of status as something that is acquired and proved through argument rather than inherited. The democratization of debate was encouraged: Gumi, for instance, was famous for allowing questions from anyone, "no matter how small." Like house fellowship leaders, Izala's youthful organizers were enabled to lead *wa'azi* (religious teachings or admonitions to follow the right path) and take the lead in organizing religious and political gatherings, which previously their inexperience and lowly status would have made impossible.[36]

Notwithstanding the emphasis on Shari'ah, the reformers, like their Born-Again counterparts, appeared to be principally concerned with framing the question of personal conduct less in terms of a strict application of the religious law than in the elaboration of a new style of life. They prescribed new ways of studying Islam and new modes of recitation of the Qur'an, built new mosques for followers to worship in, and elaborated a series of techniques of the self and new social practices, which, like the Born-Again project of moral subjectivation, appeared to focus on extricating the individual from forms of social debt and politico-historical "bondage." Larkin relates how Izala followers refused to attend Sufi mosques or even to be led in prayer by Sufi members, rejecting traditional forms of status and markers of bodily respect that went with it, such as refusing to take one's shoes off or to kneel down and salute in respect in the presence of elders. Some changed their names from Sufi to more orthodox ones, echoing the common practice among Born-Agains of changing names referring to traditional deities to Christian ones. According to Umar, Sufis spread rumors that Izala supporters, in what appears to be a symbolic bid to free themselves from the cycle of social debt, went so far as to give their mothers boxes of milk (in compensation for having nursed them) and their fathers rams (in compensation for the animal sacrificed at their birth).[37] In many respects, the Born-Again and reformist projects are doppelgangers,[38] and despite the important historical, sociopolitical, and theological differences, their projects appear to stem from many of the same aspirations and to create their pertinence and plausibility by the ways in which they give voice to these aspirations through a marriage of local and global forms. At the same time, these projects are clearly mutually exclusive. Indeed, among the most politically radical reformers, the entire Nigerian political system was understood as being profoundly neo-colonial and Christianized, and the possibility of creating new Islamic subjects, for a reformer such as Zakzaki, could only come about through the realization of an Islamic state, not the mere adoption of Islamic law.

Despite their internal differences, the reformist movements can be seen as an attempt to create on the part of northern elites—intellectual, mercantile, and religious—if not the basis for a new hegemony on religious grounds, at least a new basis for unification that would underwrite their domination of federal politics.[39] At the national level, the central issue around which such a consensus found its political expression was the question of Shari'ah, even if the bid for Shari'ah was largely promoted by the reformists against the old orthodoxy. It is thus during the first decade of the rise of both the Born-Again and reformist movements that a national religious divide found its first heated public expression, in the drawing up of a new Constitution for the Second Republic in 1977. In preparation for the return to civilian rule, the Supreme Military Council appointed a Constitutional Drafting Committee to debate the new Constitution. Discussions on the drafting process came to be almost exclusively centered on the creation of a Federal Shari'ah Court of Appeal to treat cases of Muslim civil law, and the question dominated the two years of debate around the Constitution, to the exclusion of practically any other issue.[40]

The conflict, which threatened to tear apart the fragile peace of the postwar period, was finally defused by the mediating role played by Yoruba moderates, as Laitin convincingly argues.[41] Nevertheless, it set the stage for the same debate to be revived during the drafting of the Constitution of the Third Republic, and laid the ground for the increasing politicization of religion and the exacerbation of the North-South divide. Beyond the mutual suspicion between the North and South in terms of political domination and socioeconomic disparities, the issue of Shari'ah appeared to symbolize the very survival of these different communities and their ability to determine the future form of the Nigerian nation-state. As Ibrahim points out, this debate set in motion a process of brinkmanship "that poses serious threats to the Nigerian state, because complex, multiple and overlapping divisions and contradictions are reduced to two mutually exclusive primordial camps."[42] This highly charged issue reemerged successively in the national political arena until the imposition of Shari'ah by the majority of northern states in 1999.

From the point of view of the Christians, the Shari'ah debate came to symbolize the ongoing Muslim control of national politics and the "jihadization" of Nigeria, even though as Christians, they would not fall under Islamic jurisdiction. From the point of view of the Born-Agains, it was seen as a direct challenge to their project of national conversion. The motivations behind the northern push for a Shari'ah court at the federal level should not be seen primarily in terms of the defense of Islamic law per se,[43] nor should they be seen as the expression of a desire to compromise the secular basis of the nation-state. Rather, from the point of view of Muslim reformers and conservatives alike, the push for a Shari'ah court was a means of negotiating their position and influence in the construction of the nation-state and the maintenance of northern political domination. The defense of Shari'ah must also be interpreted in the light of northern politics itself, as an anti-establishment stance on the part of "modernizing" northern political elites with increasingly radical positions on Islam, against the powerful, "traditional" northern aristocracy. The nationalistic aspects of this politicization of religious affiliation no doubt contributed to the revival of the Sokoto model of jihad under Usman Dan Fodio as a possible model for northern Nigerian political revolution, and as a bastion against Christian "crusaders," who were increasingly making their presence felt in the North in the form of evangelistic activity by Born-Agains and others.

These cleavages arose again and were sharpened in Christian protests against Nigeria's adherence to the Organisation of the Islamic Conference (OIC) in 1986 under Babangida's regime, then again in 1989 with the drafting of the Constitution of the Third Republic. In the face of increasingly bitter and divisive debates, the Constitutive Assembly took the bold step of removing government intervention in Shari'ah altogether, leaving it as a matter of private concern among Muslims. The subsequent outcry among northern Muslims, not least those constituting his principal power base, prompted Babangida to remove the question of Shari'ah from the assembly's jurisdiction and maintain the status quo. The growing divide led to repeated incidents of interreligious violence from the late 1980s on: beginning with the Kafanchan riots of 1987, regular violent clashes and riots pitted Muslims against Christians in a number of northern states.[44]

At the institutional level, the body that most outspokenly defended the political interests of the Christians at the national level was the northern branch of the Christian Association of Nigeria (CAN). While this body had originally united the Catholics, organized under the Catholic Secretariat of Nigeria, the mainline Protestant denominations under the Christian Council of Nigeria, and a nebulous group of "others" in a national ecumenical group in 1976, its original impetus came from the northern Christians, particularly those in the religiously mixed northern town of Kaduna. Enwerem cites Rev. Peter Jatua, Catholic archbishop of Kaduna and chairman of CAN for the northern region, on the organization's origins; Jatua linked CAN's formation directly to the energetic proselytization under Bello:

In 1965 or thereabouts, the Sardauna of Sokoto [Ahmadu Bello], who was the Premier of the northern region, went about trying to Islamise people, especially in the Northern Region. So he became both a political as well as a religious leader. His effort at that particular time was geared towards converting people—be they Christian or pagan—to Islam. So he paid more attention to the conversion of people to Islam than actually running the state, if one may put it that way. Many people were afraid to oppose him, else they lost their position or even their job. So because of the prevailing circumstances, some Christian leaders in the north thought it wise to come together and fight against this kind of move to forcefully make people Muslims. That gave birth to what we used to call in those days the Northern Christian Association (NCA) later changed to the Christian Association of Nigeria.[45]

Jatua's statement illustrates the northern Christians' concern, from the 1970s onward, with Muslim activists, who were seen as the central agents of the "jihadization" of Nigeria, with the added implication that religio-political leaders' central concerns were not so much good governance, as the advance of Islam.

While these developments and successive deadly religious clashes radicalized the northern members of CAN and made the issue of interreligious conflict a growing national concern, the attitudes of the broader community of Born-Again Christians (the great majority being located in the South) to the political stand of CAN and the question of "Islamization" were complex. While Islam is frequently associated in testimonies with various forms of Satanic occult activities—herbalists, mallams, and *babalawos* are often placed together in these stories— nonetheless, the dominant attitude on the part of pastors concerned the challenges such developments presented to the possibility of national evangelism rather than their political dangers for the integrity of the nation-state. Church registration, church planting, and access to populations were the central concern of Born-Again "empire builders" and, as we have seen, were at the heart of Born-Again political theology. At the same time, the conversion of Muslims was a growing priority, and in congregations Muslim converts were increasingly prized and urged to give special testimonies about their conversion experiences. Many Yoruba converts told me of struggles or clashes they had had with Muslim family members and friends in their efforts to convert them, and the growing interreligious intolerance in the highly mixed Yoruba community is undoubtedly linked to the evangelical zeal of young Yoruba Born-Agains and their increasingly aggressive public presence. In the North, evangelical activity tended to be confined to Kaduna and the Sabon Gari ("new town") neighborhoods of northern cities in which the majority of migrants from the South lived, but the increasingly aggressive presence of evangelists in these areas dramatically contributed to the degradation of interfaith relations.

Over the past two decades, institutional activity on the part of a broader Born-Again community has remained diffuse and sporadic, testifying to the ongoing difficulty of "disciplining the soldiers of the cross." Until the late 1990s the Born-Agains were not particularly active in CAN—indeed, they did not obtain a separate and official status within the organization until the early 1990s, having until that point been grouped under the category of "others." From its founding in 1986 until the late 1990s, the Pentecostal Fellowship of Nigeria's southern delegates, who made up the overwhelming majority, did not appear particularly interested in the struggles its northern delegates were waging. The PFN's first biennial meeting in 1991 was marked more by internal disputes concerning questions such as dress and comportment— the ongoing internal debate around holiness and worldliness—than by the creation of a common platform in the face of growing interreligious conflict. Still, at this first meeting, half a day was devoted to closed-door sessions on the political role of the PFN in the ongoing transition to civilian rule, and in his keynote address (quoted in chapter 2), the PFN president, Reverend Boyejo, made the organization's stand on the politicization of religion quite clear: "All good men must ensure that narrow-minded bigots and religious fanatics whose main preoccupation is to usurp delegated authority and distribute important positions in favour of one religious group as in the past should not be allowed to find their way onto the top. It's no longer a secret that Nigeria has been smuggled into the OIC, and everything that could be done to Islamise Nigeria and bring Shari'ah is being done, these things are clear to everybody. But the church must arise, men of the church must arise."[46]

However, in 1991 the great majority of Born-Agains had not even heard of the PFN, and most of those canvassed claimed that while the initiative appeared to be a good thing, they had not seen much evidence of its activities. Many expressed skepticism concerning the ability of such an organization to unite an increasingly dispersed community, although most agreed that such unification was both desirable and necessary.[47] Another survey undertaken in 1993 among RCCG parishes revealed that more than half of those surveyed had not heard of the PFN, even though the RCCG general overseer, Pastor Adeboye, was PFN president at the time.[48]

The religious cleavage may have created the grounds for legitimating a Born-Again publication's claim that Governor Michael Otedola's victory in the Lagos gubernatorial race of 1991 was God's will: "Governor Otedola was chosen by God" ran the cover story of *New Creation*. Otedola ran against a Muslim candidate from the SDP party. The article claimed that because of overwhelming belief in Lagos in the strength of the SDP before the election, his victory must have been ordained by God.[49] Otedola was not identified with the Pentecostals before the election, there was no concern whatsoever with the nature of his Christianity, and neither he nor his administration exemplified in any way the new sort of righteous authority expressed in the original Born-Again critique. Yet such claims were not necessarily representative of converts' attitudes, and indeed in discussion with converts, many expressed a certain disgust about the ways in which political opportunists appeared to be using the Born-Again movement. In canvassing attitudes to successive political regimes in the run-up to the 1993 elections, I was struck by how, out of hundreds of converts surveyed, the overwhelming majority singled out the short rule of Brigadier Murtala Muhammed as the only example of "good governance" in Nigeria's political history. Apparently, his being a Muslim had little or no bearing on Born-Agains' appreciation of him as a "courageous" individual prepared to rid the country of corruption and political violence at the cost of his life. Indeed, many converts emphasized the spirituality of what they perceived as his courage and personal conviction, some even claiming that Christians could do well to emulate the devotion and fidelity of many Muslims to their religion. Murtala's assassination and the extremely short period of his rule quite naturally lent themselves to such an idealization, and indeed, the great majority of Nigerians still hold him up as a kind of national hero. However, given the already extremely fraught relations between Christianity and Islam at the time of my inquiry, such attitudes reveal that for Born-Agains the question of government does not find its principal expression in terms of a pure logic of identity.

Born-Again attitudes to the Christian-Muslim riots of the late 1980s and early 1990s likewise reveal the ambivalence and complexity of questions of collective identity and their mobilization in political struggle and violence. Following the Zangon-Kataf religious riots of February and May 1992, I discussed with many Born-Again leaders and converts the problem of Christian-Muslim violence. While the overwhelming majority of pastors from various doctrinal tendencies were clear in their condemnation of what they saw as more evidence of the hegemonic ambitions of Islam, of its violence, and above all the of partiality of Babangida's government in punishing the perpetrators, indexing him as the principal vector for the "Islamization" of the state, ordinary members' attitudes were more nuanced. I was surprised to hear, amid the general condemnation of this violence, what appeared to be a certain ambivalence on the issue. Several members asked whether we should consider the Christian victims as true Christians, and noted that they would require more information before taking a strong political stand. Most converts did not appear overly concerned with the general problem of religious violence in the North. Much less ambivalence was demonstrated toward the killing of Christians at the hands of Muslims in Kano following the crusade of German Pentecostal evangelist Reinhard Bonnke in 1991. The theme of his crusade in Africa that year was "tearing down the strongholds of Islam," and the organization of a rally at the gates of the ancient heart of Kano was understandably felt by Muslims to be an intolerable provocation. And yet those converts I spoke with about it, while acknowledging the provocative nature of such a crusade, nonetheless condemned the violence in the strongest possible terms and invoked the democratic principles of freedom of worship, conscience, and the secular state to justify the crusade. From this point of view, only Born-Again Christians should be seen as martyrs and only their oppression or killing as worthy of political mobilization, but even in these cases, strong collective identity and rallying around a Christian cause did not appear to be the priority of the great majority of converts. Northern delegates of the PFN at both the 1991 and 1993 biennial meetings expressed severe frustration at what they explicitly stated as the lack of support from their southern brethren on the problem of Muslim oppression of Christians in the North. From the mid-1990s on, under the leadership of Idahosa, followed by Mike Okonkwo after his death in 1998, the PFN, previously dominated by holiness pastors such as Boyejo and Adeboye, came under the influence of these new Born-Again superstars who became a growing influence within CAN. By 2000 the PFN had become the single most influential group in the organization. Nonetheless, its political activities were limited to mobilizing voter support for Obasanjo and actions such as a proposed lawsuit against the adoption of Shari'ah in 1999. Over the past seven years since the adoption, the only actions have been formal protests against the destruction of churches in the North and in areas in which Muslim-dominated state governments were perceived as preventing church growth.

From the late 1980s on, within the northern Christian community, the invocation of Christian virtues of tolerance that had previously marked individual and collective Christian attitudes to violence against Islam became increasingly untenable. Christian students at ABU in Zaria, after the 1988 Christian-Muslim riots on campus, invoked the impossibility of maintaining such a position in the face of Muslim provocation. "For too long we have been pushed to the wall. . . . Both cheeks have been slapped and there is no third cheek to slap." As Enwerem argues, the students were articulating the feeling of the politicized northern CAN, "the members of whom were said to be prepared for martyrdom for the Association."[50] However, at that time the Born-Agains were by no means central members of the northern Christian vanguard, even though the odd book or tract did claim that it was time to renounce the gospel of turning the other cheek:

When a non-believer in Christ strikes a Christian, the latter (Christian) should stand up erect and look at the former direct in the face. A look can many times transform the non-believer, can pierce and melt the heart. . . . But there are moments when the Christian like the master should take up his whip and flog sense into people. Moments of open and direct confrontation may sometimes be called for. On no account should a Christian take himself as the one who always has to bear the stroke of the other. There are moments when he has to stand up on his two feet and say like the fly, "No" to the huge cow! We Christians in Nigeria want peace and unity of the nation. But on no account shall we compromise our religion for any or both of them.[51]

Over the 1990s a new and urgent sense of martyrdom developed, alongside a spirit of "crusade," according to which "soldiers of the cross" should be prepared to die for their faith. While not constituting either a radical political vanguard or united political community, the Born-Agains can be seen as having gravely exacerbated interreligious tensions through aggressive evangelism, church planting, and a discourse of intolerance. Indeed, the ways in which obedience to the project of conversion was staged as a matter of individual life and death gives added power to an ethos of martyrdom, even if the vast majority of Born-Agains, located as they were in southern cities, were never to be faced with the violence confronting their northern brethren. During outbreaks of interreligious violence in northern cities, from the late 1990s to 2004, numerous cases were reported of Christians refusing to recite the Muslim profession of faith under the threat of death by armed Muslim youth, preferring to die rather than to "renounce Jesus." Christian violence against Muslims has also grown exponentially since the late 1990s. Since the imposition of Shari'ah in 1999, both Pentecostal and mainline leaders have uttered warnings on the "limits of patience," all the while invoking democratic principles and the rule of law, which are nonetheless in contradiction to the evangelical spirit and miracle mania that increasingly animates the entire Christian community.

In 2001 the RCCG held its third Holy Ghost Congress at the 850-acre Redemption City (formerly Redemption Camp) off the Lagos-Ibadan expressway. More than 2 million people gathered from every part of Nigeria and across Africa to listen to preachers and "receive their miracle" at this mega-meeting whose theme was "Wind of Change." A reporter who was present relates: "A preacher from northern Nigeria roused the crowd with a passionate prayer. 'O God, arise! Chain every demon that comes against Your church! Bring down every government that would oppose You! May God consume every altar that has been set up against Nigeria!' A shout that followed shook the ground again. Then a million fists were raised into the air, and another million voices screamed the name of Jesus."[52] For those present, the implications in this reference by a northern pastor to demons and governments opposed to Christianity were clear. While Nigeria had a southern Christian, and ostensibly Born-Again, president at the time, strongly supported by RCCG's own general overseer, the specter of Islamic rule remains.

Both the Born-Agains and Muslim reformers conjure the devil in the name of the other. Both project political visions whose internal articulations are opposed to a representation in which power and violence are separate from right. Both emerge from the institutions and imaginaries of the colonial period, and both have engaged in complex and contradictory ways with the governmentality of postcolonial Nigeria. Both draw on increasingly intolerant global religious forms in order to carry out a project of rupture with the past. And yet both find their original impetus and popular plausibility in a quest for order, justice, and mastery; both spring from a desire to give a new account of the self and to liberate themselves from the history of enchantment, bondage, and subjection that is seen as having brought the old individual and collective subject into being. Both express a political spirituality, a quest for a new mode of distinguishing the true and the false through a new mode of governing the self and others: "the will to found entirely anew, one through the other (discover an altogether different division through another mode of self-governance, govern oneself altogether differently through another division)."[53] The promise of justice figures clearly in Christian doctrine, and the Born-Again movement began by staging its possibility through a new work on the self and a new division between the true and the false in a chaotic epistemological and moral field. The same may be said, perhaps to an even greater extent, of the popular adhesion to the Islamic reformists' program. As Last persuasively argues, the application of Shari'ah in northern Nigeria should be understood not as the sign that the practice of Islam cannot be differentiated from that of the political sphere, nor simply as an expression of the desire to be a better Muslim through a fuller application of the law. Rather, it is an extremely popular demand to which the political and religious authorities were obliged to acquiesce, a "people's quest for justice" that seeks above all a more just, equitable, and morally grounded society. As he shows, the application of Shari'ah links directly questions of personal salvation, the work of the self on the self, to a whole ensemble of practical, quotidian, and eminently political problems:

Shari'ah in this context, then, has also become much more than a practical issue. Ultimately, implementing the Shari'ah is a test of one's own faith: failure to judge a case rightly, failure to prescribe the correct punishment, results in your being destined to experiencing eternal hell-fire. So how seriously do you, as a judge, fear hell-fire; is it a reality for you? How far can you presume on Allah's mercy, on His compassion, come Judgment day, if you fail or fudge carrying out a punishment clearly specified by Him in His Qur'an? These are real, not rhetorical, questions which some individuals are having to respond to in Northern Nigeria.[54]

The development of *hisba* committees in northern states from 2000 on also draws on a religious idiom of piety and discipline. Young men invoke piety as a political act, expressing their anger at the failure of the judicial system, but above all at the inequalities, by joining *hisba* groups to enforce Shari'ah. As Pratten points out, referring to recent studies by Last and Adamu, here the problem of radical insecurity "takes the form of a widespread anxiety over the identity and activities of strangers within the Muslim *jama'a* (community) and has provided the groundswell for an impulse and imperative of 'renewal' which Adamu refers to as a 'new regime of morality.'"[55] Last sees the politics of piety as reconstituting the mode of Muslim interaction, arguing that "manifest piety is not just a personal stance, but also a conscious political effort."[56] Popular disappointment with the ways in which the application of Shari'ah has been undertaken in the North over the past eight years focuses on how its application has principally centered on the criminal and punitive aspects of the law, to the detriment of issues of social justice and equality, and the elaboration of new ways of being together, which were the impetus behind the popular demand for justice in the first instance.[57] Sheikh Zakzaki was very clear on the risks involved in the application of Shari'ah from the point of view of the reformers' project of the creation of new Muslim subjects.

You should get it clear that I have already indicated that if the Shari'ah is restricted to the courts of law, then it is not sufficient. It might end up being an instrument in the hands of those in authority which would be used to judge those in lower class, but the upper class would be above the law. So I have to differentiate between whether they are talking of a struggle to establish Islamic system to run the society in which we are living or they want the Islamic law to be applied in the courts of law. . . . The system which was established by the colonialists was meant to be against the Islamic principles. And it is the same colonial set up which is in control all through, even after the so called independence. So one naturally comes into conflict with the present system running the country which is anything but Islamic. In other words, it is not Islamic. Call it anything but it is not Islamic. And it negates Islam. To establish an Islamic system one has to do away with the present system. So when you are talking about establishment of Islam you are actually talking of removing the present system. Now the present governors of the system were elected or selected to run the system. They cannot come naturally and run a system contrary to the system they were elected to run. So it will be a sort of contradiction. They will end up using the emotions of the people and yearnings of the people to deceive the people.[58]

The "emotions and yearnings" have transformed these two faiths into a major force in contemporary Nigeria. Even if the establishment of a strong identity that could enact a violent politics of identity and exclusion is constantly interrupted by the nature of Born-Again political spirituality, nonetheless, the question posed by Mbembe remains pertinent: "At which point does the engagement with the demonic at the heart of salvation, the writing of terror and exultation, destruction and exhilaration as the law of divinity and the logos of redemption—at which point does all of this become a symptom of something even darker—a symptom of a vengeful state, of a suicidal state, one of the main justifications of which is to be permanently conscripted in settling scores—the permanent settlement of scores becoming itself an ecstatic experience?"[59] This is a question of capital importance for the future of the Nigerian nation-state. Born-Agains and Muslims are "condemned" to live together in the political space they share. While a mutual politics of vengeance has yet to take on the proportions many observers fear, nonetheless, it exists, and finds its relay within the Born-Again program of governing the self and others.

Political Spirituality and the Limits of Sovereignty

Despite its religious form that presumes the insufficiency of the human subject, Born-Again political spirituality nonetheless continues a tradition that began with the notion of platonic rulership, centered on the domination of the self and drawing its guiding principles "from a relationship established between me and myself." In this articulation, Arendt argues, "the right and wrong of relationships with others are determined by attitudes towards one's self, until the whole public realm is seen in the image of 'man writ large,' of the right order between man's individual capacities of mind, soul and body."[60] This long political tradition sees sovereignty and freedom as identical. And yet, Arendt argues, there can be neither freedom nor sovereignty, because "sovereignty, the idea of uncompromising self-sufficiency and mastership, is contradictory to the very condition of plurality. No man can be sovereign, because not one man, but men, inhabit the earth, and not, as the tradition since Plato holds, because of man's limited strength, which makes him depend upon the help of others."[61] The Born-Again ethics of submission to the sovereignty of the Holy Spirit takes the form of a compensation for this original weakness: a capturing of power by individuals that will permit their liberation from the debt and bondage imposed by others, free them from their past actions, and protect them from the actions of others. Sovereignty that is claimed in this way, as Arendt argues, is entirely spurious.[62] Divine sovereignty as employed in the messianic vocation demands above all an action toward the other, the only thing that may release all men from wandering "helplessly and without direction in the darkness of each man's lonely heart."[63]

The arresting force—the *katechon*—may be understood as a force that can release man from "the eschatological paralysis of every human action,"[64] so that the absurdity of the being-toward-death of every human life is interrupted by the possibility of beginning anew, where sovereignty may find its incarnation in human affairs. Indeed, the symbol of "new birth" has at its heart the understanding that men, though they must die, are not born to die, but to begin. But the arresting force that might rescue men cannot find its incarnation in a single sovereign entity, whether the state or the Holy Spirit in every believer. Eschatological paralysis lies in the simple fact of human mortality, but also in the recognition of the impossibility of human freedom and autonomy. Individual action—the spontaneous beginning of something new—can never be autonomous, but inevitably falls under the effects of neighboring relations and predetermined structures into which it is inserted and with which it struggles. It sets in motion a series of events in the Foucauldian sense, whose effects and outcomes cannot be foreseen and for which no one individual can either bear the burden or take the glory. Individuals thus appear to forfeit their freedom the minute they make use of it. "The only salvation from this kind of freedom seems to lie in non-acting, in abstention from the whole realm of human affairs as the only means to safeguard one's sovereignty and integrity as a person."[65] The retreat from the world of the early revival illustrates in some respects just this sort of eschatological paralysis. The prayer for redemption—"God come and take me to heaven"—expresses more than just an acknowledgment of each convert's submission or powerlessness; it also, paradoxically, expresses a being-toward-death. This paralysis is also evident in the ways in which the new birth fails to overcome the spirit of distrust and suspicion that Arendt identifies as the hallmark of our modern age.[66] In enacting a spurious individual liberation and autonomy, the Born-Again program only reinforces this spirit of distrust, forgetting that the principal recommendation of Christ was action toward the other: the messianic suspension of every law and their fulfillment in the command to "love thy neighbor as thyself."

Sovereignty, if it is to have any reality, must be based on the principle of plurality, in which concrete acts of both forgiving and promising may find their collective expression in public space. The historically constituted domain of morality "has, at least politically, no more to support itself than the good will to counter the enormous risks of action by readiness to forgive and be forgiven, to make promises and to keep them."[67] The human capacity to act depends upon the possibility of being released from the consequences of one's acts, whose effects cannot be foreseen and for which no agent may be held entirely responsible. Otherwise, "our capacity to act would, as it were, be confined to one single deed from which we would never recover." At the same time, without being bound to the fulfillment of promises, "we would never be able to keep our identities," but rather be condemned to the solitude of our own hearts and the darkness that inhabits them, which "only the light shed over the public realm through the presence of others, who confirm the identity between the one who promises and the one who fulfils can dispel." Faithfulness, if it is to have any power to redeem, depends on plurality, "on the presence and acting of others . . . forgiving and promising enacted in solitude remain without reality and can signify no more than a role played before oneself."[68]

Arendt credits Jesus with the original discovery of the politically radical potential of forgiveness, arguing that its formulation in a religious language and its connection with love, that most apolitical of forces, has prompted our political tradition to ignore its implications for an ethics of government. Jesus' formulation was totally radical—the sovereign power to forgive does not lie with God, but rather with men, and God's forgiveness of man depends upon their forgiving one another: "if ye in your hearts forgive," God shall do "likewise." The reason for the insistence on a duty to forgive is clearly "for they know not what they do," since "it is in the very nature of action's constant establishment of new relationships within a web of relations, and it needs forgiving, dismissing, in order to make it possible for life to go on by constantly releasing men from what they have done unknowingly."[69] This is why only faith enacted as a being-toward-the-other may release each person from eschatological paralysis[70], and it is also why Jesus "likened the power to forgive to the more general power of performing miracles, putting both on the same level and within the reach of man."[71] The freedom contained in Jesus' teaching is the freedom from vengeance, for forgiveness is exactly its opposite.

The Born-Again articulation stages the experiences of promising and forgiveness as a matter of the relationship between the self and the self, mediated by the Holy Spirit. Despite collective experiences of testimony, in which sins are enumerated, forgiveness demanded, and promises made, these take the form of a standardized narrative whose principal function is that of faith's performance, veridiction, and justification. The individual's release from the consequences of his or her acts—making a complete and ongoing break with the past—occurs through God's grace in private prayers of repentance, and the fulfillment of promises through the miraculous apparition of God's blessings in his or her life, not through the enactment of the central principles of the New Covenant or the public confirmation of the identity between the one who promises and the one who fulfills. The convert may thus liberate him- or herself from old forms of indebtedness or bondage, but the primacy of individual experiences of faith based on interiority, the blurring of the experiences of faith and works, interrupts the dialectic between the enactment of faith and obedience to prescriptions that would consolidate trust among men. This situation is compounded by the mistrust created by the need to counter the ever-present possibility of spiritual attacks not only for one's protection, but as both the evidence for and the performance of one's salvation. This need is called up by the impossibility of confirming the identity of the other, of dispelling the darkness of one's own heart or that of others through the Born-Again articulation of sovereignty, an impossibility that disables the messianic vocation as a being-toward-the-other. As Arendt says, "the extent and modes of self-rule justify and determine rule over others—how one rules himself, he will rule others."[72]

The original impulse of the Born-Again revolution in Nigeria responded to the urgent desire to institute forms of sovereignty that would redeem the individual and collective past from a history of subjection and auto-destruction, and rescue the individual and the nation from the experience of radical uncertainty and loss of control over the present and future. However, while this impulse has engendered new experiences of the world, the sovereignty and redemption it enacts give rise to new forms of insecurity and subjection. Within Born-Again spirituality, the experiences of faith, or grace, and of works, or the law, are blurred and merged. But as Agamben and Taubes both argue, the dialectic between these two, between spiritual powers and worldly powers, between the anomic experience of grace—what men may hope, believe, and love—and the experience of the law (what men may do or not do, know or not know), is absolutely necessary.[73] When they become confused or merged, we are facing both a crisis of religion and a crisis of the political. The explosion of Pentecostalism in Nigeria inscribes itself within a global revival of extraordinary proportions, and beyond that, a revitalization of the religious in general. In its paradoxical engagement with the ruined political and religious traditions figured as a promise throughout colonial and postcolonial history, Born-Again political spirituality reveals not only the historical forms of subjection and domination with which it engages and which it upholds, but also the central aporias and dangers inherent in both these promises. Both the democratic paradigm of the rule of law as it is projected and imposed around the world, in which all human relations are juridicized, and the theocratic ambitions of the two religions of the book signal a failure of this dialectic and a concomitant crisis of the religious and the political in our time. This is why, as Agamben argues, "the actual opposition between secular States, founded uniquely on law; and fundamentalist States, founded uniquely on religion, is only a seeming opposition that hides a similar political decline."[74]

This decline of the political in our time is taken up by philosopher Jean-Luc Nancy,[75] who draws our attention to the dangers of a hyper-religious uprising. "There where rationalities are mired in agreement [*entendement*] (technical, legal, economic, ethical and political rational-ities, or even ratiocinations), there where the instituted religions pro-long badly their traditions (through fundamentalisms or a humanist compromise) . . . an as yet almost silent expectation is steadily grow-ing, an expectation which turns in the darkness towards the possibility of bursting into flames." He warns of a "delirium which threatens to break out and spread across the desert of meaning and truth that we have created or let develop. Indeed, the place opened for its propaga-tion is that designated by the perpetual invocation of 'politics.' The demand for the restoration of reason in its entirety always focuses it-self on a political renewal or a renewal of politics."[76] He argues that the political realm today remains without a response, insofar as our "democratic lukewarmness" lacks that which the expression "civil re-ligion" designated for Rousseau, "which is to say the element in which should be exercised not only the simple rationality of governance, but that, infinitely higher and more ample, of a sentiment, indeed a pas-sion of being-together [*l'être-ensemble*]." For Nancy, the concept of "civil religion" has exhausted itself and its possibilities. Political passions are finding their expressions elsewhere and their incendiary potentialities should not be underestimated. Democracy, he argues, as it extends its form across the world, reveals that politics cannot redefine itself except as one of the following alternatives: either refounded in religion, and thus not even theologico-political (as is often mistakenly said) but well and truly theocratic; or according to a redefinition of the tension, both internal and external to politics, between the government of society and the projection of its ends or its raisons d'être. "Hyperfascism in the first instance, and something radically new to be invented in the second—a reinvention perhaps of what the secular means." Caught up within a tradition in which politics has been reduced to the simple rationality of governance, we need to be reminded of a truth that both religion and political philosophy have always engaged with: As the world becomes both global and resolutely "worldly"—without nether-worlds, heaven, or celestial powers—how and where may be inscribed the necessary affirmation that the meaning of the world must be found outside the world?[77]

Conclusion

In the twenty-five years since the Born-Again movement
began, the socioeconomic and political crisis in Nigeria
has deepened dramatically. By the turn of the millennium
the nation was characterized by extreme and growing violence against the state and among groups, in the form of
youth vigilante movements, separatist and nativist groups,
and interreligious violence; institutional collapse; staggering levels of criminality and urban violence; the failure
of the police and judiciary; predation by elites taken to
unheard-of levels; shockingly high youth unemployment;
the absolute impoverishment of the great majority; and
unprecedented levels of inequality. For many, there is a
growing absurdity in the claims and declarations of the
new Born-Again "empire builders," such as those made
by Nigeria's now largest Born-Again church, the RCCG,
in 2004:

Many considered it unrealistic, when the General Overseer announced his vision for a night of praise, worship and prayers, with
more than four million people from diverse nations gathered in one
location. Friday, December 18, 1998, was the day. The theme was:
"Divine Visitation" and by the morning of Saturday, December 19,
1998, heaven and earth bore witness that God had begun a new,
unprecedented move in Nigeria. There were miracles, signs, and the
glory of God covered the whole place. The American TV network,
CNN, estimated the attendance at seven million, while the local media gave varying figures. By 1999, the venue had to shift. There was
need for a bigger space, and the Redemption Camp, with its large

unused land, became an obvious choice. With the theme: "Victory At Last," the service lasted three days with the multitude increasing every day. It was on this occasion that the name changed from Holy Ghost Festival to Holy Ghost Congress. . . . But in December 2002, the Holy Ghost Congress, with the theme "Showers of Blessings" lasted a whole week. For six days, the power of God flowed into lives creating turning points and uncommon breakthroughs. Each day witnessed miracles of salvation, healing, deliverance and diverse wonders. Many children were born during the programme. In 2003, the theme was: "A New Song." It was indeed a glorious period in the sight of God. Many, including President Olusegun Obasanjo, attended. The president not only delivered a goodwill speech to the congress, he sang, danced, and also gave a sermon that everyone present agreed was just as good as any. Daddy G. O. [Pastor Adeboye] was so impressed that he gave Mr. President a pass mark. Many members of RCCG have given wonderful testimonies of new beginnings, new levels, and new anointing as God gave them a new song in the New Year 2004.[1]

Dr. Tony Rapu, a young, educated, and cosmopolitan pastor, fell out of grace with the Redeemed Christian Church of God in 1997. Until then, he had led the Apapa parish to become one of its most dynamic and upwardly mobile congregations in Lagos in the early to mid-1990s. As Adeboye's "favored son," he had criticized the older, "traditional" leadership for the narrowness of its vision, but also the new direction taken by Adeboye, the spirit of empire building, and the increasing emphasis on miracles to what he saw as the neglect of the holiness doctrine and the new style of life it should bring about.[2] Following a two-year period in London, Rapu returned to Nigeria in 1999, and began publicly to take the Born-Again movement severely to task, claiming that a third way between the old-fashioned holiness movement and the materialism of the prosperity or "faith" movement was vital. His organization, This Present House—Freedom Hall, made small waves in Nigerian and international Born-Again circles, and his views expressed in his publication *The Voice of One Crying in the Wilderness* echo the feelings of a growing number of converts. "I am saying that the emperor has no clothes. The church in Nigeria is in a mess. The structure must change. We must make an impact on society. You can't just camp around Pentecost."[3] He condemns prosperity preachers, moral laxity, and rampant materialism, arguing that the majority of Born-Again Christians have found themselves in a new form of bondage, and that as church growth has exploded, so have injustice, violence, poverty, sickness, corruption, and death. At the same time he unambiguously submits both the nation and government to God and the church, endorsing a vision in which the sacred and the secular, the religious and the political are merged:

A report recently circulated in the United States intelligence community predicting that Nigeria may become a failed state in the next fifteen years is currently making waves among Nigerians. The document cited incidents of ethnic unrest and political bickering and concluded that Nigeria could very likely break up in a civil conflagration. Not surprisingly both the presidency and the National Assembly condemned the reports. Our House of Representatives has directed that Nigeria's own intelligence agency investigate the reliability of the report. . . . The amusing side of the story is that we scarcely need a foreign intelligence body to convince us that this nation is potentially headed for ruin. Every social index points to just such a future. Nigerians already live in the midst of a general infrastructural collapse and grinding poverty. We are told that 70% of the country's population lives on below $1 a day. Less than half the population has access to safe drinking water. Life expectancy in Nigeria is now 49 years. The unmitigated failure of NEPA means that production costs are outrageously high. This and other factors have brought the manufacturing sector into a virtually comatose state. The educational sector is in crisis, despoiled by frequent strikes, student uprisings and violent campus cult clashes. The Central Bank of Nigeria recently disclosed that there are at least 6 million unemployed graduates currently floating around the labour market; as much for their own lack of skills as the general lack of jobs. HIV/AIDS is decimating a significant segment of the population with latest estimates placing the number of those living with the plague at one in five. The country is ranked among the bottom ten in the global human development index. Our economy has been decimated by official theft. Religious and ethnic violence still tend to break out sporadically claiming thousands of lives. . . .

There are two ways of looking at the situation we have found ourselves in. By far the easier would be to digest the information with its gory details and conclude that the end is near; that the wholesale disintegration of the Nigerian state predicted by the American intelligence analysts is inevitable and simply resign ourselves to fate. Or we can look at the seemingly insurmountable decay that surrounds us and hear within the apocalyptic tone of statistics and foreign intelligence reports a call to action. But this call is not to the institution of civil government as we know it, for that has already been weighed on the scales and found wanting. This call to arms is to the Church as the authentic custodian of the Nation's destiny to take responsibility for Nigeria. The Divine blueprint for National redemption and subsequent transformation begins with a familiar clarion call *"If My people who are called by my name . . ."* If the people of God will act purposefully, God Himself will heal the land. In practical terms this means that we must begin to understand that the redemption of Nations is tied to the purpose of the Church. But that is only as far as the Church recognizes that its mandate in the preaching of the gospel of the kingdom includes the concept of National transformation and societal reform. . . . It is only the principles of this "government," principles for an ordered society; Christian principles which many of the developed nations themselves have successfully applied that will bring reform to our land or any other land. Unfortunately many Christians are under the unscriptural impression that there is a division between the sacred and the secular. We have adopted a "church-building" mentality and have conceded the world to unruly and incompetent men. Some declare that religion and politics do not mix. They are gravely mistaken because society implicitly recognizes that all civil authority derives validity from a higher authority—God. A new consciousness of righteousness and morality is needed. A re-orientation movement where the values of the dignity of labor, discipline and orderliness would reign is a great necessity. The driving force for National Transformation will be those people who understand that only the introduction of the Divine into this complex national equation can bring a resolution.[4]

Rapu reiterates the sense of the apocalyptic that contemporary life in Nigeria inspires, and offers a choice between a paralyzed resignation in the face of the end, and purposeful action—the miraculous possibility of beginning something anew. He also relates with uncanny clarity the process of desire, debt, and enchantment at work within the Born-Again churches, and clearly links the problem of the government of the self and others to the political problem of truth:

Some of these leaders as they begin to reign as kings over their local empires, now begin to exercise rulership over the church and the people in it. . . . Very gradually a grotesque monster of control and intimidation may appear behind the concept of unity and vision. Personal liberty and the giftings of the people are then destroyed as they are brought into bondage of a man-centered organization. God warned Israel against the dangers of a man-king. . . . This is true today in that you'll find people weary, tired and burnt but serving the will of their organization yet having no intimacy with the God they claim to serve. . . . The people end up being enslaved to the vision of the king. Kings must live in comfort. Kings need money to increase the size of their empires, and unfortunately the people always have to pay for the personal ambition of the king. Those who help the king extend his empire are handsomely rewarded. And those who express concern over the king's strategies may be sidelined. Even those who started well may become ensnared in the trappings of power. . . . The lure of money, power, influence, position and a desire to be relevant in the lives of other people contributes to the creation of this monster on the pulpit. . . . The leader is trapped, the people themselves are trapped, everyone knows there is a problem but no one knows what to do. Currently, there is a raging battle in the church and the contention is between the truth and a lie being presented as the truth. . . . Unfortunately, many are caught in a strong delusion and believe this perversion of truth. Many sincere and faithful believers find themselves living and endorsing a lie.

Rapu claims it is time to make a complete break with the Born-Again past, calling upon the early interdenominational spirit and the desire to transform the self and be liberated from the cycle of debt, enchantment, and subjection, "strongholds" of bondage in the mind. He appeals to a particular ethos, one in which the government of the self by the self reestablishes the link between faith and works, a reiteration of the messianic vocation of those whose are called in His name:

Christianity is the description of prophetic life on planet earth. It is not a religion, it is not a faith, it is a lifestyle! Today Christianity is a confused term. We have people who have no idea what God is saying, calling themselves Christians. There are some activities attributable to us that are not of God, but we have just done them over time and they have basically become bondage—a stronghold that exists inside our minds. Probably, it was some printer who bound the book that first called it the Holy Bible. The printed pages in themselves are not holy, it is the Spirit and the principles of the Word, operating in the lives of those who believe which confer holiness. The true Church has no religion, what we have is a life style. It is very important we know that it is not only about something we believe, but about who we become, for the pattern of the Word is to re-incarnate itself in the lives of men. In this way the Word becomes flesh and dwells within us. This Christianity is a lifestyle that we should function in, in all dimensions of life. When we understand this in our hearts and not only in our heads, it helps us to transform what we are and how we function and operate. We don't go to church! We are the Church!

The Church has failed to redeem the Nigerian past, just as it has failed to secure its promises of security, mastery, and justice. As Rapu argues, the project of self-transformation has not led to a new mode of being-together such that "those who are called in His name" may realize the revolutionary project of collective social and political redemption they had set for themselves. The miracle of the new birth has given rise to new modes of governing the self and others, but in their internal articulations and their agonistic relations with the world in which they are enacted, Born-Again acts of faith remain prisoner of the forms of subjection and bondage they were supposed to overcome.

Rapu's project in many ways involves a new break with the past. However, despite his condemnation of the corruption of the church and his insistence that only through a new form of self-government and a style of life can bondage to the past, debt, and power be broken, he nonetheless works within a vision where faith becomes faithfulness of a narrow and exclusive form and in which he advocates the merging of the sacred and the secular. In this articulation, the principles of messianic action toward the other still remain in their state of suspended potentiality. And yet, in his reiteration of these principles, he opens up to the individual the possibility of figuring for him- or herself the meaning of the Word and the promises of justice and redemption it holds. The messianic event and its promise of justice, the possibility of redemption as expressed through divine healing and the resurrection of the dead through the Holy Spirit, is rich with symbolic import. It stages these impossibilities in such a way that the individual may see them in terms of the miraculous gift of God's love and grace, a concept that is heterogeneous to an economy of exchange and that commands a new ontology or ethology of being-together. The figure of the new birth reiterates the miracle of natality, the ontological basis for the miraculous capacity of human action, of beginning something new, "only the full experience of which can bestow upon human affairs faith and hope."[5] Even if Born-Again practice fails to enact the full experience of this capacity, and if it reinserts this gift into an economy of exchange, recreates and reinforces the cycle of bondage and enchantment of postcolonial governmentality, the urgency of the promise of justice remains. Derrida writes, "Justice—or justice as it promises to be, beyond what it actually is—always has an eschatological dimension."[6] The justice that is beyond the law cannot wait, it is always invested with urgency.[7] Beyond the immediate material promises of religious belonging, beyond the everyday, this-worldly concerns that move individuals to embrace it, beyond the petty hatreds and deadly violence and exclusions it both reveals and gives rise to, the urgency of this promise creates the force of faith. This promise, perverted by the Born-Again attempt to monopolize and control it, nonetheless reveals the general and universal hope for what is unseen, a justice to come whose horizon is unlimited and entails the resurrection of the dead and the new creation:[8] beyond the particular figure of the Christian messiah, a general messianic yearning for the "other" who will come and bestow the gift of life and justice, a hope against hope, as in Romans 8:24: "For we are saved by hope: but hope that is seen is not hope: for what a man seeth, why doth he yet hope for?"

Appendix: Grace Ihere's Testimony

This testimony was circulated throughout southern Nigeria on cassette tape from the late 1980s. I came across it in Lagos over a dozen times in different churches or ministries, and many converts suggested I listen to it. Grace Ihere's testimony is squarely within the holiness tradition. In this vivid and gruesome account, she tells of the various activities of the devil and his multiple manifestations, ending with the Christian's weapons against him. The origin of this testimony is not known, nor the date of its first recording, although the late 1980s seems likely. To my knowledge, it has never been printed, although some parts of it have appeared in Born-Again magazines. Apart from what is contained in her testimony, none of the churches or converts who proposed the tape to me could give me any information about her. The testimony fills 120 minutes of tape, and is highly emotional. I have intentionally refused to make any analysis of this testimony, preferring to let her speak for herself: its radical excess of meaning defies all reduction.

The Bible says God has highly exalted the name of Jesus and it's above any other name. That in the mention of Jesus' name, every knee shall bow and every tongue shall confess that Jesus is the Lord. Every mouth shall confess, whether on land or in the sea that Jesus is the Lord. I want to assure you that God is everywhere, God is automatic, God is authentic, God is authoritative, God is supercific, God is supernatural, God is extraordinary. He is an impossibility specialist, he is the highest order, He is above all, his story is beyond human comprehension. He is the Lord of all righteousness. He is the man that delivered me from the mark 999, the hands of the devil. I want to tell that the devil is a defeated fool, the devil is a paper, the way you tear the paper, that's how you'll tear the devil with the name of God. The devil is an ignorant in the Kingdom of God. The devil is an ignorant in the Kingdom of God. The devil is a condemned criminal in the days of his life. His work is condemned to face hell and perish. It's a pity. There is no lawyer who'll advocate and solicit for him, even though we sing we have an advocate the man called Jesus Christ. Everybody is always shaking in the pronunciation of the name Jesus Christ. The devil is in trouble ever when Christians stand on authority and pray. The devil is everywhere but he is fast as a rocket. He has got a demon and because of that he move around to look for people he can get. The devil has got no good for the Christians, the devil doesn't want any spiritual progress for the Christians. The highest thing he can do for the Christians is to break the place where he or she is seated with Christ. The devil has decided that all should die, but Jesus has come so you can have life and you have it more abundantly. I want to tell you this thing, that God did a new thing in the air and the land and sea. Because God did a new thing, that is why I am alive today. I lived under the ocean for seventeen and a half years. I was kidnapped when I was two years old. I want to tell you that my wicked mother initiated me. When my mother was alive, she was a special marine agent. She has a communication link with the demons in the water. Before she could die, she was exchanging her years, so when the demon says she has to die and that she must bring a representative, finally I was initiated to that world to take over the activities of my mother. In Proverbs 6:22 the Bible says, "Turn a child in the ways of God so that when he or she grows, she will not depart from that way." There are two powers on earth, the power of God and the power of the devil. But the power of God is bigger than the power of the devil. If your child is working with the devil you are countable to God. It was because my mother was working with the devil, that's why I was initiated to the horrible society.

I was born in 1970 and my mother died in 1972. When she died, these demons started coming to me in person. This is not the case that when I sleep they will come, but this time physically. They will come when I am in the house, they will begin to interrogate me. At first I didn't understand anything. I thought people are coming to see me, but I don't actually know where they come from and I never knew they were demons. So when they left, a time came when all the children went to the waterside to have their bath. As a kid I also followed them and went. Every other child enter the water and swim out, but as I enter, I disappear to an unknown world. The people look for me for about seven days, but I was nowhere to be found. Finally it was concluded that a fish has eaten me, but they never know I had disappeared to another world where demons exist. So on the tenth day I reappear again. One demon said I should go to a graveyard and lie down for two days. As I went there, the people of my compound ran, because this kind of thing has never happened before. So I went to the graveyard and lie down for two days. The thing just happen to me like a person who is mad or ill. Under the rain and sun I was there, I was miserable, I was helpless. When I got back my parents were afraid of me and they went and called some pastor reverends to come and ask this girl her experiences. But if they should come to me I'll look at you and not answer. When you are tired, you'll go back. In fact, I was beyond control. The fact is that nobody there touch me. If you touch me, I'll disappear in your presence. I continue until my parents were restless in mind— which kind of human being is this? They began to think whether I am Christian or not, they began to think whether a spirit or not. I was a human being, born of a human skin, but was initiated into a different world altogether.

When this had finished, I was in the house one day when this woman called the Queen of the Coast came. It was this Queen of the Coast that my mother had initiated me to. The Queen of the Coast introduced me to the Queen of the Indians. This Queen of the Indians has seven faces with two legs while the Queen of the Coast is half a human being and half a fish. If she wants to appear as a human being and walk on the land and people will take her to their house, she'll do so. Why the Queen of the Coast is able to do this is because some of her powers were covered. So you should be careful of the kind of people you pick in the street because some of these spirits are pushed into the world. Even the devil is moving to and fro. So when this woman came she bought a concoction and a very long belt. She rub the concoction over me and drape the belt around me and her so we began to fly in the air. We turned to breeze and began to fly. The first place we landed was the ocean. As we landed, our bodies were not wet because it has been transformed to the spiritual world. As we are penetrating the first ocean we jam a rock because we are breeze. As we were going we enter the second ocean, we saw demons in prison. These demons in prison said I must not pass by because I have not been their member before. And because I was with the Queen of the Coast their words were not effective. Finally, we penetrate the spiritual world. And I asked this woman why are those imprisoned. She said God has imprisoned them and they will only be released when Jesus has taken his people home. We penetrated the spiritual ring and this Queen of the Coast took me round the whole city for seven days. In fact, it's a wonderful place, It's a wonderful world altogether.

After that, I reappear physically. After that, my parents were running helter skelter. They could not understand because it was beyond their understanding. After some days this Queen of the Coast came again. I want to tell you that the devil will not give you any chance, they'll be coming often to let you deny your faith. As this woman came again, she told me this is the day they are welcoming to their Kingdom. So she come with the concoction and the belt. She rub the concoction over me and use the belt to tie us together then we begin to fly again. The ocean we landed in this time round was the Indians ocean. As we enter, we called the Queen of the Indians into the house and finally we penetrate the spiritual world. As I appear in that house, they have electricity everywhere, they have decorated everywhere. They've invited international demons, national demons, and territorial demons. They invited different kinds of pythons and crayfish. All the demons were happy that another person was coming home. As the Bible had said, the devil has come to steal. The devil is stealing God's properties. I was the unfortunate child who was initiated to the junior society which means wickedness, people having the heart without pity. I wonder how God kept his face. I wonder the feelings of God when his own property has been kidnapped. But I want to tell you that nothing has taken God unaware. When I went to the spiritual world and see the hole that we enter into the underground house. Then we enter and I saw a big chair and I went to sit down. In short, I was very happy, a little kid like me sitting on such a beautiful chair. But I never knew I'm in a dangerous trap, I never knew I was in a wicked place. If you are working with the devil, you may appear blessed and prosperous. I tell you, you are pushing yourself toward hell and you shall be there for destruction.

As I sat down, I saw a head without legs distributing blood. We were given a cup each as we sat down and a head without legs was distributing blood in these cups. They were giving people blood to drink and they were drinking it. As it reached me, they gave me and I said I'll not drink. They said they don't take anything here except blood and that if I insist it will have something to do with my life; my mother is not here, my father is not here, my brother, etc. And that I must abide with their rules and if I prove stubborn, I will see myself in a hot place. I still insisted that I will not take blood. They said when we want to do operation or when they want to turn into whatever they turn into, they said they have to drink blood. So they went into the inner chamber and so something, finally, I was compelled to drink blood. Immediately, I became half a human, half a spirit that feed on blood. After the drinking of blood, I follow them to twenty-four rings. These rings signify keeping secrets. That the day I reveal the secret, I'll die. After that, the Queen of the Coast came over me and use blade to cut me and suck my blood. I also suck her blood. Right from that moment we became intimate. I have a link with her now. No way to run away again. After that, they ask me to drink a snake's water which a demon have so I can learn demon's language. After I drank that water, I began to hear when snakes speak. They said they have to computerize my name and after they did that. They said with my human heart that I cannot do wickedness so something is going to be done. They'll pluck out my heart, it is going to be hidden under a stone. So they invited 850 intermediate demons to come and roll up a stone and as they were rolling up the stone, there were other people's heart hidden underneath the stone. You see some people, very wicked, they cannot compromise with you, their heart is under the stone. And if you tell God to come and put their heart into them, then they'll act like human beings. I told you, the devil has no good for all mankind. The devil desires that all should die and the devil gives us things in exchange of our souls. I told you that Christians are covered by a special power that no power can challenge. That's why the devil is afraid of the Christian. The devil said he will go to his computer and see how much these Christians weigh. So he went to his computer, weigh the Christians, and he came out and said that the Christians are weighing 100 degree automatic. And when the Christians are weighing 100 degree automatic, the degree of the Holy Ghost in them is great. And he said he will not keep in 100 degree automatic, but instead he will keep it in 85 automatic. Those people whose weight are like that can climb a ladder in the spiritual realm that no demon can climb. And when they climb this thing they shall subdue wickedness in high places because they've seated in heavenly places with Jesus.

They are able to subdue power, they are able subdue the devil in all activities of the devil and because of this the devil is horrible against the Christians. But where you are a Christian, the power of God will bring you up and you shall be labeled dangerous in Kingdom of the devil, and he will be focusing his attention on you because you are his target. I say he must quench the power of the Holy Ghost. If you are powerful Christian, praying continuously, it will make difference in your life. When you are praying you are able to touch the hem of God's garment and you are very powerful in the spiritual realm. So when you go out they cannot look at your face, they cannot withstand you because you have phoned heaven. So if you are prayerless Christian, powerless Christian, the devil do you harm. So because of this the devil has defined means to quench this fire, the fire is burning extensively. So the devil says, "I must quench this fire. I must not see this fire burning." So the devil has got injection to inject the Christians. When this is injected it cause laziness and fear. Before the devil inject this power into the Christians he is going to be watching how you talk. It is because how you talk against God, that the spirit of the Holy Ghost in you will be reduced. If it is reduced, the devil can have assistance to inject in you this injection. You became lazy, you cannot pray extensively again. The devil realize the power in prayer. He can then see it is through prayer you cause confusion. You'll see it because the devil inject you with laziness. If you are able to realize yourself and say "God bring me up again," God will do it. Just have a little boldness in your heart and God will assist you. The devil makes them not to read their Bibles again. The devil realize the word of God is your realize possession, you will understand where you stand. He will then be depriving [you] from reading the Bible so as not to talk with your Father. The devil is a wicked person, that is the type he inject in the Christian.

Another one he inject in the Christian is "it doesn't matter," and "it doesn't matter" has ruined Christianity, it has caused a lot of trouble in the awakening of the church. Jesus Christ said, my friend, "let's have it like that"—"it doesn't matter." My friend, it matters a lot. Don't say it doesn't matter, Christianity is not stupidity and it was because of this "it doesn't matter" that we had a meeting on April 16, 1984, at Burkina Faso to quench the power fire of the Holy Ghost to abuse God's mentality and personality. It was the devil who prescribed the meeting and as I was the secretary, I attended the meeting. The devil mix something with acid and it was presented to international demons. Finally this chemical was introduced to the church of Jesus Christ and we could see the Christian begun to fry their hair. When the Christian begun to do this act it was to tell God he's a stupid man, God, you are foolish man why did you give me this type of hair? As the heaven is higher than the earth, so is the thinking of God higher than the man's. So I want you to stop abusing God's mentality by frying your hair. God is not foolish man to give that type of hair. Today there is no difference between a Christian and a known believer, everybody wants to look alike. If you are longing for heaven, you must absent yourself from the sins of the world. When you are moving in the road, they should see the image of God in you, even without calling the name of Jesus. If you dress like a Christian, the devil will respect you even deeper because you respect yourself. So this is what the devil did and then the Christian begun to fry their hair. So if you longing [for] the heaven you must cut your coat to that size of the narrow gate. You cannot enter with your looks if you want to, you can go to the bright and wide gate. The narrow gate will not take if you want to be free. As today that the Holy Ghost start to speak in your heart, God do new thing.

The devil sent his angels around to quench the fire of the Holy Ghost. In this Pentecostal churches where there is power of the Holy Ghost, and when the Christian pray they push off the territory of the evil one. So the devil refuse to symbol 777 and 999 because he knows that place is a horrible place. The devil went to the spiritual ring and equip me very well and said I will go into this place to quench off the fire of God. So I talk to breeze and begun to fly in the air. As I was flying I never knew there was a Christian praying, that Jesus bound all the demons in the air because I was flying again, I was hanging in the air. The demons were calling me from Australia but there was nothing I could do. They were confused, what has happened to me, they don't know I was bound in the air by the name of the righteous one. I want to tell you that Christianity is trouble because they caused confusion in the air. And after three days I was loosed again so, I went back to the spiritual world to transverse again so as to enable me [to] fly. When the demon asked me what happened I said I was bound by the name of God, so I have to put myself again to fly to Australia. I couldn't enter the church because of the fire of the Holy Ghost. The church was very hot, so I turned to breeze again because they were hosting. You know in every Pentecostal church you must have some hypocritical Christians, and if you want to do something serious the devil will assist you. So as I was flying to Australia, I went with about 2,400 international demons and I entered where there is any hypocritical Christian. I'll drop the 2,400 international demons and five in their heart and they will become worse than ever. So after I finished, I decided to go to the altar and drop the demons in the man of God. As I reach the place, the man of God has a third eye, he said demons are imposing. So he said, brethren, let us get up and pray. As they were praying, any time they called the name of Jesus, I'll fly, because I cannot withstand it. After they had finished their prayer, I come back again. I was about to drop demon in the man of god. And when they call the name of Jesus again. I fell like an *iroko* tree. I slashed my stomach in the place where there is the ring and I was taken to hospital and it was stitched.

The devil sent his angel all over the world to quench the fire of Holy Ghost. Another one happened. A crusade was happening and devil sent me to go and bring the man of God alone. As I reach the crusade ground, the man of God was covered with special fire and Holy Ghost, I couldn't reach him. I was not able to look at his eyes. I reach there, I was not able to do anything. So I saw one beautiful woman there. She was not having any fun, so I told her I want to sleep in her house. She said, "Who are you?" I said, "Please don't ask me too much questions." She was still wondering, so I said, "Okay, I'm a Christian." She allowed me to come. Before I was able to talk to her, I noticed the fire of Holy Ghost. Then she took me to her house, her husband was not in. She brought food and said I should eat, I said, "I won't eat." For fifteen and a half years I was drinking blood, eating human flesh and urine. She gave me a wrapper to tie and I lay on the bed. So around 2:00 a.m. I turned into a very big python and lay across the woman. When this woman sense that something was wrong, she ask the children to turn on the light and when the light was on, she saw the python and she was unable to shout. The children begun to shout until all the people in the yard finally woke up. They come to see what was happening. And if they attempt to come, I'll open my mouth as if I want to swallow then, they will then fly away. A Born-Again Christian stood and brought a shovel to put me off the woman. If they used knife on me in that bed, I would have died, but because God has a special thing [for] my life and for you, those thinkings didn't occur to them. Jesus loves me most.

I mean the devil send his agent to all Pentecostals, he doesn't send him to the other churches, because there are handkerchief in his pocket, if they come to the church and seat comfortably, it means that church is not very hot. So he will send them to this Pentecostal churches, pretending they want to accept Jesus Christ in their life and as the man of God begins to preach they'll be moving up and down disturbing people. Careful, because the respect of the power of God will want to speak to them and you know the people have religious spirit and familiar demons, and this demon will come to make manifestation when the power of God covers. It take more of a simple eyes to know when the demons are in operations and when the power of God is in action. If you are not very strong in power, they will help in quenching the remaining fire of Holy Ghost in you. And he would throw their body to hell fire and in the spiritual world, the person will be demoted. The person will be demoted, because the person has trespassed the territory. Who told you to go and shake a Born-Again Christian?

The devil send his agent all over the world to bring the power of God low. This is one that happened. I went to a crusade, the man of

God was preaching. I was at the window with my people, so when he saw me, he left the altar and said, "This girl must be among the agent of the devil." I say, "You people are troubling us." Finally, the man called me inside the church and begin to pray. They were praying for me, but because they were ignorant of this demon, probably I was not delivered, so I was going around quenching down the power of God. The devil has advice in many way in which to quench the power of the Holy Ghost. So his power continue, but more excessive power is the fire of Holy Ghost. If you are with his fire, no devil withstand this power.

Now I want to talk on how [to] get blood. As I told you that when they are on the land, they drink blood. When I ask the devil why do they feed on blood, they told me there was a general meeting held in the spiritual world. The key of the meeting is annoying God. What are we going to do to annoy God. We'll use the image of God to annoy God. Man was made in the image of God so we will feed on man. If we feed on blood, we have power for operation, they have the power to in the air, they have the power to turn to anything they want to turn to. They have the power to dissimulate people. What happen is the devil use mostly beautiful woman as their agent, the devil will open the stomach of this beautiful woman on the land and place a very long tube with four demons and six machines into them, and if you are working with the devil and not very beautiful, the devil will take you to his land and put bone in your eyes so that when they look into your eyes you'll look very attractive. They turn into different kind things you pick on the road. They turn into different things, they turn to coffin, dead human beings. So you need to be careful the kind of people you pick on the road because the devil has agents. If they go out and see any motor coming, they will stop the motor and enter, if they enter the motor and see that it is a Born-Again Christian with the power of Holy Spirit in the motor, they will come down because they are not comfortable. No agent of the devil can sit comfortably with the presence of the power of the Holy Ghost. And even though there were hundred unbeliever in that motor and there is only a Christian in that motor and any agent of the devil enters, he or she won't stand comfortably because of the influence of the fire of the Holy Ghost. So that agent of the devil will come down and wait for another vehicle. If another vehicle land and he recognize, there is one coming to devour the driver spiritually. One of them will also disappear spiritually in his brain and his head will be ringing somehow, and because he is afraid of the lion that wants to devour him, he will lose the control and there will be a crash, and as this accident happens they will use their long tooth on the victim and their blood will flow and it will transferred into international blood bank or local blood bank. The devil also gives his agent a black thing, in this they'll transfer some international demons and they'll drop it at the middle of the road and as vehicles are coming very close together, without Christian on each side, they will cause a crash and as the accident happens they'll use their long tooth on the body and the blood will flow. The same thing happens in the ocean, the devil will send some of his agents in a particular place in the ocean and if anything happens to come across that place there will be a crash. They will look for things that are very good, even human flesh, they cause it to disappear to the spiritual realm and they will use it for fruit. The devil also send his agents to secondary school to go and get blood as the students will be on their bed sleeping, this agent of the devil will turn to breeze and breeze will enter the hostel, and they will begin to look at the one without the power of the Holy Spirit and as they place their tooth, the blood will flow. They will be transferred to their blood bank and they will become powerful in operations.

We have the occult world and we have the living world. The devil comes into this place to reach at human beings, the devil keeps his image in the heart of unbeliever, and it is the image that the devil uses and appears in the dream world to deal with people and to drink their blood. And so what happens is that in dream world, we have the first stage when you have a minor dream, we have the second stage when you have a more horrible dream, and the third stage when you have the most horrible dream. And if by chance it is in that stage you are qualified to see mister death, and it is through this way that the devil reaches at people in the dream world. If you are a woman, the devil will impersonate your husband. You know the demons don't have six ovary but within the process of impersonation. They are able to do this and for their own is a counterfeit one, so devil will impersonate your wife and you will think you were lying down with your wife or with your husband, but it is an impersonated demon, and as you come in contact with them they'll use those long tooth and suck your blood and transfer disease into you, and when you woke up physically as a human you'll be having pains here and there because your blood is contaminated and no hospital can make you well. But there is a man who can cure all sicknesses and diseases, his name is Jesus. If you are also a man the devil will impersonate your wife and when you sleep and your soul appears in the dream world, it will be as if you are lie down with your with your wife, but you are lying down with a demon, and as you lay down with them they contaminate your blood, suck your blood, transfer disease into you, remove the original sperm that God has put into you and put a demonic one and this sperm will be very hot inside the man and as he wake physically and lay with his wife, the man will push in this sperm inside the woman and this sperm will be there, very hot, and if any child happens to enter, this sperm will knock off the child and this causes miscarriages.

A lot of thing has been happening in the spiritual world. When you sleep, you see yourself eating in the dream. It is blood they use in preparing the food, and you know God is against any individual that feeds on blood. But you know because the devil is a wicked man that even as themselves, you are drinking blood and you will begin to fly as they fly. When you sleep you see yourself swimming in the water, this is a clear revelation that you have initiated to the demons' graveyard. When you sleep and a serpent pursue you, this is a revelation that you have been initiated to the serpent world. When you sleep you see a lot of behaviours in the dream. The devil has got no good intention for man in the dream. The devil is a wicked man. The devil use to put snake in the private part of woman, and when a man will go into her, he'll think he is going into the woman, but he will not know he is going into the mouth of snake. The snake will accumulate the sperm and it will seem as if nothing has happened. This has caused a lot of barrenness in most of the woman. At times, the devil will place a bottle inside the woman. He'll think he is going into the woman, but the bottle is there to accumulate his sperm. The devil use to put stones inside woman so that when they'll be going on the road they'll be receiving heaviness in the road. This is a stone that devil has put into them so that their life will be useless. This is also carried out in the spiritual realm. If you are not a Christian they'll invoke your spirit up and they'll set fire under it and as this fire will be burning, your body will be very hot and this causes internal heat and you begin to run here and there for help. No hospital can treat that case. But there is a man who can cure all cases and his name is Jesus, he is the King of Kings and Lord of Lords. It's also in the dream that they use to initiate the woman to the occultic world. They will invoke this child out of the woman's womb and the child will appear in the air and they will use the child for food. It is also in the dream that they use to exchange these children that are in the womb, they will remove the original child and put demon. It is in the dream that people also reproduce, they are not reproducing human beings, they are reproducing demons and they will grow up and become agent of the devil and they'll begin to wage war against the children. The devil has caused a lot of havocs in the lives of the women and men, but Jesus has come to destroy all the works of the devil because he said, "Whatever is not planted by my heavenly father must be uprooted out." Jesus is able to deliver you and you shall be free indeed.

It is also through this means that the Olumba-Olumba Obu people feast on blood.[1] They don't eat anything [other] than blood, and when they feast, they become powerful in operation. I want to tell you that the real Olumba has died in 1975. The one operating now is not the Holy Spirit neither is the comforter, he is a false prophet that was sent into the world to deceive man and what happens is that when the real Olumba has died these people are carried away by wonders. He has a goal for them, he says he will appear physically and will build the church and because these people are carried away by these things, they will enter the church. As it was built, they place evil spirit pins on the floor and they place a long tube from the church to their international blood bank. The rule is that no Born-Again with the fire of the Holy Ghost is allowed to enter since the fire of the Holy Ghost will burn off the pins. Those foolish and ignorant who do not know where they are going to, those the devil has succeeded to subdue by subconsciousness are the people who are allowed to be eaten without asking question, so as they enter, these evil spirit pins will suck up their blood and this blood will through those tubes to their international blood bank and every time they've feed on blood, that is why you see them high with signs and wonders.

I want to tell you that you should not be carried away by sights and wonders. But the first thing is to know Jesus as your Lord and personal saviour, and he is able to solve all your problems without anything, without collecting anything from you, and he has the power to do it. I told Olumba that I want to appear physically and laugh over the intelligent of the people, so I appear physically on earth and I went to one of their churches at G.R.A. Phase Two in Port Harcourt. When I reached there I pretended as if I had one ache or the other, so I greet the pastor and I said I have a problem with this ache, except I will be baptized by Olumba, by immersion, my problem could not be solved. So they took me to their waterside and I was immersed inside the water, so when I come out the pastor said unless I will have sex with him, my problem cannot be solved. I opened my eyes and said to the man: "Look me from head to toe, do you think you can lay down comfortably on the bed with me?" He said, "It is just five minutes." You see what they are doing? They are useless people. After that they took me into one of their inner room, they placed something on my eyes and as they kept that thing in my eyes. Olumba appear and say please I should not expose him, I told him, "Boy, cool down, you were to expose people, to deceive people and you will go on deceiving people." You know, in the spiritual realm I use to call him boy because he is operating a level 333, below level, while I was operating the level 999, higher level, so he was a junior boy to me. When I repeat it I was going around test-flying the work of Jesus Christ, one of them come to me and said, "This girl, you are exposing my master, you are degrading my master." I say, "Who is your master, do you know my master?" He says, "Who, who is your master?" I say my master is Jesus, and at the name of Jesus, Olumba will bow. When they go to their church, they will tell you he's Holy Spirit and he is the highest being here having three stars and three zeros in the air, he is powerless, foolish, illiterate and one of these days he will also die and he will accompany the devil that deceived him in hell.

Now I want to talk level 333, 666, 777, 999. If you open Ephesians 6:12, the Bible says we wrestle not against flesh and blood, but against principalities, powers, against the rulers of the dark of this world, against spiritual wickedness in high places. The devil classify principalities as level 333, powers as level 666, rulers of the darkness of this world as level 777, and spiritual wickedness in high places as level 999. This is the realm of Lucifer himself, and he is operating a level 999 higher level, we also have Satan, et cetera operating at 999 below level and they are the people responsible in causing trouble all over the world, while level 777 is the rank of the Queen of the Coast who is the matron of the sea. We have level 666, the rank of the Antichrist. These secret societies and the occultic men also operate in this level. We have also level 333, the rank of the newcomers, this demon called Leviathan is in charge of the whole demons in the water. The demon says that man can do without any other thing, but man cannot do without water, so the demon in the water decided to be very wicked and it is in the water that they train demon out of the physical realm to commit fornication with people, to abuse God and cause trouble here and there, cause confusion here and there. While the demon in the higher called Beelzebub is responsible for issuing orders with wizards to people, and there are also invisible armies on the air to wage war against the prayers of the Christian.

So levels that I've mentioned, different kinds of demons operate in this place, with different assignments. When I submitted over two thousand souls, I was promoted to level 999 higher level and also because of the number of the men of God I got low, so I was promoted to this horrible stage. You know that in the spiritual realm there is a very big blackboard that they wrote the names of powerful men of God and under they will write 'declared untouchable', and if anybody succeeds in getting any of them, you will be highly promoted. But I want to tell you that the devil's promotion will land you in hell, but when God has promoted you, you are a blessed woman or man. As I attained this level 999, I was qualified to see hell fire, you know if you operating at the other levels you won't be qualified to see a terrible hell fire. So they open hell for me and as they opened I saw horrible things, some of the people I know I submitted, I saw crying. I want to tell you that hell is a place of torment, a place of agony, place where people cry hard. I know the fire very reddish, big maggots cutting people, they are crying out aloud, no water. You cannot make friend with the devil, the devil is there to laugh over your ignorance, it is a pity when you die without Jesus Christ, your destiny will be hell. Today is the day of salvation, tomorrow will be too late for you. I want to tell you that hell is real. It is not in the air, it is on the ground. You know the day people die and their soul will appear in hell, and as they appear, the devil will ask them series of questions. The devil will ask you, "When they were telling you about that righteous man, you were shaking your head, didn't they tell you that there is a hell or you are making noise? What is actually in you that you were shaking your head, don't you know that everything in you is a borrowed one and that the owner can take any time?" And after the devil might have asked you series of questions, you will be thrown to hell. They will not joke with salvation. The fact is that people did not know what is ahead of them, that is why they pray for it. When they die, their eyes gets opened and when their souls appear in hell, they will shout a horrible shout. Hell fire is real! If you die without the master Jesus, your destiny is hell.

As I also attained level 999, they gave an honor level 999 degree 121212, ultimate 444 and this is the power behind the invocation of papers. You know I was invoking question papers and people will come to me and I'll invoke question papers and they will write their exercises, pass every paper and come out with flying colors. As I also attained level 999, I was qualified to hear any secret of secrets. The devil says before you can hear any secret of secrets, you must withstand any seven horrors. So the devil called the whole level 999, we were about 800. The devil will appear in cloud and he will be coming in a terrible form, flying, to manifest how he was thrown from heaven and as he was coming, there will be lightning, there will earthquake, and if you are not very strong, the earth will swallow you. And at the sixth horror seven hundred and ninety died and we were only nine that survived, and I was among the only thing that survived. I didn't survive because

I had power, but because God had good intuition for my life. So I with-stand the seven horrors of devil. He took us to the inner chamber and said, "Listen very well, open your ears, you want to hear the secret of secrets?" But I want to tell you that devil has got no secret, the secret things belong to our God. Praise the lord! The devil said I thought that all would have been under me.

But while I was having these thinkings in me, you know God is om-niscient, he knows what I was thinking, and he will say, "Who will go and deliver these people from the pockets of the devil? Who will go and deliver these people that the devil has imprisoned?" Finally Jesus volunteered himself and come out and said, "Father send me, I'll go and deliver them. I don't want the devil to cheat them again." So Jesus came and died on the cross, when he died on the cross the devil thought he had defeated him. They never knew it is the word of God. They never knew it is the way to deliver the people. I want to tell you that the devil doesn't know everything, when Jesus died and he was to be buried, they prepared thousands of the international demons so that the righteous man will not penetrate. You know that in the spiritual realm there are people that devil has imprisoned and there are some people the devil has cause to disappear physically on this earth and they are working for the devil. No food for them, no payment, nothing, and they are suffering like that because of the devil. God saw all these things and said, "Who shall go and deliver them?" and Jesus came. The Bible says "the earth is of the Lord and the fullness thereof." The Bible says, "God has exalted the name of Jesus, he has given him the name which is above any other name and at the mention of the name of Jesus every knee will bow and every tongue will confess that Jesus is the Lord." And because he's the King of Kings and Lord of Lords, when he was be-ing introduced, the demons bowed down, they saluted him and said: "at your worship sir."

Jesus penetrated with authority out of the spiritual world. When he entered, the devil was sitting down on his throne and Jesus walked like a king, and went where the devil was and said, "I want you to give me all the keys," and devil went down and humbly submitted the keys to Jesus. And the devil was crying, "He has collected my only power!" Jesus collected the key and went to the prison door. You know at the prison door, the devil has got efficient organized army, he has got tem-ple police soldiers who are guarding the prison door and the door is a very strong one, so when Jesus went there they could not recognize his face. They couldn't know who he was, and Jesus begun to shout "Lift up your heads, O ye gate, and be ye lifted up, ye everlasting doors that the King of glory, and the King of Kings, the Lord of Lords may enter!" They say, "Who is this King of glory?" Jesus replied, "I'm the Lord strong and mighty! I'm the Lord mighty in valour!" And Jesus collected the key and opened the door of the prison, and Jesus entered and liberated those who were in the prison. I want to tell you that Jesus has collected the key of your prosperity, the key of your possession, the key of your life. It is no longer in the hand of the devil. When Jesus got out, he said, "I die and I live for evermore and have keys of hell and of death." So the key is no longer in the hand of the devil, Jesus has collected the keys, he has given you the key and you have the power to bind, to look and to make and decree. And the decree will be established. So when these people were liberated, they were happy with Jesus and say, "Jesus we have expected you for long! We thank you for coming to liberate us!"

But I want to tell everybody there are so many people that the devil has imprisoned, but with your prayers you can be able to deliver them. So Jesus came out again with authority and made an open declaration that all powers in heaven on earth and under earth belongs to him. As Jesus was going back, the devil was not satisfied. He went and prepared demons so that Jesus will not enter. When he was going, they saluted him and say "at your lordship sir." When Jesus penetrate, he is sitting at the right hand of God. He is advocating and soliciting for you. The devil has got no good intention for mankind. After that, I ask him what is the secret of secrets, because the righteous man did like this and that is why seven hundred and ninety-nine level 999 people died. He said, "Look at this girl for talking to me and calling me a wicked man. Because you're able to challenge me, if you're brave enough you're going to overthrow me." So I overthrow the devil for two weeks. So I was sitting there in this throne, controlling the whole demons in the four corners of the world, when I was there, I suffered the demons a lot. If I send you to accomplish the mission, no blood for you. I want to tell you that devil's promotion will lead you to hell. When you are promoted, your promotion will be good to lead you to hell spoken of.

Now I want to talk on the white garment churches.[2] God is not found in those places. The devil has two forms: one he appears like the angels of the light, one when he appear in white. You know the demons also answer the names of the angels of God. So they go with this deceitful functions and prophesize to the church and say "God has spoken," when my church has not spoken. Every unbeliever has an international demon that is responsible for your problem and because they are in control of you, your spirit have been bound together to them and whenever you have a problem they direct you to these white garment churches since they have succeeded in subdividing our subconscious. So when you reach there, you will see a pastor, the pastor will ask your problem to appear. When the demon appear, they will say "What will you eat?" The demon will say I will eat goat, fowl, yam and different sort of thing, and you will ask to buy these things. They will tell you to buy red candle, black candle, and white candle, and different kind of things, a sacrifice of a devil. You will go to the market and begin to buy all these things and at time you won't have money, you'll go and begin to borrow money for the devil, when you cannot even feed fine, you cannot clothe fine, you want to spend your money for the devil. Why not you spend your money for Jesus and receive abundant blessing from him, that you won't have enough house to store them? You wonder why the Bible says the devil has come to steal. He has devised means to steal away people's money and as you bring these things to be sacrificed, they will exchange your demon. If you are steered by an international demon, it will be exchanged for a local demon accompanied by a withdrawal spirit. Because this spirit is accompanied by withdrawal spirit, it will be as if your problem is returned, because of this spirit, it will go and pinch your problem and your problem will come again. So you will be running hither and thither, buying here and there. After you buy these things, they will tell you to buy seven candles, meaning the demons of perfection. They said God created everything and on the seventh day he rested, meaning perfection. They will tell you to buy seven candles and they will round it on your head seven time and this signifies they had initiated you with the demons in the air when this is done. They will tell you to buy incense and light in your house. Let me tell you something, each incense represents thirteen demons with different assignments and as you light them in your house, you will be attracting demons. Your house will be full of demons and they possess your children and will be working on them and will come to real manifestations in their life. After seven years, you know when I had not repented, I was among one of the people supplying these white garment churches their holy water. The water is not holy because it has been contaminated with demons. So when you enter the church, the first thing they will sprinkle is this water and as they sprinkle it they have transferred demons into you and these demons will be working on you, using your children. My friend, why are you going to seek help where there is no help? Jesus is able to solve your problem without collecting money, and when your problem is being solved by God it is for once and for all. You shall not come again, it is only the devil who is a counterfeit man, and when he solve a problem, it will come again. Jesus says, "come unto me all that labour and is heavy laden, and I will give you rest." Come to Jesus, and he would be able to solve your problems, he is able to carry them. And these white garment churches also have communication links with the native doctors. They all together have communication links with the spiritual world. Their pastors have communication links with spiritual realm. And it is with the aid of their spiritual telephone that they are able to communicate with the spiritual world.

Now I want to make a description of how the kingdom of the devil looks like. And especially the kingdom in the water, it is another world altogether. I told you it is an heterogeneous society. A place where wickedness is the talk of the day. In the water they have standard computers, they have machine rooms, they have laboratories, they have hospitals, they have secondary schools, they have higher institutions. I mean it's a home of fashion and cosmetics. People use to have business with the demons in the water. You are asked to submit fifty-eight eggs. And they will give you an egg and as you throw the egg inside the water, it will direct you to the spiritual room, and as you come, you'll buy these things and come out. Remember these things are dedicated to demon, so they will have effects on you. You know all these things can have effect on you, if you are not a Christian. But whether the devil like it, he should begin to manufacture everything. But I tell you, whatever a Christian hand touches is sanctified. Most of the houses you see physically are constructed from the water. Most of these beautiful hotels that you see, that you marvel how they are built, are constructed from the water, because people have business link with the spiritual world. In the water we have renowned scientists, they have people that can invent wonderful things, and they even teach people and the people will appears physically and begun to practicalize them in this person. They would be singing he has invented this with the aid of the demon. In the spiritual realm they have torture room, if you are an agent of the devil and you're not doing any well, you're not living up to expectation, you'll be taken to the torture room and you'll be tortured so that you'll know what to do the next time. It is in the water that people come to acquire power. It's the Queen of the Coast that is responsible for issuing out power to the people. In the days that she will issue out power to the people, I will be around with her in an inner chamber, because I was very intimate with her. And the day, I'll lie down in her house, snake will be my pillow, while snake will lie by my side and another will lie by my other side and they will be exchanging duties.

When this one is dead it will roll off and on and in her room. We have drums of blood. And when these people come to acquire power in her house, they would go to an inner chamber and all the demons in the water will appear and she would invoke the power inside the ring. The ring will be given to the person who carries it, and this power is got from the water and as they give you the ring you wear it and it will always be in you and when anybody talks, you'll say who you are, because you have a little power in your pocket.

I can call the name of Jesus and this your power will disappear. I want to tell you that your power can be challenged by the power of Jesus. Who are you? Because you have a little power in your pocket. You begin to brag, you think you have power. If you want to acquire power come to Jesus, and acquire the highest power, he will give you an unchallenging power no demons, no witches, or wizards, no power of any kind will be able to challenge. Jesus will give you the real divine automatic and authentic power. Praise the lord! Now I want to talk on initiation. Devil has devised so many means he will use to initiate people. He will send his agents all around to begin to shake people's hand and anybody they see they will shake hand. They will tell you, "Please, I know you in so, so and so place," but they don't know you anywhere. They are agents of the devil. They will be moving around shaking people's hand and maybe if they had succeeded in shaking a hundred hands, and they shake the hand of believer, the hundred is lost. And it is as they shake people's hand, they initiate people. When they give people gift, eat with people, laugh with people, move together with people. They initiate people, and as they initiate them, they write down their names and you do anything they want you to do. You'll dance to their tune programmed from their computer. The devil has also sent his agents to the world to possess people and it is only non-Christians who can be possessed, because he or she is not confirmed by the power of the Holy Ghost. The devil also suppress people, both unbelievers and believers, he is not supposed to suppress believers but listen to what happens when a Christian gets off from her bed and go to her office, and as she begin to talk to people, these demons will use this as a point of contact. To your physical interaction with people you do not know, they will use it as a point of contact. If you pray very well before you sleep, they will suppress you in your dream, but if you mention the name of Jesus, this name will come and pull the demon out of you. If you don't pray before you eat you'll be eating what the demons have contaminated, but if you pray, the name of Jesus will neutralize it.

Finally, I want to talk on the weapons of the Christian. God has given Christians weapon to fight against the devil. So many people used to complain that God and the devil is putting hands together to deal with man. Some people say God was unable to withstand the devil in heaven, so he took the devil down to this place to destroy mankind. Every time devil is causing trouble here and there, man cannot rest. I want to tell you devil only do this to you if you are not a Christian, but if you are Christian you have weapons to fight with the devil and one of the weapons is the name of Jesus, and at the mention every knee shall bow, every tongue shall confess that Jesus is the Lord and as his name is mentioned to the devil, the devil will bow down and say Jesus is the Lord, so the name of Jesus is dangerous to the territory of devil. You destroy demons if you say, devil, I bind you in the name of Jesus. A rope will appear and bind the devil. There was an instance that happened in the spiritual world, something happened. You know they have different levels of blood banks and different demon drinks this blood depending on the ghost you are holding. The place they use to store blood is a very strong room and there are soldiers around to make sure that nothing will penetrate, but something happened. The devil say the Holy Spirit is a gossiper, that maybe it is the Holy Spirit that had gone to say we have blood bank. So the Christian began to pray. There was a day a Christian prayed in the name of Jesus. It turn the blood bank empty. There was a supernatural force that turn the whole blood bank empty and the demons prostrate and begun to suck the blood on the floor. If you say in the name of Jesus, it cause darkness in territory of the devil. Because there is power in the name of Jesus, it is a strong weapon of the Christian. Another weapon of the Christian is blood of Jesus, it is very acidic and it neutralize every work of the evil one. When you want to sleep, sprinkle the blood of Jesus over your house and there will be a thick darkness and no demon will see you. The demons are afraid of the blood of Jesus, when you sprinkle, the demons will stand at erect because they won't see road to move to anywhere. Another weapon of the Christian is the fire of the Holy Ghost. It is very destructive, destroys the work of the devil. Most of the people devil has written down their name in his book will be free when Christians rebuke this book by the Holy Ghost. Another weapon of the Christian is praises. You must praise the Lord!

Notes

INTRODUCTION

1. M. O. Ojewale, *A Call to Prayer for Nigeria* (Lagos: Peace and Salvation Publishers, 1990), 23–24, 37.
2. Throughout the study, I shall use the term that is the most often employed by Nigerians themselves—Born-Again Christians. This term captures the central aspect of a religious movement that is extremely diverse from the doctrinal, institutional and sociological point of view, and constitutes the central experience that enables converts to identify their co-religionists despite internal differences and conflicts. It also has the merit of avoiding the often sterile debates within the sociology of religion on the differences between Pentecostalism, neo-Pentecostalism, and evangelical movements. While the great majority of converts recognize themselves as Pentecostal, the term is not widely used in Nigeria.
3. See J. D. Y. Peel, *Religious Encounter and the Making of the Yoruba* (Bloomington: University of Indiana Press, 2000), 310–18; R. Marshall-Fratani, "Prospérité Miraculeuse: Les pasteurs pentecôtistes et l'argent de Dieu au Nigéria," *Politique Africaine* 82 (June 2001): 24–44.
4. See R. Mustapha, "Ethnicity and the Politics of Democratization in Nigeria, in *Ethnicity & Democracy in Africa*, ed. B. Berman, D. Eyoh, and W. Kymlicka (Oxford: James Currey, 2004), 257–75.; R. Mustapha, "Coping With Diversity: The Nigerian State in Historical Perspective," in *The African State: Reconsiderations*, ed. A. Samatar and I. Samatar (Portsmouth, N.H.: Heinemann, 2002), 149–75.
5. "Verily, verily I say unto thee, except that a man be born again, he cannot see the kingdom of God" (John 3:3).

Unless otherwise indicated, all biblical citations refer to the King James Version.

6. H. Arendt, *The Human Condition,* 2d ed. (Chicago: University of Chicago Press, 1998), 247.

7. G. Agamben, *The Time that Remains: A Commentary on the Letter to the Romans* (Stanford: Stanford University Press, 2005), 134.

8. J. L. Austin, *How to Do Things with Words* (Oxford: Oxford University Press, 1975).

9. P. Klassen, *Blessed Events: Religion and Home Birth in America* (Princeton: Princeton University Press, 2001).

10. N. Ngada, *Speaking for Ourselves* (Braamfontein: Institute of Contextual Theology, 1985), 21, quoted in T. Ranger, "Religious Movements and Politics in Sub-Saharan Africa," *African Studies Review* 29, no. 2 (1986): 1–69.

11. G. Anidjar, "Secularism," *Critical Inquiry* 33 (2006): 52–77.

12. M. Gauchet, *Le désenchantement du monde* (Paris: Gallimard, 1985).

13. G. C. Spivak, "Religion, Politics, Theology: A Conversation with Achille Mbembe," *boundary 2* 34, no. 2 (2007): 156.

14. M. Foucault, *Dits et Ecrits,* Vol. 3: *1976–1979* (Paris: Gallimard, 1994), 141–44.

15. R. Banégas and J.-P. Warnier, "Nouvelles figures de la réussite et du pouvoir," *Politique Africaine* 82 (June 2001): 6.

16. Spivak, "Religion, Politics, Theology," 154.

17. Ibid., 156.

18. Throughout the text I will employ the French term *véridiction,* the accepted English translation of which is "truth-telling," which I feel fails to capture the full meaning of the term. *Véridiction* implies the act or experience of telling the truth but also implies the modes or conditions in which this or that truth may be told and be accepted as true. *Véridiction* is to knowledge as *juridiction* is to power. Unless otherwise indicated, the translations of French texts in this study are my own.

19. Spivak. "Religion, Politics, Theology," 156.

20. R. Marshall-Fratani and D. Peclard, "La religion du sujet en Afrique: Introduction au thème," *Politique Africaine* 87 (October 2002): 5–20.

21. M. Foucault, *Sécurité, territoire, population: Cours au Collège de France, 1977–1978* (Paris: Gallimard/Seuil, 2005), 405.

22. M. Foucault, "Table ronde du 20 mai 1978," in *Dits et Ecrits,* Vol. 4: *1980–1988* (Paris : Gallimard, 1994), 30.

23. A. Mbembe, "La colonie: Son petit secret et sa part maudite," *Politique Africaine* 102 (July 2006): 101–27.

24. M. Foucault, "Usages des plaisirs et techniques de soi," in *Dits et Ecrits,* Vol. 4: *1980–1988,* 559.

25. Ibid.

26. Spivak. "Religion, Politics, Theology," 154.

27. For a comprehensive overview, see H. de Vries and L. E. Sullivan, *Political Theologies: Public Religions in a Post-Secular World* (New York: Fordham University Press, 2006).

28. J.-L. Nancy, *La Déclosion: déconstruction du christianisme,* vol. 1 (Paris: Editions Galilée, 2005).

CHAPTER ONE

1. See R. Marshall-Fratani and D. Peclard, eds., *Les sujets de Dieu, Politique Africaine* 87 (October 2002), especially their introduction, "La religion du sujet en Afrique: Introduction au thème," 5–20.

2. See J.-F. Bayart, *L'Illusion identitaire* (Paris: Fayard, 1996); J.-P. Chrétien, *Le défie de l'ethnisme: Rwanda et Burundi: 1990–1996* (Paris: Karthala, 1997). For a particularly egregious example of the way in which the misuse of "culture" leads to crude substantive notions of identity, see D. Laitin, *Hegemony and Culture: Politics and Religious Change among the Yoruba* (Chicago: University of Chicago Press, 1986).

3. See P. Geschiere and B. Meyer, "Introduction," in *Globalisation and Identity: Dialectics of Flow and Closure,* ed. Geschiere and Meyer (Oxford: Blackwell, 1999), 1–10.

4. The term was coined by A. Mbembe, *Afriques indociles: Christianisme, pouvoir et état en société postcoloniale* (Paris: Karthala, 1988). Even if he cannot be accused of culturalism, the idea of the "revenge of paganism" has been interpreted in a culturalist way by other analysts. For examples of such approaches, see G. Ter Haar, *L'Afrique et le monde des esprits,* (Paris: Karthala, 1996); R. Devisch, "Pillaging Jesus: Healing Churches and the Villagisation of Kinshasa," *Africa* 66, no. 4 (1996): 555–86; and "La violence à Kinshasa, ou l'institution en négatif," *Cahiers d'études africaines* 38, nos. 2–4 (1998):150–52; and "La parodie dans les églises de guérison à Kinshasa *Intinéraires et contacts de cultures* 25 (1998); R. Otayek and C. Toulabor "Innovations et contestations religieuses," *Politique Africaine* 39 (September 1990): 31–46; B. Meyer, "Delivered from the Powers of Darkness: Confessions of Satanic Riches in Christian Ghana," *Africa* 65, no. 2 (1995): 236–55; "Les églises pentecôtistes africaines: Satan et la dissociation de la 'tradition,'" *Anthropologie et société* 22, no. 1 (1998): 63–84.; "'If You Are a Devil, You Are a Witch, and If You Are a Witch, You Are a Devil': The Integration of Pagan Ideas into the Conceptual Universe of Ewe Christians in Southeastern Ghana," *Journal of Religion in Africa* 22, no. 2 (1992): 98–132. For a critique of these studies, see J. Tonda, *La guérison divine en Afrique Centrale: Congo, Gabon* (Paris: Karthala, 2002).

5. Cited by C. Coulon in order to criticize such approaches, in "Religions et Politique" in *Les Afriques politiques* (Paris: Editions La Découverte, 1991), 87.

6. One exception to this rule is the study by S. Ellis and G. Ter Haar, *Worlds of Power: Religious Thought and. Political Practice in Africa* (London: C. Hurst, 2004).

7. See the introduction to *Religion et transition démocratique en Afrique,* ed. F. Constantin and C. Coulon (Paris: Karthala, 1997).

8. J.-F Bayart, ed., *Religion et modernité politique en Afrique noire: Dieu pour tous et chacun pour soi* (Paris: Karthala, 1994). The term *cité cultuelle* is borrowed from François de Polignac, who employed it in his study of how the Greek city-state's political imaginary of civic space was developed through its relationship with its cults. See F. de Polignac, *La naissance de la cité grecque: Cultes, espace et société VIIIe–VIIe siècles* (Paris: Editions La découverte, 1984).

9. A. Mbembe, *Afriques indociles,* 18–19.

10. See the critique by Claude Lefort, "The Permanence of the Theologico-political?" in his *Democracy and Political Theory* (Cambridge: Polity Press, 1988), 213–55.

11. I use the term *rare* as it is understood by Paul Veyne, who employs it in its Latin sense as *rara* (uncommon, few).

12. This is taken from a billboard I saw in Lagos in 1989 that bore a single message: "Jesus is the Answer." Another popular Born-Again billboard slogan in Lagos and other southern cities from the late 1970s was: "I found it."

13. Lefort, *Democracy and Political Theory,* 220.

14. Ibid.

15. Lefort points out that such a position entails adopting a positivist fiction—the idea of a "presocial society" and positing as elements aspects that can only be grasped on the basis of an experience that is already social. Ibid., 218. See also P. Bourdieu, *Outline of a Theory of Practice* (Cambridge: Cambridge University Press, 1977), 21.

16. Lefort, *Democracy and Political Theory,* 220.

17. Lefort, "Introduction," in ibid., 2.

18. Bayart, ed., *Religion et modernité politique en Afrique noire;* Bayart, "Foucault au Congo," in *Penser avec Michel Foucault: Théorie critique et pratiques politiques,* ed. M.-C. Granjon (Paris: Karthala, 2005), 183–222; D. Cruise O'Brien; *Symbolic Confrontations: Muslims Imagining the State in Africa* (London: C. Hurst, 2003); J. Tonda, "De l'exorcisme comme mode de démocratisation: Eglises et mouvements religieux au Congo de 1990–1994," in *Religion et transition démocratique en Afrique,* ed. Constantin and Coulon; Tonda, *La guérison divine en Afrique Centrale,* especially chap. 7.

19. For a nonexhaustive list, see the following: J. Haynes, *Religion and Politics in Africa* (London: Zed Books, 1996); H. Hansen and M. Twaddle, eds., *Religion and Politics in East Africa: The Period since Independence* (Athens: Ohio University Press, 1991); Laitin, *Hegemony and Culture;* U. Ukiwo, "Politics,

Ethno-religious Conflicts and Democratic Consolidation in Nigeria," *Journal of Modern African Studies* 41 (2003): 115–38.; J. Ibrahim, "Religion and Political Turbulence in Nigeria," *Journal of Modern African Studies* 29, no. 1 (1991): 115–36; S. O. Ilesanmi, *Religious Pluralism and Nigerian State* (Athens: Ohio University Press, 1997); M. Kukah, *Religion, Politics and Power in Northern Nigeria* (Ibadan: Spectrum Books, 1993); E. Amucheazi, *Church and Politics in Eastern Nigeria 1945–1966: A Study in Pressure Group Politics* (Ibadan: Macmillan Nigeria, 1986); L. Danbazau, *Politics and Religion in Nigeria* (Kaduna: Vanguard, 1991). See the critique by T. Ranger, "Religious Movements and Politics in Sub-Saharan Africa," *African Studies Review* 29, no. 2 (1985): 1–70.

20. Bayart, *L'Illusion identitaire;* Chrétien, *Le défi de l'ethnisme.*

21. A. Appadurai, *Modernity at Large: Cultural Dimensions of Globalization* (Minneapolis: University of Minnesota Press, 1996), especially 165–77.

22. See discussion by Talal Asad, "Comments on Conversion," in *Conversion to Modernities: The Globalization of Christianity,* ed. P. Van der Veer (New York: Routledge, 1996), 263–74.

23. See T. Hansen and F. Stepputat, eds., *Sovereign Bodies: Citizens, Migrants and States in the Post-Colonial World* (Princeton: Princeton University Press, 2005); J. F. Bayart, *Le gouvernement du monde: Une critique politique de la globalisation* (Paris: Fayard, 2004); B. Badie and M. Smouts, *Le retournement du monde: Sociologie de la scène internationale* (Paris: Presses de la Fondation Nationale des Sciences Politiques and Dalloz, 1992).

24. See B. Lee, "Going Public," *Public Culture* 5, no. 2 (1993): 165–78; C. Calhoun, "Nationalism and Civil Society: Democracy, Diversity and Self-Determination," *International Sociology* 8, no. 4 (1993): 387–411; C. Taylor, "Modes of Civil Society," *Public Culture* 3, no. 1 (1990): 95–132; and P. Chatterjee, "A Response to Taylor's 'Modes of Civil Society,'" *Public Culture* 3, no. 1 (1990): 119–32; A. Mbembe, *De la postcolonie: Essai sur l'imagination politique dans l'Afrique contemporaine* (Paris: Karthala, 2000), especially chap. 1; J. Comaroff and J. L. Comaroff, eds., *Civil Society and Political Imagination in Africa: Critical Perspectives* (Chicago: University of Chicago Press, 2000).

25. See C. Castoriadis, *The Imaginary Institution of Society* (Cambridge, Mass.: MIT Press, 1987), chaps. 5 and 6.

26. See P. Chatterjee, *The Nation and Its Fragments* (Princeton: Princeton University Press, 1993); S. Rouse, *Shifting Body Politics: Gender, Nation, State in Pakistan* (New Delhi: Women Unlimited Edition, 2004).

27. The problematic of identity refers to the possibility of an authentic subject, one who responds to the imperative "know thyself," and through this self-knowledge affirms itself as both unique and unitary in the face of the difference of the other. See M. Foucault, *The History of Sexuality,* Vol. 1: *The Will to Knowledge* (London: Penguin Books, 1998); Foucault, *Sécurité, territoire, population: Cours au Collège de France, 1977–1978* (Paris:

Gallimard/Seuil, 2005). See also C. Taylor, *The Malaise of Modernity* (Concord, Ontario, Canada: Anansi, 1991).

28. Asad, "Comments on Conversion," 265. See also C. Taylor, *A Secular Age* (Cambridge, Mass.: Harvard University Press, 2007).

29. See B. Meyer, "Commodities and the Power of Prayer: Pentecostalist Attitudes towards Consumption in Contemporary Ghana," in *Globalisation and Identity,* ed. Geschiere and Meyer, 151–76; R. Marshall-Fratani, "Mediating the Global and Local in Nigerian Pentecostalism," *Journal of Religion in Africa* 28, no. 3 (1998): 278–315; W. Van Binsbergen, "Globalization and Virtuality: Analytical Problems Posed by the Contemporary Transformation of African Societies," in *Globalisation and Identity,* ed. Geschiere and Meyer, 273–304; Comaroff, "Consuming Passions"; J. Comaroff and J. L. Comaroff, *Modernity and Its Malcontents: Ritual and Power in Postcolonial Africa* (Chicago: University of Chicago Press, 1993); Comaroff and Comaroff, "Alien-nation: Zombies, Immigrants and Global Capitalism," *South Atlantic Quarterly* 101, no. 4 (2002): 779–805; Comaroff and Comaroff, "Second Comings: Neo-Protestant Ethics and Millennial Capitalism in South Africa, and Elsewhere," in *2000 Years and Beyond: Faith, Identity and the Common Era,* ed. P. Gifford (London: Routledge, 2002); Comaroff and Comaroff, "Naturing the Nation: Aliens, Apocalypse and the Postcolonial State," *Journal of Southern African Studies* 27, no. 3 (2001): 627–51. On witchcraft, see P. Geschiere, *Sorcellerie et politique en Afrique: La viande des autres* (Paris: Karthala, 1995).

30. See R. Banégas and J.-P. Warnier, "Nouvelles figures de la réussite et du pouvoir," *Politique Africaine* 82 (June 2001): 5–23.

31. Marshall-Fratani and Peclard, "La religion du sujet en Afrique," 6.

32. Geschiere and Meyer, "Introduction," in *Globalisation and Identity,* 1–10.

33. Van Binsbergen, "Globalization and Virtuality," 292.

34. Asad, "Comments on Conversion," 265.

35. A. Mbembe, "A propos des écritures africaines de soi," *Politique Africaine* 77 (March 2000): 16–43. Revised version published as "African Modes of Self-Writing," *Public Culture* 14, no. 1 (2002): 239–73. Quotation from Mbembe's response to critics, "On the Power of the False," *Public Culture* 14, no. 3 (2002): 631.

36. The concept of "instituting imaginary" is taken from C. Castoriadis, *Imaginary Institution of Society.* See especially chaps. 3 and 7.

37. Meyer, "Commodities and the Power of Prayer."

38. B. Meyer, *Translating the Devil: Religion and Modernity among the Ewe in Ghana* (Edinburgh: Edinburgh University Press, 1999).

39. Comaroff and Comaroff, eds., *Modernity and Its Malcontents.* See also M. Bastian, "Married in the Water: Spirit Kin and Other Afflictions of Modernity in Southeastern Nigeria," *Journal of Religion in Africa* 2 (1997): 1–19.

40. Comaroff and Comaroff, eds., *Modernity and Its Malcontents,* xxx.

41. Comaroff and Comaroff, "Alien-nation," 780.

42. Ibid., 786.

43. Ibid.

44. Comaroff and Comaroff, eds., *Modernity and Its Malcontents*, xxiii.

45. Tonda, *La guérison divine en Afrique Centrale*.

46. Devisch, "Pillaging Jesus"; Van Binsbergen, "Globalization and Virtuality."

47. Otayek and Toulabor, "Innovations et contestations religieuses,"117.

48. Tonda, *La guérison divine en Afrique Centrale*, 39. See also J. Tonda, *Le souverain moderne: Le corps du pouvoir en Afrique centrale (Congo, Gabon)* (Paris: Karthala, 2005).

49. Devisch, "Pillaging Jesus," 555.

50. Tonda, *La guérison divine en Afrique Centrale*, 34.

51. For a critical discussion of globalization studies, see Bayart, *Le gouvernement du monde;* F. Cooper, "What Is the Concept of Globalization Good For? An African Historian's Perspective," *African Affairs* 100, no. 399 (2001): 189–213.

52. J. Comaroff, 'Consuming Passions: Nightmares of the Global Village' in *Culture*, 17, 1-2, 1997. pp. 7-19. See L. White, *Speaking with Vampires: Rumor and History in Colonial Africa,* (Berkely: University of California Press, 2000).

53. J. Comaroff, "Consuming Passions: Nightmares of the Global Village," *Culture* 17, nos. 1–2 (1997): 7–19.

54. Comaroff and Comaroff, "Alien-nation."

55. Comaroff, "Consuming Passions."

56. The expression is A. Mbembe's, "La prolifération du divin en Afrique subsaharienne," in *Les Politiques de Dieu*, ed. G. Kefel (Paris: Le Seuil, 1993), 179. On Islam, see O. Kane and J.-L. Triaud, eds., *Islam et islamismes au Sud du Sahara* (Paris: Karthala, 1998); M. Gomez-Perez, ed., *L'Islam politique au sud du Sahara* (Paris: Karthala, 2005); R. Otayek, ed., *Le radicalisme islamique au sud du Sahara: Da'wa, arabisation et critique de l'Occident* (Paris: Karthala, 1993).

57. T. Asad, *Genealogies of Religion: Discipline and Reasons of Power in Christianity and Islam* (Baltimore: Johns Hopkins University Press, 1993), 163–64.

58. N. Ngada, *Speaking for Ourselves* (Braamfontein: Institute of Contextual Theology, 1985), 21, quoted in Ranger, "Religious Movements and Politics in Sub-Saharan Africa."

59. Comaroff, "Consuming Passions."

60. Ibid.; J. Lafontaine, *Speak of the Devil: Tales of Satanic Abuse in Contemporary England* (Cambridge: Cambridge University Press, 1995); J. Richardson, J. Best, and D. Bromley, eds., *The Satanism Scare* (New York: Aldine de Gruyter, 1991).

61. See *Report of the Presidential Commission of Inquiry into the Cult of Devil Worship in Kenya*, 1999. Most of the testimonies in the 204-page report do not refer to local or traditional forms of demons but to those forms— pentagrams, black masses, biblical demons—which are typically found in

global Pentecostal discourse. See also "Devil Worship Exists in Kenya—Commission Says," *The Nation,* 4 August 1999.

62. V. Mudimbe, *L'Odeur du père: Essais sur les limites de la science et de la vie en Afrique noire* (Paris: Présence Africaine, 1982).

63. Mbembe, "A propos des écritures africaines de soi"; A. Mbembe, "On the Power of the False," *Public Culture* 14, no. 3 (2002): 629–41. See also V. Mudimbe, *The Idea of Africa* (Bloomington: Indiana University Press, 1994).

64. Asad, "Comments on Conversion," 272.

65. K. Barber, "How Man Makes God in West Africa: Yoruba Attitudes towards the Orisa," *Africa* 51, no. 3 (1981): 724.

66. J.-F. Bayart, "Les églises africaines et la politique du ventre," *Politique Africaine* 35 (October 1989): 5–6.

67. J.F. Bayart, "Fait missionaire et politique du ventre: Une lecture foucauldienne," *Le Fait Missionnaire* 6 (September 1998); Bayart, "Foucault au Congo." See also J.-F. Bayart, "Total Subjectivation," in *Matière à politique: Le pouvoir, les corps et les choses,* ed. J.-F. Bayart and J.-P. Warnier (Paris: Karthala/CERI, 2004), 215–53.

68. M. Foucault, *Dits et Ecrits,* Vol. 3: *1976–1979* (Paris: Gallimard, 1994), 141–44.

69. P. Veyne, "Foucault révolutionne l'histoire," in *Comment on écrit l'histoire suivi par Foucault révolutionne l'histoire* (Paris: Seuil, Points, 1978).

70. Foucault, *Dits et Ecrits,* Vol. 3: *1976–1979,* 154.

71. Veyne, "Foucault révolutionne l'histoire," 204.

72. Ibid., 221.

73. M. Foucault, *L'Archéologie du savoir* (Paris: Gallimard, 1969), 254; cited in Veyne, "Foucault révolutionne l'histoire," 223.

74. P. Veyne, *Les Grecs ont-ils cru à leurs mythes?* (Paris: Seuil, Points, 1983), 224.

75. See Derrida's discussion of *bricolage* in J. Derrida, "Structure, Sign and Play in the Discourse of the Human Sciences," in *Writing and Difference* (Chicago: University of Chicago Press, 1978), 285.

76. Veyne, "Foucault révolutionne l'histoire," 207.

77. Asad, "Comments on Conversion," 264.

78. J. Comaroff and J. L. Comaroff, *Of Revelation and Revolution,* Vol. 1: *Christianity, Colonialism and Consciousness in South Africa* (Chicago: University of Chicago Press, 1991); J. Comaroff and J. L. Comaroff, *Of Revelation and Revolution,* Vol. 2: *The Dialectics of Modernity on a South African Frontier* (Chicago: University of Chicago Press, 1997).

79. Veyne, *Les Grecs ont-ils cru à leurs mythes?* 11.

80. Bayart, "Foucault au Congo," 192.

81. See Mbembe, "A propos des écritures africaines de soi."

82. M. Foucault, *L'Histoire de sexualité,* Vol. 1: *La volonté de savoir* (Paris: Gallimard, 1976), 121–23.

83. Ibid.

84. M. Foucault, "Le sujet et le pouvoir?" in *Dits et Ecrits,* Vol. 4: *1980–1988* (Paris: Gallimard, 1994), 233.

85. Ibid., 237.

86. Ibid., 236.

87. Foucault, *L'Histoire de sexualité,* Vol. 1: *La volonté de savoir,* 122.

88. Foucault, "Le sujet et le pouvoir?" 242.

89. Foucault, *L'Histoire de sexualité,* Vol. 1: *La volonté de savoir,* 123.

90. Foucault, "Le sujet et le pouvoir?" 243.

91. See Bayart's discussion of his *L'Etat en Afrique: La politique du ventre,* in Bayart, "Foucault au Congo."

92. Foucault, *Sécurité, territoire, population,* 397. In this form, "governmentality" refers to three things: first, the "ensemble constituted by institutions, procedures, analyses, reflections, calculations and tactics which enabled the exercise of this highly specific, but complex, form of power, which had as its principal target the population, political economy as its principal mode of knowledge, and security apparatuses as its principal technical instrument." Second, it is a line of force that over several centuries in the West has led to the preeminence of this type of power, which he calls "government," over other forms like discipline and sovereignty. Finally, it refers to the historical process in which the state of justice in the Middle Ages, which became between the fifteenth and sixteenth centuries the administrative state, became progressively "governmentalized" in the sense of employing a form of power as "conducting conduct," as opposed to power relations that express themselves as a form of confrontation, or politics as war by other means. Foucault, *Dits et Ecrits,* Vol. 3: *1976–1979:* 655.

93. Foucault, "Le sujet et le pouvoir?" 237.

94. Foucault, *Sécurité, territoire, population,* 407.

95. Ibid.

96. Mbembe, "On the Power of the False"; Mbembe, *Afriques indociles.*

97. C. Taylor, *Modern Social Imaginaries* (Durham, N.C.: Duke University Press, 2004).

98. See J. Ferguson, *The Anti-politics Machine: "Development," Depoliticisation and Bureaucratic State Power in Lesotho* (Cambridge: Cambridge University Press, 1990), for a study of Foucauldian inspiration. See also the discussion of neo-liberalism by Bayart, "Foucault au Congo," 217–19.

99. See J.-F. Bayart, ed., *La greffe de l'état* (Paris: Karthala, 1996).

100. Foucault makes clear that modern relations of power do not have their origin in the state form, but rather arise from the governmentalization of the state, tracing the genealogy of a new form of "conducting conduct" that underwrites the exercise of state power from within the Christian pastorate and what he calls "pastoral power." It is clear that while the state form may be a highly specific form of concentration of this type of power relations, whose effects are felt throughout the social body, they do not arise from the state itself, but rather from the micro-political sites within

which they find their specific expression, giving rise over time to a general rationality of power. See Foucault, *Sécurité, territoire, population*.

101. Ibid., 405.

102. Ibid., 409.

103. Mission may be seen as an example of what Foucault calls a *dispositif* (apparatus), an *explicit* program that involves "calculated and reasoned prescriptions in terms of which we should organise institutions, lay out spaces, regulate behaviour. If they have an identity, it is that of a programming which is occasionally left in suspension, it is not that of a general signification which has remained hidden. Of course, these programmings arise from much more general forms of rationality than those they put directly to work. These programmes never pass in their entirety into institutions; they are simplified, certain aspects are chosen and not others, and nothing ever goes according to plan." Foucault, "Table ronde du 20 mai 1978," in *Dits et Ecrits*, Vol. 4: *1980–1988*, 28.

104. J. D. Y. Peel, *Religious Encounter and the Making of the Yoruba* (Bloomington: University of Indiana Press, 2000); Peel, "For Who Hath Despised the Day of Small Things?: Missionary Narratives and Historical Anthropology," *Comparative Studies in Society and History* 37 (1995): 581–607; Peel, "The Pastor and the Babalawo: The Interaction of Religions in Nineteenth Century Yorubaland," *Africa* 60. (1990): 338–69; Comaroff and Comaroff, *Of Revelation and Revolution*, Vol. 1: *Christianity, Colonialism and Consciousness in South Africa;* Comaroff and Comaroff, *Of Revelation and Revolution*, Vol. 2: *The Dialectics of Modernity on a South African Frontier.* See also the novel by Mongo Beti, *Le Pauvre Christ de Bomba* (Paris: Présence Africaine, 1976).

105. I say unhappily because such a conception presumes a shared epistemological field, the possibility of a false consciousness, and the postulates of a "correct" or "true" understanding of what practices signify, and implies an approach that gives primacy to the object, and not the relation.

106. Foucault, "Table ronde du 20 mai 1978," in *Dits et Ecrits*, Vol. 4: *1980–1988*, 28.

107. Ibid.

108. Foucault, *Sécurité, territoire, population*, 391.

109. M. Foucault, "Sexualité et solitude," in *Dits et Ecrits*, Vol. 4: *1980–1988*, 171.

110. M. Foucault, "Usage des plaisirs et techniques de soi," in *Dits et Ecrits*, Vol. 4: *1980–1988*, 555.

111. M. Foucault, "L'Ethique de souci de soi comme pratique de la libérté," in *Dits et Ecrits*, Vol. 4: *1980–1988*, 719.

112. G. Deleuze, *Pourparlers 1972–1990* (Paris: Les Editions de Minuit, 1990), 135, 158.

113. G. Deleuze, "Qu'est-ce qu'un dispositif?" in *Deux régimes de fous: Textes et entretiens 1975–1995* (Paris: Les Editions de Minuit, 2003), 319.

114. Deleuze, *Pourparlers 1972–1990*, 206.
115. M. Foucault, "A quoi rêvent les Iranians?" in *Dits et Ecrits*, Vol. 3: *1976–1979*, 691.
116. Foucault, *Sécurité, territoire, population*, 204–7.
117. M. Foucault, "Inutile de se soulever?" in *Dits et Ecrits*, Vol. 3: *1976–1979*, 793.
118. Foucault, *Sécurité, territoire, population*.
119. Foucault, "Table ronde du 20 mai 1978," in *Dits et Ecrits*, Vol. 4: *1980–1988*, 30. "Le problème politique le plus général n'est-il pas celui de la vérité? Comment lier l'une à l'autre, la façon de partager le vrai et le faux et la manière de se gouverner soi-même et les autres? La volonté de fonder entièrement à neuf, l'une et l'autre, l'une par l'autre (découvrir un tout autre partage par une autre manière de se gouverner, et se gouverner tout autrement à partir d'un autre partage), c'est cela la 'spiritualité politique.'"
120. Foucault, "Inutile de se soulever?" in *Dits et Ecrits*, Vol. 3: *1976–1979*, 791.
121. Veyne, "Foucault révolutionne l'histoire," 220–21.
122. Ibid., 222.
123. H. Arendt, *The Human Condition*, 2d ed. (Chicago: University of Chicago Press, 1998), 247.
124. Mbembe, *Afriques indociles*, 27.
125. C. Lefort, "The Permanence of the Theologico-Political?" in *Democracy and Political Theory* (Cambridge: Polity Press, 1988), 254.
126. Ibid., 222.
127. I employ this term with the ambiguity of the double sense of "overcoming" and "being overcome," which takes it from the realm of pure agency or intentionality, and places it in the realm of subjectivity.
128. Foucault, "Inutile de se soulever?" in *Dits et Ecrits*, Vol. 3: *1976–1979*, 780–82.
129. Arendt, *Human Condition*, 247.

CHAPTER TWO

1. See B. Meyer, "'Make a Complete Break with the Past': Memory and Post-colonial Modernity in Ghanaian Pentecostal Discourse," in *Memory and the Postcolony: African Anthropology and the Critique of Power*, ed. R. Werbner (London: Zed Books, 1998), 182–208.
2. The "Azuza street awakening," in which a group of Methodists experienced the "baptism of the Holy Spirit" in the form of glossalalia, or speaking in tongues, in San Francisco in 1906, is often identified as the origin of global Pentecostalism, even though the movement has its roots in evangelical movements and revivals, or "awakenings," of the previous century across America and Great Britain. See M. Noll, D. Bebbington, and G. Rawlk, eds., *Evangelicalism: Comparative Studies of Popular Protestantism*

in North America, the British Isles, and Beyond, 1700–1990 (Oxford: Oxford University Press, 1994).

3. J. D. Y. Peel, *Ijeshas and Nigerians: The Incorporation of a Yoruba Kingdom 1890s–1970s* (Cambridge: Cambridge University Press, 1983), 261.

4. J. Le Goff, *History and Memory* (New York: Columbia University Press, 1992), 98.

5. V. Y. Mudimbe, *The Invention of Africa: Gnosis, Philosophy and the Order of Knowledge* (Bloomington: Indiana University Press, 1988), 47–48.

6. J. D. Y. Peel, "For Who Hath Despised the Days of Small Things? Missionary Narratives and Historical Anthropology," *Comparative Studies in Society and History* 37, no. 3 (1995): 602–3.

7. J. D. Y. Peel, *Religious Encounter and the Making of the Yoruba* (Bloomington: University of Indiana Press, 2000), 255.

8. M. de Certeau, *The Writing of History* (New York: Columbia University Press, 1988), 178–79.

9. J. D. Y. Peel, "Olaju: A Yoruba Concept of Development," *Journal of Development Studies* 14 (1978): 139–65.

10. Peel emphasizes the experiential and pneumatic nature of Evangelical Christianity, showing how missionaries articulated conversion in terms of internal conscience and the centrality of "heartfelt" conviction rather than mere obedience and the following of prescriptions. Peel, *Religious Encounter and the Making of the Yoruba*, 250–55.

11. J. Comaroff and J. L. Comaroff, *Of Revelation and Revolution*, Vol. 1: *Christianity, Colonialism and Consciousness in South Africa* (Chicago: University of Chicago Press, 1991), 250.

12. Ibid., 251.

13. This remark must be nuanced with respect to Islam, even if precolonial forms of religious allegiance to Islam did not take the form of "identity" in the modern sense, an epistemological possibility that is introduced with colonialism, as I have argued in chapter 1.

14. J. D. Y. Peel, "An Africanist Revisits *Magic and the Millennium*," in *Secularization, Rationalism and Sectarianism*, ed. E. Barker, J. Beckford, and K. Dobbelaere (Oxford: Clarendon Press, 1993), 89.

15. Peel, *Religious Encounter and the Making of the Yoruba*, 88–89.

16. Ibid., 90.

17. J. Comaroff and J. L. Comaroff, *Of Revelation and Revolution*, Vol. 2: *The Dialectics of Modernity on a South African Frontier* (Chicago: University of Chicago Press, 1997), 25.

18. A. Mbembe, "A propos des écritures africaines de soi," *Politique Africaine* 77 (March 2000): 16–43. Revised version published as "African Modes of Self-Writing," *Public Culture* 14, no. 1 (2002): 239–73.

19. E. A. Ayandele, *The Missionary Impact on Modern Nigeria, 1842–1914: A Political and Social Analysis* (London: Longman, 1966), 43.

20. This phrase in pidgin English means "a power that exceeds all power."

21. Peel shows how the military expeditions the missionaries had lobbied for also resulted in great gains for Islam. *Religious Encounter and the Making of the Yoruba,* 148–49.

22. C. C. Newton to Tupper, 12 April 1892, in *Foreign Missionary Journal* 23 (July 1892), cited in Ayandele, *Missionary Impact on Modern Nigeria,* 67.

23. Ayandele, *Missionary Impact on Modern Nigeria,* 68. Peel nuances Ayandele's rather sufficient claim that Ijebu conversion was principally the outcome of the failure of their "juju" in the face of superior material force. See J. D. Y. Peel, "Conversion and Tradition in Two African Societies: Ijesha and Buganda," *Past and Present* 77 (1977): 108–41.

24. Peel, *Religious Encounter and the Making of the Yoruba,* 93.

25. Ibid., 254–55.

26. See H. Arendt, *The Human Condition,* 2d ed. (Chicago: University of Chicago Press, 1998): "Life on earth may be only the first and most miserable stage of eternal life; it is still life, and without life that will be terminated in death, there cannot be eternal life. . . . Only with the rise of Christianity, did life on earth also become the highest good of man" (316).

27. An illustration of such pre-Christian conceptions was the practice of Yoruba political leaders or vanquished war chiefs to commit suicide as an honorable gesture whose aim was to guarantee the cohesion of the lineage, the family, and the political entity, showing the importance and endurance of the collectivity over and above the individual, much like the idea of the immortality of the *polis* among the Greeks. Another indication of this was the relative equivalence in the gravity and modes of punishment for the crimes of murder and theft, both of which could be redeemed through forms of payment to the collectivities or individuals who had been wronged.

28. See B. Meyer, "Prières, fusils et meurtre rituel: Le cinéma populaire et ses nouvelles figures du pouvoir et du succès au Ghana," *Politique Africaine* 82 (June 2001): 45–62; J. Tonda, *La guérison divine en Afrique Centrale: Congo, Gabon* (Paris: Karthala, 2002).

29. C. Lefort, "The Permanence of the Theologico-Political?" in *Democracy and Political Theory* (Cambridge: Polity Press, 1988).

30. J. D. Y. Peel, *Aladura: A Religious Movement among the Yoruba* (Oxford: Oxford University Press, 1969).

31. Comaroff and Comaroff, *Of Revelation and Revolution,* Vol. 1: *Christianity, Colonialism and Consciousness in South Africa,* chap. 6.

32. C. Lévi-Strauss, *The Savage Mind* (Chicago: University of Chicago Press, 1966).

33. J. Derrida, *Writing and Difference* (Chicago: University of Chicago Press, 1978), 285.

34. See Peel, "For Who Hath Despised the Days of Small Things?" 590. The biblical citation is: "For who hath despised the day of small things? for they shall rejoice, and see the plummet in the hand of Zerubbabel with

those seven; they are the eyes of the Lord, which run to and fro through the whole world" (Zachariah 4:10). Peel explains the use of this expression by missionaries: "Zerubbabel was governor of Judah under Persian overrule. 'This House' was the Temple, then being rebuilt after the Jews' return from Babylon; the term was later taken as a metaphor for the Church." This citation is also used commonly by Born-Agains to describe the astounding growth of the movement and the trials of the early years.

35. For an analysis of the notion of messianic time as expounded by Paul in his letter to the Romans, then two millennia later in the writings of Benjamin, Scholem, and Rosenzweig, see G. Agamben, *The Time That Remains: A Commentary on the Letter to the Romans* (Stanford: Stanford University Press, 2005). See also S. Mosès, *L'Ange de l'histoire: Rosenzweig, Benjamin, Scholem* (Paris: Gallimard Poche, 2006); J. Taubes, *The Political Theology of Paul* (Stanford: Stanford University Press, 2004).

36. Mosès, *L'Ange de l'histoire.*

37. Agamben, *Time That Remains*, 67–68.

38. Ibid.

39. Dispensationalism, originating in the early 1800s, advocates a form of premillennialism, in which it sees the past, present, and future as a number of successive administrations, or "dispensations," each of which emphasizes aspects of the covenants between God and various peoples at various times. In the dispensational scheme, the time in which the church operates, known as the church age or the Christian dispensation, represents a "parenthesis." That is, it is an interruption in God's dealings with the Jewish people as described in the Old Testament, and it is the time when the Gospel is to be preached and salvation offered to the Gentiles. However, God's continued care for the Jewish people will be revealed after the end of the church age when the Jews will be restored to their land and will accept Jesus as their messiah. According to most accounts, there are seven dispensations, and we are currently living in the sixth, known as the "church" or "grace" dispensation, beginning with the birth of Christ and the establishment of his church, which involves the evangelization of the world's peoples. This period is the last one before the seventh and final dispensation, the millennial reign of Christ. At the end of the church dispensation will occur the rapture and the premillennial tribulation of Satan's reign on earth for seven years. It thus places a heavy emphasis on prophecy and eschatology, the study of the end times.

40. Agamben, *Time That Remains*, 77.

41. W. Benjamin, "Theses on the Philosophy of History, VI," in *Illuminations* (London: Fontana, 1992), 247. "The true image of the past flees by. The past can be seized only as an image which flashes up at the instant when it can be recognized and is never seen again . . . For every image of the past that is not recognized by the present as one of its own threatens to disappear irretrievably."

42. Ibid.
43. Ibid.
44. B. Jewsiewicki, "The Subject in Africa: In Foucault's Footsteps," *Public Culture* 14 (Fall 2002): 598.
45. Data on the relative increase of this type of Christianity are notoriously difficult to ascertain. Barrett's figures from 1980 give some indication, but since there has been no reliable census data on religious populations since the early 1960s, I treat them with caution. In 1980, of a total estimated population of 75 million, 49 percent identified themselves as Christian, 45 percent as Muslim, and 5.6 percent as African Traditional Religions adherents. D. Barrett, *World Christian Encyclopedia* (Oxford: Oxford University Press, 1982), 527. The composition of the Christian population in 1980 was roughly as follows:

Religious Affiliation	Number	Percentage of Total Population
Protestants	11,034,500	15.2
Roman Catholics	8,801,700	12.1
Anglican	7,622,600	10.5
African Indigenous	7,695,200	10.6
Marginal Protestant	400,000	0.6
Total	35,572,000	49.0

Of Protestants, roughly half are considered Evangelical, and 10 percent of those are considered Pentecostal. Between 1975 and 1985, the increase in conversion for Pentecostals is given as follows: neo-Pentecostals, 38 percent; Anglican Pentecostals, 34 percent; Catholic Pentecostals, 50 percent. D. Barrett, *International Bulletin of Missionary Research* (January 1985).

46. See Peel, *Aladura*.
47. M. Ojo, "The Growth of Campus Christianity and Charismatic Movements in Western Nigeria," Ph.D. diss., University of London, 1986.
48. Ibid. See also M. Ojo, "The Contextual Significance of the Charismatic Movements in Independent Nigeria," *Africa* 58 (1988): 135–56; Ojo *The End-Time Army: Charismatic Movements in Modern Nigeria* (Trenton, N.J.: Africa World Press, 2006); R. Marshall, "Pentecostalism in Southern Nigeria: An Overview," in *New Dimensions in African Christianity*, ed. P. Gifford (Nairobi: AACC Press, 1992), 7–32.
49. See M. Ojo, "Deeper Christian Life Ministry: A Case Study of the Charismatic Movements in Western Nigeria," *Journal of Religion in Africa* 18 (1988): 141–62; Ojo, "Deeper Life Bible Church of Nigeria," in *New Dimensions in African Christianity*, ed. P. Gifford (Nairobi: AACC Press, 1992), 135–56.

50. A. Isaacson, *Deeper Life: The Extraordinary Growth of the Deeper Life Bible Church* (London: Hodder and Stoughton, 1990), 97.

51. Both the prerevival Faith Tabernacle and the Christ Apostolic Church forbade such use, and a few of the new churches carried on this practice.

52. Isaacson, *Deeper Life*, 126–28.

53. *African Guardian*, 5 July 1993.

54. Ibid.

55. For a detailed history and analysis of the Redeemed Christian Church of God, especially the changes brought about since Adeboye took over the leadership, see Azonseh F. K. Ukah, "The Redeemed Christian Church of God (RCCG), Nigeria: Local Identities and Global Processes in African Pentecostalism," Ph.D. diss., University of Bayreuth, Germany, 2003.

56. Personal communication, J. Ajayi, February 2008. See RCCG website: www.rccg.org

57. Pastor Adeboye, address at Somolu Parish, Building Dedication, Lagos, 23 May 1993.

58. Ojo, "Growth of Campus Christianity and Charismatic Movements in Western Nigeria," 12.

59. E. Eni, *Delivered from the Powers of Darkness* (Ibadan: Scripture Union, 1987). This "testimony" has been circulated throughout Africa and translated into many languages. See list of primary sources at the end of this book for more references.

60. See M. Harrison, *Righteous Riches: The Word of Faith Movement in Contemporary African American Religion* (Oxford: Oxford University Press, 2005). Word-Faith teachings trace their roots to E. W. Kenyon (1867–1948), a New England evangelical pastor who taught that health and finances were the right of every believer who would claim the promises of Scripture through faith. Kenyon coined the phrase, "What I confess, I possess." Kenneth Hagin (1917–2003) of Tulsa, Oklahoma, was heavily influenced by Kenyon's writings, and began teaching this doctrine in the late 1930s. The modern movement developed strongly in the 1970s, and Hagin is often referred to as its father. The movement has the most powerful Christian broadcasting network today in the United States, Trinity Broadcasting Network. Word-Faith preachers whose messages are distributed widely (through books and cassettes) in Nigeria include Kenneth Hagin, Kenneth Copeland, Frederick K. C. Price, Benny Hinn, Joel Osteen, Oral Roberts, Morris Cerullo, and the German Reinhard Bonnke.

61. See A. Corten and R. Marshall-Fratani, eds., *Between Babel and Pentecost: Transnational Pentecostalism in Africa and Latin America* (London: C. Hurst, 2002); D. Martin, *Tongues of Fire: The Explosion of Protestantism in Latin America* (Oxford: Blackwell, 1990); D. Stoll, *Is Latin America Turning Protestant? The Politics of Evangelical Growth* (Berkeley: University of California Press, 1990); K. Poewe, ed., *Charismatic Christianity as a Global Culture* (Columbia: University of South Carolina Press, 1994); P. Gifford, S. Rose,

and S. Brouwer, eds., *Exporting the American Gospel: Global Christian Fundamentalism* (New York: Routledge, 1996).

62. Mark 10:30 is the scriptural cornerstone of this doctrine: "But he shall receive an hundredfold in this time; houses and brethren, and sisters, and mothers, and children, and lands, with persecutions; and in the world to come, everlasting life."

63. Overcomer's Church, Aguda, 5 April 1991.

64. Interview, T. Johnson, university student, member of Christ Chapel, Lagos, 14 January 1991.

65. Interview, Dr. O. Segun, medical doctor, member of Redeemed Evangelical Mission, Lagos, 7 April 1991.

66. *African Guardian*, 5 July 1993.

67. Agbowo is an urban suburb of Ibadan, with an estimated population of 40,000, roughly divided between Muslims and Christians, most of whom are members of the lower class and lower middle class, with a few middle-class and upper middle-class pockets.

68. The number of people identifying with the Born-Again movement is likely much higher than these figures suggest, as many members of the "mainline churches," especially the Baptists, have doctrines or sections of their congregations who identify with Pentecostal doctrine and practice, and would claim to belong to the Born-Again movement, or who participate in smaller structures such as house fellowships not covered in the study.

69. The average year of establishment of mainline denominations, such as the Catholics, Anglicans, and Baptists, as well as the Aladura churches, dates to the late 1960s and early 1970s, and corresponds to the growth in the population of the area.

70. Foursquare Gospel Church, Yaba, Lagos, 27 February 1991.

71. Pastor S. O. Ibeneme, Grace of God Mission, Sabon Gari, Kano, in *His Vineyard* 4 (February–March 1993).

72. See J. B. Webster, *The African Churches among the Yoruba: 1891–1922* (Oxford: Oxford University Press, 1964).

73. See Peel, *Aladura*.

74. F. Tayo, *Nigeria Belongs to Jesus* (Ibadan: Feyisetan Press, 1988), v–vi.

CHAPTER THREE

1. See, for example, on Africa more generally: W. Zartman, ed., *Governance as Conflict Management: Politics and Violence in West Africa* (Washington, D.C.: Brookings Institution, 1997); R. Joseph and J. Herbst, "Responding to State Failure in Africa," *International Security* 22, no. 2 (1997): 175–84; J. Herbst, *States and Power in Africa: Comparative Lessons in Authority and Control* (Princeton: Princeton University Press, 2000); W. Reno, *Warlord Politics and African States* (Boulder, Colo.: Lynne Rienner, 1998); W. Zartman,

Collapsed States: The Disintegration and Restoration of Legitimate Authority (Boulder, Colo.: Lynne Rienner, 1995); P. Chabal and J. P. Daloz, *Africa Works: Disorder as Political Instrument* (Oxford: James Currey, 1998); D. Woods, "Civil Society in Europe and Africa: Limiting State Power through a Public Sphere," *African Studies Review* 35, no. 2 (1992): 77–100. And on Nigeria: W. Graf, *The Nigerian State: Political Economy, State, Class and Political System in the Post-Colonial Era* (London: James Currey, 1988); P. Lewis, T. Pearl, and R. Barnett, *Stabilizing Nigeria: Sanctions, Incentives, and Support for Civil Society* (New York: Century Foundation Press, 1998); M. H. Kukah, *Democracy and Civil Society in Nigeria* (Ibadan: Spectrum Books, 1999); R. Suberu, *Federalism and Ethnic Conflict in Nigeria* (Washington, D.C.: U.S. Institute for Peace Press, 2001). For alternative approaches in political science, see J.-F. Bayart, S. Ellis, and B. Hibou, *The Criminalisation of the State in Africa* (London: International African Institute and James Currey, 1999); R. Marshall-Fratani and R. Banégas, "Modes de régulation politique et reconfiguration des espaces publics," in *L'Afrique de l'Ouest dans la compétition mondiale: Quels atouts possibles?* ed. J. Damon and J. O. Igue (Paris, Karthala, 2004), 155–96.

2. J. Obarrio, "Time and Again: Being after Structural Adjustment," unpublished paper.

3. See J. Ferguson, *The Anti-politics Machine: "Development," Depoliticisation and Bureaucratic State Power in Lesotho* (Cambridge: Cambridge University Press, 1990); and the discussion on liberalisation in J.-F. Bayart, "Foucault au Congo," in *Penser avec Michel Foucault: Théorie critique et pratiques politiques,* ed. M.-C. Granjon (Paris: Karthala, 2005), 183–222.

4. M. Foucault, "Le sujet et le pouvoir?" in *Dits et Ecrits,* Vol. 4: *1980–1988* (Paris: Gallimard, 1994), 241.

5. J-F. Bayart, *The State in Africa: The Politics of the Belly* (London: Longman, 1993), 248.

6. See M. Foucault, *"Il faut défendre la société": Cours au College de France, 1976* (Paris: Gallimard, 1997). It is during this year that Foucault elaborates his study of power relations in terms of strategy and struggle, and bio-power. Classes of 10 and 17 March, 139–235.

7. See A. Mbembe, "Necropolitics," *Public Culture* 15, no. 1 (2003): 11–40.

8. Foucault, "Le sujet et le pouvoir?" *Dits et Ecrits,* Vol. 4: *1980–1988,* 243.

9. See Bayart, *State in Africa,* chap. 5.

10. F. Iyayi, *The Contract* (Lagos: Longman, 1982), 24–25.

11. See R. Joseph, *Democracy and Prebendal Politics in Nigeria: The Rise and Fall of the Second Republic* (Cambridge: Cambridge University Press, 1987); J. Ihonvbere and T. Shaw, *Illusions of Power: Nigeria in Transition* (Trenton, N.J.: Africa World Press, 1998); E. Osaghae, *Crippled Giant:. Nigeria since Independence* (London: Hurst, 1998); L. Diamond, "Cleavage, Conflict and Anxiety in the Second Nigerian Republic," *Journal of Modern African Studies* 20, no. 4 (1982): 629–68.

12. See L. Diamond, A. Kirk-Greene, and O. Oyediran, eds., *Transition without End: Nigerian Politics and Civil Society under Babangida* (Boulder, Colo.: Lynne Rienner, 1997).

13. Ihonvbere and Shaw, *Illusions of Power,* 49.

14. Ibid.

15. M.J. Dent, "Corrective Government: Military Rule in Perspective," in *Soldiers and Oil: The Political Transformation of Nigeria,* ed. K. Panter-Brick (London: Frank Cass, 1978), 110.

16. See R. Cohen, *Labour and Politics in Nigeria* (London: Heinemann, 1974).

17. See Osaghae, *Crippled Giant;* Ihonvbere and Shaw, *Illusions of Power.*

18. In this sense, the colonial regime was a hybrid: while this predatory form of power has its roots in an earlier monarchical model, its techniques were not only the costly and inefficient use of violence proper to this model, but also techniques and rationalities proper to the governmentality of the modern state: bio-political, disciplinary, rationalized for efficiency and control. See M. Foucault, "Les mailles de pouvoir," in *Dits et Ecrits,* Vol. 4: *1980–1988,* 190.

19. R. Tignor, "Corruption in Nigeria before Independence," *Journal of Modern African Studies,* 31, no. 2 (1993): 175–202.

20. Joseph, *Democracy and Prebendal Politics in Nigeria.* For post-1980 developments, see also P. Lewis, "From Prebendalism to Predation: The Political Economy of Decline in Nigeria," *Journal of Modern African Studies* 34, no. 1 (1996): 79–103.

21. See the detailed study of Nigeria by D. Smith, *A Culture of Corruption: Everyday Deception and Popular Discontent in Nigeria* (Princeton: Princeton University Press, 2007); also Bayart, Ellis, and Hibou, *Criminalisation of the State in Africa;* G. Blundo and J.-P. Olivier de Sardan, eds., *La corruption au quotidien, Politique Africaine* 83 (October 2001); as well as the study of economic regulation and the problem of value by J. Roitman, *Fiscal Disobedience: An Anthropology of Economic Regulation in Central Africa* (Princeton: Princeton University Press, 2005).

22. See on the Yoruba, K. Barber, "Money, Self-Realization and the Person in Yoruba Texts," in *Money Matters: Instability, Values and Social Payments in the Modern History of West African Communities,* ed. J. Guyer (Portsmouth, N.H.: Heinemann, 1995), 205–24; J. Guyer and S. Eno Belinga, "Wealth in People as Wealth in Knowledge: Accumulation and Composition in Equatorial Africa," *Journal of African History* 36, no. 1 (1995): 91–120; J. Guyer, "Wealth in People and Self-Realization in Equatorial Africa," *Man* 28, no. 2 (1993): 243–65.

23. See Roitman, *Fiscal Disobedience.*

24. See O. Oyediran, ed., *Nigerian Government and Politics under Military Rule, 1966–1979* (London: Macmillan, 1979); A. Kirke-Greene and D. Rimmer, *Nigeria since 1970* (London: Hodder and Stoughton, 1981).

25. Ihonvbere and Shaw, *Illusions of Power,* 81.

26. Ibid.

27. P. Ekeh, "The Constitution of Civil Society in African History and Politics," in *Democratic Transition in Africa,* ed. B. Caron, O. Gboyega, and E. Osaghae (Ibadan: CREDU, 1992), 83–104.

28. C. Lefort, *Democracy and Political Theory* (Cambridge: Polity Press, 1988), chap. 2, "Human Rights and the Welfare State," 39–42.

29. J. MacGaffey, *Entrepreneurs and Parasites: The Struggle for Indigenous Capitalism in Zaire* (Cambridge: Cambridge University Press, 1988).

30. John Dunn, "The Politics of Representation and Good Government in Post-Colonial Africa," in *Political Domination in Africa: Reflections on the Limits of Power,* ed. P. Chabal (Cambridge: Cambridge University Press, 1986), 163. On the problem of representation, see J. Guyer, "Representation without Taxation: An Essay on Democracy in Rural Nigeria, 1952–1990," *African Studies Review* 35, no. 1 (1992): 41–79.

31. Quoted in Bayart, *State in Africa,* 80. See T. Falola and J. Ihonvbere, *The Rise and Fall of Nigeria's Second Republic 1979–1984* (London: Zed Books, 1985).

32. A. Mbembe, *Afriques indociles: Christianisme, pouvoir et état en société postcoloniale* (Paris: Karthala, 1988), 161.

33. K. Barber, "The Religious Disaggregation of Popular Moral Discourse in Yorùbá Theatre and Video Drama," paper presented at the conference "Religion and Media in Nigeria," School of Oriental and African Studies, London, 25–26 February 1999; Barber, *The Generation of Plays: Yoruba Popular Life in Theatre* (Bloomington: Indiana University Press, 2000), especially chaps. 10 and 12.

34. J. D. Y. Peel, "Olaju: A Yoruba Concept of Development," *Journal of Development Studies* 14 (1978): 139–65.

35. Barber, *Generation of Plays.*

36. J. D. Y. Peel, *Religious Encounter and the Making of the Yoruba* (Bloomington: Indiana University Press, 2000).

37. M. Watts, "The Shock of Modernity: Money, Protest and Fast Capitalism in an Industrialising Society," in *Reworking Modernity: Capitalism and Symbolic Discontent,* ed. A. Pred and M. Watts (New Brunswick, N.J.: Rutgers University Press, 1990), 35.

38. Ibid., 36, citing B. Freund, "Oil Boom and Crisis in Contemporary Nigeria," *Review of African Political Economy* 13 (1978): 91–100.

39. A. Apter, "IBB=419: Nigerian Democracy and the Politics of Illusion," in *Civil Society and the Political Imagination in Africa: Critical Perspectives,* ed. J. Comaroff and J. L. Comaroff (Chicago: University of Chicago Press, 1999), 268.

40. Watts, "Shock of Modernity," 38.

41. Ibid., 38–41.

42. Ibid., 39.

43. S. Othman, "Classes, Crisis and Coup," *African Affairs* 27 (1984): 441–61.

44. Ihonvbere and Shaw, *Illusions of Power,* 84.
45. Falola and Ihonvbere, *Rise and Fall of Nigeria's Second Republic.*
46. K. Barber, "Popular Reactions to the Petro-Naira," *Journal of Modern African Studies* 20, no. 3 (1982): 435. See also Barber, "Popular Arts in Africa," *African Studies Review* 30, no. 3 (1987): 1–78.
47. A. Apter, *The Pan African Nation: Oil and the Spectacle of Culture in Nigeria* (Chicago: University of Chicago Press, 2005), 231.
48. D. Seers, "The Mechanism of an Open Petroleum Economy," *Social and Economic Studies* 22, no. 1 (1984): 236, cited in Watts, "Shock of Modernity," 40.
49. P. Gutkind, "The View from Below: Political Consciousness of the Urban Poor in Ibadan, *Cahiers d'études africaines* 57, no. 1 (1975): 5–35.
50. Watts, "Shock of Modernity," 39; T. Abdulraheem, A. Olukoshi, A. R. Mustapha, and G. P. Williams, "Nigeria: Oil, Debts and Democracy," *Review of African Political Economy* 13, no. 37 (1986): 6–10.
51. Ihonvbere and Shaw, *Illusions of Power,* 112.
52. Diamond, Kirk-Greene, and Oyediran, eds., *Transition without End: Nigerian Politics and Civil Society under Babangida;* T. Olagunju,, A. Jinadu, and S. Oyovbaire, *Transition to Democracy in Nigeria 1985–1993* (Ibadan: Safari Books, 1993); B. Caron, A. Gboyega, and E. Osaghae, eds., *Democratic Transition in Africa* (Ibadan: CREDU, 1992); Osaghae, *Crippled Giant.*
53. "SAPped" is a play on words referring to the effects of the unfinanced Structural Adjustment Program.
54. See C. Gore and D. Pratten, "The Politics of Plunder: The Rhetorics of Order and Disorder in Southern Nigeria," *African Affairs* 102 (2003): 211–40.
55. See J. Ihonvbere, "Are Things Falling Apart? The Military and the Crisis of Democratisation in Nigeria," *Journal of Modern African Studies* 34, no. 2 (1996): 193–225; K. Maier, *This House Has Fallen: Midnight in Nigeria* (New York: Public Affairs, 2000).
56. Apter, *Pan African Nation,* 232.
57. Ibid.
58. A. Mbembe, "Provisional Notes on the Postcolony," *Africa* 62, no. 1 (1992): 3–37.
59. L. Bourgault, *Mass Media in Sub-Saharan Africa* (Bloomington: Indiana University Press, 1995), especially chap. 7.
60. O. Esan, "Receiving Television Messages: An Ethnographic Study of Women in Nigerian Context," Ph.D. diss., University of Glasgow, 1993.
61. P. J. Dixon, "'Uneasy Lies the Head': Politics, Economics, and the Continuity of Belief among Yoruba of Nigeria," *Comparative Studies in Society and History* 23, no.1 (1991): 56–85. See also A. J. Peace, "Prestige, Power and Legitimacy in a Modern Nigerian Town," *Canadian Journal of African Studies* 13, nos. 1–2 (1979): 25–51. See Barber, "Popular Reactions to the Petro-Naira," for a discussion of distinctions among Yorubas between le-

gitimate and illegitimate wealth, and the role of medicine and witchcraft in obtaining wealth.

62. P. Nkashama, *Eglises nouvelles et mouvements religieux: L'exemple zaïrois* (Paris: L'Harmattan, 1990).

63. Dixon, "'Uneasy Lies the Head.'"

64. See conclusions in Bayart, *State in Africa*.

65. P. Geschiere, *Sorcellerie et politique en Afrique: La viande des autres* (Paris: Karthala, 1995).

66. J. O. Balogun, *Redeemed from the Clutches of Satan: Former Head of Seven Secret Cults Now an Evangelist* (Lagos: Noade Nigeria, n.d.), 12.

67. Apter, *Pan African Nation*.

68. R. Banégas and J.-P. Warnier, "Nouvelles figures de la réussite et du pouvoir," *Politique Africaine* 82 (June 2001): 6.

69. M. Ojewale, *Hope for the Sapped Generation* (Lagos: Peace and Salvation Publications, 1991), 2.

70. This is a term implying the local appropriation and (syncretic) adaptation of Christian doctrine into local cultures. "Acculturation" implies the gradual cultural change implicitly toward "modern" forms of social organization and knowledge.

71. J.-F. Bayart, *L'Illusion identitaire* (Paris, Fayard, 1996), 60.

72. P. Chatterjee, *The Nation and Its Fragments* (Princeton: Princeton University Press, 1993).

73. J. Lonsdale, "The Moral Economy of Mau Mau: Wealth, Poverty and Civic Virtue in Kikuyu Political Thought," in *Unhappy Valley: Conflict in Kenya and Africa: Book Two: Violence and Ethnicity,* ed. J. Lonsdale and B. Berman (London: J. Currey, 1992), 315–467. See also J. Lonsdale, "Moral Ethnicity and Political Tribalism," in *Inventions and Boundaries: Historical and Anthropological Approaches to the Study of Ethnicity and Nationalism,* ed. P. Kaarsholm and J. Hultin (Roskilde, Denmark: Institute for Development Studies, Roskilde University, 1994), 131–50.

74. Barber, *Generation of Plays*.

75. See T. Falola, *Violence in Nigeria: The Crisis of Religious Politics and Secular Ideologies* (Rochester: University of Rochester Press, 1998).

76. Violence broke out on the campus of the University of Ibadan in 1985–86 over the placement of the university chapel's cross, which Muslim students complained was in their direct line of vision as they faced Mecca to pray. The issue was resolved by the building of a cement wall that blocked the sight of the cross. See the account in A. Banjo, *In the Saddle: A Vice-Chancellor's Story* (Ibadan, 1997), cited in Peel, *Religious Encounter and the Making of the Yoruba,* 313. Peel notes that Wole Soyinka, in a lecture at the University of Ibadan in 1991, criticized growing religious intolerance.

77. See O. A. Ogunbameru, ed., *Readings on Campus Secret Cults,* (Ife: Kuntel, 1997).

78. Smith, *Culture of Corruption,* 163.
79. Barber, *Generation of Plays.*
80. See *L'Argent de Dieu, Politique Africaine* 35 (October 1989), especially the article by J.-F. Bayart, "Les églises chrétiennes et la politique du ventre," 3–38.
81. *African Guardian,* 5 July 1993. This accusation against the Ogbonis and the Freemasons is a longstanding theme in Nigerian Christianity, similar accusations having been made by the Aladura in the 1920s and 1930s. Personal communication, J. D. Y. Peel, 25 February 2008.
82. The intensification of American evangelism begins in the late 1950s and early 1960s, but its effects really become palpable in terms of local appropriation in the early 1970s. Among the better known evangelists of the 1970s was Franklin Hall, whose teachings emphasized "heart-felt and body-felt" and the control of carnal desires. T. L. Osborne (of the "faith" tendency) and the more biblically fundamentalist William Brahnam Ministry also had influence. See M. Ojo, "The Growth of Campus Christianity and Charismatic Movements in Western Nigeria," Ph.D. diss., University of London, 1986, 204–18.
83. Interview, T. Johnson, student and volunteer worker at Christ Chapel, Lagos, 30 April 1991.
84. Classes, Bible study, preaching, and magazine articles often focused on these questions. See various widely circulated books, such as M. O. Agboola, *The Building of a Home of Fame and Glory* (Lagos: n.p., n.d.); H. Ogbonnaya, *How to Win Your Husband* (Lagos: Ofico Enterprises, n.d.); Ogbonnaya, *How to Win Your Wife* (Lagos: Ofico Enterprises, n.d.); D. Odunze, *The Ideal Housewife* (Enugu: Family Circle Publications, 1985); E. Guti, *Sh-hh Shut Your Mouth: Marriage and Young Couples Character: Advice for Young Couples* (Harare: EGEA Publications, 1995); I. Emelife, *What Every Youth Should Know about Love, Sex and Marriage* (Owerri: Evangelistic Association International, n.d.); G. Koffuor, *Boy Meets Girl* (Ibadan: Scripture Union, 1978).
85. *Believers Fun Times,* Benin City, n.d.
86. See, for example, these sites, of which there exist dozens:

    www.christianwarfare.co.nz
    www.loveallpeople.org/deliverance.html
    www.realdeliverance.com
    www.jesusdeliverance.org
    www.jesusw.com/spiritual-warfare-christian-deliverance-healing

87. J. Butler, *Giving an Account of Oneself* (New York: Fordham University Press, 2005); Butler, "Giving an Account of Oneself," *Diacritics* 31, no. 4 (2001): 22–40. See also C. Taylor, *Sources of the Self: The Making of the Modern Identity* (Cambridge, Mass.: Harvard University Press, 1989).

88. See B. Jewsiewicki, "The Subject in Africa: In Foucault's Footsteps," *Public Culture* 14, no. 3 (2002): 593–98.

89. See J. Haynes, *Nigerian Video Films* (Athens: Ohio University Press, 2000).

90. See E. Eni, *Delivered from the Powers of Darkness* (Ibadan: Scripture Union Press, 1987); G. K. Dagunduro, *Former Satan Deputy in the World Turned Follower of Christ* (Ilesha: Rapture Evangelism International, 1987); Dagunduro, *My Journey from the Earth to Hell and My Vision of the Heaven: Where Is Your Eternal Home?* (Ilesha: Rapture Evangelism International, 1990); E. O. Omoobajesu, *My Experience in the Darkness of This World before Jesus Saved Me* (Lagos: Omoobajesu World Outreach, 1968); Balogun, *Redeemed from the Clutches of Satan;* V. Eto, *How I Served Satan until Jesus Christ Delivered Me* (Warri: Shallom Christian Mission International, 1981); I. K. Uzorma, *Occult Grand Master, Now in Christ* (Benin City: Uzorma Warfare Publications, 1993); D. K. Onuoha, *My Encounters with Lucifer: Satan, the Devil and His Agents* (Ibadan: God-Will-Do-It Publications, 1998). See also Grace Ihere's testimony in the appendix, which I have not found in published form, but which was circulated in many southern cities on cassette tapes from the mid-1980s through the early 1990s.

91. All these testimonies take up fifty or more pages in printed form (Grace Ihere's testimony of her activities as an agent of the devil fills 120 minutes of tape) and recount in gruesome detail the various ways in which these individuals served the devil and his minions. Many of these testimonies have been published since the late 1980s, but they were often circulated on tape long before appearing in print, and presented in abridged versions in front of church audiences before that. Omoobajesu's testimony was first published in 1968. Once circulated publicly, they often become the tools of an aggressive street evangelism, recounted with details added or changed, as part of public preaching and evangelism. From 1989 to 1993, when I was doing field work in Lagos using public transport, well before the video boom of the late 1990s, I heard these sorts of stories several times a week, as crowded buses were one of the privileged sites for "street" evangelism.

92. V. Eto, *The Forces of Darkness* (Warri: Shallom Christian Mission, 1988), 11.

93. E. Eni, *The Works of the Devil* (Port Harcourt: Sparks Group, 1989), 30–33.

94. Eto, *How I Served Satan,* 6.

95. See Grace Ihere's testimony in the appendix.

96. Eni, *Delivered from the Powers of Darkness,* 18.

97. Ibid., 58.

98. Balogun, *Redeemed from the Clutches of Satan,* 10.

99. Ibid., 18.

100. Ibid., 19.

101. Ibid., 41.

102. Dagunduro, *Former Satan Deputy in the World,* 37–38.

103. See Peel's discussion of the "curse of Ham" in *Religious Encounter and the Making of the Yoruba,* 297–98, 388.

104. A. Mbembe, "A propos des écritures africaines de soi," *Politique Africaine* 77 (March 2000): 16–43; revised version in English, "African Modes of Self-Writing," *Public Culture* 14, no. 1 (2002): 239–73; and his response to critics, "On the Power of the False," *Public Culture* 14, no. 3 (2002): 629–41.

105. Emeka Nwankpa, "Territorial Spirits," address given at Pentecostal conference "Combating the Powers of Darkness," National Theatre, Lagos, April 1993.

106. This term is taken from the title of another address given by Nwankpa, "Remitting the Sins of the Fathers," at the "Combating the Powers of Darkness" conference.

107. J. Comaroff, "Consuming Passions: Nightmares of the Global Village," *Culture* 17, nos. 1–2 (1997): 7–19.

108. S. Adekola, *Understanding Demonology* (Ibadan: Scripture Union Press, 1993), 10.

109. Nwankpa, "Territorial Spirits."

110. Lonsdale, "Moral Economy of Mau Mau."

111. J.-L. Nancy, *La déclosion: Déconstruction du christianisme,* vol. 1 (Paris, Editions Galilée, 2005). See also G. Bensussan, *Le Temps messianique: temps historique et temps vécu* (Paris: Librairie Philosophique J. Vrin, 2001).

112. C. Castoriadis, *The Imaginary Institution of Society* (Cambridge, Mass.: MIT Press, 1987).

113. Interview, Lagos, April 1993. This organization holds meetings in which the political future of the nation is discussed and organizes annual prayer meetings in the National Stadium in which leaders from various Born-Again churches and ministries lead "prayers for the Nation."

114. 2 Corinthians 5:17: "Therefore if any man be in Christ, he is a new creation: old things are passed away, behold, all things are become new."

115. Lee Jang Rim, leader of the Korean Mission for the Coming Days (also known as the Tami Church), predicted that the rapture would occur on this date. Lee was convicted of fraud after the prophecy failed. Lee's church was part of the larger Hyoo-Go (Rapture) movement, which took Korea by storm in 1992. "The World Did Not End Yesterday," *Boston Globe* (Associated Press), 29 October 1992.

116. See note 39 in chapter 2.

117. See, for example, the website "Rapture Ready," complete with prediction index, which the site calls "the prophetic speedometer of end-time activity": www.raptureready.com

CHAPTER FOUR

1. M. Foucault, "Table ronde du 20 mai 1978," in *Dits et Ecrits,* Vol. 4: *1980–1988* (Paris: Gallimard, 1994), 28.

2. Ibid.

3. J. Butler, *Giving an Account of Oneself* (New York: Fordham University Press, 2005).

4. M. Foucault, "What Is Enlightenment" in *The Foucault Reader,* ed. P. Rabinow (New York: Pantheon Books, 1984), 32–50. (See "Qu'est-ce que les Lumières?" in *Dits et Ecrits,* Vol. 4: *1980–1988,* 562–78.) It is within this particular epistemic structure that the question of "identity" is posed for the first time. To speak of "religious identity" in sixteenth-century Europe is thus an anachronism.

5. M. Mauss, "Body Techniques," in *Sociology and Psychology: Essays,* ed. B. Brewster (London: Routledge, 1979), 222.

6. T. Asad, "Comments on Conversion," in *Conversion to Modernities: The Globalization of Christianity,* ed. P. Van der Veer (New York: Routledge, 1996), 271.

7. M. Foucault, "Usages des plaisirs et techniques de soi," in *Dits et Ecrits,* Vol. 4: *1980–1988,* 555.

8. Ibid. Foucault clarifies: "By ethic [*morale*] we understand the ensemble of values and rules of action which are proposed to individual and groups through the intermediary of diverse prescriptive apparatuses, such as the family, educational institutions, Churches, etc. Sometimes these rules and values are very explicitly formulated in a coherent doctrine and an explicit teaching. But at times they may be transmitted in a diffused fashion, far from forming a systematic ensemble, they consist of a gamut of elements which compensate each other, correct each other, cancel each other out on certain points, thus allowing compromises or modes of escape." Here, there is a difficulty in translation. In French, a distinction can be made, and is made by Foucault, between *morale* and *éthique.* The use of "morality" in the place of *morale* does not resolve this problem, since morality normally refers to the extent to which individuals act in accordance with the codes and values that make up the *morale.* Foucault uses *éthique* to describe forms of moral subjectivation that are less oriented to the code and more oriented toward self-fashioning. I have decided to retain the term "ethic," while bearing these precisions in mind.

9. Ibid.

10. Ibid., 556–57: Foucault elaborates the study of moral subjectivation along four axes; his analysis can be broken down into the different ways in which the individual becomes a moral subject of his action: (1) how the person identifies within himself the part of himself which shall constitute the principal matter of his moral conduct, the determination of an "ethical substance"; (2) how the individual establishes his relationship to the rule and understands himself as being under an obligation to act in accordance with it; (3) the variations in the elaboration of the ethical work one performs on oneself, not merely to conform to the rule, but in an effort to transform oneself as the subject of one's moral conduct; (4) the varieties of

the "teleology of the moral subject": an action is not merely moral in and of itself, in its singularity, but also because it belongs to an ensemble of conduct, which tends to a certain way of being.

11. The use of *potens* is a misquote or a misuse: *potens* translates as "powerful." The term Asad should have used for "power" in this context is *potentia*.

12. Asad, "Comments on Conversion," 266.

13. T. Asad, *Genealogies of Religion: Discipline and Reasons of Power in Christianity and Islam* (Baltimore: Johns Hopkins University Press, 1993), 35.

14. Rev. J. B. Adeyemi, legal consultant to the Gospel Pentecostal Assembly, from his letter to the tabloid *Today's Choice* 8, no. 7 (16–27 December 1997): 10, following its publication of a story detailing the gruesome murder of one of the church's pastors, Pastor I. Alabi, accompanied by accusations that the murder was related to a struggle within the church over the nomination of a general overseer to replace the aging Reverend Badejo.

15. I was visited very regularly and urged to come back and worship again. In small congregations, as a special visitor "from abroad," I was often asked to lead the praise and worship session for a song or two.

16. Interview, Sister Yetunde, Glory Tabernacle, Ibadan, 22 February 1998.

17. Interview, Wale Abdul, university student and member of Word of Faith Fellowship, UNILAG, Lagos, April 1993.

18. Interview, Pastor Kris Okotie, Lagos, February 1993.

19. A. Mbembe, "La prolifération du divin en Afrique subsaharienne," in *Les Politiques de Dieu,* ed. G. Kefel (Paris: Le Seuil, 1993), 179.

20. J. D. Y. Peel, "For Who Hath Despised the Day of Small Things? Missionary Narratives and Historical Anthropology," *Comparative Studies in Society and History* 37 (1995): 605.

21. On global Pentecostal forms, as well as the use of media, see R. Marshall-Fratani, "Mediating the Global and Local in Nigerian Pentecostalism," *Journal of Religion in Africa* 28, no. 3 (1998): 278–315; R. Hackett, "Charismatic/Pentecostal Appropriation of Media Technologies in Nigeria and Ghana," *Journal of Religion in Africa* 28, no. 3 (1998): 1–19; B. Meyer and A. Moors, eds., *Media, Religion and the Public Sphere* (Bloomington: Indiana University Press, 2006); K. Poewe, ed., *Charismatic Christianity as a Global Culture* (Columbia: University of South Carolina Press, 1994); A. Corten and R. Marshall-Fratani, eds., *Between Babel and Pentecost: Transnational Pentecostalism in Africa and Latin America* (London: C. Hurst, 2002); A. Corten and A. Mary, eds., *Imaginaires politiques et pentecôtismes, Afrique/ Amérique Latine* (Paris: Karthala, 2000); P. Gifford, S. Rose, and S. Brouwer, eds., *Exporting the American Gospel: Global Christian Fundamentalism* (New York: Routledge, 1996); A. Anderson, *An Introduction to Pentecostalism* (Cambridge: Cambridge University Press, 2004).

22. See the list of primary sources at the end of the book for an exhaustive list.

23. I thank Karin Barber for this apt expression, used in comments she made on one of my papers in progress.

24. A. Corten, "Pentecôtisme et politique en Amérique latine," *Problèmes d'Amérique latine* 24 (January–March 1997): 17–31.

25. A. Appadurai, *Modernity at Large: Cultural Dimensions of Globalization* (Minneapolis: University of Minnesota Press, 1996).

26. J. Meyerowitz, *No Sense of Place: The Impact of Electronic Media on Social Behaviour* (Oxford: Oxford University Press, 1985), cited in ibid., 29.

27. A. Mbembe, *De la postcolonie: Essai sur l'imagination politique dans l'Afrique contemporaine* (Paris: Karthala, 2000), 212.

28. Foucault, "Usages des plaisirs et techniques de soi," in *Dits et Ecrits,* Vol. 4: *1980–1988,* 559.

29. Foucault notes that both these tendencies are found in the history of Christianity, and that we can observe at times juxtapositions, at times rivalries and conflict, and at times composition between them. The Christian system of penitence that developed from the thirteenth century up until the Reformation constituted an extremely strong form of "juridiction" against which many spiritual and ascetic movements developed just before the Reformation. Ibid.

30. S. Adekola, *Understanding Demonology* (Ibadan: Scripture Union Press, 1993), 30.

31. G. Agamben, *The Time That Remains: A Commentary on the Letter to the Romans* (Stanford: Stanford University Press, 2005). Paul, in the opening of his Letter to the Romans, calls himself "the slave of the Messiah." 1 Cor. 15:9: "For I am the least of the apostles, that I am not worthy to be called an apostle." Philem. 1:16: "Not now as a slave, but more than a slave." Ibid., 13.

32. Matt. 20:16: "So the last shall be first, and the first last: for many are called, but few are chosen." 1 Cor. 1:27–28: "But God hath chosen the foolish things of the world to confound the wise; and God hath chosen the weak things of the world to confound the things which are mighty; and the base things of the world and the things which are despised, hath God chosen, yea, and that which are not, to bring to nought things that are."

33. The rest of verse 9, and verse 10: "Most gladly therefore will I rather glory in my infirmities that the power of Christ may rest upon me. Therefore I take pleasure in infirmities, in necessities, in distresses for Christ's sake: for when I am weak, then I am strong."

34. M. Weber, *The Protestant Ethic and the Spirit of Capitalism* (Oxford: Blackwell, 2002).

35. Agamben, *Time That Remains,* 25.

36. Verses 29–32: "But this I say, brethren, time contracted itself, the rest is, that even those having wives may be as not having, and those weeping as not weeping, and those rejoicing as not rejoicing, and those buying as

not possessing, and those using the world as not using it up. For passing away is the figure of the world. But I wish you to be without care." For this whole text, I have used Agamben's translations, rather than the King James Version. Ibid., 19, 23.

37. Ibid., 26.

38. Agamben argues that the "as not" in 1 Cor. 29–31 is a special kind of tensor; "it does not push a concept's semantic field toward that of another concept. Instead, it sets itself against the form of the 'as not': weeping as not weeping. The messianic tension thus does not tend toward an elsewhere, nor does it exhaust itself in the indifference between one thing and its opposite. The apostle does not say: 'weeping *as* rejoicing' nor 'weeping as [meaning =] not weeping,' but 'weeping *as not* weeping.' In this manner, it revokes the factical condition and undermines it without altering its form." Ibid., 24.

39. Interview with T. Johnson, student and volunteer worker at Christ Chapel, Lagos, 30 April 1991.

40. Foucault sets out in a very schematic way a distinction between "spirituality" and "philosophy": "Let's call 'philosophy' that form of thought which inquires about that which permits the subject to have access to the truth, that form of thought which attempts to determine the conditions and the limits of the subject's access to truth." Unlike spirituality, these conditions and limits are not something determined by any change the subject can bring about upon himself. *L'Herméneutique du sujet: Cours au Collège de France, 1981–1982* (Paris: Gallimard/Seuil, 2001), 16.

41. Ibid., 17.

42. See E. Levinas, *Totalité et Infini: essai sur l'extériorité* (Paris: Librairie Générale Française, 1990), for a "messianic," or post-Hegelian, reading of the relationship between history, the subject, and ethics. For Levinas, Eros is that ambiguous event which engenders transcendence at the very heart of immanence, within history itself, and which bears witness both to the finitude of man and his aptitude for the infinite. Eros, in its relation to fecundity and paternity, gives rise to a radically different time than that of linear, historical time, the *time of engenderment,* a heterogeneous time of rupture and discontinuity, in terms of which the past is no longer irremediable, and where each new birth signals the possibility of the new. See the analysis of Levinas by S. Mosès, *Au déla de la guerre: trois études sur Levinas* (Paris: Editions de l'Eclat, 2004).

43. Foucault, *L'Herméneutique du sujet,* 18.

44. See M. Foucault, *Sécurité, territoire, population: Cours au Collège de France, 1977–1978* (Paris : Gallimard/Seuil, 2004); Foucault, *Naissance de la biopolitique: Cours au Collège de France, 1978–1979* (Paris : Gallimard/Seuil, 2004).

45. See Agamben, *Time That Remains,* 134; M. Foucault, "About the Beginning of the Hermeneutics of the Self: Two Lectures at Dartmouth," *Political Theory* 21, no. 2 (1993): 198–227.

46. Agamben, *Time That Remains,* 128.
47. Ibid. As in 1 Cor. 13:4–7.
48. H. Arendt, *The Human Condition,* 2d ed. (Chicago: University of Chicago Press, 1998), 242.
49. Pastor W. Kumuyi, "Foreword," in A. Isaacson, *Deeper Life: The Extraordinary Growth of the Deeper Life Bible Church* (London: Hodder and Stoughton, 1990), 10.
50. Interview, Mrs. O. Aduloju, trader and businesswoman, Lagos, November 1992.
51. Interview, Mrs. Elizabeth O., secretary, Glory Tabernacle, Ibadan, April 1998.
52. Interview, Brother. F. Agboola, assistant pastor, Redeemed Christian Church of God Campus Fellowship, University of Lagos, January 1993.
53. Interview, Pastor Kris Okotie, leader and founder of Household of God Church, Lagos, January 1993.
54. Interview, Mrs. Edith Iloh, founder of Soul Winning Ministries, secretary of Lagos Chapter, Pentecostal Fellowship of Nigeria, representative of the Christian Association of Nigeria for Lagos State, Lagos, April 1993.
55. Pastor Rapu spent three hours in a prayer session with me, in which he and an assistant pastor insisted on showing me that God wanted me to speak in tongues and had chosen Pastor Rapu to help me receive the Holy Spirit. Indeed, the creation of an emotional, highly charged atmosphere, the constant repetition of syllables in a loud voice, a certain bodily position and motion showed me that Mauss is no doubt correct to claim that there are physical, bodily modes of achieving spiritual states.
56. Jeremiah 17:5: "thus saith the Lord; Cursed be the man that trusteth in man and maketh flesh his arm, and whose heart departeth from the Lord."
57. Testimony, Sister Abassey Udom, Christ Life Church, Sword of the Spirit Ministries, Ibadan, September 1997.
58. Interview, Brother Tosin, Redeemed Evangelical Mission, Lagos, 5 March 1992.
59. Interview, Pastor B. Azmond, assistant pastor, Overcomer's Church, Lagos, 22 April 1993.
60. B. Jewsiewicki, "The Subject in Africa: In Foucault's Footsteps," *Public Culture* 14, no. 3 (2002): 569.
61. Butler, *Giving an Account of Oneself,* 39.
62. John 3:26: "And they came unto John, and said unto him, Rabbi, he that was with thee beyond Jordan, to whom thou barest witness, behold, the same baptizeth, and all men come to him."
63. Kumuyi, "Foreword," in Isaacson, *Deeper Life,* 10.
64. John 3:16: "And God so loved the world that he gave his only begotten Son that whosoever believeth in him should not perish, but have everlasting life."

65. James 2:17: "Even so faith, if it hath not works, is dead, being alone."
66. Interview, Brother Donald Uwejei, Assemblies of God, Ikate, Lagos, 12 April 1991.
67. See A. Lyons and H. Lyons, "Magical Medicine on Television: Benin City Nigeria," *Journal of Ritual Studies* 1, no. 2 (1987): 103–35.
68. Interview, Bisi O., Glory Tabernacle, Ibadan, April 1997.
69. See B. Meyer, "Prières, fusils et meurtre rituel: Le cinéma populaire et ses nouvelles figures du pouvoir et du succès au Ghana," *Politique Africaine* 82 (June 2001): 45–62. See also K. Barber, *The Generation of Plays: Yoruba Popular Life in Theatre* (Bloomington: Indiana University Press, 2000).
70. Interview with Mike Bamiloye, director, Mount Zion Productions, Ibadan, 23 February 1998. Before turning to video, this group produced Born-Again plays in the tradition of Yoruba popular theater. It is the foremost Born-Again film-producing company in the west of the country. See the section on films in the list of primary sources at the end of the book. During the interview, he told me several testimonies of people who had been converted while watching one of the films.
71. Pastor A. Oritsejafor, "Jesus on the Offensive," preached message, Lagos National Theatre, Lagos, 13 May 1993.
72. Mbembe, *De la postcolonie,* 213; J. Tonda, *La guérison divine en Afrique Centrale: Congo, Gabon* (Paris: Karthala, 2002), chap. 2.
73. Butler, *Giving an Account of Oneself.*
74. Peel, *Religious Encounter and the Making of the Yoruba.*
75. Interview, Brother T. Johnson, journalism student and lay worker, Christ Chapel, Lagos, 30 April 1991.
76. Agamben, *Time That Remains,* 130.
77. Ibid., 134.
78. This mode of subjectivation is quite unlike that achieved through confessional testimony or an exercise of penitence in which the subject is brought to speak a truth about him- or herself, whose efficacy lies in the fact of speaking the truth rather than in the assertional content itself. In this model, which Foucault calls "penitential," confession is performative in the ways in which it binds the subject to this truth and thus transforms his or her relationship to the self and others. Nor does the Born-Again model of moral subjectivation take a juridical form, which, as Foucault shows, develops out of the confessional mode and its forms of pastoral power. The central element in the juridical form is the authority who judges the subject's adherence to codes and rules, and sanctions infractions; all social relations are juridicized. In this model, testimony performs the operation of reducing the subject to "mere life," or *bios,* underwriting the modern form of power's operation, which Foucault calls bio-political and whose archetypal form is the prison camp. Nor indeed is it like the mode Foucault calls "sacrificial," as exemplified through the ancient ordeal of the oath, in which the testimony offered in or-

der that the effects of truth might perform their function of guarantee was the life of the subject. Such ordeals, it might be added, were central magico-juridical techniques for unmasking criminals and witches across precolonial and colonial West Africa. The sacrificial model also found its expression in practices of witchcraft, where the "price to pay" for access to spiritual power is the sacrifice of something that determines the life of the individual: a direct relative or kinsman.

79. G. Deleuze, "Qu'est-ce qu'un dispositif?" in *Deux régimes de fous: Textes et entretiens 1975–1995* (Paris: Les Editions de Minuit, 2003), 319.

80. G. Deleuze, *Pourparlers 1972–1990* (Paris: Les Editions de Minuit, 1990), 206.

81. Interview, Pastor "Shine" (D. Adesina), UNILAG Pastor, Redemption Fellowship, Lagos, December 1992.

CHAPTER FIVE

1. *Today's Choice* 8, no. 41 (11–17 August 1998): 2 and cover.

2. *Today's Choice* 8, no. 45 (8–14 September 1998).

3. See BBC World Service report, "Nigeria Recovers Abacha's Cash," 10 November 1998.

4. See A. Mbembe, "La colonie: son petit secret et sa part maudite," *Politique Africaine* 102 (July 2006): 101–27.

5. A. Mbembe, "Les pervers du village: Sexualité, vénalité et déréliction en postcolonie," *Africultures,* 9 March 2006: http://www.africultures.com/index.asp?menu=affiche_article&no=4346

6. See M. Foucault, *"Il faut défendre la société": Cours au College de France, 1976* (Paris: Gallimard, 1997), classes of 10 and 17 March, pp. 139–235; Foucault, *Sécurité, territoire, population: Cours au Collège de France, 1977–1978* (Paris: Gallimard, 2005).

7. A. Mbembe, "Necropolitics," *Public Culture* 15, no. 1 (2003): 11–40.

8. Mbembe, "La colonie," 103–7.

9. J.-F. Bayart, *Le gouvernement du monde: Une critique politique de la globalisation* (Paris: Fayard, 2004), 208, cited in ibid., 107.

10. Mbembe, "La colonie," 108–9.

11. C. Lefort, "The Permanence of the Theologico-political?" in *Democracy and Political Theory* (Cambridge: Polity Press, 1988), 213–55.

12. J. Tonda, *La guérison divine en Afrique Centrale: Congo, Gabon* (Paris: Karthala, 2002).

13. Mbembe, "La colonie," 110.

14. Ibid.

15. See J.-F. Bayart, *The State in Africa: The Politics of the Belly* (London: Longman, 1993); F. Cooper, *Decolonization and African Society: The Labor Question in French and British Africa* (Cambridge: Cambridge University Press, 1996); M. Klein, *Slavery and Colonial Rule in French West Africa* (Cambridge:

Cambridge University Press, 1998). The Comaroffs situate the hazard-ous quality of postcolonial political economies in the nature of millen-nial capitalism itself, and the ways in which labor has ceased to be the central site for the production of value. This argument is open to debate if one considers the ambivalent role of labor as a dominant mode for the production of value in African history. See J. Comaroff and J. L. Comaroff, "Alien-nation: Zombies, Immigrants and Global Capitalism, *South Atlantic Quarterly* 101, no. 4 (2002): 779–805; Comaroff and Comaroff, "Millennial Capitalism: First Thoughts on a Second Coming," *Public Culture* 12, no. 2 (2000): 291–343. See also S. Strange, *Casino Capital-ism* (Oxford: Blackwell, 1986); R. Weller, "Living at the Edge: Religion, Capitalism, and the End of the Nation-State in Taiwan," *Public Culture* 12, no. 2 (2000): 477–98.

16. Mbembe, "La colonie." See also J. C. Miller, *Way of Death: Merchant Capitalism and the Angolan Slave Trade 1730–1830* (Madison: University of Wisconsin Press, 1997).

17. Mbembe, "Les pervers du village."

18. Mbembe, "La colonie," 106.

19. Ibid.

20. See P. Geschiere, *Sorcellerie et politique en Afrique: La viande des autres* (Paris: Karthala, 1995).

21. The term *işe Oluwa* (the work of the Lord) was established usage among the Yoruba for church or religious business well before the Born-Again movement. J. D. Y. Peel, personal communication, 26 February 2008.

22. See, for example, the teachings in these published sermons and book-lets: M. Omodanisi, *Rehoboth: Welcome to Prosperity: Prosperity Workshop* (Kaduna: Gospel Ministries International, 1997); B. Olaoye, *Seven Biblical Principles of Prosperity* (Ibadan: Light and Love, 1996); R. K. Adeniran *You Can Live Debt-Free* (Ibadan: Hope Foundation Books, 1994); D. Davies, *Getting God's Flow into Your Finances* (Lagos: Cornywal Nigeria, 1992); B. Elushade, *Christian Principles of Prosperity* (Ibadan: Cosmo International Christian Books, 1992); J. Orogwu, *Tithe Yourself Out of Poverty: With Notes on Giving* (Enugu: Atlantic Publishers, 1990); R. Usenu, *Rehoboth: The Key to Prosperity* (Ibadan: Kingdom Designs, 1991).

23. Adeniran, *You Can Live Debt-Free*, 15.

24. Ibid., 21.

25. Davies, *Getting God's Flow into Your Finances*, 35–36.

26. Bishop D. Oyedepo, *Breaking Financial Hardship* ((Lagos: Dominion Press, 1995), back cover. See also Oyedepo, *Covenant Wealth* (Lagos: Dominion Press, 1996); and Oyedepo, *Understanding Financial Prosperity* (Lagos: Do-minion Press, 1997).

27. Elushade, *Christian Principles of Prosperity,* 12–13.

28. Digging Deep Bible Study Class, Redeemed Christian Church of God, Theme: "Traditions of Men," Pastor E. Adeboye, Lagos, 29 March 1993.

29. I thank my friend K. Johnson for this delightful expression.
30. At the time of his funeral, the exchange rate was 80 naira to 1 U.S. dollar. The casket cost $12,000, and the mausoleum around $120,000.
31. *Fame,* 7–13 April 1998, cover story and pp. 8–9.
32. Idahosa's biography is a classic rags-to-riches tale. He was born in 1938 into a poor family in Benin City, and his early life was one of privation. "Born-Again" in 1959, by 1961 he was a lay preacher at the Assemblies of God while working as a shoe salesman. He left the Assemblies in 1968 to start his own small prayer group. In 1971 he was ordained by Rev. S. Elton, an elderly British missionary who first came to Ilesha in the 1930s with the Apostolic Church. Elton developed his own ministry and played a significant role in introducing Pentecostal doctrines during the revival. In the same year, following a visit to Nigeria by Gordon Lindsay, the president of Christ for All Nations, Inc., in Dallas, Idahosa was given a scholarship to attend their Bible college. He did not complete the two-year program, but with the Lindsays' help he returned to Nigeria and began building the 7,000-seat Miracle Centre in Benin City, completed in 1975. In 1981 he became "archbishop," an unheard-of title in the Pentecostal world. By 1986 there were 50 branches of the Church of God Mission International in Benin City, and by 1994, 6,000 branches worldwide. See R. Garlock, *Fire in His Bones: The Story of Benson Idahosa, a Leader of the Christian Awakening in Africa* (Orlando: Bridge-Logos Publishing, 1982).
33. The church claims 7 million believers worldwide, and has been classed among the twenty largest Pentecostal outfits in the world. See J. Vaughan, president of Church Growth Today: www.churchgrowthtoday.com
34. *Fame,* 7–13 April 1998, 9.
35. See, for example, these cover stories: "Idahosa in Messy Land Scandal: Oba of Benin Named," *Today's Choice,* 20–26 January 1998; "Pastor Anwuzia Again! Wife Attacks Mistress," *National Enconium,* 1 September 1998; "Zoe's Pastor Anwuzia Arrested: Spends N35,000 in Sheraton," *National Enconium,* 30 September 1997; "Oduyemi's Bethel Church Collapsing: Salaries, Nepa Bills Unpaid, Members Leave in Droves," *National Enconium,* 10 February 1998; "Homosexuals Invade Okotie's Church," *Fame,* 10 November 1997; "Crisis Rocks Revival Assembly Church: Pastor Anslem Madubuko in Messy Sex Scandal, Accused of Sleeping with Female Choristers," *Today's Choice,* 3–9 February 1998; "Pastor Ashimolowo Acquires £2.6 Million Property in London," *Fame,* 14–20 April 1998; "Exclusive Details: Why Idahosa and Awuzia Don't See Eye to Eye," *Fame,* 14–20 October 1997. But see also "Deeper Life Pastor Explodes: Nigerian Seers Are Liars, Blasts Prosperity Preachers, Condemns Flamboyant Pastors," *Today's Choice,* 13–18 January 1998.
36. Pastor Adeboye, *The New Vision* (Lagos: CRFU, 1990).
37. It was Idahosa who "ordained" Oyedepo, one of his students, as "bishop."

38. This decision was reached against the members of the commune, the College of Regeneration, led by Emmanuel Odumosu, known as Jesus of Oyingbo, who died in 1988. A court ruled in favor of his family (some thirty-four wives) for the recovery of numerous properties held in the college's name in the wealthy neighborhood of Maryland, Lagos. Churches and ministries are exempt from tax and are obliged to register under the Companies and Allied Matters Act of 1990, under Part I, Article 26.1.

39. See M. Harrison, *Righteous Riches: The Word of Faith Movement in Contemporary African American Religion* (Oxford: Oxford University Press, 2005); K. Poewe, ed., *Charismatic Christianity as a Global Culture* (Columbia: University of South Carolina Press, 1994); P. Gifford, S. Rose, and S. Brouwer, eds., *Exporting the American Gospel: Global Christian Fundamentalism* (New York: Routledge, 1996).

40. Glory Tabernacle is a large (membership 2,500) Ibadan Born-Again church (although still modest by Lagos standards), situated in a relatively modest neighborhood. The congregation is middle- to lower middle-class. Preaching is focused on miracles, but the prosperity gospel is not emphasized, and woman are still expected to come to church with their hair covered and to refrain from wearing trousers or excessive makeup or jewelry.

41. Figures are notoriously hard to come by. An intelligence report shared in the Western diplomatic community in Abuja in 2006 claimed that American missions had spent over $3 million on evangelism and support for Nigerian ministries in 2005. In discussion with the diplomat who shared this report with me, I pointed out in the face of his alarm over the figure, how small such a sum was in comparison to the tens of millions if not billions of dollars generated locally by the ensemble of Born-Again churches and missions. Interview, French diplomat, Abuja, 10 November 2006.

42. See A. Corten and R. Marshall-Fratani, "Introduction," in *Between Babel and Pentecost: Transnational Pentecostalism in Africa and Latin America,* ed. A. Corten and R. Marshall-Fratani (London: C. Hurst, 2002), 1–21; B. Meyer, "Commodities and the Power of Prayer: Pentecostalist Attitudes towards Consumption in Contemporary Ghana," in *Globalization and Identity: Dialectics of Flow and Closure,* ed. B. Meyer and P. Geschiere (Oxford: Blackwell, 1999), 151–76; B. Meyer, "The Power of Money: Politics, Occult Forces, and Pentecostalism in Ghana," *African Studies Review* 41, no. 3 (1998): 15–38.

43. Pastor Acmond, Overcomer's Church, Lagos, 7 April 1992.

44. "Nigeria's Miracle Workers . . . Sources of Power Revealed," *Fame,* 3–9 February 1998, 4.

45. *Aworo* in Yoruba means "possessed medium" of an *orisa* (fetish priest). "Crowd Puller" was the English title used by the filmmaker.

46. See "Mystery Man behind Successful Pastors," *National Enconium,* 7 October 1997, 11.

47. *The Week,* 13 April 1998.

48. J. Lee Grady, "Famed Nigerian Faith Healer 'Dangerous to the Body of Christ': But Some Western Leaders Still Maintain T. B. Joshua Is God's Man," *Charisma News Service,* www.charismanews.com (2 October 2002). "Prominent Nigerian church leaders have labelled T. B. Joshua a fraud, but that has not stopped Christians in South Africa, Europe and the United States from continuing to support the controversial faith healer. Joshua, 39, hosts daily services that attract thousands of visitors to his Synagogue Church of All Nations in Lagos. Pilgrims flock to the sprawling compound seeking cures from terminal diseases, infertility and other ailments. Reports of alleged healings from cancer, AIDS and multiple sclerosis have circulated widely through videotaped testimonies. . . . Pastors of Nigeria's largest churches say Joshua mixes Christianity with occult practices. During a leadership summit held near Lagos in July, they firmly denounced him while discussing the issue with a group of Americans that included theologian C. Peter Wagner, Colorado pastor Ted Haggard and prayer leader Chuck Pierce. 'Without exception the Nigerian leaders said they believe [T. B. Joshua] is not a legitimate minister of the gospel. There was no debate about it,' said Haggard, pastor of New Life Church in Colorado Springs. 'T. B. Joshua is dangerous to the body of Christ, both in Nigeria and globally,' said Joseph Thompson, a facilitator of the summit who is an associate pastor at Haggard's church. A Nigerian himself, Thompson said he is concerned that some charismatics who tend to 'chase after miracles' will be duped by Joshua's use of Christian terminology. 'Americans don't realize that witchdoctors have healed many people' in Nigeria, he said. Yet several prominent charismatic leaders have visited Joshua's compound and returned with favorable impressions. These include Canadian renewal leader John Arnott, Pittsburgh pastor Joseph Garlington, Louisiana evangelist Marvin Gorman and New Zealand minister Bill Subritzky."

49. D. Smith, "'The Arrow of God': Pentecostalism, Inequality and the Supernatural in Southeastern Nigeria," *Africa* 71, no. 4 (2001): 587–613. See also Smith, *Culture of Corruption.*

50. A. Apter, *The Pan African Nation: Oil and the Spectacle of Culture in Nigeria* (Chicago: University of Chicago Press, 2005), 248.

51. Ibid., 228.

52. "Idahosa: 300 Pastors Go to Jail," *Prime People,* 7–13 May 1993; Abdulateef Ottan, "The Big Money Scam," *The News* (Lagos), 10 September 2001.

53. I also witnessed the beating to death of a woman in Lagos in February 2000. The driver of the car I was in queried bystanders, who explained that the woman in question had been seen earlier that morning in the form of a vulture and was a powerful member of the vulture cult.

54. J. Haynes, *Nigerian Video Films* (Athens: Ohio University Press, 2000). See also Karin Barber, "The Religious Disaggregation of Popular Moral Discourse in Yorùbá Theatre and Video Drama," paper presented at the

conference "Religion and Media in Nigeria," School of Oriental and African Studies, London, 25–26 February 1999; B. Larkin, "Degraded Images,
Distorted Sounds: Nigerian Video and the Infrastructure of Piracy," *Public
Culture* 16, no. 2 (2004): 289–314; F.-K. U. Asonzeh, "Advertising God:
Nigerian Video-Films and the Power of Consumer Culture," *Journal of
Religion in Africa* 33 (2003): 203–31.
55. *Today's Choice* 8, no. 35, 30 June–6 July 1998, 10.
56. Ibid.
57. Matthew 7:15–20: "Beware of false prophets, which come to you in sheep's
clothing, but inwardly they are ravening wolves. Ye shall know them
by their fruits. Do men gather grapes of thorns, or figs of thistles? Even
so every good tree bringeth forth good fruit; but a corrupt tree bringeth
forth evil fruit. A good tree cannot bring forth evil fruit, neither can a
corrupt tree bring forth good fruit. 19: Every tree that bringeth not forth
good fruit is hewn down and cast into the fire. Wherefore, by their fruits
ye shall know them."
58. A. Corten, "Miracles et obéissance: Le discours de la guérison divine à
l'Eglise Universelle," *Social Compass* 44, no. 2 (1997): 283.
59. T. Hobbes, *Leviathan* (London: Penguin, 1981), Part III, chap. 37, "Of
Miracles and Their Use": "In this aptitude of mankind to give too hasty
belief to pretended miracles, there can be no better nor I think any other
caution than that which God hath prescribed, first by Moses (as I have
said before in the precedent chapter), in the beginning of the thirteenth
and end of the eighteenth of Deuteronomy; that we take not any for
prophets that teach any other religion than that which God's lieutenant,
which at that time was Moses, hath established; nor any, though he teach
the same religion, whose prediction we do not see come to pass. . . . For
in these times I do not know one man that ever saw any such wondrous
work, done by the charm or at the word or prayer of a man, that a man
endued but with a mediocrity of reason would think supernatural: and
the question is no more whether what we see done be a miracle; whether
the miracle we hear, or read of, were a real work, and not the act of a
tongue or pen; but in plain terms, whether the report be true, or a lie.
In which question we are not every one to make our own private reason
or conscience, but the public reason, that is the reason of God's supreme
lieutenant, judge; and indeed we have made him judge already, if we have
given him a sovereign power to do all that is necessary for our peace and
defence. A private man has always the liberty, because thought is free,
to believe or not believe in his heart those acts that have been given out
for miracles, according as he shall see what benefit can accrue, by men's
belief, to those that pretend or countenance them, and thereby conjecture
whether they be miracles or lies. But when it comes to confession of that
faith, the private reason must submit to the public; that is to say, to God's
lieutenant."

60. See T. Jennings, *Reading Derrida, Thinking Paul* (Stanford: Stanford U. Press, 2006), especially chaps. 4 and 5.

61. See J. Derrida, *Given Time: I. Counterfeit Money* (Chicago: University of Chicago Press, 1992), 7. See also Derrida, *Spectres of Marx: The State of the Debt, the Work of Mourning and the New International* (New York: Routledge, 1994); and Derrida, *The Gift of Death* (Chicago: University of Chicago Press, 1995).

62. G. Agamben, *The Time That Remains: A Commentary on the Letter to the Romans* (Stanford: Stanford University Press, 2005), 120.

63. Derrida, *Gift of Death*, 105.

64. See "Oyakhilome's Miracles: Real or Fake?" *Newswatch*, 15 April 2002.

65. Ibid.

66. See BBC World Service report, "Crackdown on Nigeria TV Miracles," 30 April, 2004 (accessed online).

67. Evangelist John Nkwocha, *Sun Newspaper*, 1 February 2005.

68. Apter, *Pan African Nation*, 235.

69. Lagos slang from the early 1990s used to refer to young upwardly mobile people, from the fad of saying "whassup?" in greeting, in an affectation of American slang.

70. Interview, Brother Bernard Chukwu, tailor, Bethel Church, 18 November 1992.

71. J. O. Balogun, *Redeemed from the Clutches of Satan: Former Head of Seven Secret Cults Now an Evangelist* (Lagos: Noade Nigeria, n.d.).

72. See M. Ofoegbu, *Victory over Evil Dreams* (Lagos: Holy Ghost Anointed Books, 1995); D. Olukoya, *Victory over Satanic Dreams* (Lagos: Mountain of Fire and Miracles Ministries, 1996). See also M. Ofoegbu, *Dangerous Prayers Part 1–3* (Lagos: Holy Ghost Anointed Books, 1996–98); Ofoegbu, *Exposing Satanic Manipulations* (Lagos: Holy Ghost Anointed Books, 1996); Ofoegbu, *How to Destroy Satanic Manipulations* (Lagos: Holy Ghost Anointed Books, 1998). See also S. Arowobusoye, *Powerful Prayers for Deliverance and Total Breakthrough (In English and Yoruba Languages) with Over 100 Revival Songs* (Ibadan: Gospel Teacher's Fellowship International, 1999); D. K. Olukoya, *Personal Spiritual Checkup* (Lagos: Mountain of Fire and Miracles Ministries, 1995).

73. "Wetin you dey carry?" is pidgin for "What do you have to declare?" S. Arowobusoye, *Satanic Immigration Officers* (Ibadan: Gospel Teachers Publications, 1996), 16 and 21. See also A. Akoria, *The Spiritual Barbers and Barbing Saloons* (Sapele: Christian Life Publications, 1998).

74. Arowobusoye, *Powerful Prayers for Deliverance and Total Breakthrough*, 43–44.

75. This term is extremely difficult to render in English. *Génie* means "spirit," but also "genius," as in aptitude or talent. *Sorcier* implies sorcery, witchcraft, or magic. I have chosen to leave it in the French. Tonda, *La guérison divine en Afrique Centrale*, 28.

76. B. Meyer, "Les églises pentecôtistes africaines: Satan et la dissociation de la 'tradition,'" *Anthropologie et société* 22, no. 1 (1998): 63–84; Meyer, "'Make a Complete Break with the Past': Memory and Postcolonial Modernity in Ghanaian Pentecostal Discourse," in *Memory and the Postcolony: African Anthropology and the Critique of Power,* ed. R. Werbner (London: Zed Books, 1998), 182–208; R. Devisch, "Pillaging Jesus: Healing Churches and the Villagisation of Kinshasa," *Africa* 66, no. 4 (1996): 555–86. See also U. Danfulani, "Exorcising Witchcraft: The Return of the Gods in New Religious Movements on the Jos Plateau and the Benue Regions of Nigeria," *African Affairs* 98 (1999): 167–93.

77. Tonda, *La guérison divine en Afrique Centrale,* 225.

78. "By this notion of Modern Sovereign we want to designate the hegemonic force of the civilising mission, in the name of which 'modernisation' has been legitimated in Africa. The Modern Sovereign is in consequence the figure of the Christian God as he was introduced in the interaction between the work of translation of Christian missionaries and those of indigenous appropriations. But the Modern Sovereign is also the colonial and postcolonial state and money." Ibid., 22.

79. Ibid., 19.

80. Citing G. Balandier, when he argues that the accusation of witchcraft is effected on the basis of exceeding the limits that define the status (condition) of each individual, an attack against the precarious equilibrium that maintains social relations. *Le Pouvoir sur scènes* (Paris: Baillard, 1992), 104; cited in Tonda, *La guérison divine en Afrique Centrale,* 49. Here I have deliberately played on the ambiguity of the French word *dépassement.* Tonda implies it in a negative sense, of being overtaken, overwhelmed. But I would like to read it in a more positive sense, overcoming as well as being overcome.

81. W. Benjamin, "Theses on the Philosophy of History, VI," in *Illuminations* (London: Fontana, 1992), 247.

82. A. Mbembe, "On the Power of the False," *Public Culture* 14, no. 3 (2002): 639.

83. J-F. Bayart, "Fin de partie au sud du Sahara? La politique africaine de la France," in *La France et l'Afrique: Vade-mecum pour un nouveau voyage,* ed. S. Michaïloff (Paris, Karthala, 1993), 115.

84. Bayart, *State in Africa,* 265.

85. V. Y. Mudimbe, *L'Odeur du père: Essais sur les limites de la science et de la vie en Afrique noire* (Paris: Présence Africaine, 1982), 44.

86. M. Foucault, *Dits et Ecrits,* Vol. 3: *1976–1979* (Paris: Gallimard, 1994), 141.

87. Ibid.

88. Mbembe, "On the Power of the False," 634.

89. "Abacha was a devil incarnate—Beko," *Fame,* 23–29 June 1998, 6.

90. Mbembe, "On the Power of the False," 639.

CHAPTER SIX

1. "Who Is on the Lord's Side?" Pastor E. A. Adeboye, address, PFN Biennial Conference, Lagos, 13 February 1993.
2. I have used Agamben's translation of this text, as the King James Version is opaque and convoluted. G. Agamben, *The Time That Remains: A Commentary on the Letter to the Romans* (Stanford: Stanford University Press, 2005), 109.
3. See C. Schmitt, *Political Theology: Four Chapters on the Concept of Sovereignty* (Chicago: University of Chicago Press, 1985).
4. W.-D. Hartwick, A. Assman, and J. Assman, "Afterword," in J. Taubes, *The Political Theology of Paul* (Stanford: Stanford University Press, 2004), 138.
5. Ibid.
6. See Agamben, *Time That Remains,* 109. He notes Tertullian, who writes: "We pray for the permanence of the world [*pro status saeculi*], for peace in all things, for the delay of the end [*pro mora finis*]."
7. Schmitt, *Political Theology.* As Taubes and Agamben argue, Schmitt is from this point of view a fundamentally antimessianic thinker, as the messianic is precisely the release of such paralysis, through its effect of suspension, which returns the law to its state of potentiality, to be fulfilled through faith, as expressed in the Pauline "use it rather." The messianism of 2 Thessalonians 2 shows that this passage cannot in any way be used as a foundation for divine authority or a theory of the state. Agamben, *Time That Remains,* 111.
8. Taubes, *Political Theology of Paul,* 103.
9. Hartwick, Assman, and Assman, "Afterword," in Taubes, *Political Theology of Paul,* 131.
10. *Ausnahmezustand* (the state of emergency, the suspension of the legal order) literally means "the state of exception." For Carl Schmitt, it is central to his doctrine of sovereignty: the sovereign is the one who can proclaim a state of exception. According to Schmitt, the functioning of the legal order rests in the last instance on an arrangement, the state of exception, whose aim is to make the norm applicable by a temporary suspension of its exercise. Schmitt, *Political Theology.* Schmitt's analysis of the state of exception was criticized by Walter Benjamin, in terms of the problem of "pure" violence, which would be outside the law. In his Eighth Thesis on the Philosophy of History, Benjamin posed the problem of the "permanent" state of exception. Giorgio Agamben shows how Schmitt's articulation is paradoxical and how it opens up the possibility of the exception becoming the rule. G. Agamben, *Etat d"Exception: Homo Sacer II* (Paris: Seuil, 2003).
11. C. Lefort, "Human Rights and the Welfare State," in *Democracy and Political Theory* (Cambridge: Polity Press, 1988), 40–41.
12. Ibid.

13. W. Benjamin, "Critique of Violence," in *Walter Benjamin: Selected Writings,* Vol. 1: *1913–1926,* ed. M. Bullock and M. W. Jennings (Cambridge, Mass.: Belknap Press of Harvard University Press, 1996), 236–53; Agamben, *Etat d'Exception.* See also J. Derrida, *Force de Loi* (Paris: Galilée, 1994).

14. Agamben, *Etat d'exception,* 145.

15. Agamben, *Time That Remains,* 135; Taubes, *Political Theology of Paul,* 103.

16. Schmitt, *Political Theology.*

17. *Weekend Concord,* 12 December 1992, 13.

18. Ibid.

19. Interview, Lagos, 6 April 1991.

20. J. Lee Grady, "Nigeria's Miracle," cover story, *Charisma,* May 2002, 4.

21. Ibid.

22. Excerpt from Bible School lesson, Voice of Faith Ministries International, Lagos, October 1992.

23. G. C. Spivak. "Religion, Politics, Theology: A Conversation with Achille Mbembe," *boundary 2* 34, no. 2 (2007): 154.

24. My preliminary studies of Pentecostalism in Côte d'Ivoire reveal that it has been mobilized in support of a xenophobic form of ultra-nationalism based on territorial autochthony and nativism, in which deliverance from bondage takes the form of the demonization of Islam and the rejection of strangers of whatever religion. See also A. Mary, "Prophètes pasteurs: La politique de la délivrance en Côte d'Ivoire," *Politique Africaine* 87 (October 2002): 69–94. Ellis shows how Pentecostalism was a central symbolic resource in the Liberian civil wars. See S. Ellis, *The Mask of Anarchy: The Destruction of Liberia and the Religious Dimensions of an African Civil War* (New York: NYU Press, 2001).

25. M. Ojo, "The Growth of Campus Christianity and Charismatic Movements in Western Nigeria," Ph.D. diss., University of London, 1986.

26. See O. Kane, "Le réformisme musulman au Nigeria du Nord," in *Islam et Islamismes au Sud du Sahara,* ed. O. Kane and J.-L. Triaud (Paris: Karthala 2003); C. Coulon, "Les nouveaux oulémas et le renouveau islamique au Nord Nigeria," in *Le radicalisme Islamique au sud du Sahara,* ed. R. Otayek (Paris: Karthala, 1998). See also J. Kenny, "Sharia and Christianity in Nigeria: Islam and a 'Secular' State," *Journal of Religion in Africa* 26, no. 4 (1996.): 338–64.

27. See R. Loimeier, *Islamic Reform and Political Change in Northern Nigeria* (Chicago: Northwestern University Press, 1997); J. N. Paden, *Religion and Political Culture in Kano* (Berkeley: University of California Press, 1973).

28. R. Loimeier, "Playing with Affiliations: Muslims in Northern Nigeria in the Twentieth Century," in *Entreprises religieuses transnationales en Afrique de l'Ouest,* ed. L. Fourchard, A. Mary, and R. Otayek (Paris: Karthala, 2005), 349–72; and Kane, "Le réformisme musulman au Nigeria du Nord."

29. Loimeier, *Islamic Reform and Political Change in Northern Nigeria.* See also A. Gumi, with I. Tsiga, *Where I Stand* (Ibadan: Spectrum Books, 1992).

30. See O. Kane, *Muslim Modernity in Postcolonial Nigeria: A Study of the Society for the Removal of Innovation and Reinstatement of Tradition* (Leiden: Brill, 2003); Coulon, "Les nouveaux oulémas et le renouveau islamique au Nord-Nigeria"; Loimeier, "Playing with Affiliations"; A. B. Nouhou, *Islam et politique au Nigéria: Genèse et évolution de la charia* (Paris: Karthala, 2005). See also M. Watts, "The Shock of Modernity: Money, Protest and Fast Capitalism in an Industrialising Society," in *Reworking Modernity: Capitalism and Symbolic Discontent,* ed. A. Pred and M. Watts (New Brunswick, N.J.: Rutgers University Press, 1990), 21–64; P. Lubeck, "Islamic Protest under Semi-industrial Capitalism: 'Yan Tatsine explained,'" *Africa* 55, no. 4 (1985): 368–89.

31. Loimeier, "Playing with Affiliations"; Nouhou, *Islam et politique au Nigéria.*

32. See M. D. Sulaiman, "Shiaism and the Islamic Movement in Nigeria: 1979–1991," *Islam et sociétés au Sud du Sahara* 7 (1993): 5–16. In particular, Zakzaki, who studied political science at ABU in the mid-1970s and was a leading organizer of campus riots in Zaria in the late 1970s and early 1980s, challenged northern military governors, leading to his imprisonment on several occasions (1984, 1987, 1996). Zakzaki's ally, Malam Yayaha, established the Islamic Movement in Katsina in 1984, which claimed it was struggling against the arbitrary nature of the Nigerian military regime and was at the forefront of highly politicized conflicts with several military governors, provoking a number of violent clashes in 1990–91.

33. Loimeier, "Playing with Affiliations."

34. B. Larkin, "Bandiri Music, Globalization and Urban Experience in Nigeria," *Social Text* 22, no. 4 (2004): 91–112. See also B. Larkin and B. Meyer, "Pentecostalism, Islam and Culture: New Religious Movements in West Africa," in *Themes in West African History,* ed. E. Akyeampong (Oxford: James Currey, 2006), 286–312.

35. M. S. Umar, "Changing Islamic Identity in Nigeria from the 1960s to the 1980s: From Sufism to Anti-Sufism," in *Muslim Identity and Social Change in Sub-Saharan Africa,* ed. L. Brenner (Bloomington: Indiana University Press, 2003).

36. Larkin and Meyer, "Pentecostalism, Islam and Culture," 286.

37. Umar, "Changing Islamic Identity in Nigeria from the 1960s to the 1980s," 166.

38. R. Marshall-Fratani, "Mediating the Global and Local in Nigerian Pentecostalism," *Journal of Religion in Africa* 28, no. 3 (1998): 278–315; A. Corten and R. Marshall Fratani, eds., Between Babel and Pentecost: Trasnnational Pentecostalism in Africa and Latin America (London: C. Hurst, 2002), 80.

39. Coulon, "Les nouveaux oulémas et le renouveau islamique au Nord-Nigeria."

40. The question was simple from a juridical point of view: with the breakup of the Northern Region into several states in 1967, a legal anomaly became apparent. While the northern states had each created their own Shari'ah courts of appeal, the role of final appellate court played for the Muslim community by the Shari'ah Court of Appeal (set up in 1960 by the northern assembly) no longer existed. To create a court of appeal for the northern region alone amounted to recognizing the continued existence of this defunct political entity, a politically impossible move. At the same time, northern interests insisted upon a formal acknowledgment of the role of Shari'ah in the Second Republic. To address these two problems, the Constitutional Drafting Committee recommended a Federal Shari'ah Court of Appeal. D. Laitin, "The Sharia Debate and the Origins of Nigeria's Second Republic," *Journal of Modern African Studies* 20, no. 3 (1982): 411–30.

41. Ibid.

42. J. Ibrahim, "Religion and Political Turbulence in Nigeria," *Journal of Modern African Studies* 29, no. 1 (1991): 131.

43. Indeed, as more moderate Muslims pointed out, the appeals courts themselves are not part of the Islamic legal tradition, in which individual qadis may judge which rule is relevant, and different strands of rules may operate simultaneously. With the exception of the Ottoman empire, institutionalized procedures such as appellate courts are not part of an Islamic tradition. Kenny, "Sharia and Christianity in Nigeria."

44. See J. Ibrahim, "Politics and Religion in Nigeria: The Parametres of the 1987 Crisis in Kaduna State," *Review of African Political Economy* 45–46 (1989): 65–82; M. H. Kukah, *Religion, Politics and Power in Northern Nigeria* (Ibadan: Spectrum Books, 1993).

45. I. Enwerem, *A Dangerous Awakening: The Politicization of Religion in Nigeria* (Ibadan: IFRA, 1995), 77.

46. Keynote Address, PFN Annual Meeting, Foursquare Gospel Church, Lagos, 27 February 1991.

47. Results of a survey conducted among five hundred converts from various churches and ministries in Lagos, November 1991–January 1992.

48. Results of a survey conducted among three hundred members of the Redeemed Christian Church of God: Ebute Meta, Apapa, Surulere, Ikeja, and Somolu parishes, Lagos, February–April 1993.

49. *New Creation* 1, no. 11 (1991): 20.

50. Enwerem, *Dangerous Awakening,* 150.

51. K. Bongo, *Christianity in Danger (As Islam Threatens): The Five Whys* (n.p.: Diquadine Admiral Productions, 1989), 11–12.

52. Grady, "Nigeria's Miracle."

53. M. Foucault, *Dits et Ecrits,* Vol. 4: *1980–1988,* 30.

54. M. Last, "The Shari'a in Context: People's Quest for Justice Today and the Role of Courts in Pre- and Early-Colonial Northern Nigeria," paper

presented at the International Conference on Muslim Family Law in Sub-Saharan Africa, Centre for Contemporary Islam, University of Cape Town, March 2002. See also Last, "Terrain: La charia dans le Nord Nigeria," *Politique Africaine* 79 (October 2000): 141–51.

55. D. Pratten, "The Politics of Protection: Perspective on Vigilantism in Nigeria," *Africa* 78, no. 1 (2008): 1–15.

56. M. Last, "The Search for Security in Muslim Northern Nigeria," *Africa* 78, no. 1 (2008): 41–63.

57. S. M. O'Brien, "La charia contestée: Démocratie, débat et diversité musulmane dans les 'États charia' du Nigeria," *Politique Africaine* 106 (2007): 46–68.

58. Interview with Sheikh Ibraheem Zakzaki, *Weekly Trust* 2, no. 31 (8–14 October 1999), accessed online.

59. Spivak. "Religion, Politics, Theology," 154.

60. H. Arendt, *The Human Condition*, 2d ed. (Chicago: University of Chicago Press, 1998), 234.

61. Ibid.

62. Ibid., 235.

63. Ibid., 237.

64. Schmitt, *Political Theology.*

65. Arendt, *Human Condition*, 234.

66. Ibid., 319.

67. Ibid., 245.

68. Ibid., 237.

69. Ibid., 240. See Matthew 18:35: "And when ye stand praying, forgive, . . . that your Father also which is in Heaven may forgive your trespasses"; Matthew 6:14–15: "If ye forgive men their trespasses, your heavenly Father will also forgive you your trespasses. But if ye forgive not men their trespasses, neither will your Father forgive your trespasses."

70. Here, Arendt's thought can be seen to rejoin that of Levinas in *Totalité et Infini*. For Levinas, the encounter with the "face of the other" is the epiphany that opens the subject up to transcendence and that grounds ethics, an encounter that each time interrupts the course of history, producing a reality of a different nature, which breaks the continuity of historical time and enables it to begin anew. See S. Mosès, *Au-déla de la guerre.*

71. Arendt, *Human Condition*, 247.

72. Ibid., 238.

73. Taubes, *Political Theology of Paul*, 105; Agamben, *Time That Remains*, 135.

74. Agamben, *Time That Remains.*

75. J.-L. Nancy, *La Déclosion: déconstruction du christianisme*, vol. 1 (Paris: Editions Galilée, 2005).

76. Ibid., 12.

77. Ibid., 15.

CONCLUSION

1. See the RCCG's website for this report: http://hgs.rccg.org/story%20of%20 HG2.htm

2. I "worked" in Tony Rapu's church for three months between February and April 1993. I had many occasions to discuss his vision for the RCCG, which had yet to take on the emphasis on miracles that became its central characteristic of the period from 1995 onward. Nonetheless, one of the central reasons for the RCCG's astounding success in the latter part of the 1990s is not merely the "performance of miracles," but the continuing conviction of many that Adeboye still represents a holiness- and "righteousness"-oriented doctrine in comparison to other name-it-and-claim-it mega-stars. People regularly refer to his modest demeanor and lifestyle, demonstrating that this model still constitutes a powerful form of legitimacy or guarantee of spiritual authority.

3. Interview in *Charisma*, J. Lee Grady, "Nigeria's Miracle," 6.

4. Dr. Tony Rapu, "A Call to Order." 2002. See http://www.thispresenthouse .org/home/firstword.cfm?ContentID=241

5. H. Arendt. *The Human Condition,* 2d ed. (Chicago: University of Chicago Press, 1998), 247.

6. J. Derrida and M. Ferraris, *A Taste for the Secret* (Cambridge: Polity Press, 2001), 20.

7. J. Derrida, *The Force of Law: The Mystical Foundation of Authority,* in *Acts of Religion,* ed. G. Anidjar (New York, Routledge, 2001), 255, cited in T. Jennings, *Reading Derrida, Thinking Paul* (Stanford: Stanford University Press, 2006), 107.

8. Jennings, *Reading Derrida, Thinking Paul,* 167.

APPENDIX

1. Reference to Olumba Olumba Obu, the leader of an extremely heterodox movement, who claimed to be a special envoy of Christ and an incarnation of the Holy Spirit. He was strongly rejected by the Born-Again Christians.

2. Reference to Aladura churches.

Bibliography

NOTE ON REFERENCES

The references for this work are divided into Primary and Secondary Sources. Under Primary Sources, readers will perhaps be surprised to find a number of university dissertations from Nigerian universities at the Bachelor's and Master's level. The reason for their inclusion in Primary Sources is that while they do contain a certain amount of verifiable factual information on their subjects, they nonetheless do not meet the requirements for analytical objectivity expected of a secondary source, very often appearing closer to a form of Pentecostal proselytism than to an academic work.

BIBLIOGRAPHY OF PRIMARY SOURCES

Abina, E. O. *Biblical Evangelism and the Twentieth Century Church.* Ibadan: Afolabi Press, 1989.

Abiona, F. *To God Be the Glory: The Story of Pastor E. A. Adeboye.* Lagos: Boom of Blessing Printing, 1991.

Adeboye, E. A. *The Making of a Leader: An Abridged Version of Moses—A Man of Destiny.* Lagos: Adonay House, 1991.

———. *The New Vision.* Lagos, 1990.

———. *Our Comprehension Insurance Policy: The Hiding Place.* Lagos: Christ the Redeemer's Ministries, 1995.

Adekanmbi, J. *The Choice Is Ours.* Ibadan: Gospel Literature Writers/Distributors, 1989.

Adekola, S. *Understanding Demonology.* Ibadan: Scripture Union Press, 1993.

Adekoya, S. *You Could Be a Missionary.* Kaduna: Baraka Press, 1995.

Adeniran, R. K. *You Can Live Debt-Free.* Ibadan: Hope Foundation Books, 1994.

Aderibigbe, G., and D. Ayegboyin. *Religion, Medicine and Healing.* Lagos: Free Enterprise, 1995.

Adeyokunnu, A. *Why God Became Man.* Lagos: Christ the Redeemer's Press, 1990.

Agba, A., and L. Owo. *Ihuwasi Onigbagbo ati Irin Ajo Wa ninu Aye yii.* Ibadan: Gospel Faith Mission Press, n.d.

Agboola, M. O. *The Building of a Home of Fame and Glory.* Lagos: n.p., n.d.

Agorom, M. N. *Family Fear Proof (365 Fear Nots for 365 Days): Daily Devotions for Second Quarter, April–June.* Vol. 2. Lagos: Powerline Books, 1989.

———. *Family Fear Proof (365 Fear Nots for 365 Days): Daily Devotions for Third Quarter, July–September.* Vol. 3. Lagos: Powerline Books, 1989.

———. *Family Fear Proof (365 Fear Nots for 365 Days): Daily Devotions for Fourth Quarter, October– December.* Vol. 4. Lagos: Powerline Books, 1989.

Aguape, O. B. *Wake Up, Stand Up!* Lagos: Saigers, 1997.

Ajayi, G. *The Rapturable Church.* Ibadan: Olu Ajayi Publications, 1992.

Ajibulu, S. *Passing Examination without Tears.* Ibadan: God-Will-Do-It Publications, 1992.

Akindele, M. *What's All This Born Again Stuff Anyway?.* Ibadan: Victory Publishing House, 1997.

Akoria, A. *The Spiritual Barbers and Barbering Saloons.* Sapele: Christian Life Publications, 1998.

Amedari, D. O. *Be Fruitful and Multiply.* Ilorin: Endtime Power Books, 1989.

Amuta, B. A. *Advice to Unmarried Teenagers, Suitable for Secondary School Students and Above.* Lagos, n.p., 1995.

Arowobusoye, S. *Powerful Prayers: For Deliverance and Total Breakthrough (In English and Yoruba Languages) with over 100 Revival Songs.* Ibadan: Gospel Teacher's Fellowship International, 1999.

———. *Satanic Immigration Officers.* Ibadan: Gospel Teachers Publications, 1996.

Ashimolowo, M. *Take Giant Leap.* London: Mattison Media Publications, 1992.

Balogun, J. O. *Redeemed from the Clutches of Satan: Former Head of Seven Secret Cults Now an Evangelist.* Lagos: Noade Nigeria, n.d.

Bamiloye, M. *Lost Forever . . . in Hell!* Lagos: Faith Fellowship Books, 1992.

———. *The Unprofitable Servant.* Ibadan: Mount Zion Publications, 1988.

Banjo, D. *Child Redemption Campaign: For the Redemption of Their Soul Is Precious.* Lagos: Good News Printers, n.d.

Bongo, K. C. *Christianity in Danger (As Islam Threatens): The Five Whys.* n.p.: Diquadine Admiral Publications, 1989.

Bonnke, R. *Evangelism by Fire: Igniting Your Passion for the Lost.* London: Kingsway Publications, 1989.

———. *How to Have Assurance for Salvation.* n.p.: Christ for All Nations, 1991.

Brown, R. *Prepare for War.* Lagos: Academic Press, 1987.

Building the Body. Lagos: Deeper Christian Life Ministry, n.d.

Collins, T. *The Baptist Mission of Nigeria: 1850–1993.* Ibadan: Nigerian Baptist Bookstore, 1994.

Dagunduro, G. K. *Former Satan Deputy in the World Turned Follower of Christ.* Ilesha: Rapture Evangelism International, 1987.

———. *My Journey from the Earth to Hell and My Vision of the Heaven: Where Is Your Eternal Home?* Ilesha: Rapture Evangelism International, 1990.

Daily Power 1991: Notes for Daily Reading for the Whole Year. Ibadan: Scripture Union (Nigeria) Press and Books, 1990.

Daily Power 1993: Notes for Daily Reading for the Whole Year. Ibadan: Scripture Union (Nigeria) Press and Books, 1993.

Daoud, M. A. *The Real Way to Heaven: The Grace of God That Brings Salvation.* Dallas: M. A. Daoud's Ministry, 1986.

Davies, D. *Getting God's Flow into Your Finances.* Lagos: Cornywal Nigeria, 1992.

Durojaye, J. O. *Magic of Miracles.* Ibadan: Calvary Publishers, 1994.

Eckhardt, J. *Deliverance and Spiritual Warfare Manual.* Lagos: Highways Publications, 1987.

Ededeji, B. *All That You Need.* Lagos: Salem Media (Nigeria), 1988.

Eghagha, G. *The Races of Mankind: Whence and Whither.* Lagos: G.K.S. Press, 1993.

Elushade, B. *Christian Principles of Prosperity.* Ibadan: Cosmo International Christian Books, 1992.

Emelife, I. *What Every Youth Should Know about Love, Sex and Marriage.* Owerri: Evangelistic Association International, n.d.

Emmanuel, F. *Say No to Compromise: The Danielic Experience.* Ibadan: Feyisetan Press, 1996.

Engel, J. F. *Getting Your Message Across.* Lagos: Salem Media Nigeria, n.d.

Eni, E. *Delivered from the Powers of Darkness.* Ibadan: Scripture Union Press, 1987.

———. *The Works of the Devil.* Port Harcourt: Sparks Group, 1989.

Esekie, P.A. *Born Again: What It Is Not.* Lagos: Peter Esekie Ministries, 1990.

———. *What It Means to Be Born Again.* Vol. 1. Lagos: Peter Esekie Ministries, 1989.

Eto, V. *Exposition on Water Spirits.* Warri: Shallom Christian Mission International, 1983.

———. *The Forces of Darkness.* Warri: Shallom Christian Mission, 1988.

———. *How I Served Satan until Jesus Christ Delivered Me.* Warri: Shallom Christian Mission International, 1981.

Eyiyere, D. O. *The Priesthood and Names of Blasphemy.* n.p. (Nigeria): Doe-Sun Publishers, 1993.

Famonure, B. *Training to Die.* Lagos: Capro Media Services, 1989.

Fomum, Z. T. *Deliverance from Sin.* n.p. (Cameroon): I. G. H., 1990.

Guti, E. *Sh-hh Shut Your Mouth: Marriage and Young Couples Character: Advice for Young Couples.* Harare: EGEA Publications, 1995.

Hammond, F., and I. M. Hammond. *Pigs in the Parlor.* Impact Books, 1973.

Heaven, U. *How to Cast Out Demons or Evil Spirits.* Lagos: Heaven and Blessing Books, 1992.

Henderson, W. Guy. *Passport to Missions.* Nashville, Tenn.: Broadman Press, 1979.

Idahosa, B. *Faith for Doing the Impossible.* Benin City: Idahosa World Outreach, 1994.

Iheme, U. *Jesus: The Holy Communion.* Port Harcourt: Water of Life Ministries, 1991.

Ijagbulu, Dele O. *For Husbands Only 1.* Lagosi: Olu-Ibukun Counselling Centre, n.d.

———. *For Wives Only 2.* Lagosi: Olu-Ibukun Counselling Centre, n.d.

———. *For Younger Boys Only.* Lagos: Olu-Ibukun Counselling Centre, n.d.

Ilugbusi, T. O. T. *The Jesus Project.* Katsina: Kole Printers, 1990.

Jegede, J. A. *Godliness Invites Trouble.* Lagos: Latter House of God Ministry, n.d.

Koffuor, G. *Boy Meets Girl.* Ibadan: Scripture Union, 1978.

Kumuyi, W. F. *Call to Commitment.* Lagos: Zoe Publishing and Printing, 1989.

———. *Complete Bible Study Series in One Volume.* Lagos: Zoe Publishing and Printing, 1983.

———. *God's Answers to Man's Questions.* Lagos: Zoe Publishing and Printing, 1989.

———. *Have Compassion on Them.* Lagos: Zoe Publishing and Printing, 1991.

———. *The Heartbeat of the Almighty.* Lagos: Zoe Publishing and Printing, 1990.

———. *The Hour of Decision.* Lagos: Zoe Publishing and Printing, 1990.

———. *How to Know God's Will in Marriage.* Lagos: Zoe Publishing and Printing, 1990.

———. *How to Receive Divine Healing.* Lagos: Zoe Publishing and Printing, 1976.

———. *Sanctification: A Christian Experience.* Lagos: Zoe Publishing and Printing, 1988.

———. *Standing on the Promises.* Lagos: Zoe Publishing and Printing, 1991.

Lindsay, D., and G. Lindsay. *Evolution: The Incredible Hoax.* Dallas: Christ for the Nations, 1988.

Lindsay, G. *The Miracle of Israel.* Ibadan: Olusseyi Press, 1990.

———. *Satan: Fallen Angels and Demons.* Dallas: Christ for the Nations, n.d.

———. *Signs of the Soon Coming of Christ.* Christ for the Nations, n.d.

McDowell, J. *More Than a Carpenter.* London: Kingsway Publications, 1977.

Ngwoke, I. B. *Islam, the O.I.C and Nigerian Unity.* Enugu: SNAAP Press, 1986.

Nnamdi-Ronnie, V. School of Deliverance. Lagos: Frontline Christian Publications, 1997.

Obu, Olumba Olumba. *If You Saw God Would You Know Him?* Ibadan: Exquisite Printers, 1990.

Odunze, D. *The Ideal Housewife.* Enugu: Family Circle Publications, 1985.

Ofoegbu, M. *Dangerous Prayers Parts 1–3.* Lagos: Holy Ghost Anointed Books, 1996–98.

———. *Exposing Satanic Manipulations*. Lagos: Holy Ghost Anointed Books, 1996.

———. *How to Destroy Satanic Manipulations*. Lagos: Holy Ghost Anointed Books, 1998.

———. *Victory over Evil Dreams*. Lagos: Holy Ghost Anointed Books, 1995.

Ogbonnaya, H. U. *How to Win Your Husband*. Lagos: Offico Enterprises, n.d.

———. *How to Win Your Wife*. Lagos: Offico Enterprises, n.d.

Ogunbusola, M. O. *The Dangers of Backsliding*. Ibadan: Jecem Publications, 1994.

Ogunsusi, G. O. *My Journey from Earth to Hell and My Vision of the Heaven*. Lagos: Gate of Perfection, 1990.

Ojewale, M. O. *A Call to Prayer for Nigeria*. Lagos: Peace and Salvation Publishers, 1990.

———. *Hope for the Sapped Generation*. Lagos: Peace and Salvation Publications, 1991.

———. *Pathway to Peace*. Lagos: M.O.O. & A. Publications, 1987.

Okafor, L. E. *Urgent Warnings to the End-time Church*. Ibadan: Lamcall Ministries, 1992.

Okediji, O. O. *On Spiritual Madness: A Biblical Perspective*. Lagos: Triumphal Press, 1991.

Okonwo, M. *Faith Is Now or Never*. Lagos: TREM Publication Committee, 1990.

Olaoye, B. *Seven Biblical Principles of Prosperity*. Ibadan: Light and Love, 1996.

Olukoya, D. K. *Brokenness*. Lagos: Mountain of Fire and Miracles Ministries, 1997.

———. *Personal Spiritual Checkup*. Lagos: Mountain of Fire and Miracles Ministries, 1996.

———. *Pray Your Way to Breakthroughs*. Lagos: Mountain of Fire and Miracles Ministries, 1994.

———. *Victory over Satanic Dreams*. Lagos: Mountain of Fire and Miracles Ministries, 1996.

Omodanisi, M. *Rehoboth: Welcome to Prosperity: Prosperity Workshop*. Kaduna: Gospel Ministries International, 1997.

Omoobajesu, E. O. *My Experience in the Darkness of This World before Jesus Saved Me*. Lagos: Omoobajesu World Outreach, 1968.

Onaiyekan, J. *Religion: Peace and Justice in Nigeria*. Ilorin: Ilorin Diocese Catechetical Resource Centre, 1989.

Oniororo, N. *Lagos Is a Wicked Place*. Ibadan: Ororo Publications, 1967.

Onotu, J. J. *Christian-Muslim Relationship in Nigeria: Muslim Master Plan and Method*. Anambra: Diocesan Priests Association of Anambra and Imo (ANIM), 1988.

Onuoha, D. K. *My Encounters with Lucifer: Satan, the Devil and His Agents*. Ibadan: God-Will-Do-It Publications, 1998.

———. *Satan the Devil and His Agents*. Ibadan: God-Will-Do-It Publications, 1998.

Opatayo, A. *Too Late to Wait?* Ibadan: Scripture Union (Nigeria) Press and Books, 1990.

Oreweme, L. *The Men the World Needs.* Lagos: Meg-Comm Network, n.d.

Orogwu, J. *Tithe Yourself Out of Poverty: With Notes on Giving.* Enugu: Atlantic Publishers, 1990.

Oyedepo, D *Breaking Financial Hardship* Lagos: Dominion Press, 1995.

———. *Covenant Wealth.* Lagos: Dominion Press, 1996.

———. *Understanding Financial Prosperity.* Lagos: Dominion Press, 1997.

Oyor, G. F. *Alcohol, the Devil's Weapon.* Ibadan: God-Will-Do-It Publications, 1997.

———. *Complete Deliverance and Healing in Jesus' Name.* Ibadan: God-Will-Do-It Publications, 1987.

———. *Covenants, Curses and the Way Out.* Ibadan: God-Will-Do-It Publications, 1991.

———. *Knowing God Intimately.* Ibadan: God-Will-Do-It Publications, 1989.

———. *Ministering Deliverance.* Ibadan: God-Will-Do-It Publications, 1992.

———. *Who Needs Deliverance.* Ibadan: God-Will-Do-It Publications, 1995.

Praise and Prayer Bulletin: Praying for Nigeria. n.p. (Nigeria): Christian Missionary Foundation, 1999.

Prayer Is the Key : A Decade of Harvest Prayer Lessons. Enugu: General Council of the Assemblies of God Nigeria, n.d.

The Praying Youth: Youth Prayer Guide. Ibadan: Youth Ministries Division, 1997.

The Redeemed Christian Church of God: Sunday School in English. Lagos: CRM Press, n.d.

Satguru Maharaj Ji. *Nigeria Is The New Holy Land!* Ibadan: One Love Family, 1992.

Search the Scriptures. Vols. 2, 4, 14, 24, 25, 26. Lagos: Deeper Life Christian Ministry, n.d.

Search the Scriptures: For Children 3–8. Vol. 23. Lagos: Deeper Life Christian Ministry, n.d.

Search the Scriptures: For Children—Senior. Vol. 24. Lagos: Deeper Life Christian Ministry, n.d.

Tayo, F. *Nigeria Belongs to Jesus.* Ibadan: Feyisetan Press, 1988.

Timmons, J. P. *Mysterious Secrets of the Dark Kingdom.* Austin, Texas: CCI Publishing, 1991.

Usenu, R. *Rehoboth: The Key to Prosperity.* Ibadan: Kingdom Designs, 1991.

Uzorma, I. N. *Exposing the Rulers of Darkness.* n.p. (Nigeria): Perfect Blood of Our Lord Jesus-Christ, 1994.

———. *Occult Grand Master, Now in Christ.* Benin City: Uzorma Warfare Publications, 1993.

Walsh, V. M. *A Key to Charismatic Renewal in the Catholic Church.* n.p.: Key of David Publications, 1974.

Watson, D. *You Are My God: A Pioneer of Renewal Recounts His Pilgrimage in Faith.* Wheaton, Ill.: Harold Sha Publishers, 1950.

Wurmbrand, R. *Was Karl Max a Satanist?* New Delhi: Sabina Printing Press, 1981.

Yusuf, A. B. *Maitatsine: Peddler of Epidemics.* Lagos: Publication Division of SYRECO, 1988.

Yusuf, S. L. O. *God's Intervention in World Affairs.* Ibadan: Straight Channel Nigeria, 1997.

Zahradeen, N. B. *The Maitatsine Saga.* Zaria: Hudahuda Publishing, 1988.

Dissertations

Abikoye, E. O. "Paul's Method of Church Planting with Particular Reference to the Foursquare Gospel Church in Nigeria." B.A. thesis, Department of Religious Studies, Obafemi Awolowo University, Ile-Ife, Nigeria, 1987.

Adegoroye, B. A. "Deeper Life Campus Fellowship: A Study of Student Evangelism in Obafemi Awolowo University." B.A. thesis, Department of Religious Studies, Obafemi Awolowo University, Ile-Ife, Nigeria, 1991.

Akade, G. O. "The Role of Good Women Association in the Christ Apostolic Church." B.A. thesis, Department of Religious Studies, University of Ibadan, 1994.

Ayandiji, E. O. "The Origin of Indigenous Pentecostal Churches in Nigeria: A Case Study of the Redeemed Christian Church of God." B.A. thesis, Department of Religious Studies, University of Ibadan, 1997.

Bamidele, M. O. "The History of the Evangelistic Ministry of Prophet, Evangelist Dr. Timothy Oluwale Obadare up to 1985." B.A. thesis, Department of Religious Studies, Obafemi Awolowo University, Ile-Ife, Nigeria, 1986.

Folake, O. F. "Contradictions in Yoruba Witchcraft Belief." B.A. thesis, Department of Religious Studies, University of Ibadan, 1995.

Idamarhare, A. O. "The Healing Miracles of Jesus: Healing in Some Pentecostal Churches in Nigeria as a Case Study." B.A. thesis, Department of Religious Studies, University of Ibadan, 1997.

Iyiola, T. "The Life and Works of Pastor E. T. Latunde: The Late President of the Christ Apostolic Church in Nigeria and Overseas." B.A. thesis, Department of Religious Studies, Obafemi Awolowo University, Ile-Ife, Nigeria, 1984.

Ogbuji, G. N. "Religion and Social Change: Its Sociological Implications with Particular Reference to Assemblies of God, Nigeria." B.A. thesis, Department of Religious Studies, University of Ibadan, 1992.

Okwuoma, J. C. "Glory Tabernacle Ministry: History, Doctrines and Impact on Society." B.A. thesis, Department of Religious Studies, University of Ibadan, 1994.

Olaniyi, F. A. "Christ Apostolic Church and the Use of Medicine: A Study of Change in Attitude in the Church." B.A. thesis, Department of Religious Studies, University of Ibadan, 1991.

Olayemi, O. I. "Women in the Church: A Study of Vine Branch Charismatic Church, Ibadan." M.A. thesis, Department of Sociology, University of Ibadan, 1997.

Olojo, O. R. "The Meaning of Matthew 16:17–19 to the Deeper Life Bible Church: An Exegetical Approach." B.A. thesis, Department of Religious Studies, Obafemi Awolowo University, Ile-Ife, Nigeria, 1988.

Omiyale, B. A. "History and Doctrines of Christ Ministries Pentecostal Church." B.A. thesis, Department of Religious Studies, University of Ibadan, 1991.

Onwidiegwu, M. J. N. "Catholic Church in Dialogue with the Pentecostal Churches: Prospect for Evangelization 2000." B.A. thesis, Department of Religious Studies, University of Ibadan, 1992.

Somoyi, A.A. "Charismatic Movements in Ile-Ife: A Case Study of the Christ Way Fellowship International." B.A. thesis, Department of Religious Studies, Obafemi Awolowo University, Ile-Ife, Nigeria, 1992.

Taped Sermons and Messages

Deeper Life Christian Ministry, Lagos, Life Tapes, Pastor William O. Kumuyi

"Love is the Key." 29 April 1990.

"The Mission of Church." 25 June 1990.

"The Gospel Truth." 13 August 1990.

"Reconciliation with God." 8 October 1990.

"Healing of the Blind." 21 October 1990.

"Total Healing for Christians." 23 December 1990.

"Christian Unity among Brethren." 17 February 1991.

"Deliverance for the Oppressed." 21 February 1991.

"Question and Answer: Consecration and Submission." 24 February 1991.

"Submission to God's Will." 24 February 1991.

"Causes and Cure for Spiritual Blindness'." 3 February 1992.

"God's Unfailing Promises." 3 October 1992.

"The Centrality of Holiness and Sanctity." 16 October 1992.

"Escaping the Great Tribulation." 16 October 1992.

"Bride's Preparation for the Bridegroom's Return." 30 October 1992.

"Christ: High Priest and Sanctifier." 30 October 1992.

"Double Cure for Sin." 12 November 1992.

"Temptation and the Trials of Saints." 12 November 1992.

"Spread and Keep the Faith." 30 November 1992.

"The Great Decision." 24 December 1992.

"Let Your Light So Shine." 27 December 1992.

"Dealing with the Demonised and Possessed." Annual Retreat. January 1998.

"Dealing with Disappointment and Discouragement." Annual Retreat. January 1998.

"God's Whole Armour for End-time Spiritual Warfare." Annual Retreat. January 1998.

"The Kind of Mother Every Child Needs." Annual Retreat. January 1998.

Redeemed Christian Church of God, Apapa Parish, Lagos,
Word and Sound Ministries
Rapu, Pastor Tony.
"Financial Blessings I." 8 April 1992.
"Financial Blessings II." 13 April 1992.
"Kingdom Currency." 1 November 1992.
"Equipping the Spirits." n.d.
Odeyemi, Pastor E. A.
"We Declare War." 28 July 1991.
Nwankpa, Emeka.
"Spiritual Warfare." Lagos. 1 July 1992.
Itsuelli, Sister Bridget.
"Relationships." Lagos. 10 October 1992.
"Relationships II." 10 November 1992.
Obanure, Brother Olu.
"Signs of His Coming." 15 November 1992.

Redeemed Christian Church of God, Ebute Meta, Lagos,
Pastor E. A. Adeboye

"Feeding of the 5000." 27 October 1991.
"A Voice to the Nation." 27 October 1991.
"First Anniversary Service." 3 May 1992.
"Freedom from Poverty into Abundance." n.d., 1998.
"The Glory of the Latter House." n.d., 1998.

Overcomers Mission, Lagos, Archbishop Benson Idahosa

"Divine Change." 4 April 1991.

Idahosa World Outreach, Benin City, Archbishop Benson Idahosa "Come from
the Top." n.d. "Power Against." n.d.
Hour of Deliverance, Lagos, Pastor Ayo Oritsejafor

"God Cannot Lie." n.d.
"How to Pray and Get an Answer." n.d.

Redeemed Evangelical Mission, Lagos, Power in the Word Tapes,
Bishop Mike Okonkwo
"Power in the Word." n.d., 1989.
"Practising Union with Deity." n.d., 1989.
"As Long as You Are a Jew." 8 February 1990.
"Commendation or Condemnation." 10 February 1991.
"Preparing for the Storm." 15 February 1991.
"Secret Chamber of Satan." 26 February 1991.

Christ Chapel—Voice of Faith Ministries, Lagos

Joda, Rev. Tunde
"Paul's Revelation." 3 April 1991.
"Understanding God's Will for Your Life." n.d., 1992.
"The Resurrection Power." n.d., 1992.
Dada, Rev. Gbolahan
"Breaking Through Your Barriers." n.d., 1992.
"Brokenness and the Servant's Heart." n.d., 1992.
"Divine Healing." n.d., 1992.
"Faith Work's in Two Places." n.d., 1992.
"The Vital Key to Supernatural." n.d., 1992.
"A Way through the Wilderness." n.d., 1992.
Ashimolowo, Rev. Matthew
"The Secrets of Solomon's Success." n.d., 1992.

Conference: "Combating the Powers of Darkness," National Theatre, Lagos,
11–13 April 1993
Onuzo, Dr. Okey
"Overcoming the Strong Man."
"Overcoming the Strongman II."
"Spiritual Power in Evangelism."
Nwankpa, Emeka
"Remitting the Sins of the Father." "Territorial Spirits."
Adeboye, Pastor E. A.
"Preparation for Battle."
Oritsejafor, Pastor Ayo
"Jesus on the Offensive."
Okonkwo, Bishop Mike
"Equipping the Warriors."

Pentecostal Fellowship of Nigeria Biennial Meeting, Lagos, 11–12 February 1993
Adeboye, Pastor E. A.
"Laziness on the Part of Leader."
"Reaching Your Goal."
"Rudiment of Spiritual Warfare."
"What You Must Do to Be Well with You."
Okonkwo, Bishop Mike
"Gospel, the Power of God." Lagos, 11 February 1993.

Kingdom Life World Conference, Redeemed Evangelical Mission, Lagos,
23–28 November 1992
Jonathan, Pastor Dan. 27 November 1992.
Nweka, Dr. Paul. 24 November 1992.
Oke, Rev. Reuben. 23 November 1992.
Okah, Pastor Simeon. 23 November 1992.

Omobude, Dr. Felix. 22 November 1992.

Wilson, Rev. Jerry. 28 November 1992.

Conference on Missions, Assemblies of God, Aguda, Lagos, 22 April 1992

Abuka, Barrister P. C. "Challenges of Professionals in Local Missions."

Asiedu, Pastor S. "The World from a Missions Perspective."

Macauley, Rev. J. W. "International Partnership in Missions in the 90s: Prospects, Problems and Solutions."

Offodile, Dr. C. "Reaching the African Child by the Year 2000."

Video Films

Note: Format is home video cassettes; average length, 80 minutes.

Mount Zion Film Ministry Productions

The Great Mistake, Part I. Mount Zion Productions, Ibadan; KAY Technical Video and Film Co., Ibadan. n.d.

The Great Mistake, Part II. Mount Zion Productions, Ibadan; KAY Technical Video and Film Co., Ibadan. n.d.

The Great Mistake, Part III. Mount Zion Productions, Ibadan; KAY Technical Video and Film Co., Ibadan. n.d.

Ide Esu, Part I. Mount Zion Productions, Ibadan; KAY Technical Video and Film Co., Ibadan. n.d.

Ide Esu, Part II. Mount Zion Productions, Ibadan; KAY Technical Video and Film Co., Ibadan. n.d.

Ide Esu, Part III. Mount Zion Productions, Ibadan; KAY Technical Video and Film Co., Ibadan. n.d.

Ide Esu, Part IV. Mount Zion Productions, Ibadan; KAY Technical Video and Film Co., Ibadan. n.d.

The Perilous Times. Mount Zion Productions, Ibadan; KAY Technical Video and Film Co., Ibadan. n.d.

The Story of My Life. Mount Zion Productions, Ibadan; KAY Technical Video and Film Co., Ibadan. n.d.

Other Productions

Agbara Ajinde (Power of Resurrection). Refuge Films, Refuge Drama Ministry, Lagos. n.d.

The Backslidden Giant. Step Films, Stage Evangelism Production Ministries, Ibadan. n.d.

Blood Money I: The Vulture Men. OJ Productions, Onitsha. 1996.

Blood Money II: The Vulture Men. OJ Productions, Onitsha. 1997.

Cursed from Beyond. Great Movie Productions/Ossy Affason Productions, Onitsha. n.d.

Daughters of the River Part I. Watchtower Evangelical Drama Ministries, Ilorin; KAY Technical Video and Film Co., Ibadan. n.d.

Died Wretched, Buried in a N 3.2 Million Casket. NEK Video Links Production, Lagos. 1998.

Egun Aimo. Evangelical Outreach Ministries, Ilorin. n.d.

Endtime. NEK Video Links Production, Lagos. 1999.

Eni Nla. KAY Technical Evangelical Films Production, God's Camera Ministries, Ibadan. 1997.

Etan. Calvary Drama Ministries, Ilorin. n.d.

Ewu-Nla (Great Danger). Cornerstone Film Ministry, Lagos. n.d.

Faces. J. A. Shamma Films, Zelex Nigeria Ltd., Onitsha. n.d.

Ipe Oluwa (The Call of the Lord). Chosen Generation Ministries; CORAD Nigeria Enterprises, Ibadan. n.d.

Ipinnu (The Decision). KAY Technical Evangelical Films Production, God's Camera Ministries, Ibadan. 1996.

Itusile. Grace of Christ Ministry and Decross Drama Group, Lagos. n.d.

Karishaka. Tony Jackson Nigeria Ltd., Lagos. n.d.

Karishaka 2: Satan Is the Trouble. Tony Jackson Nigeria Ltd., Lagos. 1999.

Metamorphosis. B. S. F. Drama Group, Sound on Vision Frames, Ilorin. n.d.

The New Bride. C-Team Christian Ministry; Petez Communications, Lagos. n.d.

The Price. Liberty Films Productions, Lagos. n.d.

Sins of the Fathers. Great Movies Productions, Onitsha. n.d.

Witches. Great Movie Productions/Ossy Affason Productions, Onitsha. n.d.

Television Programs

Note: 25 hours of programs were recorded from Ogun State television channels (NTA, BCOS, OGTV) over a period of six months in 1998. The programs included revivals, sermons, and "healing and miracle" hours from the following ministries:

By Faith Christian Ministries, Ibadan
Christ Embassy, Lagos
Christ Power Divine Church, Ibadan
Christ Revival Miracle Church, Ibadan
Christ Searchlight Evangelistic Ministry, Ibadan
Ever Increasing Faith Ministry, Lagos
Fountain Grace Ministry, Ibadan
Fountain of Life Harvest Church, Ibadan
Full Gospel Business Men's Fellowship, Ibadan
Full Stature International Mission, Ibadan
Gospel Mission International, Ibadan
Kingsway International Church, London
Miracle Life Prophetic Ministry, Lagos
Synagogue Church of God of All Nations, Lagos
Victory Life Ministry, Ilesa
World Soul Winning Evangelistic Ministry, Lagos

BIBLIOGRAPHY OF SECONDARY SOURCES

Abdulraheem, T. A. Olukoshi, A. R. Mustapha, and G. P. Williams. "Nigeria: Oil, Debts and Democracy." *Review of African Political Economy* 13, no. 37 (1986): 6–10.

Agamben, G. *Etat d'exception: Homo Sacer II*. Paris: Seuil, 2003.

———. *The Time That Remains: A Commentary on the Letter to the Romans*. Stanford: Stanford University Press, 2005.

Amucheazi, E. *Church and Politics in Eastern Nigeria, 1945–1966: A Study In Pressure Group Politics*. Ibadan: Macmillan Nigeria, 1986.

Anderson, A. *An Introduction to Pentecostalism*. Cambridge: Cambridge University Press, 2004.

Anidjar, G. "Secularism." *Critical Inquiry* 33 (2006) 52–77.

Appadurai, A. *Modernity at Large: Cultural Dimensions of Globalization*. Minneapolis: University of Minnesota Press, 1996.

Apter, A. "IBB = 419: Nigerian Democracy and the Politics of Illusion." In *Civil Society and the Political Imagination in Africa: Critical Perspectives*, ed. J. Comaroff and J. L. Comaroff, 267–308. Chicago: University of Chicago Press, 1999.

———. *The Pan African Nation: Oil and the Spectacle of Culture in Nigeria*. Chicago: University of Chicago Press, 2005.

Arendt, H. *The Human Condition*. 2d ed. Chicago: University of Chicago Press, 1998. Originally published 1958.

Asad. T. "Comments on Conversion." In *Conversion to Modernities: The Globalization of Christianity*, ed. P. Van der Veer, 263–74. New York: Routledge, 1996.

———. *Formation of the Secular: Christianity, Islam, Modernity*. Stanford: Stanford University Press, 2003.

———. *Genealogies of Religion: Discipline and Reasons of Power in Christianity and Islam*. Baltimore: Johns Hopkins University Press, 1993.

Asonzeh F-K. U. "Advertising God: Nigerian Video-Films and the Power of Consumer Culture." *Journal of Religion in Africa* 33 (2003): 203–31.

———. "The Redeemed Christian Church of God (RCCG), Nigeria: Local Identities and Global Processes in African Pentecostalism." Ph.D. diss., University of Bayreuth, Germany, 2003.

Austin, J. L. *How to Do Things with Words*. Oxford: Oxford University Press, 1975.

Ayandele, E. A. *The Missionary Impact on Modern Nigeria, 1842–1914: A Political and Social Analysis*. London: Longman, 1966.

Badie, B., and M. Smouts. *Le retournement du monde: Sociologie de la scène internationale*. Paris: Presses de la Fondation Nationale des Sciences Politiques and Dalloz, 1992.

Banégas, R., and J.-P. Warnier. « Nouvelles figures de la réussite et du pouvoir. » *Politique Africaine* 82 (June 2001): 5–23.

Barber, K. *The Generation of Plays: Yoruba Popular Life in Theatre.* Bloomington: Indiana University Press, 2000.

———. "How Man Makes God in West Africa: Yoruba Attitudes towards the Orisa." *Africa* 51, no. 3 (1981): 724–44.

———. "Money, Self-Realization and the Person in Yoruba Texts." In *Money Matters: Instability, Values and Social Payments in the Modern History of West African Communities,* ed. J. Guyer, 205–24. Portsmouth, N.H.: Heinemann, 1995.

———. "Popular Arts in Africa." *African Studies Review* 30, no. 3 (1987): 1–78.

———. "Popular Reactions to the Petro-Naira." *Journal of Modern African Studies* 20, no. 3 (1982): 431–50.

———. "The Religious Disaggregation of Popular Moral Discourse in Yorùbá Theatre and Video Drama." Paper presented at the conference "Religion and Media in Nigeria," School of Oriental and African Studies, London, 25–26 February 1999.

Bastian, M. "Married in the Water: Spirit Kin and Other Afflictions of Modernity in Southeastern Nigeria." *Journal of Religion in Africa* 2 (1997): 1–19.

Bayart, J.-F. « Les églises africaines et la politique du ventre, » *Politique Africaine* 35 (October 1989).

———. « Les églises chrétiennes et la politique du ventre: le partage du gâteau ecclésial. » *L'Argent de Dieu, Politique Africaine* 35 (October 1989) : 3–26.

———. « Fait missionnaire et politique du ventre: Une lecture foucauldienne. » *Le Fait Missionnaire* 6 (September 1998).

———. « Fin de partie au sud du Sahara? La politique africaine de la France. » In *La France et l'Afrique: Vade-mecum pour un nouveau voyage,* ed. S. Michaïloff, 112–29. Paris, Karthala, 1993.

———. « Foucault au Congo. » In *Penser avec Michel Foucault: Théorie critique et pratiques politiques,* ed. M.-C. Granjon, 183–222. Paris: Karthala, 2005.

———. *Le gouvernement du monde: Une critique politique de la globalisation.* Paris: Fayard, 2004.

———. *L'Illusion identitaire.* Paris: Fayard, 1996.

———. *The State in Africa: The Politics of the Belly.* London: Longman, 1993.

———. « Total Subjectivation. » In *Matière à politique: Le pouvoir, les corps et les choses,* ed. J.-F. Bayart and J.-P. Warnier, 215–53. Paris: Karthala/CERI, 2004.

Bayart, J.-F., ed. *La Greffe de l'Etat.* Paris: Karthala, 1996.

Bayart, J.-F., ed. *Religion et modernité politique en Afrique noire: Dieu pour tous et chacun pour soi.* Paris: Karthala, 1994.

Bayart, J.-F., S. Ellis, and B. Hibou. *The Criminalisation of the State in Africa.* London: International African Institute and James Currey, 1999.

Bayart, J.-F., and P. Geschiere. « 'J'étais là avant': Problèmes politiques de l'autochtonie. » *Critique Internationale* 10 (January 2001) : 5–10.

Bayart, J.-F., P. Geschiere, and F. Nyamnjoh. « Autochtonie, démocratie, et citoyenneté en Afrique. » *Critique Internationale* 10 (January 2001) : 177–94.

Bayart, J.-F., and J.-P. Warnier, eds. *Matière à politique: Le pouvoir, les corps et les choses*. Paris: Karthala/CERI, 2004.

Benjamin, W. « Critique of Violence." In *Walter Benjamin: Selected Writings*, Vol. 1: *1913–1926*, ed. M. Bullock and M. W. Jennings, 236–53. Cambridge, Mass.: Belknap Press of Harvard University Press, 1996.

———. *Illuminations*. London: Fontana, 1992.

Bensussan, G. *Le temps messianique: temps historique et temps vécu*. Paris: Librairie Philosophique J. Vrin, 2001.

Beti, M. *Le Pauvre Christ de Bomba*. Paris: Présence Africaine, 1976. Originally published 1954.

Blundo, G., and J.-P. Olivier de Sardan, eds. *La corruption au quotidien. Politique Africaine* 83 (October 2001).

Bourdieu, P. *Outline of a Theory of Practice*. Cambridge: Cambridge University Press, 1977.

Bourgault, L. *Mass Media in Sub-Saharan Africa*. Bloomington: Indiana University Press, 1995.

Brenner, L., ed. *Muslim Identity and Social Change in Sub-Saharan Africa*. Bloomington: Indiana University Press, 2003.

Butler, J. "Giving an Account of Oneself." *Diacritics* 31, no. 4 (2001): 22–40.

———. *Giving an Account of Oneself*. New York: Fordham University Press, 2005.

Calhoun, C. "Nationalism and Civil Society: Democracy, Diversity and Self-Determination." *International Sociology* 8, no. 4 (1993): 387–411.

Caron, B., A. Gboyega, and E. Osaghae, eds. *Democratic Transition in Africa*. Ibadan: CREDU, 1992.

Castoriadis, C. *The Imaginary Institution of Society*. Cambridge, Mass.: MIT Press, 1987.

Chabal, P., and J. P. Daloz. *Africa Works: Disorder as Political Instrument*. Oxford: James Currey, 1998.

Chatterjee, P. *The Nation and Its Fragments*. Princeton: Princeton University Press, 1993.

———. "A Response to Taylor's Modes of Civil Society." *Public Culture* 3, no. 1 (1990): 119–32.

Chrétien, J.-P. *Le défie de l'ethnisme: Rwanda et Burundi: 1990–1996*. Paris: Karthala, 1997.

Cohen, R. *Labour and Politics in Nigeria*. London: Heinemann, 1974.

Comaroff, J. "Consuming Passions: Nightmares of the Global Village." *Culture* 17, nos. 1–2 (1997): 7–19.

Comaroff, J., and J. L. Comaroff. "Alien-nation: Zombies, Immigrants and Global Capitalism." *South Atlantic Quarterly* 101, no. 4 (2002): 779–805.

———. "Millennial Capitalism: First Thoughts on a Second Coming." *Public Culture* 12, no. 2 (2000): 291–343.

———. "Naturing the Nation: Aliens, Apocalypse and the Postcolonial State." *Journal of Southern African Studies* 27, no. 3 (2001): 627–51.

———. *Of Revelation and Revolution*. Vol. 1: *Christianity, Colonialism and Consciousness in South Africa*. Chicago: University of Chicago Press, 1991.

———. *Of Revelation and Revolution.* Vol. 2: *The Dialectics of Modernity on a South African Frontier.* Chicago: University of Chicago Press, 1997.

———. "Second Comings: Neo-Protestant Ethics and Millennial Capitalism in South Africa, and Elsewhere." In *2000 Years and Beyond: Faith, Identity and the Common Era*, ed. P. Gifford,106–26. London: Routledge, 2002.

Comaroff, J., and J. L. Comaroff, eds. *Civil Society and Political Imagination in Africa: Critical Perspectives.* Chicago: University of Chicago Press, 2000.

———. *Modernity and Its Malcontents: Ritual and Power in Postcolonial Africa.* Chicago: University of Chicago Press, 1993.

Constantin, F., and C. Coulon, eds. *Religion et transition démocratique en Afrique.* Paris: Karthala, 1997.

Cooper, F. *Decolonization and African Society: The Labor Question in French and British Africa.* Cambridge: Cambridge University Press, 1996.

———. "What Is the Concept of Globalization Good For? An African Historian's Perspective." *African Affairs* 100, no. 399 (2001): 189–213.

Corten, A. « Miracles et obéissance: Le discours de la guérison divine à l'Eglise Universelle. » *Social Compass* 44, no. 2 (1997).

———. « Pentecôtisme et politique en Amérique latine. » *Problèmes d'Amérique latine* 24 (January–March 1997): 17–31.

Corten, A., and R. Marshall-Fratani. "Introduction." In *Between Babel and Pentecost: Transnational Pentecostalism in Africa and Latin America*, ed. A. Corten and R. Marshall-Fratani, 1–21. London: C. Hurst, 2002.

Corten, A., and R. Marshall-Fratani, eds. *Between Babel and Pentecost: Transnational Pentecostalism in Africa and Latin America.* London: C. Hurst, 2002.

Corten, A., and A. Mary, eds. *Imaginaires politiques et pentecôtismes, Afrique/ Amérique Latine.* Paris: Karthala, 2000.

Coulon, C. *Les Afriques politiques.* Paris: Editions La Découverte, 1991.

———. « Les nouveaux oulémas et le renouveau islamique au Nord Nigeria. » In *Le radicalisme Islamique au sud du Sahara*, ed. R. Otayek, 123–50. Paris: Karthala, 1998.

Cruise O'Brien, D. *Symbolic Confrontations: Muslims Imagining the State in Africa.* London: C. Hurst, 2003.

Danbazau, L. *Politics and Religion in Nigeria.* Kaduna: Vanguard, 1991.

Danfulani, U. "Exorcising Witchcraft: The Return of the Gods in New Religious Movements on the Jos Plateau and the Benue Regions of Nigeria." *African Affairs* 98 (1999): 167–93.

De Certeau, M. *The Writing of History.* New York: Columbia University Press, 1988.

Deleuze, G. *Deux régimes de fous: Textes et entretiens 1975–1995.* Paris: Les Editions de Minuit, 2003.

———. *Pourparlers 1972 –1990.* Paris: Les Editions de Minuit, 1990.

Dent, M. J. "Corrective Government: Military Rule in Perspective." In *Soldiers and Oil: The Political Transformation of Nigeria*, ed. K. Panter-Brick. London: Frank Cass, 1978.

De Polignac, F. *La naissance de la cité grecque: Cultes, espace et société VIIIe–VIIe siècles*. Paris: Editions La Découverte, 1984.

Derrida, J. *Foi et savoir: Le siècle et le pardon: Entretien avec Michel Wievorka*. Paris: Seuil Poche, 2001.

———. *Force de Loi*. Paris: Galilée, 1994.

———. "The Force of Law: The Mystical Foundation of Authority." In *Acts of Religion*, ed. G. Anidjar, 230–98. New York: Routledge, 2001.

———. *The Gift of Death*. Chicago: University of Chicago Press, 1995.

———. *Given Time: I. Counterfeit Money*. Chicago: University of Chicago Press, 1992.

———. *Spectres of Marx: The State of the Debt, the Work of Mourning and the New International*. New York: Routledge, 1994.

———. *Writing and Difference*. Chicago: University of Chicago Press, 1978.

Derrida, J., and M. Ferraris. *A Taste for the Secret*. Cambridge: Polity Press, 2001.

Devisch, R. « La parodie dans les églises de guérison à Kinshasa. » *Itinéraires et contacts de cultures* 25 (1998): 143–76.

———. "Pillaging Jesus: Healing Churches and the Villagisation of Kinshasa." *Africa* 66, no. 4 (1996): 555–86.

———. « La violence à Kinshasa, ou l'institution en négatif. » *Cahiers d'études africaines* 38, nos. 150–52 (1998): 441–69.

Diamond, L. "Cleavage, Conflict and Anxiety in the Second Nigerian Republic." *Journal of Modern African Studies* 20, no. 4 (1982): 629–68.

Diamond, L., A. Kirk-Greene, and O. Oyediran, eds. *Transition without End: Nigerian Politics and Civil Society under Babangida*. Boulder, Colo.: Lynne Rienner, 1997.

Dixon, P. J. "'Uneasy Lies the Head': Politics, Economics, and the Continuity of Belief among Yoruba of Nigeria." *Comparative Studies in Society and History* 23, no.1 (1991): 56–85.

Dunn, John. "The Politics of Representation and Good Government in Post-Colonial Africa." In *Political Domination in Africa: Reflections on the Limits of Power*, ed. P. Chabal, 58–74. Cambridge: Cambridge University Press, 1986.

Ekeh, P. "The Constitution of Civil Society in African History and Politics." In *Democratic Transition in Africa*, ed. B. Caron, O. Gboyega, and E. Osaghae, 83–104. Ibadan: CREDU, 1992.

Ellis, S. *Mask of Anarchy: The Destruction of Liberia and the Religious Dimensions of an African Civil War*. New York: NYU Press, 2001.

Ellis, S., and G. Ter Haar. *Worlds of Power: Religious Thought and Political Practice in Africa*. London: C. Hurst, 2004.

Enwerem, I. *A Dangerous Awakening: The Politicization of Religion in Nigeria*. Ibadan: IFRA, 1995.

Esan, O. "Receiving Television Messages: An Ethnographic Study of Women in Nigerian Context." Ph.D. diss., University of Glasgow, 1993.

Falola, T. *Violence in Nigeria: The Crisis of Religious Politics and Secular Ideologies*. Rochester: University of Rochester Press, 1998.

Falola, T., and J. Ihonvbere. The Rise and Fall of Nigeria's Second Republic 1979–1984. London: Zed Books, 1985.

Ferguson, J. The Anti-politics Machine: "Development," Depoliticisation and Bureaucratic State Power in Lesotho. Cambridge: Cambridge University Press, 1990.

Foucault, M. "About the Beginning of the Hermeneutics of the Self: Two Lectures at Dartmouth." Political Theory 21, no. 2 (1993): 198–227

———. L'Archéologie du Savoir. Paris: Gallimard, 1969.

———. Dits et Ecrits. Vol. 3: 1976–1979. Paris: Gallimard, 1994.

———. Dits et Ecrits. Vol. 4: 1980–1988. Paris: Gallimard, 1994.

———. L'Herméneutique du sujet: Cours au Collège de France, 1981–1982. Paris: Gallimard/Seuil, 2001.

———. L'Histoire de sexualité. Vol. 1: La volonté de savoir. Paris: Gallimard, 1976.

———. The History of Sexuality. Vol. 1: The Will to Knowledge. London: Penguin Books, 1998.

———. « Il faut défendre la société »: Cours au Collège de France, 1976. Paris: Gallimard, 1997.

———. Naissance de la biopolitique: Cours au Collège de France, 1978–1979. Paris: Gallimard/Seuil, 2004.

———. Sécurité, territoire, population: Cours au Collège de France, 1977–1978. Paris: Gallimard/Seuil, 2005.

———. "What Is Enlightenment." In The Foucault Reader, ed. P. Rabinow, 32–50. New York: Pantheon Books, 1984.

Fourchard, L., A. Mary, and R. Otayek, eds. Entreprises religieuses transnationales en Afrique de l'Ouest. Paris: Karthala, 2005.

Freund, B. "Oil Boom and Crisis in Contemporary Nigeria." Review of African Political Economy 13 (1978): 91–100.

Garlock, R. Fire in His Bones: The Story of Benson Idahosa, a Leader of the Christian Awakening in Africa. Orlando: Bridge-Logos Publishing, 1982.

Gauchet, M. Le désenchantement du monde. Paris: Gallimard, 1985.

Geschiere, P. Sorcellerie et politique en Afrique: La viande des autres. Paris: Karthala, 1995.

Geschiere, P., and B. Meyer, eds. Globalisation and Identity: Dialectics of Flow and Closure. Oxford: Blackwell, 1999.

Geschiere, P., and F. Nyamnjoh. "Capitalism and Autochthony: The Seesaw of Mobility and Belonging." Public Culture 12, no. 2 (2000): 423–52.

Gifford, P., ed. New Dimensions in African Christianity. Nairobi: AACC Press, 1992.

Gifford, P., ed. 2000 Years and Beyond: Faith, Identity and the Common Era. London: Routledge, 2002.

Gifford, P., S. Rose, and S. Brouwer, eds. Exporting the American Gospel: Global Christian Fundamentalism. New York: Routledge, 1996.

Gomez-Perez, M., ed. L'Islam politique au sud du Sahara. Paris: Karthala, 2005.

Gore, C., and D. Pratten. "The Politics of Plunder: The Rhetorics of Order and Disorder in Southern Nigeria." *African Affairs* 102 (2003): 211–40.

Graf, W. *The Nigerian State: Political Economy, State, Class and Political System in the Post-Colonial Era.* London: James Currey, 1988.

Gumi, A., with I. Tsiga, *Where I Stand.* Ibadan: Spectrum Books, 1992.

Gutkind, P. "The View from Below: Political Consciousness of the Urban Poor in Ibadan." *Cahiers d'études africaines* 57, no. 1 (1975): 5–35.

Guyer, J. "Representation without Taxation: An Essay on Democracy in Rural Nigeria, 1952–1990." *African Studies Review* 35, no. 1 (1992): 41–79.

———. "Wealth in People and Self-Realization in Equatorial Africa." *Man* 28, no. 2 (1993): 243–65.

Guyer, J., ed. *Money Matters: Instability, Values and Social Payments in the Modern History of West African Communities.* Portsmouth, N.H.: Heinemann, 1995.

Guyer, J., and S. Eno Belinga. "Wealth in People as Wealth in Knowledge: Accumulation and Composition in Equatorial Africa." *Journal of African History* 36, no. 1 (1995): 91–120.

Hackett, R. "Charismatic/Pentecostal Appropriation of Media Technologies in Nigeria and Ghana." *Journal of Religion in Africa* 28, no. 3 (1998): 1–19.

Hansen, T., and F. Stepputat, eds. *Sovereign Bodies: Citizens, Migrants and States in the Post-Colonial World.* Princeton: Princeton University Press, 2005.

Hansen, H., and M. Twaddle, eds. *Religion and Politics in East Africa: The Period since Independence.* Athens: Ohio University Press, 1991.

Harrison, M. *Righteous Riches: The Word of Faith Movement in Contemporary African American Religion.* Oxford: Oxford University Press, 2005.

Haynes, J. *Nigerian Video Films.* Athens: Ohio University Press, 2000.

———. *Religion and Politics in Africa* London: Zed Books, 1996.

Herbst, J. *States and Power in Africa: Comparative Lessons in Authority and Control.* Princeton: Princeton University Press, 2000.

Hobbes, T. *Leviathan.* London: Penguin, 1981.

Ibrahim, J. "Politics and Religion in Nigeria: The Parameters of the 1987 Crisis in Kaduna State." *Review of African Political Economy* 45–46 (1989): 65–82.

———. "Religion and Political Turbulence in Nigeria." *Journal of Modern African Studies* 29, no. 1 (1991): 115–36.

Ihonvbere, J. "Are Things Falling Apart? The Military and the Crisis of Democratisation in Nigeria." *Journal of Modern African Studies* 34, no. 2 (1996): 193–225.

Ihonvbere, J., and T. Shaw. *Illusions of Power: Nigeria in Transition.* Trenton, N.J.: Africa World Press, 1998.

Ilesanmi, S. O. Religious Pluralism and Nigerian State. Athens: Ohio University Press, 1997.

Isaacson, A. Deeper Life: The Extraordinary Growth of the Deeper Life Bible Church. London: Hodder and Stoughton, 1990.

Isichei, E. "The Maitatsine Risings in Nigeria, 1980–85: A Revolt of the Disinherited." *Journal of Religion in Africa* 17, no. 3 (1987): 194–208.

Iyayi, F. *The Contract.* Lagos: Longman, 1982.

Jennings, T. *Reading Derrida, Thinking Paul.* Stanford: Stanford University Press, 2006.

Jewsiewicki, B. "The Subject in Africa: In Foucault's Footsteps." *Public Culture* 14, no. 3 (2002): 593–98.

Joseph, R. *Democracy and Prebendal Politics in Nigeria: The Rise and Fall of the Second Republic.* Cambridge: Cambridge University Press, 1987.

Joseph, R., and J. Herbst. "Responding to State Failure in Africa." *International Security* 22, no. 2 (1997): 175–84.

Kane, O. *Muslim Modernity in Postcolonial Nigeria: A Study of the Society for the Removal of Innovation and Reinstatement of Tradition.* Leiden: Brill, 2003.

———. « Le réformisme musulman au Nigeria du Nord. » In *Islam et Islamismes au Sud du Sahara,* ed. O. Kane and J.-L. Triaud, 117–36. Paris: Karthala, 2003.

Kane, O., and J.-L. Triaud, eds. *Islam et islamismes au Sud du Sahara.* Paris: Karthala, 1998.

Kastfelt, N. "Rumours of Maitatsine: A Note on Political Culture in Northern Nigeria." *African Affairs* 88 (1989): 83–90.

Kenny, J. "Sharia and Christianity in Nigeria: Islam and a 'Secular' State." *Journal of Religion in Africa* 26, no. 4 (1996): 338–64.

Kepel, G., ed. *Les politiques de Dieu.* Paris: Seuil, 1993.

Kirke-Greene, A., and D. Rimmer. *Nigeria since 1970.* London: Hodder and Stoughton, 1981.

Klassen, P. *Blessed Events: Religion and Home Birth in America.* Princeton: Princeton University Press, 2001.

Klein, M. *Slavery and Colonial Rule in French West Africa.* Cambridge: Cambridge University Press, 1998.

Kukah, M. H. *Democracy and Civil Society in Nigeria.* Ibadan: Spectrum Books, 1999.

———. *Religion, Politics and Power in Northern Nigeria.* Ibadan: Spectrum Books, 1993.

Lafontaine, J. *Speak of the Devil: Tales of Satanic Abuse in Contemporary England.* Cambridge: Cambridge University Press, 1995.

Laitin, D. *Hegemony and Culture: Politics and Religious Change among the Yoruba.* Chicago: University of Chicago Press, 1986.

———. "The Sharia Debate and the Origins of Nigeria's Second Republic." *Journal of Modern African Studies* 20, no. 3 (1982): 411–30.

Larkin, B. "Bandiri Music, Globalization and Urban Experience in Nigeria." *Social Text–81* 22, no. 4 (2004): 91–112.

———. "Degraded Images, Distorted Sounds: Nigerian Video and the Infrastructure of Piracy." *Public Culture* 16, no. 2 (2004): 289–314.

Larkin, B., and B. Meyer. "Pentecostalism, Islam and Culture: New Religious Movements in West Africa." In *Themes in West African History,* ed. E. Akyeampong, 286–312. Oxford: James Currey, 2006.

Last, M. "The Search for Security in Muslim Northern Nigeria." *Africa* 78, no. 1 (2008): 41–63.

———. "The Shari'a in Context: People's Quest for Justice Today and the Role of Courts in Pre- and Early-Colonial Northern Nigeria." Paper presented at the International Conference on Muslim Family Law in Sub-Saharan Africa, Centre for Contemporary Islam, University of Cape Town, March 2002.

———. « Terrain: La charia dans le Nord Nigeria'. » *Politique Africaine* 79 (October 2000): 141–51.

Lee, B. "Going Public." *Public Culture* 5, no. 2 (1993): 165–78.

Lefort, C. *Democracy and Political Theory*. Cambridge: Polity Press, 1988.

Le Goff, J. *History and Memory*. New York: Columbia University Press, 1992.

Levinas, E. *Totalité et Infini: essai sur l'extériorité*. Paris: Librairie Générale Française, 1990.

Lévi-Strauss, C. *The Savage Mind*. Chicago: University of Chicago Press, 1966.

Lewis, P. "From Prebendalism to Predation: The Political Economy of Decline in Nigeria." *Journal of Modern African Studies* 34, no. 1 (1996): 79–103.

Lewis, P., T. Pearl, and R. Barnett. *Stabilizing Nigeria: Sanctions, Incentives, and Support for Civil Society*. New York: Century Foundation Press, 1998.

Loimeier, R. *Islamic Reform and Political Change in Northern Nigeria*. Chicago: Northwestern University Press, 1997.

———. "Playing with Affiliations: Muslims in Northern Nigeria in the Twentieth Century." In *Entreprises religieuses transnationales en Afrique de l'Ouest*, ed. L. Fourchard, A. Mary, and R. Otayek, 349–72. Paris: Karthala, 2005.

Lonsdale, J. "The Moral Economy of Mau Mau: Wealth, Poverty and Civic Virtue in Kikuyu Political Thought." In *Unhappy Valley: Conflict in Kenya and Africa: Book Two: Violence and Ethnicity*, ed. J. Lonsdale and B. Berman, 315–467. London: J. Currey, 1992.

———. "Moral Ethnicity and Political Tribalism." In *Inventions and Boundaries: Historical and Anthropological Approaches to the Study of Ethnicity and Nationalism*, ed. P. Kaarsholm and J. Hultin, 131–50. Roskilde, Denmark: Institute for Development Studies, Roskilde University, 1994.

Lubeck, P. "Islamic Protest under Semi-industrial Capitalism: 'Yan Tatsine Explained.'" *Africa* 55, no. 4 (1985): 368–89.

Lyons, A., and H. Lyons. "Magical Medicine on Television: Benin City Nigeria." *Journal of Ritual Studies* 1, no. 2 (1987):103–35.

MacGaffey, J. *Entrepreneurs and Parasites: The Struggle for Indigenous Capitalism in Zaire*. Cambridge: Cambridge University Press, 1988.

Maier, K. *This House Has Fallen: Midnight in Nigeria*. New York: Public Affairs, 2000.

Marie, A. « Du sujet communautaire au sujet individuel. » In *L'Afrique des individus: Itinéraires citadins dans l'Afrique contemporaine (Abidjan, Bamako, Dakar, Niamey)*, ed. A. Marie, 53–110. Paris: Karthala, 1997.

Marshall, R. "Pentecostalism in Southern Nigeria: An Overview." In *New Dimensions in African Christianity*, ed. P. Gifford, 7–32. Nairobi: AACC Press, 1992.

Marshall-Fratani, R. "Mediating the Global and Local in Nigerian Pentecostalism." *Journal of Religion in Africa* 28, no. 3 (1998): 278–315.

———. « Prospérité miraculeuse: Les pasteurs pentecôtistes et l'argent de Dieu au Nigeria. » *Politique Africaine* 82 (June 2001): 24–44.

———. "The War of 'Who is Who': Autochthony, Nationalism and Citizenship in the Ivorian Crisis." *African Studies Review* 49 (October 2006): 9–43.

Marshall-Fratani, R., and R. Banégas. « Modes de régulation politique et reconfiguration des espaces publics. » In *L'Afrique de l'Ouest dans la compétition mondiale: Quels atouts possibles ?* ed. J. Damon and J. O. Igue. (Paris: Karthala, 2004): 155–96.

Marshall-Fratani, R., and D. Péclard. « La religion du sujet en Afrique: Introduction au thème. » *Politique Africaine* 87 (October 2002): 5–20.

Marshall-Fratani, R., and D. Péclard, eds. *Les sujets de Dieu. Politique Africaine* 87 (October 2002).

Martin, D. *Tongues of Fire: The Explosion of Protestantism in Latin America.* Oxford: Blackwell, 1990.

Mary, A. « Prophètes pasteurs: La politique de la délivrance en Côte d'Ivoire. » *Politique Africaine* 87 (October 2002): 69–94.

Mauss, M. « Body Techniques." In M. Mauss, *Sociology and Psychology: Essays*, ed. B. Brewster, 97–123. London: Routledge, 1979.

Mbembe, A. "African Modes of Self-Writing." *Public Culture* 14, no. 1 (2002): 239–73.

———. *Afriques indociles: Christianisme, pouvoir et état en société postcoloniale.* Paris: Karthala, 1988.

———. « La colonie: Son petit secret et sa part maudite. » *Politique Africaine* 102 (2006): 101–27.

——— « A propos des écritures africaines de soi. » *Politique Africaine* 77 (March 2000): 16–43.

———. « La colonie: Son petit secret et sa part maudite. » *Politique Africaine* 102 (July 2006): 101–27.

———. *De la postcolonie: Essai sur l'imagination politique dans l'Afrique contemporaine.* Paris: Karthala, 2000.

———. « Necropolitics. » *Public Culture* 15, no. 1 (2003): 11–40.

———. "On the Power of the False." *Public Culture* 14, no. 3 (2002): 629–41.

———. « Les pervers du village: Sexualité, vénalité et déréliction en postcolonie. » *Africultures* 9 March 2006, http://www.africultures.com/index .asp?menu=affiche_article&no=4346

——— « La prolifération du divin en Afrique subsaharienne. » In *Les Politiques de Dieu*, ed. G. Kepel, 177–201. Paris: Le Seuil, 1993.

——— « A propos des écritures africaines de soi. » *Politique Africaine* 77 (March 2000): 16–43.

———. "Provisional Notes on the Postcolony." *Africa,* 62, no. 1 (1992): 3–37.

Meyer, B. "Commodities and the Power of Prayer: Pentecostalist Attitudes towards Consumption in Contemporary Ghana." In *Globalisation and Identity: Dialectics of Flow and Closure,* ed. P. Geschiere and B. Meyer, 151–76. Oxford: Blackwell, 1999.

———. "Delivered from the Powers of Darkness: Confessions of Satanic Riches in Christian Ghana." *Africa* 65, no. 2 (1995): 236–55.

———. « Les églises pentecôtistes africaines: Satan et la dissociation de la 'tradition.' » *Anthropologie et société* 22, no. 1 (1998): 63–84.

———. " 'If You Are a Devil, You Are a Witch, and If You Are a Witch, You Are a Devil': The Integration of Pagan Ideas into the Conceptual Universe of Ewe Christians in Southeastern Ghana." *Journal of Religion in Africa* 22, no. 2 (1992): 98–132.

———. " 'Make a Complete Break with the Past': Memory and Postcolonial Modernity in Ghanaian Pentecostal Discourse." In *Memory and the Postcolony: African Anthropology and the Critique of Power,* ed. R. Werbner, 182–208. London: Zed Books, 1998.

———. « The Power of Money: Politics, Occult Forces, and Pentecostalism in Ghana." *African Studies Review* 41, no. 3 (1998): 15–38.

———. « Prières, fusils et meurtre rituel: Le cinéma populaire et ses nouvelles figures du pouvoir et du succès au Ghana. » *Politique Africaine* 82 (June 2001): 45–62.

———. *Translating the Devil: Religion and Modernity among the Ewe in Ghana.* Edinburgh: Edinburgh University Press, 1999.

Meyer, B., and A. Moors, eds. *Media, Religion and the Public Sphere.* Bloomington: Indiana University Press, 2006.

Meyerowitz, J. *No Sense of Place: The Impact of Electronic Media on Social Behaviour.* Oxford: Oxford University Press, 1985.

Miller, J. C. *Way of Death: Merchant Capitalism and the Angolan Slave Trade 1730–1830.* Madison: University of Wisconsin Press, 1997.

Mosès, S. *L'Ange de l'histoire: Rosenzweig, Benjamin, Scholem.* Paris: Gallimard Poche, 2006.

———. *Au déla de la guerre: trois études sur Levinas.* Paris: Editions de l'Eclat, 2004.

Mudimbe, V. Y. *The Idea of Africa.* Bloomington: Indiana University Press, 1994.

———. *The Invention of Africa: Gnosis, Philosophy and the Order of Knowledge.* Bloomington: Indiana University Press, 1988.

———. *L'Odeur du père: Essais sur les limites de la science et de la vie en Afrique noire.* Paris: Présence Africaine, 1982.

Mustapha, R. "Coping with Diversity: The Nigerian State in Historical Perspective." In *The African State: Reconsiderations,* ed. A. Samatar and I. Samatar, 149–75. Portsmouth, N.H.: Heinemann, 2002.

———. "Ethnicity and the Politics of Democratization in Nigeria." In *Ethnicity and Democracy in Africa,* ed. B. Berman, D. Eyoh, and W. Kymlicka, 257–75. Oxford: James Currey, 2004.

Nancy, J.-L. *La déclosion: Déconstruction du christianisme, 1.* Paris, Editions Galilée, 2005.

Ngada, N. *Speaking for Ourselves.* Braamfontein: Institute of Contextual Theology, 1985.

Nkashama, P. *Eglises nouvelles et mouvements religieux: L'exemple zaïrois.* Paris: L'Harmattan, 1990.

Noll, M., D. Bebbington, and G Rawlks, eds. Evangelicalism: Comparative Studies of Popular Protestantism in North America, the British Isles, and Beyond, 1700–1990. Oxford: Oxford University Press, 1994.

Nouhou, A. B. *Islam et politique au Nigeria: Genèse et évolution de la charia.* Paris: Karthala, 2005.

Obarrio, J. "The Spirit of the Laws in Mozambique." Ph.D. diss., Columbia University, 2006.

———. "Time and Again: Being after Structural Adjustment." Unpublished paper.

O'Brien, S. M. « La charia contestée: Démocratie, débat et diversité musulmane dans les 'États charia' du Nigeria. » *Politique Africaine* 106 (2007): 46–68.

Ogunbameru, O. A., ed. *Readings on Campus Secret Cults.* Ife: Kuntel, 1997.

Ojo, M. "The Contextual Significance of the Charismatic Movements in Independent Nigeria." *Africa,* 58 (1988): 175–92.

———. "Deeper Christian Life Ministry: A Case Study of the Charismatic Movements in Western Nigeria." *Journal of Religion in Africa* 18 (1988): 141–62.

———. "Deeper Life Bible Church of Nigeria." In *New Dimensions in African Christianity,* ed. P. Gifford, 135–56. Nairobi: AACC Press, 1992.

———. *The End-Time Army: Charismatic Movements in Modern Nigeria.* Trenton, N.J.: Africa World Press, 2006.

———. "The Growth of Campus Christianity and Charismatic Movements in Western Nigeria." Ph.D. diss., University of London, 1986.

Okri, B. *Infinite Riches.* London: Orion Books, 1999.

Olagunju, T., A. Jinadu, and S. Oyovbaire. *Transition to Democracy in Nigeria 1985–1995.* Ibadan: Safari Books, 1993.

Osaghae, E. *Crippled Giant: Nigeria since Independence.* London: Hurst, 1998.

Osaghae, E., and R. Suberu. "A History of Identities, Violence and Stability in Nigeria." CRISE Working Paper no. 6. Queen Elisabeth House, January 2005.

Otayek, R., ed. *Le radicalisme islamique au sud du Sahara: Da'wa, arabisation et critique de l'Occident.* Paris: Karthala, 1993.

Otayek, R., and C. Toulabor. « Innovations et contestations religieuses. » *Politique Africaine* 39 (September 1990): 31–46.

Othman, S. "Classes, Crisis and Coup." *African Affairs* 27 (1984): 441–61.

Oyediran, O., ed. *Nigerian Government and Politics under Military Rule, 1966–1979.* London: Macmillan, 1979.

Paden, J. N. *Religion and Political Culture in Kano.* Berkeley: University of California Press, 1973.

Peace, A. J. "Prestige, Power and Legitimacy in a Modern Nigerian Town." *Canadian Journal of African Studies* 13, nos. 1–2 (1979): 25–51.

Peel, J. D. Y. "An Africanist Revisits *Magic and the Millennium.*" In *Secularization, Rationalism and Sectarianism,* ed. E. Barker, J. Beckford, and K. Dobbelaere,81–100. Oxford: Clarendon Press, 1993.

———. *Aladura: A Religious Movement among the Yoruba.* London: Oxford University Press, 1969.

———. "Conversion and Tradition in Two African Societies: Ijesha and Buganda." *Past and Present* 77 (1977): 108–41.

———. "For Who Hath Despised the Day of Small Things?: Missionary Narratives and Historical Anthropology." *Comparative Studies in Society and History* 37 (1995): 581–607.

———. *Ijeshas and Nigerians: The Incorporation of a Yoruba Kingdom 1890s–1970s.* Cambridge: Cambridge University Press, 1983.

———. "Olaju: A Yoruba Concept of Development." *Journal of Development Studies* 14 (1978): 139–65.

———. "The Pastor and the Babalawo: The Interaction of Religions in Nineteenth Century Yorubaland." *Africa* 60 (1990): 338–69.

———. *Religious Encounter and the Making of the Yoruba.* Bloomington: University of Indiana Press, 2000.

Poewe, K., ed. *Charismatic Christianity as a Global Culture.* Columbia: University of South Carolina Press, 1994.

Pratten, D. "The Politics of Protection: Perspective on Vigilantism in Nigeria." *Africa* 78, no. 1 (2008): 1–15.

Pred, A., and M. Watts, eds. *Reworking Modernity: Capitalism and Symbolic Discontent.* New Brunswick, N.J.: Rutgers University Press, 1990.

Ranger, T. "Religious Movements and Politics in Sub-Saharan Africa." *African Studies Review* 29, no. 2 (1985): 1–70.

Ranger, T., and O. Vaughan, eds. *Legitimacy and the State in Twentieth-Century Africa: Essays in Honour of A. H. M. Kirk-Greene.* Oxford: St Antony's College, 1993.

Reno, W. *Warlord Politics and African States.* Boulder, Colo.: Lynne Rienner, 1998.

Report of the Presidential Commission of Inquiry into the Cult of Devil Worship in Kenya. Nairobi, 1999.

Richardson, J., J. Best, and D. Bromley, eds. *The Satanism Scare.* New York: Aldine de Gruyter, 1991.

Roitman, J. *Fiscal Disobedience: An Anthropology of Economic Regulation in Central Africa.* Princeton: Princeton University Press, 2005.

Rouse, S. *Shifting Body Politics: Gender, Nation, State in Pakistan.* New Delhi: Women Unlimited Edition, 2004.

Schmitt, C. *Political Theology: Four Chapters on the Concept of Sovereignty.* Chicago: University of Chicago Press, 1985.

Seers, D. "The Mechanism of an Open Petroleum Economy." *Social and Economic Studies* 22, no. 1 (1984): 233–42.

Sklar, R. *Nigerian Political Parties: Power in an Emergent African Nation.* New York: Nok Publishers International, 1963.

Smith, D. "'The Arrow of God': Pentecostalism, Inequality and the Supernatural in South-eastern Nigeria." *Africa* 71, no. 4 (2001): 587–613.

———. *A Culture of Corruption: Everyday Deception and Popular Discontent in Nigeria.* Princeton: Princeton University Press, 2007.

Spivak, G. C. "Religion, Politics, Theology: A Conversation with Achille Mbembe." *boundary 2* 34, no. 2 (2007): 149–70.

Stoll, D. *Is Latin America Turning Protestant? The Politics of Evangelical Growth.* Berkeley: University of California Press, 1990.

Strange, S. *Casino Capitalism.* Oxford: Blackwell, 1986.

Suberu, R. *Federalism and Ethnic Conflict in Nigeria.* Washington, D.C.: U.S. Institute for Peace Press, 2001.

Sulaiman, M. D. "Shiaism and the Islamic Movement in Nigeria: 1979–1991." *Islam et sociétés au Sud du Sahara* 7 (1993): 5–16.

Taubes, J. *The Political Theology of Paul.* Stanford: Stanford University Press, 2004.

Taylor, C. *The Malaise of Modernity.* Concord, Ontario, Canada: Anansi, 1991.

———. *Modern Social Imaginaries.* Durham, N.C.: Duke University Press, 2004.

———. "Modes of Civil Society." *Public Culture* 3, no. 1 (1990): 95–132.

———. *A Secular Age.* Cambridge, Mass.: Harvard University Press, 2007.

———. *Sources of the Self: The Making of the Modern Identity.* Cambridge, Mass.: Harvard University Press, 1989.

Ter Haar, G. *L'Afrique et le monde des esprits.* Paris: Karthala, 1996.

Tignor, R. "Corruption in Nigeria before Independence." *Journal of Modern African Studies* 31, no. 2 (1993): 175–202.

Tonda, J. « De l'exorcisme comme mode de démocratisation: Eglises et mouvements religieux au Congo de 1990 à 1994. » In *Religion et transition démocratique en Afrique,* ed. F. Constantin and C. Coulon, eds. Paris: Karthala, 1997.

———. *La guérison divine en Afrique Centrale: Congo, Gabon.* Paris: Karthala, 2002.

———. *Le souverain moderne: Le corps du pouvoir en Afrique centrale (Congo, Gabon).* Paris: Karthala, 2005.

Ukah, F. K. A. "Poster Publicity and Religious Proselytization: A Study of Pentecostalism in Ibadan." M.A. thesis, Department of Sociology, University of Ibadan, 1999.

———. "The Redeemed Christian Church of God (RCCG), Nigeria: Local Identities and Global Processes in African Pentecostalism." Ph.D. diss., University of Bayreuth, Germany, 2003.

Ukiwo, U. "Politics, Ethno-religious Conflicts and Democratic Consolidation in Nigeria." *Journal of Modern African Studies* 41 (2003): 115–38.

Umar, M. S. "Changing Islamic Identity in Nigeria from the 1960s to the 1980s: From Sufism to Anti-Sufism." In *Muslim Identity and Social Change in*

Sub-Saharan Africa, ed. L. Brenner, 154–78. Bloomington: Indiana University Press, 2003.

Van Binsbergen, W. "Globalization and Virtuality: Analytical Problems Posed by the Contemporary Transformation of African Societies." In *Globalisation and Identity: Dialectics of Flow and Closure,* ed. P. Geschiere and B. Meyer, 273–304. Oxford: Blackwell, 1999.

Veyne, P. *Comment on écrit l'histoire suivi par Foucault révolutionne l'histoire,* Paris: Seuil Points, 1978.

———. *Les Grecs ont-ils cru à leurs mythes?* Paris: Seuil, Points, 1983.

Watts, M. "The Shock of Modernity: Money, Protest and Fast Capitalism in an Industrialising Society." In *Reworking Modernity: Capitalism and Symbolic Discontent,* ed. A. Pred and M. Watts, 21–64. New Brunswick, N.J.: Rutgers University Press, 1990.

Weber, M. *Economie et société: Tome 1.* Paris: Plon, 1971.

———. *The Protestant Ethic and the Spirit of Capitalism.* Oxford: Blackwell, 2002.

Webster, J. B. *The African Churches among the Yoruba: 1891–1922.* Oxford: Oxford University Press, 1964.

Weller, R. "Living at the Edge: Religion, Capitalism, and the End of the Nation-State in Taiwan." *Public Culture* 12, no. 2 (2000): 477–98.

Woods, D. "Civil Society in Europe and Africa: Limiting State Power through a Public Sphere." *African Studies Review* 35, no. 2 (1992): 77–100.

Zartman, W. *Collapsed States: The Disintegration and Restoration of Legitimate Authority,* Boulder, Colo.: Lynne Rienner, 1995.

Zartman, W., ed. *Governance as Conflict Management: Politics and Violence in West Africa.* Washington, D.C.: Brookings Institution, 1997.

Index